What Works in Offender Compliance

International Perspectives and Practice

Edited by

Pamela Ugwudike
Lecturer in Criminology, Swansea University

and

Peter Raynor
Professor of Criminology and Criminal Justice, Swansea University

First published 2013 by
PALGRAVE MACMILLAN

Palgrave Macmillan in the UK is an imprint of Macmillan Publishers Limited,
registered in England, company number 785998, of Houndmills, Basingstoke,
Hampshire RG21 6XS.

Palgrave Macmillan in the US is a division of St Martin's Press LLC,
175 Fifth Avenue, New York, NY 10010.

Palgrave Macmillan is the global academic imprint of the above companies
and has companies and representatives throughout the world.

Palgrave® and Macmillan® are registered trademarks in the United States,
the United Kingdom, Europe and other countries.

ISBN 978–1–137–01951–6

This book is printed on paper suitable for recycling and made from fully
managed and sustained forest sources. Logging, pulping and manufacturing
processes are expected to conform to the environmental regulations of the
country of origin.

A catalogue record for this book is available from the British Library.

A catalog record for this book is available from the Library of Congress.

Contents

Section III Evidence-Led Compliance Mechanisms: Recent Developments in International Research

Section IV Offender Diversity: Contextualizing Compliance Theory, Policy and Practice

Tables and Figures

Tables

Figures

Acknowledgements

The idea for this book emerged from a realization by the editors that very little has been written about offender compliance. Therefore, unsurprisingly, it was a challenge to identify suitable contributors to this volume. Eventually we did succeed in identifying academics and researchers who have through their previous work revealed a commitment to understanding offender compliance and its mechanisms. We are therefore very grateful to all the contributors for responding favourably to our request to contribute to the book and for the time and effort they invested in making this work a reality.

We are also grateful to the Swansea University Criminology Department for allowing one of us a period of sabbatical leave during the production of the book. Finally, we wish to express our thanks to all those who worked in various capacities to support the production of this book, especially Julia Willan and Harriet Barker at Palgrave Macmillan and Devasena Vedamurthi at Integra.

Contributors

Melissa Alexander received her PhD in clinical psychology from the University of Texas Southwestern Medical Center at Dallas, USA. She has worked as a clinical psychologist in the criminal justice system and now serves as the chief probation officer for the US probation office in the Middle District of North Carolina. She has authored or co-authored over 20 publications on substance abuse, mental illness, motivational interviewing and STARR, and has been involved in numerous trainings focused on helping officers utilize evidence-based practices with clients.

Tim Bateman is Reader in Youth Justice at the University of Bedfordshire, UK, where his responsibilities include managing a doctoral programme for professionals working in the field of youth justice or services to disadvantaged young people. Tim has a background in youth justice policy and has extensive experience as a youth justice social worker. He has written widely on youth justice, youth crime and young people in conflict with the law. He has a particular interest in the experiences of children within the criminal justice system. Tim is co-editor of *Safer Communities* journal, news editor for *Youth Justice* journal, editorial board member of *Child and Families Law Quarterly*, deputy chair of the National Association for Youth Justice, secretary of the London Association for Youth Justice and associate member of the Standing Committee for Youth Justice.

Kristel Beyens holds a PhD in criminology and is Professor of Penology at the Criminology Department of the Vrije Universiteit Brussel (Free University of Brussels, Belgium). She is a member of the research group Crime and Society (CRiS). Her PhD was a penological study of sentencing decision making as a social practice. She has also published on prison overcrowding and the implementation of prison sentences and community sanctions. Together with Mike Nellis and Dan Kaminski, she published a book on electronic monitoring from a critical and international comparative perspective (2013). She is a member of the editorial board of the *European Journal of Probation* and a founding member of the ESC working group on community sanctions (chair 2009–2012). She is the vice-chair of a COST action on offender supervision.

Anthony E. Bottoms is Emeritus Wolfson Professor of Criminology at Cambridge, and Honorary Professor of Criminology at the University of

Sheffield. He is also a life fellow of Fitzwilliam College, Cambridge. His interests within criminology include desistance from crime, socio-spatial criminology, penology and theoretical criminology.

Guy Bourgon is a clinical psychologist specializing in correctional and criminal justice psychology. He has over 25 years clinical experience in the assessment and treatment of adults and youths involved in the criminal justice system. Dr Bourgon has been involved in the development of various empirically validated correctional programmes and has extensive international experience in the training and supervision of numerous front-line professionals. He is presently a senior researcher for Public Safety Canada, conducting research on effective correctional services and practices. As the co-lead on the Strategic Training Initiative in Community Supervision, he plays a significant role in the development of its community supervision model, the training and clinical supervision of probation officers across Canada, as well as the evaluation of this Risk-Need-Responsivity approach to offender supervision. He has published articles on effective correctional treatment across a range of offender populations and programmes, risk assessment, research methodology and effective knowledge transfer to everyday practice. He maintains a private practice, and is an adjunct professor at Carleton University and a member of the Editorial Board on *Criminal Justice and Behavior*.

Ben Crewe is Deputy Director of the Prisons Research Centre at the Institute of Criminology, University of Cambridge, UK. He has published widely on prison culture, prisoner relations, public and private sector prisons, and other areas of prison life. His monograph *The Prisoner Society: Power, Adaptation and Social Life in an English Prison* was published in 2009.

Stef Decoene completed a PhD in experimental cognitive psychology before starting work as a forensic psychologist in a high security prison. He is a part-time lecturer in the Criminology Department of the Vrije Universiteit Brussel, where he teaches forensic and criminological psychology. His research centres on (the development of) psychopathic features, risk assessment and desistance, the development of microcriminogetical accounts of an individual offence as a key to linking individualized risk assessment and treatment, and, more recently, responsivity factors in forensic treatment related to therapist characteristics. He is involved in supervising the change processes of a number of clinical settings making the step from clinical to forensic case management.

Loraine Gelsthorpe is Professor of Criminology and Criminal Justice and Director of the MPhil Programme at the Institute of Criminology, University of Cambridge, UK. She has published extensively in the area of women, crime and justice, as well as community penalties more generally, and she maintains an active interest in youth justice and methodological and policy-related developments. Recent research has focused on the criminalization of women migrants and on deaths under probation supervision. In 2009 she became a Fellow of the Royal Society of Arts for her distinguished contribution to criminal justice, and she is the current president of the British Society of Criminology.

Leticia Guiterrez is a research analyst in the Corrections Research Unit of the Department of Public Safety and a doctoral student in the Forensic Psychology Program at Carleton University, Canada. Her areas of research include problem-solving courts, offender rehabilitation and aboriginal offenders.

Laura J. Hanby is currently completing her PhD in forensic psychology at Carleton University, Canada. Since 2008, Laura has also been employed with the Correctional Service of Canada in various capacities. Her master's work focused on the role of offender competencies in predicting treatment programme performance as well as release outcome. This research has important implications for correctional practice and, more generally, advances our understanding of the processes underlying offender change. While this research is ongoing, Laura's doctoral dissertation has taken a different focus on dynamic risk assessment. This study examines whether the assessment of dynamic risk factors and protective factors using the Dynamic Risk Assessment for Offender Re-entry (DRAOR) improves risk assessment and case management. It is expected that this systematic assessment and reassessment of dynamic and protective factors will provide insight into the mechanisms by which risk changes over time.

Martine Herzog-Evans teaches law and criminology at Reims University, Law Faculty, France. She also teaches at the Universities of Nantes and Bordeaux IV/National Penitentiary Academy. Her majors are criminal law, sentences, probation, prisons and re-entry. Publications include *Droit de l'application des peines*, 4th ed. (2012–2013); *Droit pénitentiaire*, 2nd ed. (2012–2013); *Transnational Criminology Manual* (2010); *L'évasion* (2009); and *L'intimité du détenu et de ses proches en droit comparé* (2000). She is a member of the European Society of Criminology and works with three of its subgroups: Community Sentences and Measures; Sentencing; and Prisons.

Caleb D. Lloyd is a PhD candidate in forensic psychology at Carleton University, Ottawa, Canada. His research examines various aspects of offender change and desistance from crime. He has authored a variety of published research papers on correctional psychology, including desistance from crime, judges' perceptions of psychopathy, sex offender risk, and treatment change among offenders. His other recent presentations and projects have examined gambling and impulsivity among offenders, the role of community volunteers in the criminal justice system, differences among violent offenders and re-entry.

Christopher T. Lowenkamp received his PhD in criminal justice from the University of Cincinnati, USA. He has served as the director of the Center for Criminal Justice Research and the associate director of The Corrections Institute at the University of Cincinnati. He has also held the positions of research associate and research professor at the University of Cincinnati. He served as a probation officer and jail emergency release coordinator in Summit County, Ohio. He is the co-author of EPICS-II, STARR, EPICS, two cognitive–behavioural curricula for clients and the Ohio Risk Assessment System (ORAS), and the developer of the Post Conviction Risk Assessment (PCRA) and the Pretrial Risk Assessment (PTRA), which are used in the federal probation and pre-trial services systems. He has co-authored over 60 publications on risk assessment and correctional programming.

Trish McCulloch is Senior Lecturer in Social Work, based in the School of Education and Social Work at the University of Dundee, UK. Prior to joining the University in 2003 she worked as a social worker within youth and adult justice settings. Her research activity has focused on various areas of criminal justice social work/probation practice, and includes a focus on the social and community contexts of change. She is currently completing her doctorate and has recently completed a research review exploring the value and outcomes associated with user involvement in criminal justice.

Mike Nellis is Emeritus Professor of Criminal and Community Justice in the Centre for Law, Crime and Justice, Law School University of Strathclyde, UK. He was formerly a social worker with young offenders in London, has a PhD from the Institute of Criminology in Cambridge, and was involved in the training of probation officers at the University of Birmingham. He has written widely on the fortunes of the probation service, alternatives to imprisonment and particularly the electronic monitoring of offenders. He has recently co-edited *Electronically Monitored Punishment: International and Critical Perspectives*, with Kristel Beyens and Dan Kaminski.

Peter Raynor is Professor of Criminology and Criminal Justice at Swansea University in Wales. A former probation officer and social work educator, he has been carrying out and publishing research on effective practice in probation services since the 1970s. His previous books include *Social Work, Justice and Control* (1985); *Probation as an Alternative to Custody* (1988); *Effective Probation Practice* (with Smith and Vanstone, 1994); *Understanding Community Penalties* (with

Vanstone, 2002); *Race and Probation* (with Lewis, Smith and Wardak, 2005); *Developments in Social Work with Offenders* (with Gill McIvor, 2007); *Rehabilitation, Crime and Justice* (with Gwen Robinson, 2009) and *Offender Supervision: New Directions in Theory, Research and Practice* (with McNeill and Trotter, 2010).

Charles R. Robinson received his BS degree from Grambling State University, USA. He is a probation administrator for the Administrative Office of the US Courts, Office of Probation and Pretrial Services. Prior to working with the Administrative Office, he worked for the Dallas County Community Supervision and Corrections Department. He has focused on developing and training corrections professionals to use cognitive–behavioural strategies with clients.

Gwen Robinson is Reader in Criminal Justice in the School of Law at the University of Sheffield, UK. Her principal research interests are community penalties and their administration; offender management and rehabilitation; penal policy and practice; and restorative justice. She has published widely in these areas, and her recent publications include *Restorative Justice in Practice: Evaluating What Works with Victims and Offenders* (with Joanna Shapland and Angela Sorsby, 2011).

Ralph C. Serin received his PhD from Queen's University in 1988 and has been registered with the Ontario College of Psychologists since 1990. He worked in federal correction from 1975 to 2003 in various capacities and is now an associate professor at Carleton University, where he is Director of the Criminal Justice Decision Making Laboratory and a member of the Forensic Psychology Research Center. He has consulted with the National Institute of Corrections and the Centre for Effective Public Policy, and is an advisor to the National Parole Resource Centre (USA). He has also provided training and is currently engaged in research collaboration with the Departments of Corrections in numerous US states and internationally regarding violent offenders, dynamic risk assessment, evidence-based practice, parole decision making and offender change. He is co-principal investigator (co-PI) for a recently funded innovation grant from BJA to develop e-learning materials for probation/parole officers, and is also co-PI for a re-entry model adopted by the National Institute of Justice for a national field demonstration experiment under the Second Chance Act on offender re-entry (USA). He has recently been appointed to the Correctional Services Advisory and Accreditation Panel in the UK.

Marianna Shturman is Director of Addiction and Mental Health Services at the Wabano Centre for Aboriginal Health and serves as a member of the Board of Directors of the Ottawa Institute of Object Relations Therapy. She has 15 years' clinical experience in not-for-profit sector work and began her career in offender rehabilitation in the USA. Her research interests include the importance of therapeutic relationships in the effectiveness of treatment outcomes, motivation to change, self and relational needs, and holistic prevention and intervention approaches.

Paul Sparrow is currently Associate Dean (Law) at Wolverhampton University, UK. Working initially with drug misusers at the Maudsley Hospital's National Addiction Centre, he then practised as a probation officer, before finally moving to Nottingham Trent University, where he headed Criminology. Dr Sparrow's research interests lie in the history of probation practice generally and in the probation service's work with drug misusers more particularly.

Christopher Trotter is Professor in Social Work at Monash University, Australia, and Director of the Monash Criminal Justice Research Consortium. He has published widely and is well known for his work on offender supervision and prosocial modelling. His book *Working with Involuntary Clients*, now in its second edition, has sold widely and has been published in multiple languages.

Pamela Ugwudike is Lecturer in Criminology at Swansea University in Wales. She trained as a lawyer and went on to obtain a Master's degree in Criminology and Criminal Justice (with distinction). She was awarded a University of Wales PhD studentship in 2004. After completing her PhD, she took up a position as a research officer at the Centre for Criminal Justice and Criminology, Swansea University. She was appointed a lecturer in September 2009. Her research interests include developing insights into evidence-based offender rehabilitation and exploring the dynamics of compliance with legal authorities. She is currently working (with Professor Peter Raynor and Professor Maurice Vanstone, who are also based in Swansea University) on a research project that is evaluating the delivery and impact of supervision programmes. The project is funded by the Jersey Probation and Aftercare Service. She is also working (with Professor Peter Raynor) on two projects that are also exploring the delivery and impact of supervision programmes. One of the projects is funded by the Welsh Government and the second project is funded by the London Probation Trust. Her recent publications and conference papers have explored the relevance of criminal justice policy and practice to compliance with court orders.

Maurice Vanstone is Emeritus Professor of Criminology and Criminal Justice in the Department of Criminology, Swansea University, UK. His many publications include *Supervising Offenders in the Community: A History of Probation Theory and Practice* (2004) and *Offenders or Citizens?: Readings in Rehabilitation* (with Philip Priestly, 2010).

Section I

Setting the Scene – Probation and Compliance: Historical and Contemporary Policy Developments

1
Introduction

Pamela Ugwudike and Peter Raynor

This book's main objective is to draw together the latest international research and theoretical literature on offender compliance during criminal justice supervision and after supervision ends. As far as we know, no text has focused exclusively on the subject-matter of offender compliance. This book addresses the gap in knowledge by providing a useful analysis of the extant international research and theoretical literature. It examines compliance across two broad domains: short-term compliance during criminal justice supervision[1] and long-term compliance[2] after supervision ends.

Compliance is a broad concept. To demonstrate the multidimensionality of compliance, we may turn to Bottoms's (2001) framework for understanding compliance. According to this framework, there are several forms of legal compliance, namely: constraint-based compliance; habit compliance; instrumental compliance; and normative compliance. Constraint-based compliance may stem from physical constraints such as the electronic monitoring devices that seek to reduce opportunities for non-compliance. Habit or routine compliance may manifest as established non-criminogenic routines and habits. With instrumental compliance, people comply because of perceived benefits or because they believe that the costs of non-compliance outweigh its benefits. Normative compliance is the product of internalized mechanisms that can produce compliance. It is a form of compliance that has several dimensions. It could be the product of bonds or attachments people form with others in authority, such as probation officers. It could also stem from the belief that a representative of authority has used their authority fairly (Tyler 2010, 2013; Tyler and Huo 2002). Compliance in this sense occurs irrespective of personal beliefs or principles because the authority in question is perceived to be legitimate.

Bottoms's fourfold classification of compliance and its mechanisms has greatly informed recent work in the field of offender compliance. Indeed, several chapters in this volume draw on, or attempt to critically analyse, the fourfold classification.

Robinson and McNeill's (2008) useful conceptual framework for understanding compliance also demonstrates the multidimensionality of the concept. This framework is another commonly cited piece of work and several chapters in this text also refer to it. In their description of compliance, Robinson and McNeill highlight the difference between formal and substantive compliance (see also McNeill and Robinson 2013). Formal compliance entails adhering to the minimum requirements of a court order. Substantive compliance involves the 'active engagement and co-operation of the offender with the requirements of his or her order' (Robinson and McNeill 2007:434). Regulatory theorists persuasively argue that formal compliance is superficial, it typically involves complying with the most basic requirements of the order and it may involve an unwillingness to fully engage with the change process (see also Murphy 2005). Substantive compliance, on the other hand, is normative because it is also underpinned by an acceptance that an authority can legitimately exercise power over the offender.

The nature of compliance as a multidimensional concept is also evident in the claim put forward by several commentators who argue that compliance is a construct that emerges from the interactions between practitioners and the people they supervise. From this perspective, in order to understand the nature of compliance, one has to examine the micro-dynamics of compliance, that is, the policy and practice contexts in which the key actors (practitioners and supervisees) negotiate and define compliance (see also McCulloch, this volume; Robinson, this volume; Ugwudike 2008). It follows that we may not simply presume that the definition of compliance is commonsensical and may be taken for granted. Compliance is a broad term, and its explication lies in detailed theorization and empirical analysis.

The foregoing suggests that anyone attempting to study compliance and its mechanisms is undertaking a mammoth task, given that the concept has several possible dimensions. Nevertheless, the chapters in this book do develop useful insights that can help us understand the concept, its diverse forms and its diverse mechanisms. There are numerous reasons why we should explore the factors that can encourage compliance. An important reason is that, as mentioned earlier, there is a dearth of academic research in this field. Therefore, a text is needed which brings together new and emerging insights into effective compliance strategies. These insights are also needed in the light of what official statistics, evaluations of offender behaviour programmes and other studies suggest about the extent of non-compliance. For example, recent official statistics reveal that many offenders in England and Wales are reconvicted shortly after their court orders expire (Ministry of Justice 2012). The Ministry of Justice recognizes this in its statement that: 'nearly half of adult offenders released from prison are reconvicted within a year, and overall one in five offenders spent some time in custody in the year after they were released from prison or started a non-custodial sentence' (Ministry of Justice 2011: 6). Equally, many offenders fail to complete community orders (Ministry of Justice 2012). Worryingly, the statistics also tell us that high rates of conviction for non-compliance have inflated the already burgeoning prison population (see, generally, Ministry of Justice 2010). In 2009, the Ministry of Justice observed that 'tougher enforcement' represents one of two factors that 'caused the increase in the prison population of England and Wales from 1999 to 2009' (Ministry of Justice 2010). Several offender behaviour programmes have also recorded high rates of offender attrition and non-completion (Hollin et al. 2008; Kemshall et al. 2002; Palmer et al. 2007). In drawing together emerging international perspectives on compliance, this book offers useful insights on what works best in offender compliance. We hope that practitioners, managers, academics, students, policy makers and others interested in offender rehabilitation research, policy and practice will find this text a useful resource.

This book comprises four sections. In Section I which sets the scene, Chapter 1 describes the book's objectives and presents an overview of how the book is structured. The subsequent three chapters in Section 1 focus on compliance during community-based supervision. In Chapter 2, Maurice Vanstone provides an overview of the historical and contemporary contexts of probation policy and practice. The chapter also examines how probation practitioners navigate evolving policy provisions and the implications of their actions for compliance during probation supervision. In Chapter 3, Gwen Robinson draws attention to the nature of compliance as a multidimensional concept and argues that the concept should not be decontextualized from the policy and practice developments from which it emerges. Trish McCulloch expands our understanding of compliance in Chapter 4 which emphasizes that compliance is a co-produced phenomenon. The chapter also identifies the policy developments that shape its definition; and highlights the active role of supervisees in its production.

Section II brings to the fore the typically ignored voices in criminal justice research: the perspectives and experiences of the key actors whose actions shape compliance. The key actors are: the practitioners and the people they supervise. The section comprises six chapters. In Chapter 5, Anthony Bottoms introduces an innovative approach to understanding compliance. The approach departs from the traditional focus on using external mechanisms such as threats, incentives or other criminal justice interventions to promote compliance. By contrast, the chapter provides insights into self-applied situational mechanisms of compliance that stem from the self-motivation of the individual offender. Building on the theme of offender self-motivation, in Chapter 6 Ralph Serin and his colleagues propose a departure from the traditional focus of theory and research on extrinsic compliance mechanisms. They emphasize instead, the importance of acknowledging and building on the motivation and strengths of the offenders as key mechanisms of desistance. In Chapter 7, Peter Raynor presents the findings of a study that examined offenders' views about the supervision experiences that encourage them to comply. The chapter describes the compliance strategies employed by probation practitioners in Jersey. In Chapter 8, Ben Crewe also expands existing understandings of compliance and its dynamics by exploring compliance and its mechanisms in prison contexts. By focusing its analysis within the contexts of supervision in a medium security prison, Ben Crewe's chapter clearly draws attention to the contextual nature of compliance. It presents the findings of a study that equips us with a better understanding of offenders' perspectives regarding compliance, and how offenders' levels of motivation can affect compliance. Mike Nellis also alerts us to the contextual nature of compliance in Chapter 9. He offers a detailed and insightful analysis of yet another context of criminal justice supervision – electronic monitoring. Like the other chapters in Section I, the chapter also describes the factors that can affect compliance. These range from perceived legitimacy to levels of offender motivation. In Chapter 10, Pamela Ugwudike describes the findings of a study that examined probation practitioners' views about effective compliance strategies.

Section III of the book explores new and emerging insights in compliance theory, research and practice. In Chapters 11 to 15, the authors present empirical findings from different jurisdictions, including Australia; North America – Canada and the United States; and Western Europe – England and Wales, Scotland, France and Belgium. There is an examination of how different criminal justice practitioners involved in encouraging offender compliance interpret and implement the policy provisions that govern or guide their work. The practitioners include probation, prison and youth justice practitioners and judicial professionals. The objective of this section is to draw together emerging international perspectives and international research on the skills, knowledge and strategies that are central to effective offender engagement. The section should also provide insights that can significantly inform policy and evidence-based practice across multidisciplinary contexts. Opening up the discussion in Chapter 11, Martine Herzog-Evans presents insights from France. In that chapter, Martine Herzog-Evans directs attention to the role of the courts in encouraging compliance. Indeed, the role of the courts in this context has been overlooked. Yet one can see from Martine's chapter that the courts can occupy a productive role. In Chapter 12, Stef Decoene and Kristel Beyens offer a multidisciplinary account of compliance. The chapter focuses mainly on policy and practice in Belgium. Christopher Trotter follows on in Chapter 13 with insights from Australia. The chapter draws on a study that demonstrates the impact of specific evidence-based supervision skills on compliance in youth justice contexts. Melissa Alexander and colleagues extend the discussion about evidence-based compliance strategies in Chapter 14. The chapter emphasizes that adequate staff training is required for the effective implementation of evidence-based supervision skills. Guy Bourgon and Leticia Guiterrez offer further insights on evidence-based compliance mechanisms in Chapter 15 which sets outs findings from Canada.

In Section IV, the contributing authors contextualize compliance theory, policy and practice by identifying the compliance issues that may arise during the supervision of offenders with specific demographic attributes. This group comprises women, young people and supervisees involved in drug use. In Chapter 16 Loraine Gelsthorpe describes the compliance issues that affect how women serving community orders comply. Tim Bateman explores compliance in youth justice contexts in Chapter 17 and critically explores the policy and other factors that are relevant in these contexts. In Chapter 18, Paul Sparrow examines the policy developments that pose implications for compliance in penal contexts involving drug-using offenders. The final chapter of the book draws together the key themes covered by each of the chapters and attempts to answer the question: what works in offender compliance?

Notes

1. Short-term compliance in this context may be defined as: 'compliance with the specific legal requirements' of a court order (Bottoms 2001). For example, attending statutory appointments with a probation practitioner may constitute a form of short-term compliance.
2. According to Bottoms (2001), long-term compliance can be described as compliance with the criminal law after the period of supervision. For a broad description of the difference between short-term and long-term compliance, please see Bottoms (2001).

References

Bottoms, A. E. (2001) 'Compliance and Community Penalties'. in A. E. Bottoms, L. Gelsthorpe and S. Rex (Eds) *Community Penalties: Change and Challenges*. Devon: Willan.

Dowden, C. and Andrews, D. A. (2004) 'The Importance of Staff Practice in Delivering Effective Correctional Treatment: A Meta-Analytic Review of Core Correctional Practice'. *International Journal of Offender Therapy and Comparative Criminology* 48(2), 203–214.

Hollin, C. R., McGuire, J., Hounsome, J. C., Hatcher, R. M., Bilby, C. A. L., and Palmer, E. J. (2008) 'Cognitive Skills Behaviour Programs for Offenders in the Community: A Reconviction Analysis'. *Criminal Justice and Behavior* 35, 269–283.

Kemshall, H. and Canton, R. with Bailey, R., Dominey, J., Simpkin B. and Yates, S. (2002) *The Effective Management of Programme Attrition: A Report for the National Probation Service (Welsh Region)*. Leicester: De Montfort University. http://www.design.dmu.ac.uk/Images/ATTRITION%20%20REPORT%20-%20PDF_tcm6-10440.pdf (accessed June 2003).

McNeill, F. and Robinson, G. (2013) 'Liquid Legitimacy and Community Sanctions'. in A. Crawford and A. Hucklesby (Eds) *Legitimacy and Compliance in Criminal Justice* (pp. 116–137). NY, London: Routledge.

Ministry of Justice. (2010) *Offender Management Caseload Statistics 2009*. Ministry of Justice Statistics Bulletin. London: Ministry of Justice.

Ministry of Justice. (2011) Adult Reconvictions: Results from the 2009 Cohort. www.justice.gov.uk/publications/statistics-and-data/reoffending/adults.htm (accessed January 2013).

Ministry of Justice. (2012) Criminal Justice Statistics: Quarterly Update to December 2011. Ministry of Justice Statistics bulletin. http://www.justice.gov.uk/downloads/statistics/criminal-justice-stats/criminal-justice-stats-dec- 2011.pdf (accessed January 2013).

Palmer, E. J., McGuire, J., Hounsome, J. C., Hatcher, R. M., Bilby, C. A. L., and Hollin, C. R. (2007) 'Offending Behaviour Programmes in the Community: The Effects on Reconviction of Three Programmes with Adult Male Offenders'. *Legal and Criminological Psychology* 12, 251–264.

Robinson, G. and McNeill, F. (2008) 'Exploring the Dynamics of Compliance with Community Penalties'. *Theoretical Criminology* 12, 431.

Tyler, T. R. (1990) *Why People Obey the Law*. New Haven, CT: Yale University Press.

Tyler, T. R. (2013) 'Legitimacy and Compliance: The Virtues of Self-Regulation'. in A. Crawford and A. Hucklesby (Eds) *Legitimacy and Compliance in Criminal Justice* (pp. 8–28). NY, London: Routledge.

Tyler, T. R. and Huo, Y. J. (2002) *Trust in the Law: Encouraging Public Cooperation with the Police and Courts*. New York: Russell-Sage Foundation.

2
Compulsory Persuasion in Probation History

Maurice Vanstone

What follows in this chapter is a series of reflections on the probation service's function of supervising people within a legal framework which requires them to comply with certain conditions in exchange for escaping the stigma of a criminal conviction or, in some cases, prison – what Fielding (1984: 3) describes as 'a role which is gravely problematic in its combination of contradictory functions'. For most of its history, the probation service has cherished a social work identity, but what Raynor (1978) has described as 'compulsory persuasion' and others as 'authoritative and compulsory power' (Howard Association 1881: 4) has ever hovered in the background like the ghost of Banquo. It was there when Matthew Davenport Hill applied the concept of recognizance, when John Augustus bailed his first drunkard, and when the first probation officers began to advise, assist and befriend people in the United Kingdom. The driving motivation might always have been to help, but the largely unspoken dilemma has always been about how to persuade people to submit to the authority inherent in the probation contract and, perhaps more importantly, to participate in the helping process on offer. In his account of work with a man with a drink problem, Thomas Holmes (1900: 210), the police court missionary, set out his approach:

> At night I waited for him in his own room. He returned one morning about two, when I quickly took possession of him. About four o'clock he insisted on going out, but I had locked the door, so he had to remain. The next day I cut short his debauch, by taking him home with me, and putting him under lock and key. This he was most indignant about, and questioned my right to make a prisoner of him. I told him might was right, and that he had got to remain.

His successors in the forthcoming probation project were to be far more reticent about infringing the liberty of the individual, although, interestingly, echoes of his approach can be heard some 80 years later in claims made about the Kent Control Unit that 'in real terms the Probation Control Unit exceeds in severity any institutional sentence currently available to the Magistrate's Court for a single offence.'[1] Seemingly, they, like Holmes, had few qualms about their approach and were confident about its simple efficacy. The real story of compliance and enforcement exposes greater complexity than this and is interesting, if less remarkable.

So, what kind of story is this? Emphatically, it is not a detailed elaboration of how probation officers have attempted to encourage compliance, because, as a number of commentators have indicated, there is a dearth of documented evidence and a paucity of empirical investigation into compliance (Robinson and McNeill 2010; Ugwudike 2010). The knowledge base has been succinctly summed up by Ugwudike: breach action has most often been taken for total non-cooperation, members of probation staff have displayed a reluctance to enforce legal requirements rigidly, and the use of professional discretion has been widespread. Early research shows that cooperative probationers (or, at least, those who were not breached) had high levels of contact, rapport with their supervisors, and support; and low levels of control. Moreover, they had been supervised by a probation officer with social work experience prior to entry into the probation service (Folkard et al. 1966). In community service, breach remained a last resort until at least the 1970s (Vass 1990), and, as Deering (2010: 171) explains, even at the beginning of the 21st century probation workers are 'clear that it [is] their role to decide on the acceptability of absences and that this [is] not applied in a uniform or apparently consistent manner'. So, even in the current 'tougher framework', practitioners share the same 'care versus control concerns' of previous times (Raynor 1985).

A strictly historical account of this aspect of practice could be summed up in a few words – probation workers used their discretion and, if at all possible, avoided breach action. However, there is legitimacy in a more reflective approach which pays more attention to organizational, political and social contexts through which the service has passed. Before embarking on an exploration of the probation service's engagement with these authority-laden issues, it is necessary to be clear about what is meant by compliance and enforcement.

Definitions

Both emanate from the simple definition of the authority of a probation order in an early handbook on sentencing (Home Office 1964: 5):

> [Probation] involves the discipline of submission by the offender while at liberty to supervision by a probation officer.

So, compliance relates to the behaviour of the probationer and involves '[o]bserving the legal requirements of the order of the court or the terms of a licence or, more broadly, conforming with the purpose and expectations of supervision' (Canton 2007: 56). Enforcement, on the other hand, relates not only to the actions of the practitioner but also to the policy and procedures of the organization within which they work. It involves '[a]ction taken by the Probation Service in response to non-compliance, either through the courts in relation to community orders, or through executive recall to prison in the case of the vast majority of post-release licences' (Nicholls 2007: 120). Bottoms (2001) has provided helpful further clarification with his distinction between short-term cooperation with the legal requirements (the keeping of appointments and so on) and long-term desistance from offending (engagement in the processes of change). Even more helpfully, he has addressed the complexity of the latter by breaking it down into three types, namely: instrumental/prudential (rational calculation of pros and cons); normative (sense of moral responsibility and/or commitment to others); constraint-based (submission to discipline); and habit/routine. More recently, Robinson and McNeill (2010) have given added depth to Bottoms's definitions with the introduction of a further distinction between formal compliance (following the letter of the law) and substantive compliance (engagement with the spirit of the order's purpose).

Although these contributions add significantly to current thinking about compliance and enforcement, it is important to be aware that a focus on breach action or its absence alone does not tell the whole story. Enforcement short of breach action, in the past at least, involved a range of practices to encourage the probationer to comply with the requirements of an order: in particular, this included letters and home visits. Up until the 1980s, faced by the failure of a probationer to keep an appointment, there was an expectation of follow-up by letter and home visits. It was the responsibility of the officer to encourage, cajole and persuade probationers to maintain regular contact, but the locus of blame in the event of a breakdown of a probation order has shifted. So, when attempts to influence and modify behaviour through moral exhortation underpinned by Christian mores failed, this could be attributed to moral deficiencies in the character of the probationer, but, as the professionalization of the service led to more emphasis on the application of psychological theories and the technical skill of the probation officer, failure was more likely to be attributed to the probation officer. Now, coming full circle, with the stress on changing behaviour through control, surveillance and the policing of conditions, blame for failure can once again be placed firmly on the shoulders of the probationer. Inevitably, perhaps, *staying* with the probationer has become less of a priority. In an interesting observation, Drakeford (1992: 204) has described the detrimental effect of the rapid decline of home visiting on the principle of 'active stickability: [that is the] capacity to stick with individuals who have never had or have exhausted the ordinary process of social sustenance'. Any understanding of the processes of compliance and enforcement, therefore, has to take account of a parallel understanding of how this principle of 'stickability' has had impact on practice, as illustrated by this quote from an experienced officer:

> I was also quite prepared to bring back to court those who broke the rules of their probation order [...] I saw no real conflict in these two roles [...] On the other hand the fact that the client had failed did not mean that you gave up on them. To take a client back to court was usually done to re-establish the probation order [...] 'hang in there' was my motto in almost all cases.[2]

It was a way of working under the threat posed by a change of climate which, in Drakeford's view, began at the beginning of the 1980s and culminated in National Standards, regulation, the 'replacement of cooperative by coercive relationships' and probation practice becoming 'an activity to be carried out upon, rather than with, its recipients' (p. 203). The keynote of National Standards, introduced in the 1990s, was, indeed, enforcement, and, although this argument might be criticized for contributing to an oversimplified version of the history of the probation service's involvement in control (Vanstone 2004a, 2004b), it does point accurately to a pivotal change in the mechanics of enforcement and attempts to invoke compliance operated as they are now, mainly from the office desk.

Early preoccupations

As some reports in *The Times* indicate, magistrates wanted to give the new Probation Act a fair chance of success, albeit not always with high levels of confidence. In the case of a 28-year-old charged with being a suspected person, it was reported that the magistrate 'could not be very enthusiastic about the success of the new Act, but [...] thought it was desirable that the Act should be given a fair trial'.[3] In another, it was reported that in 'dealing with the prisoner, the magistrate remarked that the Home Secretary was most anxious to secure the good working of the Act'.[4] So goodwill there was, and by the end of the first year of probation's existence a mere 5 per cent of people placed on orders were brought back before the court in breach (Dersley 2000, cited in Hedderman and Hough 2004), and it is probable that this remained the position for the next 70 years, as confirmed by Lawson's (1978) study of 55 probationers in Essex, which revealed a breach rate of 3.7 per cent.[5]

Authority had been at the heart of police court missionary work, and its place in the newly created probation officer role was established at the outset. The clear expectation in the 1908 Probation Rules that probation officers had to bring any failure to comply to the attention of the court (Bochel 1976) reveals the exercise of control as an undeniable feature of early probation practice (Vanstone 2004a). By the time of the first set of guidelines for probation officers, enforcement was an established part of the professional language. Specific attention was drawn to enforcement as 'the *ultimate* sanction of probation, [which] *must* be *resorted* to if there is a reason to believe that the offender will not respond to the opportunities given him' in order to ensure that the probationer does not 'think that the promise which he has made by his recognizance is of little effect' (Le Mesurier 1935: 81; my italics). It is defined, however, as a last resort, and the handbook stresses the importance of officer discretion by pointing out that when a breach occurs the 'spirit, not the letter, of the law, should guide the officer in such an emergency' and although the 'probation officer has the power of the Court behind him [...] he must refrain from using it arbitrarily' (pp. 130–131). Le Mesurier cautioned against the counter-productive nature of issuing threats, and, although she made the duty placed on the officer explicit, she engaged with the conflict and tension in the role that persist today:

> The probation officer is in a peculiar position. He is an officer of the Court, and his first duty is to the Court: he is also a social worker. There need be no conflict in principle between the probation officer as a social worker and as a Court officer, but under existing conditions the occasion may arise when he has to subordinate his feelings as a social worker. (p. 131)

The next handbook (Jarvis 1974), first published in the late 1960s, made no reference to discretion but set out the position purely in legal terms:

> If a probationer fails to comply with one or more of the requirements of a probation order made by a magistrates' court he is liable to be brought before the supervising court or before the court which made the order. (p. 66)

Obviously, care should be taken about how this difference is interpreted, but it seems reasonable to speculate that by the time Jarvis produced his guidance the discretion used by probation officers in their interpretation of the letter of the law was taken for granted and did not need reiteration.

Although it is easy to overplay the place of authority in what was essentially a social work role, as several writers have argued (and as these guidelines demonstrate), the social work element of probation, while clearly an important ingredient, was not viable until it was placed in a legal framework and provided with a coercive element (Harris 1995; Hedderman and Hough 2004; Vanstone 2008) – a point summed up neatly by one probation officer working in the late 1950s when she explained that help comes from 'self-discipline or the discipline the order imposes [...] through the court, and its servant, the probation officer' (Todd 1963: 30). Indeed, control and the use of authority were very much at the heart of political thinking at the time of the reading of the Probation of Offenders Bill in 1907 when additional clauses were being introduced:

> Another clause will enable the Court to lay down additional conditions in the recognizance, failure to observe any of which will render the offender liable to apprehension and imprisonment.[6]

Despite the validity of this rendition of the early history, it remains true that, for the first 70 years or so of the life of probation, the social work element was in focus, with coercion part of a blurred background. Indeed, the dominance of this aspect of probation practice is illustrated by the fact that, up until the 1970s at least, probation officers were involved in matrimonial work and divorce court reports, and acted as Guardian ad Litem in adoption cases (Rimmer 1995). In fact, work in the divorce court was made a statutory duty in the 1959 probation rules (Mair and Burke 2012).

Of course, all of this is not to suggest that the probation service had settled its nervousness about use of authority. King (1964: 78), for example, asserted that the probation service had not solved 'the problem of practicing social work in an authoritarian setting', but in her discussion of the compulsory nature of supervision even she revealed her own social work pedigree by defining submission to authority as 'an opportunity for growth and change' in the probationer (p. 86). Although he found senior probation officers were more likely to take breach action than main grade officers, Lawson (1978: 61) concluded that variations in breach rates revealed a reluctance by some officers to take such action when required because 'they may find the idea of formal sanctions impalatable, and seek to avoid the problem by avoidance and drift.' There is no such fudge in what may be regarded as the first independent account of probation practice: St John (1961: 72–73) understood that officers, while trying to avoid giving the impression that the service was 'a crooks' protection service', faced a problem when taking on the role of prosecutor and becoming 'starkly identified with Authority' and imposing 'at least temporary damage' on the 'friendly relationship'.

A very real and present problem

The more frequent attention being paid to these conflicts and problems in written discourse from the 1970s onwards is evidence of growing concern. For example, while acknowledging that probation officers have always been involved to some extent in a minimal degree of controlling probationers' lives through the maintenance of contact, Goslin (1975: 56), in a paper which seems in retrospect to be a precursor to Raynor's (1978) choices made under constraint thesis and to be a harbinger of the eventual removal of consent from the process of making a probation order, argued that the direction heralded by the Younger Report (Advisory Council on the Penal System 1974) represented a 'marked advance into the territory of personal freedom'. Both parole and probation retained consent as essential, but the new direction being proposed meant that 'control-to-enforce-contact' was to be transformed into 'control-to-enforce-conduct'. In a critique of the report, Wright (1974: 103–104) attacked what he judged to be the fallacy that the extension of controls and sanctions would induce compliance, and instead conjured up an alternative vision of the structured use of a whole range of different methods designed to improve such things as problem-solving and survival skills to accompany one-to-one work. In his model, control would be invoked, but on 'the level of personal influence', and return to court would be 'a last resort'.

However, the increasing concern was given a voice by Harris (1977: 434), who, in a stark warning, expressed the view that the probation service had not adjusted effectively to new demands. As he bluntly put it:

> in spite of the vast social and professional changes which have occurred since the early days, the probation service's organization remains geared to the performing of its original tasks, and its expectation remains that philosophically its relationship to the magistracy will stay much as it always has. The probation service has not kept pace with the developing roles demanded of the main social service agency operating in the penal field, while the expectation of courts and public alike that it will continue to provide a rather odd mixture of discipline for its own sake and treatment has rendered innovations of limited value and has reduced the extent to which probation officers can use their considerable training for the benefit of their clients.

Though perhaps not as pessimistic as Harris, Vass (1980) identified further complexity when he pointed out the three-fold nature of the conflict facing probation officers who juggled with the roles of helper, defence counsellor and prosecutor. For Harris (1980), reconciling these roles was becoming impossible and he argued, therefore, that the probation service should accept defeat in its quest to find ways of reducing offending by means of social work, and concede that it was too difficult to respond to the genuine needs for help of poor probationers within a statutory supervisory framework. His proposed solution was a separation of the roles, with probation becoming a court-based welfare service offering voluntary help, leaving the delivery of punishment in the community to a new agency. The problems of adjustment highlighted by Harris were recognized, too, by Haxby (1978: 149) in his analysis of a growing, changing service, but he advocated a markedly different solution. While still valuing the place of social work in the *treatment* of people who offend, he articulated the need for a new correctional service – 'a unified administration for a variety of penal provisions in the community' – which would prioritize diversion from custody, base itself in the community and link with formal and informal community groups, diversify its methods beyond the casework relationship, and involve itself in what he termed semi-custodial provisions.

Haxby's proposal was firmly rooted in a social work tradition and encompassed the responsibilities of trying to control behaviour, but the new agency advocated by Harris would have been a perfect fit for what Senior (1984) has termed the *surveillance model* and Raynor (1985) *controlism*, and it had an early champion. Griffiths (1982) created controversy within the service and particularly its union, the National Association of Probation Officers, with his proposal that the probation service should embrace the goal of containment and place its emphasis on surveillance and control, perhaps the kind of 'intensive controlling supervision' a probation officer had suggested five years earlier (Sterry 1977: 98). Certainly, alarm bells began to ring and, in a no-holds-barred critique, Drakeford (1983: 7–10) accused Griffiths of peddling a simplistic thesis based on a view of human nature 'which appears to owe considerably more to religion than to science' and a definition of probation as punishment. If Griffiths's ideas were to prevail, he warned, the humanitarian roots of probation would be uprooted and the goal of rehabilitation eschewed, and, as a consequence, the probation service would become 'an irrelevant accretion on the back of an already over-punitive system'.

The emergence of *controlism* (probably most aptly symbolized by the short life of the Kent Control Unit with its curfew, restrictive conditions, and its intensification of the care versus control issue) and other attempts to resolve the conflict between help and control have been aired fully in many accounts, so only need summarizing here (Raynor 1985; Raynor and Vanstone 2002; McWilliams 1987). Walker and Beaumont (1981) advocated progressive, humanistic, socialist practice; Bryant et al. (1978) established a practical experiment based on a primary contract relating to the basic conditions of the probation order and a secondary contract relating to the voluntary acceptance of needs-linked help; Bottoms and McWilliams (1979) set out a collaborative non-treatment model which encompassed aims of implementing statutory supervision, diverting from custody and reducing crime; and Raynor and Vanstone (1994) attempted to adjust that model to fit the reality of the probation service's modern context. What these attempts have in common is that they were all concerned with maintaining the notion of the probationer as a citizen with as much freedom to make choices as the constraints and reality of a court order allowed. Furthermore, it can be claimed that they also shared a faith in probation officers as custodians of the principle of freedom, a faith, incidentally, not shared by Lord Bridge of Harwich in the Cullen v. Rogers case (Cullen v. Rogers [1982] 1 W.L.R 729). He expressed his concern about the 'unfettered discretionary control' of probation officers and determined that 'any discretion conferred on the probation officer pursuant to the terms of the order to regulate a probationer's activities, had in itself to be confined within well-defined limits'.

These doubts about the benevolence of state-sponsored help had been raised earlier by C. S. Lewis (1949: 5) in his critique of humanitarian theory and humanitarians, when he argued that the 'things done to a criminal, even if they are called cures, will be just as compulsory as they were in the old days when we called them punishments'. This resonates with Fielding's (1984: 77) later observation that probation officers '[faced] by realistic and idealistic reasons for reluctance to expand control at the expense of care [...] have developed an operating ideology that defines control as care'. Bean (1976) alluded to the same issue with his tellingly sceptical phrase 'a system of rampant discretions'. Paradoxically, for others it was the loss of discretion that posed the greatest threat to personal liberty. The report of a NAPO (National Association of Probation Officers) Hampshire Branch study group on the Sentenced to Social Work experiment forecast that control would eclipse care functions and that probationers would experience a more rigid system. The new system, they argued, placed 'an inappropriate emphasis on control and surveillance whilst removing officer discretion'. According to the group, many probationers experienced 'great difficulty with the concept and [found] themselves faced with a reduced choice and little opportunity for negotiation'.[7] A few years earlier, in a critique of the Sentenced to Social Work model, James (1979) prefigured the very same concern that probationers would be sentenced to surveillance and control as opposed to social work help. So, underpinning the care versus control controversy was an equally divisive, highly pertinent and still unresolved philosophical dispute about whether the law or probation practice was the more trusted custodian of personal liberty.

A changing environment

Uncertainty, ambivalence and tension, therefore, have always permeated the probation role, but undoubtedly their intensity and degree was increased by the shift of probation practice into deeper waters. Traditionally the probation service operated in shallower waters, supervising people with less serious criminal profiles and in a benign political and social climate. The shift began with what Nellis (2001) has described as Labour's strategy of modernization, which increased the service's role in after-care and introduced practitioners to higher-risk criminal profiles through the inauguration in 1967 of parole or, as Fielding (1984: 76) put it, 'this stimulus to control-oriented work'. James (1979: 16) also identified the 1960s as the time when the probation service came more under central government control (principally because of statutory after-care and parole) and when 'concern for the client' was subordinated to concerns about risk to the public, with the result that officers became responsible for 'more duties which involved control and coercion'.

This introduction to higher-risk probationers may have also brought the notion of protection of the public more to the fore, and heightened supervisors' sense of responsibility for monitoring the behaviour of those they were supervising. A short time after this, Community Service Orders and Day Training Centres were introduced, and their status as alternatives to custody ensured that the service actively sought out people with more serious offending careers. As one principal officer put it about DTCs:

> We expect that the majority of potential trainees will have had at least one prior custodial sentence.

> Current offences and previous offences make likely a prison sentence whether suspended or not. The day training centre must be seen as a definite alternative to a custodial sentence [...][8]

Their history, too, has been well documented (Wright 1985) and they are mentioned here merely to argue that one of their effects was to reinforce the effect of the introduction of parole and familiarize probation staff with greater numbers of a hitherto rare category of probationer. The radical new approach to juvenile justice inaugurated by academics from Lancaster University (Thorpe et al. 1980) compounded this effect in so far as, when the probation service began to encounter the small percentage of juveniles who had continued offending and moved into adulthood, they already had well-developed criminal careers, albeit obscured by the new system of cautioning. Ultimately, this drift into deeper waters became an all-embracing official policy through the introduction of management by objectives and the specified target of radically reducing the number of probation orders given to those first convicted by the courts: the service declared its intent to divert higher-risk probationers from custody.

Each of these changes produced a partially accurate, though incomplete, account of the changes in probation practice. The complete story takes into account not only the fact that during this period many practitioners continued to base their work on traditional social work values (Vanstone 2004a), but also the reality that changes in the broader context within which practitioners struggled with these issues began to change significantly and irrevocably. It is a contention of this chapter that these changes have proved to be far more significant than any others in the story of late 20th-century and early

21st-century probation. As Feeley and Simon (1992) put it, a new penology with a distinctively different discourse was emerging. The old discourse had focused on individual morality and culpability, and reasons for offending: essentially, it was concerned with the moral and the clinical. It featured diagnosis and assessment and was concerned with punishment, rehabilitation, the causes and correlates of criminal behaviour, and interventions to effect change and reconcile the individual with the community. Family, employers and various community institutions provided positive influence and social restraint. In contrast, the new discourse is concerned with categorization, targeting and management of groups that threaten social stability, such as the small group of young people who are deemed responsible for the majority of crime. Major preoccupations are prediction, risk and statistical analysis, and it is characterized by reference to 'high risk offenders' and 'career criminals': managerialism holds sway, the prison population ever increases and mechanisms of control spread.

This discourse has its roots, perhaps, in the penal crisis of the 1980s (Cavadino and Dignan 2002), flourishes in Young's (1998, 1999) exclusive society, is sustained by the politicization of crime (Downes and Morgan 1997) and is given added power by the scandals surrounding high-profile professional failure (Fitzgibbon 2011). Cavadino and Dignan (2002) argued that by the early 1990s, because of, among other things, increasing concerns about cost, loss of belief in rehabilitation, erosion of the legitimacy of prisons, prison riots, greater public scrutiny and charges of being overindulgent, the need for changes in the penal system had reached a critical point. Young (1999) theorized that the long-standing social contract under which troublesome groups of people retained their status as citizens had broken down and been replaced by an agenda of separation and exclusion. Parallel to these developments, Downes and Morgan (1997) showed that, from the point when the Conservative Party successfully exploited crime as leverage for their election to office in the 1979 election, crime had slowly become an increasingly difficult issue for politicians who wanted to either maintain or achieve power. All had impact on the new discourse, but a more direct effect on the developmental context of community sentences can be discerned in Fitzgibbon's account of how recent scandals of professional shortcomings (the murders of the French students Gabriel Ferez and Laurent Bonomo, and Baby P) have had a significantly greater detrimental effect on probation and social work than earlier scandals (the murder of Maria Colwell and the case of the poisoner, Graham Young, in the 1970s). In a broad-ranging analysis, she shows how changes in media responses, community structure, political culture and institutional change have led to a particular political construction of public protection which itself has undermined the skills and status of professional workers and produced a clamour for greater control, inappropriate levels of media influence, and political indifference to, and denial of, the effect of cuts in resources.

Tragically, the effect of all this has occurred during a prolonged period when the social circumstances of probationers 'in terms of unemployment and poverty, have worsened significantly' and when the service is dealing with more people who fall into this category and who are the likely targets of breach action (Drakeford 1993: 292). Just over 20 years ago, Drakeford, in what he acknowledged as a polemic, expressed his fears about the new regime of breach heralded by the 1991 Criminal Justice Act and suggested that assessment of seriousness would have a negative impact on probation practice, destroy the alternatives to custody model and encourage probation officers in pre-sentence reports to propose disproportionate restrictions of liberty. He exposed what he saw as four fallacies relating to breach: first, that it has a positive therapeutic effect on the probationer and his or her relationship with the supervisor; second, that those taken back before the courts are likely to be fined or admonished; third, that breach action is fair; and fourth, that it increases credibility with sentencers. On the latter point, Drakeford used an amusing analogy of Ford Motor Company producing more faulty cars and highlighting the fact to customers in order to encourage them to buy. In the face of all this, he advocated new, sensible policies which use the whole range of National Standards requirements (e.g., the minimum requirement for enforcement and the issue of chaotic lifestyles) to create greater flexibility and use of discretion, encourage the traditional practice of practitioners making 'every effort to keep contact alive' (p. 300), implement anti-discriminatory measures and employ 'breach gatekeeping panels' (p. 301). He concluded by asserting that '[strong arm tactics in probation are a sign of weakness in the thinking of the service [and, therefore, less] coercion and more consideration are the ingredients suggested here for a defensible as well as a successful future' (p. 303).

Interestingly, 11 years later Hedderman and Hough (2004: 128) seemed to endorse aspects of Drakeford's argument for what they termed 'a graduated response' when they pointed out that the revisions of National Standards had increased the chances of failure and 'may be at odds with effective practice'. According to them, the need was to find ways of ensuring that compliance processes increased the chances of successful completions of orders and programmes in order to increase rather than reduce effectiveness.[9] Hedderman (2003) had recognized previously, however, that, in as much as research evidence showed that completers of programmes were less likely to reoffend, National Standards might assist effective practice. That said, she, too, underlined the value of a graduated response and urged greater emphasis on positive normative actions to encourage attendance: these included rewarding rather than punishing good responses to supervision, and making appointments easier by coinciding them with signing on or other times that suited the probationer. An interesting study, drawing 882 probationers from 11 probation areas with harsh or lenient approaches to breach, provided evidence that harshness or leniency seemed to have no effect on reconviction rates, and advocated, first, some realism about the reduction of offending effect of tough enforcement and, second, greater emphasis on positive reinforcement as a means of improving compliance (Hearndon and Millie 2003). This resonates with Waterhouse's (1983: 63) conclusion that there is 'scant evidence to support the general argument that the effective supervision of offenders should be based on techniques associated with authority and control'. Yet, as though to ensure that the need for uncertainty was not forgotten, Hedderman and Hough (2004) argued that a clearer emphasis on enforcement which ensures that probationers are clearer about their position is likely to improve engagement and make effective supervision more achievable.

Some concluding thoughts

In this new world of probation with its National Offender Management Service (NOMS) and Probation Trusts, the language of rehabilitation and reintegration lingers on, surviving in the imaginations of some practitioners and academics (Deering 2010), but the emphasis is not on individual success or failure but, rather, correctional programmes designed to control and manage behaviour deemed a threat to society. Rather than assisting the process of reintegrating people into their communities, NOMS is primed to control problematical people in the community in as cost-effective a way as possible. This is not to say that control is necessarily a problem simply juxtaposed to abuse of power: after all, probation workers quite rightly do not shrink from the positive use of power and control in order to combat discrimination or protect the vulnerable. The fundamental problem is the growing detachment of practitioners from the people they supervise. Perhaps what is needed is reconnection and an unashamed commitment to a transparent humanitarianism so that probationers have clear guidelines, know what is expected of them and understand the nature of the collaborative contractual relationship (Robinson and McNeill 2010). Transparent humanitarianism of necessity involves the positive use of power. Raynor's (1978) assertion is as relevant today as it was 34 years ago:

> Constraints or controls imposed for the benefit or protection of persons other than the subject of the constraint may well be necessary, but their nature and purpose should be explicit and not presented in a mystifying or mystified way. In this way choices and contracts, instead of being overlooked or obscured, can be made more informed and more real, confirming a sense of identity and responsibility rather than undermining it.

Probation was conceived out of Victorian philanthropic concern for the poor and disadvantaged, and it grew up with the idea that positively expressed care and practical help in face to face relationships with people was not only worthwhile but likely to benefit those people and society generally. The rather simple idea that people are moved and influenced by such relationships is gaining renewed currency – an old world truth resuscitated in a modern context (Ugwudike 2010; Robinson and McNeill 2010; Turner 2010). Ugwudike's (2010: 340) study demonstrates, first, that enforcement which is based on positive relationships and pays heed to the relevant individual circumstances of each case is more likely to achieve compliance; and, second, that practitioners need to 'develop an individualised approach that is responsive to the practical, structural and situational factors that affect compliance'. Turner (2010: 361), drawing on Australian research findings, stresses the importance of the 'continuity, consistency and commitment of worker-client relationships' to increased compliance. Finally, Robinson and McNeill (2010: 377), in highlighting the importance of substantive compliance, assert that practitioners must establish 'the moral right to influence another human subject with their consent'. Each of these contributions has this simple idea at its core. Whether it can survive, as Deering (2010: 188) quite correctly asserts, depends more than anything else on whether governments choose 'positive, curious, humanistic practice' over media-friendly macho posturing. Perhaps we should not hold our breath.

Notes

1. Unpublished paper by the Kent Probation and After-Care Service, *The Widening Scope of the Probation and After-Care Service* (No date: page 6).
2. Taken from an interview undertaken during my research into the history of the service: Vanstone (2001).
3. *The Times* 8 January 1908, p. 17, Issue 38537.
4. *The Times* 2 January 1908, p. 11, Issue 38532.
5. By comparison, in 2007 21 per cent of community service orders for females were terminated for failure to comply (22 per cent for men) (Ministry of Justice 2008).
6. *The Times* 18 June, p. 14, Issue 38362.
7. Unpublished report by the NAPO branch of the probation area in which the pilot projects operated. No date is given for the report, but the study was undertaken after the projects were started in 1981 and it drew on the views of officers involved in the projects.
8. Paper prepared by H. Sanders for a residential conference of principal probation officers held at Leicester University in September 1972.
9. On this point, it is interesting to reflect back to Lawson's (1978) small-scale study, which showed that probationers who were taken back to court subsequently reported more regularly.

References

Advisory Council on the Penal System. (1974) *Young Adult Offenders*. London: HMSO.
Bean, P. (1976) *Rehabilitation and Deviance*. London: Routledge and Kegan Paul.

Bochel, D. (1976) *Probation and After-care: Its Development in England & Wales*. Edinburgh: Scottish Academic Press.

Bottoms, A. (2001) 'Compliance and Community Penalties'. in A. Bottoms, L. Gelsthorpe and S. Rex (Eds) *Community Penalties. Changes and Challenges*. Cullompton: Willan.

Bottoms, A. E. and McWilliams, W. (1979) 'A Non-Treatment Paradigm for Probation Practice', *British Journal of Social Work* 9, 159–202.

Bryant, M., Coker, J., Estlea, B., Himmel, S. and Knapp, T. (1978) 'Sentenced to Social Work'. *Probation Journal* 25(4), 110–114.

Canton, R. (2007) 'Compliance'. in R. Canton and D. Hancock (Eds) *Dictionary of Probation Offender Management*. Cullompton: Willan.

Cavadino, M. and Dignan, J. (2002) *The Penal System: An Introduction*. Third Edition. London: Sage.

Deering, J. (2010) *Probation Practice and the New Penology. Practitioner Reflections*. Farnham: Ashgate.

Dersley, I. (2000) 'Acceptable or Unacceptable? Local Probation Service Policy on Non-Compliance and Enforcement'. Unpublished dissertation. Birmingham University School of Social Sciences.

Downes, D. and Morgan, R. (1997) 'Dumping the "Hostages to Fortune"? The Politics of Law and Order in Post-War Britain'. in M. Maguire, R. Morgan and R. Reiner (Eds) *The Oxford Handbook of Criminology*. Second Edition. Oxford: Clarendon Press.

Drakeford, M. (1983) 'Probation: Containment or Liberty?' *Probation Journal* 30(1), 7–10.

Drakeford, M. (1992) 'Quietly, but not at Home'. *Probation Journal* 39(4), 202–204.

Drakeford, M. (1993) 'The Probation Service, Breach and the Criminal Justice Act 1991'. *Howard Journal* 32(4), 291–303.

Feeley, M. and Simon, J. (1992) 'The New Penology: Notes on the Emerging Strategy of Corrections and its Implications'. *Criminology* 30, 449–474.

Fielding, N. (1984) *Probation Practice. Client Support Under Social Control*. Aldershot: Gower.

Fitzgibbon, W. (2011) *Probation and Social Work on Trial*. Basingstoke: Palgrave Macmillan.

Folkard, S., Lyon, K., Carver, M. M. and O'Leary, E. (1966) *Probation Research. A Preliminary Report*. HORS 7 London: HMSO.

Goslin, J. (1975) 'Mission: Control?' *Probation Journal* 22(2), 55–57.

Griffiths, W. A. (1982) 'Supervision in the Community'. *Justice of the Peace*, 21 August.

Harris, R. (1977) 'The Probation Officer as Social Worker'. *British Journal of Social Work* 7(4), 432–442.

Harris, R. (1980) 'A Changing Service: The Case for Separating Care and Control in Probation Practice'. *British Journal of Social Work* 10(2), 163–184.

Harris, R. (1995) 'Probation Round the World: Origins and Development', in K. Hamai, R. Villé, R. Harris, M. Hough and U. Zvekic (Eds) *Probation Round the World: A Comparative Study*. London: Routledge.

Haxby, D. (1978) *Probation: A Changing Service*. London: Constable.

Hearndon, I. and Millie, A. (2003) *Investigating Links Between Probation Enforcement and Reconviction*. Home Office Research Findings 225. London: Home Office.

Hedderman, C. (2003) 'Enforcing Supervision and Encouraging Compliance'. in W. H. Chui and M. Nellis (Eds) *Moving Probation Forward. Evidence, Arguments and Practice*. Harlow: Pearson Longman.

Hedderman, C. and Hough, M. (2004) 'Getting Tough or Being Effective: What Matters?' in G. Mair (Ed.) *What Matters in Probation*. Cullompton: Willan.

Holmes, T. (1900) *Pictures and Problems from London Police Courts*. London: Thomas Nelson and Sons.

Home Office (1964) *The Sentence of the Court. A Handbook for Courts on the Treatment of Offenders*. London: HMSO.

Howard Association (1881) *Annual Report of the Howard Association*. London: Howard Association.

James, A. (1979) 'Sentenced to Surveillance?' *Probation Journal* 26(1), 15–20.

Jarvis, F. (1974) *Probation Officers' Manual*. London: Butterworths.

King, J. (1964) *The Probation and After-Care Service*. Second Edition. London: Butterworth.

Lawson, C. (1978) *The Probation Officer as Prosecutor. A Study of Proceedings for Breach of Requirements in Probation*. Institute of Criminology Occasional papers No. 3. Cambridge University.

Le Mesurier, L. (1935) *A Handbook of Probation*. London: National Association of Probation Officers.

Lewis, C. S. (1949) 'The Humanitarian Theory of Punishment'. *20th Century: An Australian Quarterly Review* 3(3), 5–12.

Mair, G. and Burke, L. (2012) *Redemption, Rehabilitation and Risk Management. A History of Probation*. London: Routledge.

McWilliams, W. (1987) 'Probation, Pragmatism and Policy'. *Howard Journal Of Criminal Justice* 26, 97–121.

Nellis, M. (2001) 'Community Penalties in Historical Perspective'. in A. Bottoms, L. Gelsthorpe and S. Rex (Eds) *Community Penalties. Changes and Challenges*. Cullompton: Willan.

Nicholls, G. (2007) 'Enforcement'. in R. Canton and D. Hancock (Eds) *Dictionary of Probation Offender Management*. Cullompton: Willan.

Raynor, P. (1978) 'Compulsory Persuasion: A Problem for Correctional Social Work'. *British Journal of Social Work* 8(4), 411–424.

Raynor, P. (1985) *Social Work, Justice and Control*. Oxford: Blackwell.

Raynor, P. and Vanstone, M. (2002) *Understanding Community Penalties; Probation, Change and Social Context*. Buckingham: Open University Press.

Raynor, P. and Vanstone, M. (1994) 'Probation Practice, Effectiveness and the Non-Treatment Paradigm'. *British Journal of Social Work* 24(4), 387–404.

Rimmer, J. (1995) 'How Social Workers and Probation Officers in England Conceived Their Roles and Responsibilities in the 1930s and 1940s'. in J. Schwieson and P. Pettit (Eds) *Aspects of the History of British Social Work*. University of Reading.

Robinson, G. and McNeill, F. (2010) 'The Dynamics of Compliance with Offender Supervision'. in F. McNeill, P. Raynor and C. Trotter (Eds) *Offender Supervision. New Directions in Theory, Research and Practice*. Abingdon: Willan.

Senior, P. (1984) 'The Probation Order: Vehicle of Social Work or Social Control?' *Probation Journal* 31(2), 64–70.

Sterry, D. (1977) 'Control in After-Care Licences'. *Probation Journal* 24(3), 97–99.

St John, J. (1961) *Probation – The Second Chance*. London: Vista Books.

Thorpe, D. H., Smith, D., Green, C. J. and Paley, J. (1980) *Out of Care*. London: Allen and Unwin.

Todd, M. (1963) *The Probation Officer and His World*. London: Victor Gollancz.

Turner, S. (2010) 'Case Management in Corrections: Evidence, Issues and Challenges'. in F. McNeill, P. Raynor and C. Trotter (Eds) *Offender Supervision. New Directions in Theory, Research and Practice*. Abingdon: Willan.

Ugwudike, P. (2010) 'Compliance with Community Penalties: The Importance of Interactional Dynamics'. in F. McNeill, P. Raynor and C. Trotter (Eds) *Offender Supervision. New Directions in Theory, Research and Practice*. Abingdon: Willan.

Vanstone, M. (2001) *Making Sense of Probation: A History of Professional Discourse*. PhD Thesis. University of Wales, Swansea.

Vanstone, M. (2004a) *Supervising Offenders in the Community: A History of Probation Practice*. Aldershot: Ashgate.

Vanstone, M. (2004b) 'Mission Control: The Origins and Early History of Probation'. *Probation Journal* 51(1), 34–47.

Vanstone, M. (2008) 'The International Origins and Initial Development of Probation: An Early Example of Policy Transfer'. *British Journal of Criminology* 48(6), 735–755.

Vass, A. A. (1980) 'Law Enforcement in Community Service: Probation, Defence of Prosecution?' *Probation Journal*, 27 (4), 114–117.

Vass, A. A. (1990) *Alternatives to Prison: Punishment, Custody and the Community*. London: Sage Publications.

Walker, M. and Beaumont, B. (1981) *Probation Work: Critical Theory and Practice*. Oxford. Blackwell.

Waterhouse, J. (1983) 'The Effectiveness of Probation Supervision'. in Lishman, J. (Ed.) *Social Work with Adult Offenders. Research Highlights Number 5*. University of Aberdeen.

Wright, M. (1974) 'Probation, with Teeth?' *Probation Journal* 21(4), 103–105.

Wright, M. (1985) *Day Centres for Offenders. Enabling the Unable*. Report for the Crime and Justice Foundation. Boston: Crime and Justice Forum.

Young, J. (1998) 'From Inclusive to Exclusive Society. Nightmares in the European Dream'. in V. Ruggiero, N. South and I. Taylor (Eds) *The New European Criminology. Crime and Social Order in Europe*. London: Routledge.

Young, J. (1999) *The Exclusive Society*. London: Sage.

3
What Counts? Community Sanctions and the Construction of Compliance

Gwen Robinson

> *...social groups create deviance by making the rules whose infraction constitutes deviance,* and by applying those rules to particular people and labelling them as outsiders [...] Deviance is [therefore] not a quality that lies in behaviour itself, but in the interaction between the person who commits an act and those who respond to it.
>
> (Becker 1963: 9, 14; emphasis in original)

Introduction

A notable trend in the recent academic and policy literature on community penalties is a turn toward 'compliance' as a topic of interest. In the United Kingdom, this has been particularly true of England and Wales, where the probation service has come under increasing pressure to improve rates of offenders' compliance with both community penalties and post-custodial licences,[1] not least because of the significant contribution made by those deemed non-compliant to chronically high imprisonment rates, via so-called back-door sentencing (Ministry of Justice 2009a). To date, academic contributions to this topic have centred on developing theoretical explanations for compliance with community-based sanctions, and developing thinking about strategies for increasing offenders' compliance with community sanctions (e.g. Bottoms 2001; Hucklesby 2009; McCulloch 2010; Robinson and McNeill 2008; Ugwudike 2010).

This chapter adopts a different and more critical approach to the issue of compliance, eschewing analysis of the possible mechanisms underpinning compliant behaviour in favour of an exploration of the policies, rules, mechanisms and processes involved in the construction of the 'compliant offender' in the context of community sanctions. Drawing upon the labelling theory of Becker and other scholars in the 'social constructionist' tradition, it argues that compliance is not an objective quality of behaviour, but, rather, a label which comes to be applied to some individuals and not others. It is also an inherently elastic construct: 'what counts' as compliance can shift, to privilege different definitions and dimensions of compliance, and to encompass larger or smaller populations within the 'compliance net' (Cohen 1985). Compliance, then, is very much a moving and historically contingent target.

This chapter begins with a discussion of compliance as a construct with a number of possible dimensions, before going on to analyse changing 'official' constructions of compliance in the context of community sanctions in England and Wales. The next part of the chapter examines what we know about how those official constructions or rules are perceived and applied by practitioners, and the role of discretion in that process. In this section, some empirical findings from a small qualitative study conducted in one probation area (now Probation Trust) are presented. The final part of the chapter considers some of the implications of changing constructions of compliance, for offenders, practitioners and the legitimacy of community sanctions and the probation service.

Dimensions of compliance

In the context of non-custodial sanctions of all kinds, compliance is an important issue. As 'mid-range' penalties which involve placing requirements and restrictions on offenders while they remain at liberty, community sanctions rely to a particularly high degree upon the compliance of offenders to render them meaningful or effective (Bottoms 2001). This is true however we understand the purposes of such sanctions, whether in punitive, rehabilitative or, indeed, other terms: where an offender fails to comply with a community sanction it is (in the absence of any enforcement action) tantamount to having imposed no penalty at all.[2] Here, then, lies an important contrast between community and custodial sanctions: as Mair and Canton (2007: 270) have observed, 'a passive or recalcitrant prisoner is still being punished', whereas it is difficult to argue that the community sanction is achieving anything when the offender fails or refuses to comply with it. Establishing compliance with community sanctions, then, is a particularly important objective.

However, establishing just what compliance means – or should mean – in the context of community sanctions is not so straightforward. In a key contribution to the limited literature on compliance with community penalties, Bottoms (2001) has drawn a useful distinction between two principal types of compliance. The first of these, 'short-term requirement compliance', refers to compliance with the specific legal requirements of the community penalty. Short-term legal compliance is illustrated by Bottoms with reference to an offender who:

completes [a community sentence] with no breach of the formal requirements of the order: for example, an offender given community service
attends regularly at community service work sessions, and works hard and
diligently during those sessions. (2001: 88)

The second type of compliance Bottoms describes as 'longer-term legal
compliance'. This, he explains, is a broader category which refers to the 'more
fundamental issue' of the offender's compliance with the criminal law (2001:
89). Longer-term compliance, then, equates with desistance: it implies no
further reoffending within a specified time frame.

This is a very useful starting point for thinking about dimensions of compliance with community penalties. However, as Fergus McNeill and I have argued
elsewhere (Robinson and McNeill 2008), short-term requirement compliance is
arguably more complex than Bottoms suggests. Let us return to the example
offered by Bottoms, cited above. It would be difficult to argue that the offender
described here is not worthy of the 'compliant' label. However, what we cannot
ascertain from this brief illustration is precisely where the line between compliance and non-compliance is to be drawn. Much will depend upon what the
'formal requirements' of the order are. So, for example, do these simply specify
regular attendance, or do they go further, setting out expectations about the
quality of the work to be completed? Is it necessary that the offender works
'hard and diligently' at the assigned task; or is it sufficient that s/he simply
turns up and 'goes through the motions'?

Prompted by these sorts of questions, Fergus McNeill and I have argued
that it is useful to think about compliance as a construct with more than one
possible dimension (Robinson and McNeill 2008). We have argued that there
is a distinction to be made between behaviour that technically conforms
to rules and that which reflects a genuine engagement with a particular
sanction and its purposes. Drawing on Christine Parker's (2002: 27) differenti-
ation, in the context of corporate compliance systems, between 'legalistic/rule'
and 'goal-oriented/substantive' compliance, we have proposed a distinction
between *formal* and *substantive* compliance. The former denotes behaviour
which technically meets minimum behavioural requirements, such as attending appointments (or work placements) at designated times. The latter implies
rather more: namely, the active engagement and cooperation of the offender
with the requirements of his or her order and its broader objectives. It is
achieved when (for example) the offender subject to community service works
hard and diligently; or when the offender on probation shows a genuine desire
to tackle his or her problems.

This distinction between formal and substantive compliance reflects an
acknowledgement of the possibility of both behavioural and attitudinal dimensions of compliance. Substantive compliance implies that the sanction and its
purposes have psychological legitimacy for the offender: he or she 'buys into'

it in a way that someone who is only formally compliant will not necessarily do. Tyler's distinction between compliance and cooperation is relevant here (e.g. see Tyler and Fagan 2008). The 'ideal type' would be in the overlapping area of the diagram, where there is evidence of both formal and substantive compliance/compliance and cooperation; and it is here that the offender described by Bottoms (see above) seems to fall. However, like most ideal types, this combination of formal and substantive compliance may not often be in evidence. In other words, it is theoretically possible that an offender could fall into any of the shaded areas in the diagram and still attract a 'compliant' label.

Once we open up the possibility that compliance is not clear-cut or one-dimensional, we start to see that compliance and non-compliance are far from objective 'social facts', but are, rather, categories which are likely to be defined and operationalized differently between jurisdictions, localities and individual actors. A number of questions then start to suggest themselves. For example, what counts as compliance, in what context(s), and who decides? Are there significant differences in constructions of compliance over time, between places, or by different individuals? These are all questions with significance both for comparative research and for historical research within single jurisdictions. In the following section, the latter approach is adopted with reference to changing constructions of compliance in England and Wales. It is argued that we can, in this jurisdiction, identify four distinct phases in the construction of compliance in the community sanctions context.

Official constructions of compliance with community sanctions in England and Wales (1907–2012): A case study

The following analysis of official constructions of compliance centres on developments in a single jurisdiction: England and Wales. Arguably this represents an extreme case study: the probation service in England and Wales has witnessed particularly rapid and significant policy developments in the last 30 years or so, which have not necessarily been experienced to the same degree in other parts of the world. It might also be argued that the analysis presents a somewhat crude characterization of a complex history. Nonetheless, the objective in presenting it here is to illustrate the elasticity of 'compliance' as a label that can be applied to – or denied – offenders who are subject to community sanctions, and to begin to think about some of the consequences of changing constructions of compliance: for offenders; for practitioners; and for the legitimacy of the probation service.

Phase 1: An era of discretion (1907–1989)

Until the 1990s, those orders of the court that we now refer to as community penalties had the legal status of 'alternatives to sentencing'. The probation order – the oldest of such 'alternatives' – had operated since 1907 according to a voluntary contractual model which was accepted by the court on condition of good behaviour on the part of the offender. Under the 1907 Act the standard 'condition of recognizance' was that the offender 'be under the supervision' of a probation officer and, where specified by the court, that s/he comply with up to three further conditions pertaining to: association with 'undesirables' or in prohibited areas; abstention from alcohol; and the pursuit of 'an honest and industrial life'. Central to the general notion of 'good behaviour' – and, importantly, linked with the legal status of the probation order as an alternative to sentencing – was an expectation of desistance: in other words, commission of a further offence was a clear indicator of default, and grounds for both breach and 'sentencing proper'. The supervising probation officer was responsible for monitoring the offender's compliance with the conditions of the order, such as they were, and for informing the court of any failure to comply. Discretion thus fell to probation officers to draw the distinction between compliance and non-compliance, and, as far as it is possible to ascertain, there were no detailed specifications of the expected content of probation orders and little, if any, formal oversight of probation officers' work. During this phase, then, it would appear that the discretion of practitioners to define and delimit compliance was at its height.

Phase 2: An era of standardization (the 1990s)

The 1991 Criminal Justice Act has long been considered a 'watershed' in the history of community sanctions in England and Wales, and this is no less true in the context of the present discussion. The 1991 Act was crucial with regard to constructions of compliance because it changed the legal status of those orders, which had formerly been alternatives to sentencing, rendering them sentences in their own right, with a necessary punitive component (reflected in the new discourse of 'punishment in the community'). In this regard, the probation order was brought into line with the community service order, the first example of a community-based order of the court with the legal status of a sentence, which had been introduced in the 1970s.

Rendering community orders sentences in their own right had the important, and arguably ironic, effect of severing the traditional connection between compliance and desistance: so, for example, compliance with a probation order was reconceived after 1991 such that it now meant following rules that no longer included a condition to be of good behaviour beyond the probation office or work placement specified by the court. Desistance from offending, in other words, ceased to be a component of 'formal compliance'. New specifications of formal compliance were, however, set out in National Standards published by the Home Office from the early 1990s.[3] These were largely shaped by the requirement of the new community sentences to demonstrate the deprivation of offenders' liberty.

Thus, from the outset, the emphasis in National Standards was on frequency of reporting: the compliant offender was conceived as one who attended regular, scheduled appointments.[4] National Standards were silent on the desired content or quality of contact between practitioner and offender. Policy dictated that breach action should be taken after a third 'failure to comply', although probation officers retained some discretion to set the 'compliance bar', namely, to decide upon the legitimacy of any excuse offered by the offender when his or her behaviour fell short of the minimum formal requirements (e.g. see Home Office 1995). It is in this period, and in the broader context of the managerialization of probation practice, that we see the seeds of the idea of the compliant *probation officer* coming to the fore: he or she being someone who kept accurate records and enforced orders in accordance with policy.

Phase 3: An era of enforcement (the late 1990s to 2004)

As the decade progressed, a punitive shift in penal policies saw probation areas and their staff come under increasing pressure to both 'tighten' and 'toughen up' their enforcement practice. Indeed, by the late 1990s, enforcement had become one of the key preoccupations of community penalties policy (Robinson and Ugwudike 2012). This was to have significant consequences for both probation staff and offenders. Probation staff experienced increased managerial oversight of their discretion in respect of when it was appropriate to take enforcement action. Meanwhile, offenders found that the likelihood of breach increased significantly, and that 'compliance' became increasingly difficult to demonstrate.

Tonry (2010) has characterized the period under the New Labour government (which came to power in 1997) as a period during which policy tended toward 'defining deviance up': that is, more and more people came to attract deviant labels. We can discern a similar trend in the community sanctions context. In 2000, revised National Standards reduced the number of written warnings that could be issued to an offender before formal breach action was triggered: a 'three strikes' policy became 'two strikes', and practice guidance reduced practitioners' discretion to count as 'acceptable' a range of (formerly reasonable) excuses. The underlying assumption here was that a tougher approach toward enforcement would ultimately drive up rates of compliance, through the mechanism of deterrence (e.g. HMIP, HMICA and HMIC 2007). However, the toughening of enforcement policy actually achieved the opposite, essentially making it more difficult for offenders to evade 'non-compliant' labels and both 'widening' and 'thinning' the mesh of the net in which non-compliers were captured (Cohen 1985). Official data revealed that between 1994 and 2004 breach rates doubled from 18 per cent to 37 per cent, a trend which could not be explained with reference to the other possible explanation: namely, a trend toward higher-risk offenders receiving community orders[5] (Home Office 2005; Morgan 2003).

Phase 4: An era of pragmatism (2004 to 2012)

By 2004 probation's failure to 'produce' high levels of compliance via a strategy centred on tough enforcement – evidenced in published statistics on breach rates – was beginning to attract concern and criticism. The Home Office announced that 'Ministers want a rapid improvement in compliance levels' and, in an effort to achieve that, a 'compliance target' for the National Probation Service was introduced (alongside existing enforcement targets) for the first time (Home Office 2004). In other words, the service's performance was henceforth to be judged, in part, with reference to its ability to demonstrate acceptable levels of compliance on the part of those offenders subject to statutory orders and licences. For a government committed to (quantitative) performance measurement and the auditing of practice, this meant deciding how to measure compliance levels at an aggregate level.

Initially, compliance was measured in terms of the proportion of offenders completing their order or licence without two (three in the case of licences) or more 'unacceptable failures' on their record, and the 'overall compliance target' for probation areas in 2004–2005 was set at 70 per cent. However, compliance targets were revised a number of times in the following years. Targets also multiplied, to include both principal targets (also known as 'key performance indicators') and subsidiary ones. For example, in 2006–2007 compliance was principally measured with reference to *the proportion of arranged appointments attended by the offender in the first 26 weeks* (with a target of 85 per cent) and *the proportion of cases reaching the 6 month stage without requiring breach action* (with a target of 70 per cent), alongside two additionally subsidiary measures (NOMS 2006).[6] By 2009–2010 the key performance indicator for compliance was *orders and licences successfully completed* (target 70 per cent), with the subsidiary measure of *cases reaching the 6 month stage without requiring breach action* (target 71 per cent) (Ministry of Justice 2009b: 41, 52). Quite why these particular measures and their accompanying targets were selected was not made clear. However, the proliferation and shifting of targets around compliance in this period does appear to indicate a failure to agree on just how compliance ought to be measured.

Meanwhile, there were signs of a slight relaxation of the rules that previously sought to limit practitioners' discretion in respect of defining compliance. National Standards published in 2007 specified that practitioners should make a judgement about the validity of any excuse provided by the offender for any apparent failure to comply, and that this decision should 'take account of the nature of the failure, the circumstances of it and the circumstances of the offender' (Ministry of Justice 2007, s2 f.4; see also NOMS 2008). The

2007 Standards further stated that offenders should 'experience their relation-ships with staff as being characterized by the encouragement of compliance and cooperation' (s3.6). These insertions could be read as more or less explicit attempts to encourage and enable the widening of the 'compliance net' (i.e. enabling greater numbers of offenders to be labelled 'compliant'), and they were indicative of an important shift in how the legitimacy of the service was henceforth to be judged: that is, with reference to its ability to secure offenders' compliance. This was underlined in January 2008, when it was announced that an additional £40 million would be made available to probation areas able to demonstrate 'good' performance in relation to achieving aggregate compliance targets.[7] If there were questions about the appropriateness of such targets, the suitability of the specific measures adopted, or any unintended consequences of the new 'compliance drive', these were not articulated in public.

That the service's legitimacy was now to be evaluated against its ability to secure compliance was further underlined in 2010 when the National Offender Management Service (NOMS) launched a three-year programme of projects and research aimed at 'improving the effectiveness of one-to-one engagement between the probation practitioner and the offender' (Rex 2012: 6), and in April 2011 it was announced that over the coming year National Standards for pro-bation were to be replaced by Probation Trusts' own policies.[8] The press release which announced this development declared that the new standards would 'remove the unnecessary proscription and red tape that restricts frontline deci-sion making', including (at the level of national policy, at least) decisions about what ought to 'count' as compliance, and when enforcement action should be taken.

Front-line constructions of compliance

We have seen, in the previous section, that 'official' constructions of compliance in England and Wales have evolved in ways that have sought to apply the compliance label to both qualitatively and quantitatively variable groups of offenders. We have also seen a shifting tolerance toward the use of professional judgement on the part of practitioners in their applications of those labels. As far as policy is concerned, there has, until very recently, been a squeezing of practitioners' discretion in respect of deciding what does and what does not count as compliance, and such decisions have increasingly come to be subject to managerial oversight in a target-driven culture. How-ever, we know very little about how this has played out in practice, and how practitioners themselves understand and prefer to construct compliance in the context of their day-to-day work. We do, on the other hand, know (from empir-ical research in other areas of probation and social work practice) that it can be unwise to equate attempts to impose structure and standardization with the 'death of discretion' at the level of practice, and that practitioners are as likely to find ways to subvert and resist rules as they are to apply them unquestioningly (e.g. see Robinson 2003).

Indeed, in the only published study in England and Wales to date which has examined front-line decision making in respect of compliance, it was found that discretion, albeit constrained, was far from completely quashed (Ugwudike 2008; Robinson and Ugwudike 2012; Ugwudike, this volume). Ugwudike's research, which involved interviews with 19 Welsh practitioners in 2005–2006, revealed that there was limited 'buy-in' to the sanctioning/deterrence model of enforcement set out in policy documents, and that practitioners continued to exercise their professional judgement – albeit under managerial scrutiny – when it came to individual decisions about compliance. Typically, this meant making decisions about when to define an offender's failure to attend a scheduled appointment as 'acceptable' or 'unacceptable'. In these circumstances, discretion was not used lightly, and it had to be professionally defensible in the eyes of practitioners. This meant drawing upon their knowledge of the particular case: the practitioners interviewed by Ugwudike talked about the importance of understanding the individual circumstances behind an offender's failure to comply, and responding accordingly.

Ugwudike's enlightening study was conducted at a time when policy was beginning to shift in line with the transition from Phase 3 to Phase 4 in the chronology described above, but before the 'compliance drive' had really begun to bite at the level of practice. In the following section, some of the findings of a more recent exploratory study of practitioners' perspectives on compliance, conducted by the author, are presented. The study, conducted in the latter part of 2008, involved three focus group interviews with practitioners in one English probation area. The 14 participants had a range of roles and included probation officers, probation service officers and supervisors of unpaid work, and their probation careers ranged from 12 months to in excess of 20 years. Although it is not possible to make any claims of 'representativeness' in such a small sample, the views of participants were nonetheless illuminating, and would appear to confirm the importance of discretion and 'professional defensibility' in practitioners' constructions of compliance.

Moving the goalposts: Constructing compliance in the era of pragmatism

In the first part of each of the three focus group interviews, practitioners were asked to talk in general terms about the perceived importance of compliance as a topic or issue, and there was a clear consensus among participants that compliance had, in the six months prior to the research, become a key issue, both nationally and in their own probation area. More than once this was referred to as a 'culture shift', and the contemporary context was seen as one in which ways of thinking about and defining compliance were being challenged. One interviewee described it as 'compliance mania' within the service. There was less clarity about why this was happening, but some awareness of additional resources from the Ministry of Justice being deployed locally to improve rates of compliance, particularly with a view to reducing the number of breaches and subsequent short custodial sentences. Hitting centrally determined compliance targets was also understood to be linked with areas' eligibility for Trust status. As one interviewee explained, 'basically you've got to hit various targets to be able to become a Trust and if we don't hit the targets then we don't get it.'

Views about this recent emphasis on compliance were, in principle, generally positive, and participants said that they generally welcomed the move away from a strict/inflexible culture of enforcement, particularly in respect of 'chaotic' offenders who struggled to keep appointments, and people with other 'genuine' barriers to formal compliance (such as childcare responsibilities or mental health needs). It was also reported that recent weeks had seen significant reductions in breach rates (and, as a corollary of that, higher rates of recorded compliance). However, it emerged that different teams within the probation area had some quite different experiences of the 'compliance drive', and not all were entirely positive about the means via which targets were being met.

Participants with knowledge of practice in the south of the county reported that practitioners there were being encouraged to take a more tolerant approach toward non-compliance than in the past, in order to improve performance in respect of compliance targets; and they were largely being left to exercise their own judgement in that regard. For a minority, this was a source of some uncertainty and a degree of discomfort. As one interviewee explained:

> it [used to be] dead straightforward, in many ways, wasn't it, it was quite simple, we knew what we needed to do, and I think now there seems to be, there's a whole number of debates in our office as to what is acceptable, what isn't; if somebody hasn't come in, how much leeway do you give somebody, and it sort of muddies the waters, and I suppose in that respect, compliance itself becomes an uncertain sort of issue, erm, and I think we're a bit confused, well I feel confused.

Notwithstanding a few comments along these lines, the majority – in line with Ugwudike's findings – saw discretion as a necessary element in making decisions, on a case by case basis, about how and where to 'draw the line' between compliance and non-compliance, and they welcomed the move away from a rigid 'enforcement culture'. In one focus group, discussion focused on the importance of the relationship between practitioner and offender as a basis for communicating, reinforcing and, sometimes, (re)negotiating the 'ground rules', particularly in the wake of lapses in formal compliance. This did not, however, mean overlooking, ignoring or 'turning a blind eye' to non-compliance, which many felt *was* beginning to happen in other parts of the county.

It became clear that some managers were taking a much more assertive approach to reducing breach rates/improving performance against compliance targets. In their teams, practitioners felt that they were not experiencing increased discretion: rather, they reported feeling under considerable pressure to avoid enforcement action, at almost any cost. This entailed, in practice, a redefinition of behaviours as 'acceptable' that would, six months previously, have been deemed 'unacceptable'. Examples offered included use of bad language; a poor attitude generally; being under the influence of drugs or alcohol; or (in the context of unpaid work) being in possession of a mobile phone. Formerly all grounds for enforcement action, these were now cited as behaviours unlikely to meet new working definitions of 'non-compliance'. In addition, much more strenuous efforts were being taken to follow up non-attendance (traditionally the clearest example of non-compliance) in an effort to relabel an absence as 'acceptable'; and the legitimacy of offenders' excuses for absence was not being challenged as before.[9] Observations included the following:

> Before, it would be first fail, final warning; second fail, breach – but now they've introduced like a verbal warning that you can use at your discretion or almost giving people a third chance. It kind of feels like almost any sniff of a reason you can justify to make this acceptable, no-one's going to question it, I think.

> I think that's what they're actually asking us to do to be honest, if someone just sits there for five minutes and grunts at everything you say, it's a tick in a box.

Participants said that this was happening even in cases where they felt offenders were deliberately flouting the rules or 'playing the system':

> Sometimes when you think these people are taking you for a ride, we're sort of still looking for ways to, you know, get them back in ...

> That's the thing at the moment, we're encouraged to let people off, to give them leeway, when really they don't warrant it.

Concerns were expressed about what one practitioner called the 'integrity' of new policies which were focused on meeting compliance targets by simply redefining previously unacceptable behaviours as acceptable. Rather than being enabled to adopt discretion in assessing, on a case by case basis, when it might be appropriate to take enforcement action, practitioners were reporting that discretion was in fact being 'stolen' by managers. Examples were offered of instances where line managers had blocked practitioners' attempts to take enforcement action, even when practitioners felt that they were being 'taken for a ride', or where the offender's behaviour was disruptive to others (e.g. in the context of a group programme). This policy of 'extreme tolerance' was thought to be problematic in a number of ways.

First, concern was expressed that such a policy would send out mixed messages to offenders with experience of both 'old' and 'new' regimes:

> I mean it all comes down to defensibility because when it was enforcement based I had somebody who was on an order who missed an appointment and I thought, well, give him the benefit of the doubt, and, you know, my manager said 'it's not defensible, we can't do that', and he had to go back to court. Whereas now, it would be, discuss it with your manager, [they say] that's defensible, you give him the benefit of the doubt, so it's like, completely the opposite message.

Second, it was thought that, far from encouraging compliance, such an approach could reinforce poor behaviour:

> 'Cos they all talk to each other: 'oh yeah, it doesn't matter, just miss it, won't matter' [...] that's the downside of it: they do talk to each other.

> I've got a case that's been so chaotic and he's had that much help and he still isn't bothered, and it's like, you're basically saying, continue to behave like this because you won't get any, you know, punishment for it.

> The negative side to it is you're not putting any ownership on the offender, you're not putting any, er, routines in their life, you're not giving them any responsibility, it's just as and when you want, if you don't want to come in on Monday, you come in on Wednesday [...] there's got to be a wide line in terms of flexibility, accommodating somebody and basically, on the opposite side is giving the offender some sort of responsibility and keeping appointments.

Third, it could indirectly penalize 'genuine' compliers:

> There's other people who toe the line, they do everything they're expected to, you don't even have to ask them to get a doctor's note 'cos they've been, they've paid for it themselves, but you know, they do everything and in a way it seems like you're actually discriminating against them because they don't get any reward for that, you know.

Fourth, it could mask increasing risk:

> If you look at the main aims of probation, reducing the risk of harm, protection of the public, they're the two main ones, obviously rehabilitation etc., punishment, whatever, but the main one is reducing the risk of harm, so if you're allowing people to be too flexible, not turn up, they could be doing anything, and be anywhere, you know.

> I don't like it, probation being a revolving door: someone comes in, signs a piece of paper and leaves. Well it happens too often. Because it's all very much target driven. But it only takes something serious to happen [...] and suddenly everyone feels it.

For all of these reasons, the new strategy of extreme tolerance was seen as a strategy that could damage the legitimacy of community sanctions, and the probation service, in the eyes of the public and other external audiences.

The practitioners involved in this small study, then, described mixed experiences and expressed mixed views about the service's 'compliance turn'. Many, it seemed, had thought through the unintended consequences and risks of prioritizing (quantitative) compliance targets at the expense of more nuanced constructions of compliance and substantive definitions of the concept. As one interviewee commented:

> I think, you know, like compliance is obviously a huge issue in the service at the minute [...] but for me, *I'm not sure whether we're looking at the right compliance*, 'cos it's one thing to get, like you say, get people in, that hits numbers, that hits, you know, reduced numbers into court, but we're not looking at the quality of what we do when we get them in [...] so, for me, it's a huge issue but [is it enough] to get people through the doors, and hit our targets, or is compliance bigger than that?

For the practitioners I interviewed, compliance clearly *was* bigger than that. When, at the start of the focus group interviews, they were asked to offer a definition of compliance, National Standards (pertaining to frequency of reporting) were typically mentioned, but participants tended to say that, for them, compliance was not simply a quantitative issue. They said that, for them, compliance was not just about physical presence (e.g. attending appointments on time) but also about what several participants referred to as 'active engagement', as the following quotations illustrate:

> Turning up for appointments on time [...] and actually engaging in the work when they actually come to probation, not just sitting there looking through the window.

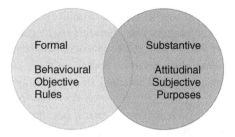

Figure 3.1   Dimensions of compliance (adapted from Robinson and McNeill 2008)

Engaging with relevant services as well, not just turning up, ticking a box...

> They agree certain things, don't they; they agree to be basically pro-social while they're with us [on unpaid work] and if they're not in any way, that then becomes unacceptable.

In other words, practitioners were clearly looking for substantive, as well as formal, compliance – and preferably both in tandem (see Figure 3.1).

Choices, choices: Legitimacy and the construction of compliance

A key argument of this chapter has been that regulators of community sanctions are faced with and have to make choices about just what constitutes compliance and how it should be understood and defined. These choices are reflected in the 'formal requirements' (Bottoms 2001) of such penalties as set out in statute, and in published practice guidance, such as the National Standards for offender supervision in England and Wales. As we have seen with reference to the example of England and Wales, these formal requirements are not necessarily stable over time, but are, rather, subject to the influences of changing political winds and, hence, priorities for the organizations and sanctions concerned.

In England and Wales, the twin influences of managerialism (as manifested in the setting of quantitative targets, performance measurement and the oversight of practice by managers) and a 'punitive turn' in criminal justice have both impacted significantly on constructions of compliance in the last 20 years, with some intended and unintended consequences for the probation service (Robinson and Ugwudike 2012). On the one hand, the less tolerant approach characteristic of the 'era of enforcement' (Phase 3) served to reinforce probation's punitive credentials at a time when this was considered politically necessary. However, it was a strategy which, ultimately, damaged rather than boosted the legitimacy of the probation service. Chronically high breach rates were ultimately interpreted as evidence of a failure on the part of the service and its staff to effectively 'engage' the offenders on its caseload, and this sense of 'failure' was exacerbated by the service's (increasingly unaffordable) contribution to a rapidly expanding prison population.[10] In 2009 the Ministry of Justice published a report which indicated that the incarceration (on breach) of offenders subject to community sanctions was responsible for 16 per cent of the 66 per cent overall increase in the prison population between 1995 and 2009 (Ministry of Justice 2009a). Data such as these were a key driver of the transition to Phase 4: the service's legitimacy in the eyes of powerful external stakeholders is now to be evaluated with reference to its ability to hold offenders in the compliance net, and, reflecting that, we have witnessed a significant relaxation of the formal rules – not least the replacement of National Standards for the supervision of offenders in England and Wales. How compliance is measured and what 'counts' as compliance, then, are far from trivial issues: they are, in fact, intimately linked with the legitimacy of the service and the sanctions it is charged with delivering, as well as having significant implications for offenders, who face enforcement action (and, often, more severe sanctions) when they fail to attract 'compliant' labels.

Formal rules and requirements are, of course, only part (albeit a significant part) of the mosaic of compliance: at the front line, practitioners are charged with interpreting and applying the formal rules, and have always retained a degree of discretion as decision makers and rule enforcers, albeit subject to varying degrees of oversight and surveillance at the level of management. This chapter has reviewed the findings of two small-scale studies which have examined practitioners' perspectives on the construction of compliance. Both have revealed that practitioners place a high value on substantive compliance and that their perceptions of substantive engagement on the part of the offender play a significant role in their decisions about whether and how to enforce the formal rules. They also value the exercise of discretion in decisions about compliance, but they see discretion as something which should be exercised within the boundaries of what they consider to be 'professionally defensible', and most likely to facilitate substantive compliance – preferably in addition to formal compliance. When discretion is too wide, or when it rests in the wrong hands, it can lack legitimacy, not just in the eyes of practitioners, but also in the eyes of offenders and powerful external stakeholders, with (as we have seen) potentially damaging consequences. Unregulated discretion, then, may present reputational risks that are as significant as those associated with rules that are too narrow and circumscribed.

In reviewing the changing approaches to the construction of compliance with community sanctions in England and Wales, it has hopefully become evident that how compliance is defined speaks to the key issue of how the purposes of such sanctions are understood. Ultimately, how we construct the purposes or 'ends' of such sanctions dictates, to a large extent, how we think about compliance and the weight we give to its different dimensions. When we see community sanctions in principally managerial and/or punitive terms, then it makes perfect sense to prioritize the 'formal', quantitative dimension, because this is both more easily auditable and more straightforwardly related to the deprivation of offenders' liberty. Thus, we saw that, when the probation order came to be recast as 'punishment in the community', the *quantity* of the offender's engagement with the order came into much sharper focus. During the 1990s, as penal policy developed in a more punitive vein, formal compliance came to focus even more on quantitative measures, and minimum expectations increased, as did sanctions for non-compliance. If, however, we see the task of community sanctions as being to any degree productive or transformative, then compliance should arguably entail both formal and substantive dimensions. Equally, if we are serious about managing risk and protecting the public, then we need to be counting more than just frequency of contact. Narratives for community sanctions that emphasize risk and/or rehabilitation thus offer a critique of a purely formal/superficial definition of compliance, and it is these narratives which appear to be in the minds of practitioners when they talk and think about compliance.

Notes

1. In this chapter the term 'community sanctions' is used to encompass both community sentences/orders and periods of statutory post-custodial supervision.
2. The same, of course, can be said of a fine or compensation order that goes unpaid.
3. The first National Standards applied only to community service orders, and were published prior to the 1991 Act (Home Office 1989). Subsequent editions of National Standards, however, covered the full range of orders (e.g. Home Office 1992, 1995).
4. Indeed, a Home Office research study conducted in the mid-1990s in five probation areas revealed that failure to attend scheduled appointments without a reasonable excuse was the most common basis for breach action (Ellis et al. 1996).
5. These statistics mask substantial variation between different types of community orders (which were proliferating in this period – see Bottoms et al. 2004).
6. These subsidiary measures were (i) the average number of acceptable failures to attend appointments (orders and licences) during the first 26 weeks; and (ii) the proportion of orders and licences that terminated successfully.
7. There were also incentives for probation areas to meet compliance targets that were linked with gaining Trust status.
8. Ministry of Justice press release 5 April 2011, at http://www.justice.gov.uk/news/features/feature050411a.htm
9. In one group reference was made to the practice of recording 'rearranged appointments' instead of 'acceptable absences' in order to avoid missing nationally set targets for the latter – see above (Phase 4).
10. During Phase 3, punitive policies affecting sentencers meant harsher sanctions – and more custodial sentences – on breach than in the past.

References

Becker, H. S. (1963) *Outsiders: Studies in the Sociology of Deviance*. New York: Free Press.

Bottoms, A. E. (2001) 'Compliance with Community Penalties'. in A. Bottoms, L. Gelsthorpe and S. Rex (Eds) *Community Penalties: Change and Challenges*. Cullompton: Willan.

Bottoms, A., Rex, S. and Robinson, G. (2004) 'How Did We Get Here?' in A. Bottoms, S. Rex and G. Robinson (Eds) *Alternatives to Prison: Options for an Insecure Society*. Cullompton: Willan.

Cohen, S. (1985) *Visions of Social Control*. Cambridge: Polity Press.

Ellis, T., Hedderman, C. and Mortimer, E. (1996) *Enforcing Community Sentences*. Home Office Research Study 158. London: Home Office.

HMIP, HMICA and HMIC. (2007) *A Summary of Findings on the Enforcement of Community Penalties from Three Joint Area Inspections*. London: Home Office.

Home Office. (1989) *National Standards for Community Service Orders*. Home Office Circular 18/1989.

Home Office. (1992) *National Standards for the Supervision of Offenders in the Community*. London: Home Office.

Home Office. (1995) *National Standards for the Supervision of Offenders in the Community*. London: Home Office.

Home Office. (2004) *Managing Compliance and Enforcement of Community Penalties*. Probation Circular 43/2004. London: Home Office.

Home Office. (2005) *Offender Management Caseload Statistics 2004*. Home Office Statistical Bulletin 17/05. London: Home Office.

Hucklesby, A. (2009) 'Understanding Offenders' Compliance: A Case Study of Electronically Monitored Curfew Orders'. *Journal of Law and Society* 36(2), 248–271.

Mair, G. and Canton, R. (2007) 'Sentencing, Community Penalties and the Role of the Probation Service'. in L. Gelsthorpe and R. Morgan (Eds) *Handbook of Probation*. Cullompton: Willan.

McCulloch, T. (2010) 'Exploring Community Service, Understanding Compliance'. in F. McNeill, P. Raynor and C. Trotter (Eds) *Offender Supervision: New Directions in Theory, Research and Practice*. Cullompton: Willan.

Ministry of Justice. (2007) *National Standards for the Management of Offenders*. London: Ministry of Justice.

Ministry of Justice. (2009a) *Story of the Prison Population 1995–2009 England and Wales*. Ministry of Justice Statistics Bulletin. London: Ministry of Justice.

Ministry of Justice. (2009b) *National Offender Management Service Strategic and Business Plans. 2009–10 to 2010–11*. London: Ministry of Justice.

Morgan, R. (2003) 'Foreword', *Her Majesty's Inspectorate of Probation Annual Report 2002/2003*. London: Home Office.

National Offender Management Service. (2006) *NPS Performance Targets and Measures 2006–2007: Guidance*. Probation Circular 28/2006. London: NOMS.

National Offender Management Service. (2008) *Determining Unacceptable Absences*. Probation Circular 05/2008. London: NOMS.

Parker, C. (2002) *The Open Corporation*. Cambridge: Cambridge University Press.

Rex, S. (2012) 'The Offender Engagement Programme: Rationale and Objectives'. *Eurovista*, 2(1), 6–9.

Robinson, G. (2003) 'Technicality and Indeterminacy in Probation Practice: A Case Study'. *British Journal of Social Work* 33, 593–610.

Robinson, G. and McNeill, F. (2008) 'Exploring the Dynamics of Compliance with Community Penalties'. *Theoretical Criminology* 12(4), 431–449.

Robinson, G. and Ugwudike, P. (2012) 'Investing in "Toughness": Probation, Enforcement and Legitimacy'. *Howard Journal of Criminal Justice* 51(3), 300–316.

Tonry, M. (2010) 'The Costly Consequences of Populist Posturing: ASBOs, Victims, "Rebalancing" and Diminution in Support of Civil Liberties'. *Punishment and Society* 12(4) 387–413.

Tyler, T. and Fagan, J. (2008) 'Legitimacy and Cooperation: Why do People help the Police Fight Crime in their Communities?' *Ohio State Journal of Criminal Law* 6, 231–275.

Ugwudike, P. (2008) *Developing an Effective Mechanism for Encouraging Compliance with Community Penalties*. Unpublished PhD Thesis, Swansea University.

Ugwudike, P. (2010) 'Compliance with Community Penalties, the Importance of Interactional Dynamics'. in F. McNeill, P. Raynor and C. Trotter (Eds) *Offender Supervision: New Directions in Theory, Research and Practice*. Cullompton: Willan.

4
Reanalysing the Compliance Dynamic: Toward a Co-Productive Strategy and Practice

Trish McCulloch

Introduction

In the opening pages of his text *Status Anxiety* (2004), Alain De Botton aptly captures the nonsense, the reality and (some of) the consequences of the differential treatments sometimes afforded to penal actors within late-modern penal systems and processes:

> It is common to describe people who hold important positions in society as 'somebodies' and their inverse as 'nobodies' – nonsensical terms, for we are all by necessity individuals with identities and comparable claims on existence. But such words are apt in conveying the variations in the quality of treatment meted out to different groups. Those without status remain unseen, they are treated brusquely, their complexities are trampled upon and their identities ignored.
>
> (De Botton 2004, p. 12)

In this deeply stratified context, typically, those with status include criminal justice policy makers, professionals and academics, and those without include both the victims and the perpetrators of criminal activity.[1] In this chapter I wish to revisit the status afforded to offender actors in the context of community penalties, and more specifically in the increasingly salient context of compliance.

As will be argued, recent attention to the concept and pursuit of compliance in community penalties arises from more long-standing penal concerns with the development of effective and credible community penalties. More recently, however, compliance has re-emerged as a 'new penological discourse' (Feeley and Simon 1992) in which the traditional (if understated) pursuit of *offender* compliance (as demonstrated, for example, in the engagement, participation and progression of the individual offender within community penalties) is being supplanted by a more rationalized and short-term preoccupation with the management, control and regulation of the 'dangerous' (Feeley and Simon 1992; Nellis 2004, 2006). In policy and practice terms, this has contributed to an unprecedented preoccupation with 'enforcement' in community penalties, a consequence of which is that community penalties are now increasingly required to demonstrate effectiveness in terms of their capacity to manage and control 'dangerous' groups. However, notwithstanding the considerable impact of this shift on contemporary penal policy and practice (and perhaps in part because of it), there has also emerged a new theorizing of compliance that suggests that there is much more to achieving effectiveness in community penalties than forced or constrained compliance with penal 'products'. Indeed, recent theoretical attention to the concept and dynamic of compliance very powerfully attests to the 'inextricable link' (Bottoms 2001) between *offender* compliance and the more holistic pursuit of effectiveness in community penalties.

This paper seeks to trace the impact of these divergent compliance narratives within emerging compliance policy and practice and the implications of that for those required to comply. A principal observation of this paper is that, despite the clear co-existence of the above outlined compliance narratives, policy and practice developments in this area have continued to progress in a fairly straightforward managerialist fashion. In the few examples where the impact of recent compliance thinking can be observed – in the form of a considered or applied compliance strategy – at best we can trace a move from 'enforced' compliance toward a practice of 'professionally produced'[2] compliance. In both strategies, compliance is reduced to a quantitative output arrived at by state and professional manipulation, and offenders are reduced to the objects on which that manipulation occurs. As will be argued, neither of these processes appears to be particularly effective in producing 'short-term' compliance, and they may in fact be counterproductive to the more complex, and arguably more important, process of supporting longer-term compliance outcomes (in the form of, for example, offender progression and change). Noting, then, recent calls to think more holistically about compliance and effectiveness in community penalties (Bottoms 2001), and acknowledging the recognized role of offender actors in making compliance efforts – and by extension community penalties – 'work' (McNeill and Robinson 2013; Nellis 2006; Robinson and McNeill 2008), this chapter considers the ways in which emerging research in this area might be utilized to develop a more coherent, connected and co-productive compliance strategy and practice.

I begin by charting the rise and pursuit of compliance in the United Kingdom penal context, giving due attention to the managerialist pursuit of short-term formal compliance, while also acknowledging the new theorizing, and necessary problematizing, of compliance as a dynamic concept. In tracing the impact of these developments within recent compliance policy and practice, I question the potential of short-term managerialist strategies of compliance, dominated as they are by professional actors and actions. In an attempt to explore a more constructive way forward, consideration is given to emerging research literature relating to 'normative' mechanisms of compliance and to the implications of this literature for developing compliance policy and practice. In conclusion, I explore the possibility of a more coherent and co-productive approach to compliance policy and practice, in which professionals take greater cognizance of their supporting role in the compliance dynamic toward the meaningful progression of the offender/compliance actor.

Before proceeding further, it is necessary to provide some preliminary mapping of what is meant by compliance and how it is here defined and understood. For the purpose of this discussion, compliance is defined as the act of adhering to a rule or order. In the context of community penalties, then, the act of compliance is located principally with the individual required to comply, albeit in a context of constraints and, increasingly, compulsion. In this respect, compliance is distinguished from the act of enforcement, which might be defined as the response of a given authority to an act of non-compliance.

More broadly, drawing on the work of Tyler (1990), Bottoms (2001) and Robinson and McNeill (2008), compliance is understood as a dynamic process which occurs across a continuum and in response to multiple and interactive mechanisms. Specifically, this discussion recognizes Bottoms's (2001) distinction between short and long-term compliance, and Robinson and McNeill's (2008) distinction between formal and substantive compliance. In the context of community penalties, short-term compliance refers to an offender's compliance with the specific legal requirements of a penalty, for example, successful completion of a court order. Longer-term compliance refers to an offender's compliance with the criminal law, that is, future law-abiding behaviour or 'non-offending' within a specified time period. Importantly, Robinson and McNeill (2008) propose a further distinction within short-term compliance – between formal and substantive compliance (though it seems to me that this distinction may also be applicable to longer-term compliance). Here, formal compliance is used to denote an offender's 'technical' compliance with the legal requirements of an order and/or the criminal law. Substantive compliance, by contrast, is used to refer to the offender's active and meaningful engagement with the requirements of an order and/or its prescribed purposes. This might be evidenced, for example, in an offender's positive attitude to and engagement with unpaid work requirements, or, in respect of long-term compliance, an ex/offender's internalized decision (and capacity) to desist from criminal activity.

My interest in this chapter lies principally in the concepts of substantive and long-term compliance, that is, in the 'types' of compliance that rely less on the power of penal products and those who enforce them, and more on the engagement, cooperation and contribution of the offender 'required' to comply. This is not to suggest that this chapter is not concerned with the role of the state and/or justice authorities in *supporting* compliance. Quite the opposite: a key concern of this chapter is the extent to which community penalties, and those who deliver them, can more effectively create the contexts, conditions and contents required to support offenders to progress their own compliance journeys, toward the achievement of meaningful progression and change.

The rise and problematizing of compliance

Though there may be some appeal in constructing compliance as a late-modern penal concern – spawned, it might be argued, by recent global preoccupations with risk, security and control– even a cursory reading of probation's origins, development and evolving purposes attests that compliance is an old–new concept. That is, the pursuit of compliance has long occupied a central place in probation endeavours, to the extent that compliance with and completion of court orders consistently emerges as a primary measure of the service's success and effectiveness (see, for example, Duguid 1982; McNeill and Whyte 2007; Pease et al. 1975; Vanstone 2004).

However, though there exist clear continuities between early and more recent compliance strategies (in the existence, for example, of incentives and disincentives for compliant/non-compliant behaviour; see also Garland 1985), we can also observe important points of departure. For example, while there is no question of who held the greater power in early accounts of probation, both McNeill's (2010) and Vanstone's (2004) accounts of this process portray the pursuit of compliance as a negotiated, progressive and substantive endeavour. Looking, as we will, to more recent compliance activity, the same claim is less easily made. Indeed, it might be argued that, as compliance has come to occupy a more pronounced place in late-modern penal strategy, so the offender's capacity to contribute to and progress toward substantive compliance has become increasingly constrained.

The more recent *rise* of compliance – observable in the United Kingdom from the mid-1980s onwards – is reasonably well documented and tells a more tangled story of various and largely unsuccessful efforts on the part of the state to 'produce' or 'enforce' offender compliance. From the 1980s to the late 1990s this was predominantly pursued in the United Kingdom via an array of policies, practices and strategies of 'tougher and tougher' enforcement – most vividly demonstrated in the perpetual revision and 'toughening up' of prescribed National Standards for community penalties in England and Wales (Hedderman and Hough 2004). Though this ratcheting up of enforcement practice may have originated with a concern to improve both formal and substantive compliance with community penalties – arguably informed by a small number of studies which suggested a link between *effective* enforcement practice, offender compliance and reduced recidivism (McIvor 1995; Trotter 2006; May and Wadwell 2001) – as concerns with effectiveness in the pursuit of compliance gave way to more myopic preoccupations with appearing 'tough', so the more complex pursuit of compliance gave way to compliance by enforcement. Here, compliance was not an outcome to be fostered in the context of an evolving and participatory relationship, but an outcome required and enforced from the outset.[3] Considered in the context of offenders' demonstrated tendencies toward noncompliance (at least in the face of instrumental mechanisms of control), the consequences of this penal 'strategy' are not difficult to fathom.

By way of summary, in England and Wales breach rates for community penalties soared, doubling from 18 per cent in 1994 to 37 per cent in 2004 (Home Office 2005). In the same period, prison rates escalated and the existing link between effective enforcement practice, offender compliance and reduced reconviction collapsed under the force and myopia of a strategy of enforced compliance. More problematically, as the above outputs began to impact on the United Kingdom government's much lauded (and heavily invested in) 'What Works' project – which now risked derailment on the basis of the service's inability to retain sufficient numbers of offenders on orders for sufficient periods of time – at the very least it produced a truce of sorts. Politicians, policy makers and probation chiefs were forced to acknowledge that neither formal nor substantive compliance was particularly amenable to being systematically (en)forced; rather, organizations seeking to secure compliance needed to look beyond short-term strategies of enforcement toward the progression of more participatory and prosocial processes thought to foster compliant behaviour.

Occurring alongside (and not unrelated to) the rise of enforced compliance, there has developed what I here refer to as a new theorizing – and necessary problematizing – of compliance in the context of community penalties. The work of Bottoms (2001) has been particularly influential in this regard and was the first to outline a need to shift attention from the practicalities of enforcing compliance toward a more conceptual engagement with compliance as a complex and multidimensional dynamic (see also Robinson and McNeill 2008; McNeill and Robinson 2013). As previously outlined, one of the key contributions of Bottoms's analysis lies in his distinction between short-term and longer-term compliance, and his assertion that individuals and organizations involved with the delivery of community penalties 'are (or should be) inescapably involved in trying to maximise both' (p. 89). In outlining the important distinction between 'formal' and 'substantive' compliance, Robinson and McNeill (2008) reach a similar, though no less important, conclusion – that is, that the task of those supervising community penalties is 'not just to establish formal compliance but to move beyond it into substantive and (then) longer term compliance' (p. 440). Each of the above contributions proceeds to map out the principal mechanisms underpinning the various dimensions of compliant behaviour, and in doing so begins to engage with the many and varied implications of this new theorizing for those seeking to influence and support compliant behaviour (see also McNeill and Robinson 2013). Significantly, building on the work of Tyler (1990, 2006), connecting theories of social order and recent scholarship on tax regime compliance (Braithwaite 2003; McBarnet 2003), these new analyses highlight the limitations of our long-standing reliance on instrumental mechanisms of compliance (i.e. the building in of incentives and, more frequently, disincentives into the legal frameworks of community penalties) and point to the need now also to attend to other compliance mechanisms, and to the role of normative mechanisms in particular (i.e. the influence of what citizens consider moral and just; Tyler 1990).

We will return to the detailed implications of this new theorizing of compliance below. For now, the significance of this work is that it underscores the need to look beyond current preoccupations with short-term, formal compliance (in the form of, for example, attendance and completion targets) to also consider more complex questions relating to the progression of substantive and long-term compliance outcomes (in the form of, for example, offender engagement, progression and change). Relatedly, in demonstrating the multiple and interactive mechanisms variously impacting on offender compliance, these same analyses underscore that there is much more to developing an effective compliance strategy than the creation of robust, transparent and standardized mechanisms of control.

To summarize, in the last two decades we have witnessed the rise of compliance as a 'new penological discourse'. Yet, in the same period we have been made to recognize that compliance – both formal and substantive – is not an outcome to be systematically (en)forced; rather, it is a complex dynamic and process that we need to understand and support. Notwithstanding the significance of this discovery for the pursuit of compliance in and through community penalties, as we turn now to consider emerging practice in this area it would be naive to overstate the progress made.

Practising compliance

As is the case in many areas of criminal justice policy and practice, the emerging picture of compliance efforts is quite a muddled and conflicting one. On the one hand, the value of qualitative, substantive and longer-term compliance outcomes (in the form of offender engagement, rehabilitation and desistance) continues to be explicitly endorsed in the ascribed purposes and practices of community penalties, both in the United Kingdom and beyond (see, for example, Ministry of Justice 2011; Robinson 2008; Scottish Government 2010). Relatedly, we have recently witnessed a distinct (though not altogether coherent) 'relaxing' of enforcement practices, alongside explicit attempts to restore reasonable levels of discretion to offender managers and criminal justice social workers (Ministry of Justice 2007, 2011; NOMS 2007; Scottish Government 2010). Yet, at the same time, even these more 'relaxed' approaches to enforcement continue to be very closely aligned with short-term managerialist notions of effectiveness and credibility in community penalties (i.e., how to get offenders to turn up, meet prescribed targets and complete orders). Relatedly, there is an emerging sense that many of the tools and technologies being deployed to engage and motivate offenders are either overly prescriptive, patronizing or simply inadequate for the task (Hughes 2012). Also, emerging punishment 'initiatives' and technologies continue to reveal a distinct privileging of 'external credibility' (i.e. what the public think about punishment), without accompanying consideration of how new initiatives might impact on offenders' internal journeys toward compliance and desistance (see, for example, Maruna 2008). Perhaps most significantly, in almost all of these developments, the opportunities for offenders to actively engage in, contribute to and progress their own compliance journeys appear to be significantly and increasingly constrained.

By way of example, let us consider the findings of a recent empirical study conducted in this area by Phillips (2011). Drawing on research observations and interviews conducted in two English probation teams, Phillips set out to examine the way in which offender managers sought to improve offender compliance. Importantly, the findings provide some encouraging evidence of a shift in focus from a culture and practice of enforcement toward an appreciation of the importance of *supporting* and *improving* compliance in community penalties (and to the important place of discretion within that process). However, in examining how offender managers progressed this 'move toward compliance', Phillips observes that it was both driven and 'produced' through managerialist means. As the author explains:

> I noticed that increased compliance was being achieved through managerialist means such as targets which stipulate that '70 per cent of orders and licences must be successfully completed'. This meant that [offender managers] 'just have to get [offenders] through' the Order.
>
> (TPO, Fieldnotes, p. 1)

Phillips goes on to describe how compliance was most frequently achieved (and non-compliance avoided) by the various and creative strategies deployed by offender managers. The strategies described by Phillips – for example, arranging appointments on days that were convenient to the offender, conducting appointments on the telephone or at the offender's home, or sending offenders text messages about appointments to make non-attendance less likely – are not unusual to those familiar with the methods sometimes deployed by workers attempting to support and/or build compliance, and might be seen as the effective and appropriate use of professional discretion. However, what is concerning about Phillips's account is that it describes a process in which compliance is achieved (and non-compliance avoided) not by the active engagement, cooperation or commitment of offender actors but by the enhanced and closed manoeuvrings of offender managers. As Phillips concludes:

> What is key about both methods…is that they tend to happen behind closed doors with little or no input from the offender. (p. 2)

Though there exists a very limited body of empirical research literature examining this aspect of practice, Phillips's findings are not isolated. Ugwudike's (2010) study, for example, reaches broadly similar conclusions. In exploring the nature and pursuit of compliance in probation areas in Wales and Jersey, Ugwudike begins by observing that, in the probation area examined, 'a narrow definition of compliance prevails', whereby 'compliance is typically defined in terms of attending routine appointments' (p. 330). More significantly, Ugwudike concludes that, in the probation areas examined, 'compliance [was] linked to a series of processes through which *officers manage* several structural, situational and practical contradictions' (pp. 330–332, emphasis added).

Though Ugwudike's study gives important attention to the many structural, situational and practice contradictions variously impacting on offender compliance within community penalties, and to the important role of individualized and interactive supervisory processes in responding to these contradictions, in common with Phillips's findings, the emerging picture is one in which the pursuit of compliance is not only narrowly defined but progressed and produced through the discretionary 'management' of supervising officers. Interestingly, Ugwudike speculates that the positive relationships developed between officers and probationers in this more discretionary management of compliance may provide fertile ground for cultivating more substantive compliance outcomes (in the form, for example, of normative compliance). However, as Phillips (2011) observes, it is equally possible that the micromanagement of compliance in this way might impede and obstruct the types of processes necessary for the effective progression of substantive and longer-term compliance outcomes (including, for example, the acquisition of motivation, agency and responsibility for compliance and change). There are parallels to be drawn here with recent research findings in the area of assisted desistance. One of the principal findings of that body of research is that desistance is achieved and sustained not merely through offenders meeting or achieving desired targets – in the form, for example, of maturation, the development of prosocial relationships, or finding employment. Rather, the key to desistance is seen to lie in what those outcomes come to mean to offenders/desisters in their journey toward desistance (McCulloch and McNeill 2007).

While, then, we can trace some impact of recent theorizing about compliance in emerging compliance policy and practice, at the time of writing the transfer of knowledge, so to speak, appears partial, fragmented and dangerously incoherent. On the one hand, the above provides some encouraging evidence of a shift from a practice of enforcement toward a more creative, relationship-based and discretionary pursuit of compliance in the practice of community penalties. On the other, the fact that this shift has been set and progressed within a managerialist framework raises a number of important questions about the place of the offender actor in this process, the nature (and value) of the compliance achieved, and the extent to which the methods adopted to produce compliance on these terms are in any way conducive to the types of processes required to progress substantive and longer-term compliance outcomes.

Progressing compliance

Of course, none of the above means that it is impossible to progress contemporary compliance policy and practice from its current preoccupation with securing and/or producing short-term formal compliance, or from the above observed leaning toward a practice of professionally produced compliance. However, in attempting to progress such a shift, we perhaps need to begin by more explicitly acknowledging the nature and challenge of that task. We might begin by recognizing that the present (and long-standing) pursuit of short-term, formal compliance in community penalties is unlikely to wane. Short-term, formal compliance remains a primary and important measure of effectiveness in community penalties. Moreover, the existence of robust, transparent and consistent systems of enforcement is considered – by both the actors and audiences of community penalties – critical to the credibility and legitimacy of those penalties (see, for example, Hucklesby 2009; McCulloch 2010). In this respect, the pursuit and progression of short-term formal compliance are reasonably straightforward (though see Hucklesby 2009). Punishment is administered as a consequence of wrong-doing, and strategies of enforcement are about creating transparent and standardized mechanisms of control to ensure orders are robustly enforced. The problem, however, arises when we expect (and, increasingly, 'require') these strategies also to produce or progress substantive and longer-term compliance outcomes. Unlike short-term formal compliance, substantive and longer-term compliance is a much more complex outcome and process, as it relates not just to a penal product (in the form of managed or controlled offenders) but to a more complex and vexed process of rehabilitation. In other words, we can quite easily compel or require offenders to formally comply with the requirements of a community sanction (and invoke punishment when they fail to do so). We cannot, however, compel or require offenders to engage with the substantive and longer-term purposes of these penalties, that is, achieve progression and change. As offender accounts of desistance attest, these outcomes, and the processes that support them, are achieved only when offenders themselves (often with the support of significant others) commit to the pursuit and progression of those outcomes (Davies 1979; Farrall 2002b). Considered from this vantage point, the critical challenge facing those seeking to support formal, substantive and long-term compliance lies much less in questions of how we can manage or produce compliance within community penalties, and much more in questions of how we can create the context, conditions and content in which offenders might meaningfully engage in, take responsibility for and progress their own compliance journeys.

There are many theoretical and empirical resources that might be drawn upon in attempting to progress such an approach to compliance (McCulloch 2012). In the remainder of this chapter I wish to consider the contribution of recent research findings relating to the concept and dynamics of normative compliance. In a penal climate simultaneously dominated, seduced and let down by the promise of instrumental mechanisms of control (i.e. the use of incentives and disincentives to influence or control individual behaviour), recent attention to the role of normative mechanisms in compliance invites us to consider the ways in which offenders might be motivated and supported to comply for reasons beyond the instrumental, as well as the ways in which justice authorities might more effectively support this process.

Normative theories of compliance are primarily concerned with the influence of what people regard as moral and just on law-abiding (or compliance) behaviour. In this respect, normative theories start from a focus on the individual citizen (or offender) and on his or her 'internal mechanisms' of compliance. Accordingly, normative compliance is often referred to as 'internalized obligations' – that is, obligations for which the citizen has taken personal responsibility (Tyler 1990). In the context of community penalties, normative compliance might be considered as the ideal 'type' of compliance, in so far as it encompasses both the formal and substantive elements of compliance for which community penalties purportedly strive. Looking more closely at the dynamics of normative compliance, Tyler (1990) distinguishes between two 'types' of normative compliance. The first is compliance that occurs through personal morality, that is, a person's conscious belief in, or moral acceptance of, the norm in question (see also Bottoms 2001). The second is compliance that occurs through legitimacy, that is, 'the belief that authorities, institutions, and social arrangement are appropriate, proper, and just' (Tyler 2006, p. 376).

Tyler's study (1990) was the first large-scale study to explore the significance and dynamics of normative compliance with the law. The overarching conclusion of that study is that normative issues matter in compliance. That is, people obey the law not only for instrumental reasons but *also* because they believe, or come to believe, that it is proper and just to do so. According to Tyler, the practical implication of this conclusion is that:

> police officers and judges who recognise and respond to people's normative concerns can exercise their authority more effectively; their rules and decisions will be accepted and obeyed voluntarily. (p. 178)

Though Tyler may be at risk of overstating the impact of normative mechanisms on individual compliance behaviour (at least as it applies to persistent offenders), in a penal climate that is sometimes hostile to the idea of attending to or improving offenders' experience of community sanctions, his findings in this area have much to contribute to our discussion here.

One of the primary implications of normative theories of compliance is that those seeking to support compliance in community penalties need first to recognize the critical role of the offender *actor* in that pursuit. If normative compliance occurs through the 'internalized obligations', 'personal responsibility' and 'voluntary actions' (Tyler 1990) of those made subject to community penalties, then authorities concerned with the progression of compliance need (now on effectiveness grounds) to recognize offenders as actors – not objects – in the compliance pursuit. This is not to negate the multiple constraints variously impacting on offenders' compliance decisions and actions, or the role of professionals in supporting and, where necessary, enforcing compliance. Rather, it is to recognize that, if compliance is to have any real or lasting value in late-modern community penalties (for actors and audiences alike), then it needs to be both constructed and progressed as a co-productive endeavour: that is, an endeavour that focuses as much on shared and collaborative processes of production – and the relationships and resources required to progress these – as it does on the outcomes and targets to be achieved (see, for example, Beresford 2002; Bovaird 2007; Weaver 2011).

Relatedly, normative theories of compliance suggest a need to more explicitly attend to offenders' understanding of the purposes and 'requirements' of community penalties. Again, if offenders are to develop an internalized obligation to, personal responsibility for, or voluntary actions toward desired compliance outcomes, then community penalties need to be more explicitly orientated toward helping offenders to understand what those outcomes are, as well as why they are deemed to be important. Though this may appear to be a reasonably straightforward observation, recent empirical research in this area suggests that offenders (and sometimes supervising officers) often have a very limited grasp of the broad purposes of community penalties (beyond the retributive); such that, for some, substantive and longer-term compliance outcomes – in the form of offender progression and change – were seen to begin on completion of a community penalty rather than within it (McCulloch 2010).

With regard to Tyler's two 'types' of compliance, the idea of progressing compliance by appealing to or influencing an offender's personal morality has received relatively little attention in the existing compliance literature (though the recent rise of cognitive behavioural approaches is clearly relevant here). As Tyler (1990) observes, 'from the perspective of the authorities...legitimacy is a far more stable base on which to rest compliance than personal or group morality' (p. 26). Though Tyler is right to acknowledge the limitations of the state in shaping personal or group morality, again, recent accounts of assisted desistance make clear that the journey toward substantive and longer-term compliance very often involves a shifting and shaping of moral values (and/or compliance attitudes); a process which, in turn, appears to be influenced variously and interactively by processes of maturation, the influence of significant relationships (formal and informal) and changing social circumstances (see, for example, Farrall 2002b; Maruna 2001; McCulloch 2005). Consider, for example, the following account of the many and interactive processes impacting on one probationer's journey toward normative compliance:[4]

> It was just kenning [knowing] about all your stuff, all like in the one room, rather than just waking up in the morning and going what's happening. Kenning about everything and sort of like that's when I realized. Then wi' being on probation you have to be of good behaviour too so I was sort of like being alright and then once I got the job that was it. I've got a new job now too. That one was only temporary but the one I'm at now is permanent.

> [How did you get the new job? (Researcher)]

> My dad, like cos fae I got probation and I was trying to calm down, with stopping going out, not getting charged, getting a job. I think it sort of showed my dad tae I was able to dae it like, so he got [me] an application for his work and then I got a job.

In this account – and the many others like it – 'changing' an offender's normative values, or perceived moral obligations, is not something that is achieved by professional efforts (or programmes) alone. Rather, it is a process and outcome that occur as a result of the active and interactive engagement of offenders *and* others in a process of change. Again, the message emerging from accounts such as these is that shifting or shaping an offender's moral values and obligations appears to depend less on what professionals do to produce change and much more on the ways in which offenders, often with the help of significant others, engage with and make use of these processes. The practical implication of this message is that, if community penalties are to become spaces in which offenders are enabled to develop and demonstrate normative compliance, then they need to become more explicitly and practically orientated toward supporting rather than (en)forcing that process.

Tyler's second identified 'type' of compliance, that is, compliance that occurs through legitimacy, has long been considered relevant to the effective exercise of authority and has typically focused on understanding and influencing what 'the public' think about the legitimacy of the state and its various mechanisms of law enforcement (including, for example, the judiciary, police officers, lawyers and the like; see Beetham 1991). Only very recently, however, has the concept of legitimacy been extended to include consideration of the 'internal' experience of penal sanctions; that is, the perception and experience of a sanction as viewed from the person made subject to it. To summarize a developing and complex literature, the key message arising from this area of analysis is that offenders are more likely to comply, cooperate with and commit to community penalties (and their purposes) if they perceive and experience those penalties, and the exercise of authority within them, to be reasonable, fair and just (Bottoms 2001; Robinson and McNeill 2008; McIvor 2009).

The implications of this conclusion for the pursuit of compliance in community penalties are, potentially, considerable and far-reaching. Tyler's work, for example, highlights the importance of attending to issues of 'procedural justice' (1990), that is, the exercise of fair procedures in supporting compliance with legal requirements; a finding recently echoed and expanded in McIvor's (2009) analysis of the role of procedural justice within the newly established Scottish Drug Courts. Relatedly, Bottoms (2001), Ugwudike (2010) and McNeill and Robinson (2010, 2013) draw attention to the importance of the supervisory relationship as a key site or resource within which legitimacy can be built and developed. Further, McCulloch's (2010) recent study highlights the importance of issues of social justice in supporting and sustaining substantive compliance, a finding also highlighted in Farrall's (2002a) analysis of the factors associated with non-compliance in community penalties.

Notwithstanding the significance of these emerging messages, in lieu of the preceding discussion, the challenge of these findings perhaps lies in the extent to which they can be meaningfully progressed as part of a coherent compliance strategy. As a regulatory and coercive institution, there is a natural tendency within the criminal justice system (and, arguably, some of its actors) to appropriate and apply the above discussed research findings in an instrumental way – that is, from a position of: how can we use this new thinking about compliance to get offenders to do what we want? (The earlier discussed findings from

1

Phillips's study arguably illustrate such a tendency.) The problem, however, is that normative theories of compliance require us to think (and act) differently. They require us to recognize that the key to normative compliance (as manifest in substantive and longer-term compliance behaviour) does not reside within professional activity – that is, in what professionals do to manage or produce normative values, just procedures or legitimate relationships. Rather, it resides within the developing offender/desister attitudes, actions and commitments that are *sometimes* triggered when professional 'aids' to compliance are in place and working well. When conceptualized in this way, the role of (and relationships between) penal actors in progressing compliance is significantly altered, as is the role of research knowledge in supporting compliance efforts. In short, there is no single or simple means by which justice agencies and/or professional actors can secure or produce normative compliance. At best, those who wish to support compliance on these terms can strive to develop the types of environments, relationships and opportunities (even painful and 'punishing' ones) that are more, not less, likely to assist offenders to engage in, take responsibility for and progress their own compliance journeys.

If this message were not sufficiently challenging in the contemporary climate of corrections, as McNeill and Robinson's (2013) recent engagement with these issues cautions, it is not enough to merely attend to how we might progress normative compliance in community penalties (and/or the building of legitimacy within that); we must also, and at the same time, attend to the regular and routine ways in which community penalties, and those who deliver them, can act to damage and erode normative compliance (see also the above discussion of Phillips's research findings). In charting the many aspects of contemporary corrections practice that might be vulnerable to accusations of procedural injustice and/or perceptions of illegitimacy, McNeill and Robinson highlight the earlier discussed culture and practice of enforcement currently dominating penal practice in England and Wales, the associated privileging of 'external' legitimacy over 'internal' legitimacy, and the increasing orientation toward discontinuity and fragmentation within routine supervisory relationships and processes. Importantly, the argument being presented is not simply that an increasingly robust, punitive and depersonalized approach to enforcement, punishment and supervision runs the risk of damaging the development of positive supervisory relationships (and, in turn, the legitimacy of those relationships). Rather, it is that offenders' experience of these processes, particularly when they are perceived to be unreasonable, unfair or unjust, runs the risk of undermining the perceived legitimacy of the sanction itself and, thus, the motivations, attitudes and actions of compliance potentially developing within it.

This interactive and counteractive relationship between normative compliance, legitimacy and offenders' perceptions and experience of (social) justice (see also Bottoms 2001; Duff 2001, 2003) finds further and fuller expression in offenders' own accounts of what matters in compliance, such as they are. For example, in McCulloch's (2010) recent examination of the factors impacting on offender compliance within community service in Scotland, respondents were clear that the positive, respectful and fair behaviour of staff toward them supported attendance and compliance with community service. Offenders were equally clear that 'negative' attitudes and behaviour on the part of staff 'made you think twice' about complying. However, when considered in the context of their individual experiences of compliance and, more frequently, non-compliance, staff attitude and approach were not considered to be *as* critical to compliance as 'other' factors. Amidst the array of other factors deemed to be 'more important', one aspect that emerged as particularly significant was referred to as 'other stuff going on in your life [that] might have nothing to do with CS'. Here, what was being described was the array of personal and social problems which offenders dealt with on a daily basis. Importantly, for this and many of the other offenders interviewed, such factors were seen to matter a lot more than 'what people here say and do to you'. Farrall's (2002a) study reaches broadly similar conclusions (albeit via a different route). In attempting to identify the correlates and features of long-term absence from supervision (i.e. non-compliance), Farrall found that non-compliance was highly associated with the experience of financial problems, depression, mental health problems, unstable accommodation, substance dependency and, for some, a sense that supervision had little to offer in the face of these problems.

In each of these recent studies the complex, interactive and counteractive nature of compliance (and non-compliance) looms large in offender accounts of what matters in compliance and its pursuit, as do issues and experiences of social (in)justice. Yet, these same studies consistently reveal a compliance strategy and practice that appears to be narrowly focused, disconnected from offenders' lived experience and, more often than not, ill-equipped to respond to offenders' compliance 'needs' and aspirations (Farrall 2002a; Hughes 2012; McCulloch 2010; Ugwudike 2010). As Ugwudike (2010) concludes in respect of her findings on this issue:

> In sum, there appeared to be no coherent compliance strategy for alleviating the obstacles to compliance. Individual officers developed their unique approach based on subjective considerations of the appropriateness of each strategy. (p. 333)

These messages raise important questions about the purpose and possibilities of the contemporary compliance pursuit (and of community penalties more broadly). If the pursuit of compliance is to be about more than the robust enforcement and administration of punishment; if it is also about engaging, motivating and supporting offenders to develop and sustain the 'types' of normative compliance necessary for the progression and maintenance of substantive and longer-term compliance outcomes, then there is a need to develop a more coherent, connected and co-productive compliance strategy and practice. This is a strategy and practice that starts from a more coherent engagement with compliance as a complex and multidimensional concept and dynamic; that proceeds from an understanding of the offender's pivotal place in (and experience of) progressing compliance; and that is both attentive and responsive to the multiple, interactive and counteractive mechanisms variously impacting on offender compliance over and beyond the life of a community penalty. The idea that such a strategy can be produced or progressed independently of the offender actors required to demonstrate compliance is nonsensical. The extent to which community penalties can provide the context and conditions in which a more coherent and co-productive compliance strategy and practice can be developed and progressed remains to be seen.

Concluding comment

The above discussion demonstrates that the pursuit of compliance in community penalties is, necessarily, a complex, challenging and far-reaching endeavour (for all of the actors involved). It is so because compliance with community penalties, if meaningful, is about much more than forced or professionally produced compliance with an abstract penal product. Rather, in its ideal form, it relates to a normative process of cooperation with, commitment to and progression through the purposes and practices of penal sanctions. Supporting compliance on these terms in the contemporary climate of corrections is challenging. Producing or (en)forcing compliance on these terms is impossible.

At the heart of this chapter, then, lies the conviction that compliance, properly constructed, belongs principally to the offender actor 'required' to comply. Accordingly, I have argued that, to the extent that justice authorities are committed to the progression of substantive and longer-term compliance outcomes within community penalties, there is a need to more explicitly recognize (and engage with) offenders as actors, not objects, in the compliance pursuit. Moreover, I have argued that the role of justice authorities in this pursuit ought to be much less about how to manage or produce compliance (though there will always be a place for the former), and much more about how to create the environments, relationships and resources known to motivate and *support* offenders to take responsibility for and progress their own compliance journeys. The evidence base regarding what matters in this dynamic is only just emerging – and the need now to develop our understanding in this area is clear. However, within emerging analyses there can be traced a rising recognition of the need now to construct and progress compliance as a more co-productive endeavour. Further, there is evidence to suggest that offenders are more likely to engage in such an endeavour if they perceive and experience community penalties to be purposeful, legitimate and just, and if they experience some alignment between their developing compliance goals and the personal and social circumstances required to progress these.

Admittedly, in a penal climate that seems ever keen to demonstrate and display its punitive capacities, it may seem counterintuitive and even fanciful to construct the pursuit of compliance in these terms (see, for example, Raynor 2012). Certainly, the above-described pursuit of compliance sits some way from the short-term managerialist pursuit documented in the first half of this paper, and which recent empirical studies suggest continues to prevail in practice. In such circumstances we cannot fail to question whether the pursuit of compliance in these terms is possible, far less practical. Perhaps encouragingly, the concept and practice of co-production is now (re-)emerging within criminal justice debate, policy and practice, and there are a number of encouraging examples of offender and ex-offender involvement in the design, delivery and evaluation of penal services (see, for example, Weaver 2011; Weaver and Lightowler 2012). However, developments in this area are modest, robust research evidence is scarce, and there remain a number of questions about the value, possibilities and potential of a co-productive approach in a service that seems determined to align itself with the business of punishment, and which (no doubt for these reasons) remains ambivalent about the place and contribution of offenders in that process (Weaver and McCulloch 2012). Similar questions emerge when we explore the possibilities of developing more purposeful, legitimate and just community penalties (as perceived by those made subject to them) (McNeill and Robinson 2013), and/or when we consider what might be required to make meaningful the social justice responsibilities that now loiter ignominiously yet persistently around the multiple and contested purposes of community penalties.

Of course, these questions and tensions are not new to probation and criminal justice social work efforts, and it might be argued that the service (and its actors) has long grappled with and sought to manage these tensions. However, in a context of increasing scrutiny regarding the outcomes of community penalties, and the near-constant reporting of 'disappointing results' (and, however problematic these results may be, let us not forget that they portray the lived experience and outcomes of an already troubled and troubling group of individuals), to argue that this is how it has always been does not now seem sufficient.

The remaining space and focus of this chapter preclude engagement with the question of how community penalties might constructively move beyond these tensions and contradictions (though readers will note that there already exist a number of compelling and 'game-changing' responses to this question, emerging as they have at different points in probation's history and in response to a notably cognate series of contradictions and crises; see, for example, Bottoms 1980; Bottoms and McWilliams 1979; Christie 1977; Duff 2001, 2003; McNeill 2010; Raynor 1985; Raynor 2012; Rotman 1990, 1994). My point here is simply that, if we wish to progress the pursuit of compliance (and community penalties more broadly), then these questions – and the insights and responses they have given rise to – now need to move to the fore.

Certainly there exist many obstacles and problems to be navigated in progressing a more coherent and co-productive approach to compliance in the contemporary penal/political climate. However, we cannot deny that there exist as many obstacles and problems in the progression of a short-term, managerial or professionally produced approach to compliance: not least that, even if compliance can be produced on those terms, its value as a criminal justice outcome remains questionable in a society which, for all its doubts and ambivalence, seems still to 'require' of offenders substantive compliance outcomes – in the form of responsibility, progression and change. Therein lies the principal driver for the progression of a more coherent and co-productive compliance practice. We now have at our disposal a developing understanding of what that might look like, involve and require. The key question is whether we have, or can arouse, the political, public, professional and offender will required to take that forward.

Notes

1. For those seeking an overview of why this might be the case, see Sander and Young's (2007) discussion of the criminal justice system as a complex regulatory social institution. Essentially they argue that, in operating within a society in which power, status and wealth are unequally distributed along lines such as age, gender, race and class, the criminal justice system – as a regulatory and coercive social institution – both reflects and compounds these inequalities in its routine activity.
2. This phrase is used to refer to a process in which compliance is achieved through the managerial and sometimes discretionary strategies of supervising officers, with little or no input from the offender actor (more of which below).
3. see also Nellis (2004, 2006) for an overview of the role of surveillance and electronic monitoring technologies in this process.
4. This was recorded as part of a small-scale study (McCulloch 2005) which sought to understand the interplay of factors impacting on offenders' compliance and desistance journeys.

References

Beetham, D. (1991) *The Legitimation of Power.* London: Macmillan.

Beresford, P. (2002) 'User Involvement in Research and Evaluation: Liberation or Regulation?' *Social Policy and Society* 1(2), 95–105.

Bottoms, A. (1980) 'An Introduction to "The Coming Crisis"'. in A. Bottoms and R. Preston (Eds) *The Coming Penal Crisis*. Edinburgh, UK: Scottish Academic Press.

Bottoms, A. (2001) 'Compliance and Community Penalties'. in A. Bottoms, L. Gelsthorpe and S. Rex (Eds) *Community Penalties: Change and Challenges*. Cullompton: Willan.

Bottoms, A. and McWilliams, W. (1979) 'A Non-Treatment Paradigm for Probation Practice'. *British Journal of Social Work* 9, 159–202.

Bovaird, T. (2007) 'Beyond Engagement and Participation: User and Community Co-production of Public Services'. *Public Administration Review* 67(5), 846–860.

Braithwaite, V. (2003) 'Dancing with Tax Authorities: Motivational Postures and Non-Compliant Actions'. in V. Braithwaite (Ed.) *Taxing Democracy: Understanding Tax Avoidance and Evasion*. Aldershot: Ashgate.

Christie, N. (1977) 'Conflicts as Property'. *British Journal of Criminology* 17, 1–15.

Davies, M. (1979) 'Through the Eyes of the Probationer'. *Probation Journal* 26(3), 84–88.

De Botton, A. (2004) *Status Anxiety*. London: Penguin.

Duff, A. (2001) *Punishment, Communication and Community*. Oxford University Press: New York.

Duff, A. (2003) 'Probation, Punishment and Restorative Justice: Should Altruism Be Engaged in Punishment?' *Howard Journal of Criminal Justice* 42(1), 181–197.

Duguid, G. (1982) *Community Service in Scotland: The First Two Years*. Edinburgh: Scottish Office Central Research Unit.

Farrall, S. (2002a) 'Long-Term Absences from Probation: Officers' and Probationers' Accounts', *The Howard Journal of Criminal Justice* 41(3), 263–278.

Farrall, S. (2002b) *Rethinking 'What Works with Offenders': Probation, Social Context and Desistance from Crime*. Cullompton: Willan.

Feeley, M. and Simon, J. (1992) 'The New Penology: Notes on the Emerging Strategy of Corrections and Its Implications'. *Criminology* 30(4), 449–474.

Garland, D. (1985) *Punishment and Welfare: A History of Penal Strategies*. Aldershot: Gower.

Hedderman, C. and Hough, M. (2004) 'Getting Tough or Being Effective: What Matters?' in G. Mair (Ed.) *What Matters in Probation*. Cullompton: Willan.

Home Office (2005) *Offender Management Caseload Statistics 2004*. Home Office Statistical Bulletin 17/05. London: Home Office.

Hucklesby, A. (2009) 'Understanding Offenders' Compliance: A Case Study of Electronically Monitored Curfew Orders'. *Journal of Law and Society* 36(2), 248–271.

Hughes, W. (2012) 'Promoting Offender Engagement and Compliance in Service Planning: Practitioner and Service User Perspectives in Hertfordshire'. *Probation Journal* 59(1), 49–65.

Maruna, S. (2001) *Making Good: How Ex-Convicts Reform and Rebuild Their Lives*. Washington: American Psychological Association.

McBarnet, D. (2003) 'When Compliance Is not the Solution but the Problem: From Changes in Law to Changes in Attitude'. in V. Braithwaite (Ed.) *Taxing Democracy: Understanding Tax Avoidance and Evasion*. Aldershot: Ashgate.

McCulloch, T. (2005) 'Probation, Social Context and Desistance: Retracing the Relationship'. *Probation Journal* 52(1), 8–22.

McCulloch, T. (2010) 'Realising Potential: Community Service, Pro-social Modelling and Desistance'. *European Journal of Probation* 2(2), 3–22.

McCulloch, T. (2012) 'Giving Compliance Back: Re-Analysing and Re-Orientating the Debate'. *Eurovista* 2(1), 27–30.

McCulloch, T. and McNeill, F. (2007) 'Consumer Society, Commodification and Offender Management'. *Criminology and Criminal Justice* 7(3), 223–242.

McIvor, G. (1995) *Working with Offenders*. London: Jessica Kingsley.

McIvor, G. (2009) 'Therapeutic Jurisprudence and Procedural Justice in Scottish Drug Courts'. *Criminology and Criminal Justice* 9(1), 29–49.

McNeill, F. (2010) 'Supervision in Historical Context: Learning the Lessons of (Oral) History'. in F. McNeill, P. Raynor and C. Trotter (Eds) *Offender Supervision: New Directions in Theory, Research and Practice*. Cullompton: Willan.

McNeill, F. and Robinson, G. (2013) 'Liquid Legitimacy and Community Sanctions'. in A. Crawford and A. Hucklesby (Eds) *Legitimacy and Compliance in Criminal Justice*. Cullompton: Willan.

McNeill, F. and Whyte, B. (2007) *Reducing Reoffending: Social Work and Community Justice in Scotland*. Cullompton: Willan.

Ministry of Justice. (2007) *National Standards for the Supervision of Offenders in the Community*. London: Ministry of Justice.

Ministry of Justice. (2011) *National Standards for the Management of Offenders*. London: Ministry of Justice. https://www.gov.uk/government/uploads/system/uploads/attachment_data/file/162202/national-standards-management-offenders-2011.pdf.pdf (accessed 9 July 2013).

Nellis, M. (2004) 'Electronic Monitoring and the Community Supervision of Offenders'. in A. Bottoms, S. Rex and G. Robinson *Alternative to Prison: Options for an Insecure Society*. Cullompton: Willan.

Nellis, M. (2006) 'Surveillance, Rehabilitation and Electronic Monitoring: Getting the Issues Clear'. *Criminology and Public Policy* 5(1), 103–108.

NOMS (2007) *National Standards for the Management of Offenders: Standards and Implementation Guidance*. London: Ministry of Justice.

Phillips, J. (2011) 'The Exercise of Discretion in the Probation Service and Bottoms' Model of Compliance'. *Howard League for Penal Reform, Early Career Academics Network Bulletin*, October 2011.

Raynor, P. (1985) *Social Work, Justice and Control*. Oxford: Blackwell.

Raynor, P. (2012) 'Is Probation Still Possible'. *The Howard Journal of Criminal Justice* 51(2), 173–189.

Robinson, G. (2008) 'Late-Modern Rehabilitation: The Evolution of a Penal Strategy'. *Punishment and Society* 10(4), 429–445.

Robinson, G. and McNeill, F. (2008) 'Exploring the Dynamics of Compliance with Community Penalties'. *Theoretical Criminology* 12(4), 431–449.

Rotman, E. (1990) *Beyond Punishment. A New View of the Rehabilitation of Criminal Offenders*. New York, NY: Greenwood Press.

Rotman, E. (1994) 'Beyond Punishment'. in A. Duff and D. Garland (Eds) *A Reader on Punishment*. Oxford: Oxford University Press.

Sanders, A. and Young, E. (2007) *Criminal Justice*. Third Edition. Oxford: Oxford University Press.

Scottish Government (2010) *National Outcomes and Standards for Social Work Services in the Criminal Justice System*. Available at: http://www.scotland.gov.uk/Resource/Doc/925/0103556.pdf

Trotter, C. (2006) *Working with Involuntary Clients: A Guide to Practice*. Second Edition. London: Sage.

Tyler, T. (1990) *Why People Obey the Law*. New Haven: Yale University Press.

Tyler T. (2006) 'Psychological Perspectives on Legitimacy and Legitimation'. *Annual Review of Psychology* 57, 375–400.

Ugwudike, P. (2010) 'Compliance with Community Penalties: The Importance of Interactional Dynamics'. in F. McNeill, P. Raynor and C. Trotter (Eds) *Offender Supervision: New Directions in Theory, Research and Practice*. Cullompton, Willan.

Vanstone, M. (2004) 'Mission Control: The Origins of a Humanitarian Service'. *Probation Journal* 51(1), 34–47.

Weaver, B. (2011) 'Co-Producing Community Justice: The Transformative Potential of Personalisation for Penal Sanctions'. *The British Journal of Social Work* 41(6), 1038–1057.

Weaver, B. and McCulloch, T. (2012) *Co-producing Criminal Justice: Executive Summary*. The Scottish Centre for Crime and Justice Research. http://www.sccjr.ac.uk/publications/co-producing-criminal-justiceexecutive-summary/

Weaver, B. and Lightowler, C. (2012) 'Shaping the Criminal Justice System: The Role of Those Supported by Criminal Justice Services'. IRISS Insights, no.13. http://www.iriss.org.uk/resources/shaping-criminal-justice-system-role-those-supported-criminal-justice-services

Section II

In the Front Line: The Importance of Offender Motivation

5

Learning from Odysseus: Self-Applied Situational Crime Prevention as an Aid to Compliance

Anthony E. Bottoms

In Homer's great epic poem, *The Odyssey*, the Greek hero Odysseus makes a ten-year journey home to Ithaca after the Trojan War, beset by innumerable threats and misadventures. In Book Twelve, we find Odysseus being warned by the goddess Circe of a significant danger on the next stage of his sea voyage. His ship, he learns, must sail past the island of the Sirens:

> those creatures who spellbind any man alive,
> whoever comes their way. Whoever draws too close,
> off guard, and catches the Sirens' voices in the air –
> no sailing home for him, no wife rising to meet him,
> no happy children beaming up at their father's face.
> The high, thrilling song of the Sirens will transfix him,
> Lolling there in their meadow, round them heaps of corpses
> rotting away....

> (Homer 1997: 200)

But Circe also instructs Odysseus how to avoid being fatally enticed by these seductive but deadly temptresses. He must, she says, soften some beeswax, and place it in the ears of every member of his crew, so that they cannot hear the song of the Sirens (and therefore will not be tempted). However, Circe recognizes that Odysseus himself might be 'bent on hearing' the Sirens. If that is the case, she advises, the danger can still be avoided, but only if Odysseus takes some specific precautionary steps. Odysseus must therefore order his shipmates:

> [to] tie you hand and foot in the swift ship
> erect at the mast-block, lashed by ropes to the mast
> so you can hear the Sirens' song to your heart's content.

> But if you plead, commanding your men to set you free,
> then they must lash you faster, rope on rope.
>
> (Homer 1997: 200)

Of course, Odysseus follows Circe's instructions. It is just as well that he does, because the temptation turns out to be very real. Odysseus later records that, as he heard the Sirens' 'ravishing voices', so 'the heart inside me throbbed to listen longer…I signalled the crew with frowns to set me free.' However, the crew, as previously instructed, ignored him, and the danger was duly averted.

What has all this to do with criminology? The answer is: rather more than one might initially suppose. Consider, for example, the case of Darren (not his real name), a male young adult offender who had decided to try to desist from crime. Darren was very close to his grandmother, and he realized that he would need her help and support if he was to stay out of trouble. However, his grandmother – who was largely housebound – lived in a block of flats where Darren and his family used to live, and several of his criminal friends also lived in those flats. Darren was afraid that, if he visited his grandmother at her home, he would meet some of these friends on his way in or out of the flats, and he thought that he might not be strong-willed enough to say 'no' to them if they proposed committing further offences. He therefore agreed with his grandmother that, in order to avoid such temptations, he would, at least for a time, contact her only by telephone and not by visiting her. Is there not a remarkable similarity between this plan and that recommended to Odysseus by Circe?

'Self-binding'

Although criminologists have not (to my knowledge) previously shown much specific interest in the Odysseus story, other social scientists have done so; particularly important in this regard has been Jon Elster's (1984) *Ulysses and the Sirens*, and his later revisiting of similar themes in *Ulysses Unbound* (Elster 2000, esp. ch. 1).[1] In these works, Elster discussed, among other things, what he described as 'constraints that an agent imposes on himself for the sake of some expected benefit to himself' (Elster 2000: 4), a phenomenon that he called 'pre-commitment' or, more graphically, 'self-binding'. He further hypothesized that feared future situations involving the emotions (what he calls 'passions') might be one potential reason for self-binding, because, as he put it: 'When we act under the influence of passions, they may cause us to deviate from plans laid in a cooler moment. Knowledge of this tendency creates an incentive to pre-commit ourselves, to help us stick to our plans' (Elster 2000: 7). Of course, this exactly describes Circe's stratagem to assist Odysseus and his crew, and it also exactly describes Darren's mindset in deciding to set up the agreement with his grandmother. If we then analyse such situations a little more closely, we can see that such 'self-bindings to avoid the possible influence of emotionally-led choices' are put in place by actors in response to a train of thought of a particular kind, namely: 'How can I avoid doing a certain thing that, all things considered, I really think I should not do (e.g., committing a burglary) when I know that in certain circumstances (e.g., meeting my old friends and getting excited in their company), I might be swayed by emotion and therefore very strongly tempted to act again in that fashion?'

Philosophy students are used to considering situations of this kind, which are known generically in that discipline as raising problems relating to 'the weakness of the will'. Indeed, since the time of the ancient Greeks, some philosophers have questioned whether 'weakness of the will' truly exists, notwithstanding the near-universal common-sense assumption that it does.[2] Here, I shall leave aside such scepticism, and instead ask a different question, namely: can we identify the main *mechanisms* by which temptations of this kind can in principle be avoided, and successful self-binding achieved? (On the importance of a mechanism-based analytical approach in the social sciences, see Hedström 2005.) I would suggest that there are three principal mechanisms potentially available, and these can be illustrated by the following vignettes about a hypothetical habitual shoplifter, 'Ryan', who wishes to stop offending. Ryan might try to avoid temptation by planning his life in one of these ways:

(i) Ryan might decide to shop only in stores which have internal CCTV cameras. His belief is that there will be a high probability of getting caught and punished in such stores; he hopes, therefore, that this will prevent him from offending because of the fear that any further thefts will result in unpleasant consequences (arrest, etc.). This would be *instrumental compliance* with Ryan's preferred course of action, based on a rational calculation of his long-term self-interest: the deterrent threat will, he hopes, prevent the action.

(ii) Because Ryan is deeply religious, and has been taught by his church that theft is wrong, he might decide deliberately to try to remember this teaching every time he goes into a shop (perhaps by carrying a rosary and touching it as he enters the store). His hope will then be that the teaching will be stronger than the urge to steal; accordingly (though this will probably happen only after an internal struggle) the religious norms will prevail over the temptation. This would be *normative compliance* with his preferred course of action, based on the moral teaching of the church.

(iii) Ryan might decide to plan his daily routines so that – as far as possible – he completely avoids going into shops with tempting displays. For example, he might decide to abandon his previous habit of stocking up at the local supermarket every week, and instead order his groceries online; and/or he might devise a fresh way of going to and from his workplace so that no

shops are passed on the way. This is *situational compliance* with Ryan's preferred course of action, based not on prudential calculation (see (i) above)
nor on normative influences at the potential crime scene (see (ii)), but
on the manipulation of the physical relationship between the potential
offender (himself) and the potential crime site (a shop).

Thus, self-binding can be achieved using instrumental, normative, or situational mechanisms (or, of course, some combination of them). Using this
typology,[3] Odysseus's successful encounter with the Sirens was clearly accom-
plished by *situational* means alone: had it not been for the wax in the ears of
the crew, and the ropes tying Odysseus to the mast, they would undoubtedly
have joined the 'heaps of corpses rotting away' on the Sirens' island. Similarly, Darren's deliberate avoidance of the block of flats where his grandmother
lived is a version of the situational avoidance of temptation. It is this kind of
situational self-binding that is the principal focus of this chapter.

While the term 'situational self-binding' does not appear anywhere in the
criminological literature, there are three criminological concepts that have
some affinity with it, namely: *situational crime prevention, self-control* and *'knifing
off'*. In the next two sections of this chapter, I shall consider the first and
second of these concepts, which are, of course, central topics, familiar to all
criminologists. 'Knifing off' is a concept of a more specialist kind, but in the
last decade it has become well known within the literature on desistance from
crime. I shall therefore consider it in the final main section of this chapter, having first considered the evidence relating to 'situational self-binding' from the
Sheffield Desistance Study.

Situational crime prevention

Criminologists' familiarity with the concept of situational compliance has been
derived especially from the policy approach known as *situational crime prevention* (SCP). This type of policy was first formally articulated in the 1970s under
the leadership of Ronald Clarke (then the head of the Home Office Research
Unit in Britain), and it has since been considerably – and very influentially –
elaborated and developed by Clarke and others.[4] A recent description of SCP,
taken from an encyclopaedia entry by Clarke (2010), is as follows:

> SCP is the science of reducing opportunities for crime. It focuses on specific
> forms of crime or disorder and analyses the opportunity structure giving
> rise to those problems – in particular, the immediate settings in which
> they occur. It then seeks to identify changes in the design and manage-
> ment of these settings that will reduce crime with the fewest economic and
> social costs. These changes are intended to discourage potential offenders

by increasing the risks or difficulties of crime, making it less rewarding or excusable and reducing temptations and provocations.

It is instructive to consider this description alongside Darren's use of situational tactics to try to avoid reoffending. The first half of the encyclopaedia entry rather perfectly describes Darren's plan: he has indeed decided on a strategy of 'reducing opportunities for crime'; he has carefully considered the 'immediate settings' that might lead to his offending; and he has then sought 'to identify [possible] changes in... these settings that will reduce crime' – that is, he will not himself visit the 'immediate setting' in question (the flats). However, already by this stage the encyclopaedia entry has begun to diverge from the specifics of Darren's case, because the quotation mentions 'changes *in the design and management of'* the settings in question; and, of course, no such changes are proposed in Darren's case. The reason for the mismatch becomes very clear when we reach the last sentence of the encyclopaedia entry, because there we learn that the planned changes in the local environment 'are intended to discourage potential offenders by increasing the risks or difficulties of crime'. In other words, in SCP as classically formulated, it was simply assumed that the offender and the person modifying the situation are different people; or, more starkly put, the offender was always seen as 'the other'. Less problematically when applied to a case such as that of Darren, classical SCP also assumed the rationality of potential offenders; hence, a close connection developed between SCP and a version of 'rational choice theory' (see Cornish and Clarke 1986).

It will be valuable to explore these issues a little more fully. In an honest appraisal of their own work, Cornish and Clarke (2008: 39) have conceded that 'the rational choice perspective [in criminology] has had rather little to say about the nature of the offender.' They continue:

> In accordance with good-enough theorising the original depiction was of an individual bereft of moral scruples – and without any defects such as lack of self-control that might get in the way of rational action. He (or she) was assumed to arrive at the crime scene already motivated and somewhat experienced in committing the crime in question, and to evaluate criminal opportunities on the basis of the likely rewards they offered, the effort they required, and the risks they were likely to involve. Although this picture has been modified over the years..., the offender as antisocial predator has remained the perspective's default view.

The phrase 'good-enough theorising', used in this quotation, is telling. As Richard Wortley (2012: 192) has argued in an important essay included in a recent *festschrift* for Ron Clarke, such a phrase probably reflects Clarke's 'single-minded focus on utility' and a wish 'not to complicate [SCP] with unnecessary theoretical baggage'. However, Wortley continues, while these characteristics have in many ways 'served [Clarke's] case well', the pragmatic, 'good-enough' approach has also '[come] at a price' – and the price has included the rather limited degree of integration that SCP has been able to achieve with mainstream psychology, and even with mainstream criminology (especially, perhaps, in the United States). But, given the successful 35-year track record of SCP as a crime prevention strategy, Wortley suggests – surely with justice – that it is now safe for this perspective to become theoretically more ambitious 'without compromising Clarke's original mission'. To this end, Wortley particularly recommends '*exploring the person-situation interaction in more depth*', in order to provide '*a more sophisticated rendering of the intimate relationship between [potential] offenders and their [putative] crime scenes*' (p. 192, emphasis added).[5] If SCP were to develop in this way, it would, of course, easily be able to encompass self-applied SCP by offenders like Darren who are trying to desist. It would seem to be important for SCP theorization to make an adjustment of this kind, given the well-known fact that most offenders (even persistent offenders) eventually try to desist (Laub and Sampson 2003, ch.5). Once a desire to desist has developed, the assumption made by Cornish and Clarke (see above) that the offender is an 'antisocial predator...bereft of moral scruples' is clearly no longer fully accurate (see, further, Shapland and Bottoms 2011).

Self-control

'Self-control' is a central concept in contemporary criminological theory, for the obvious reason that (in very general terms) a lack of self-control seems likely to be related to criminality. However, the meaning of this concept is by no means settled. The most influential theoretical discussion of self-control in contemporary criminology has been that of Gottfredson and Hirschi (1990), which has generated a substantial empirical research literature (for an overview, see Gottfredson 2006). Gottfredson and Hirschi regard low self-control as the primary individual characteristic causing criminal behaviour, and they conceptualize self-control (or the lack of it) as a cluster of personal traits that is established very early in life, producing behavioural differences between individuals that are relatively invariant over the life-span. As they put it:

> [P]eople who lack self-control will tend to be impulsive, insensitive, ... risk-taking, short-sighted, and nonverbal, and they will tend therefore to engage in criminal and analogous acts. Since these traits can be identified prior to the age of responsibility for crime, since there is considerable tendency for these traits to come together in the same people, and since the traits tend

to persist through life, it seems reasonable to consider them as comprising a stable construct useful in the explanation of crime.

(pp. 90–91)

For the purposes of the present chapter, the most important critique of Gottfredson and Hirschi's work is that by Per-Olof Wikström and Kyle Treiber (2007), who offer a very different understanding of the concept of 'self-control'. According to Wikström and Treiber, 'self-control is something we *do*...rather than something we *are*' (p. 243, emphasis in original); accordingly, their formal definition of self-control (originally stated in Wikström 2006) is 'the successful inhibition of perceived action alternatives, or interruption of a course of action, that conflict with an individual's morality' (Wikström and Treiber 2007: 244, 258, Table 1). In subsequent work, Wikström et al. (2012) have provided substantial empirical support for their contention that an individual's 'crime propensity' (comprising the two interacting dimensions of 'morality' and 'ability to exercise self-control') interacts with situational contexts and a process of choice to create criminal or non-criminal outcomes.

In their 2007 paper, Wikström and Treiber make several important claims about self-control. It is worth setting out two of these in full, because I shall shortly argue that the first statement is more fundamental than the second.

The first statement is, in its essentials, an elaboration of the authors' formal definition of the concept of self-control (see above). They postulate that:

> [S]elf-control comes into play in [an agent's] process of choice only when the temptations and provocations an individual faces *in a particular setting* conflict with his/her moral rules (i.e. the rules guiding his/her choices about what it is right or wrong to do).[6] We argue that, when an individual acts in accordance with his/her morality when faced with conflicting temptations or provocations, he/she exercises self-control, whereas if an individual acts upon a temptation, or responds to a provocation contrary to his/her moral beliefs, he/she fails to exercise self-control.

(pp. 243–244, emphasis added)

It is important to note, in the above quotation, the italicized words 'in a particular setting'. This limits the geographical and temporal ambit of the exercise of self-control, given that the authors also define 'setting' as 'the social and physical environment (objects, persons, events) that an individual, *at a particular moment in time, can access with his/her senses*' (p. 245, emphasis added).

This focus on the setting leads directly to the second quotation:

> Whereas Gottfredson and Hirschi view self-control as a trait, we suggest that self-control is best analysed as a *situational concept*. We define a *situation* as

an individual's perception of action alternatives and process of choice that arise from his/her intersection with a particular setting.... We submit that self-control is *part of the process of choice*, not an individual trait.

(p. 243, emphasis in original)

Wikström and Treiber's paper constitutes, in my view, a clear advance in criminological understanding. They are to be warmly congratulated, in particular, on the central insight that self-control should be conceptualized as an *action*, not a bundle of traits,[7] and on their insistence that the need for self-control arises only when what they call an individual's 'morality' potentially conflicts with a temptation or provocation that he/she experiences (as in the hypothetical case of Ryan the habitual shoplifter, discussed earlier in this chapter). It is also of very great interest that these aspects of Wikström and Treiber's work are highly congruent with the earlier analysis of a moral philosopher, Jeanette Kennett, although the two accounts were developed completely independently. At the beginning of a chapter of outstanding clarity and interest called 'A Taxonomy of Agent-Control', Kennett (2001: 119) tells her readers that she is primarily concerned to develop and explain what she describes as the concept of 'full-blooded self-control', the understanding of which she regards as 'of central moral importance'. She suggests that there is 'a hierarchy of control which agents may exercise over their actions', and 'full-blooded self-control' is at the apex of this hierarchy. This strong form of self-control arises, according to Kennett, when there is a divergence between, on the one hand, one's judgement 'about what is, all things considered, [morally] desirable in the circumstances' (p. 132); and, on the other hand, desires or temptations that provide a motivation to act otherwise than in accordance with this judgement. In these circumstances of temptation, the 'strictly orthonomous agent'[8] exercises true self-control; otherwise stated, to act with self-control is 'to bring one's action into line with one's judgements of value' (Kennett 2001: 119).

The similarity in these independent analyses by a moral philosopher (Kennett) and two criminologists (Wikström and Treiber) is truly striking. There is, however, also a point of divergence, which is of special relevance to the discussion in this chapter. In a nutshell, Kennett's definitions are *general* in character, whereas Wikström and Treiber's discussion stipulates that self-control comes into play only when the individual faces temptations *in a particular setting* (where 'setting', as we have seen, is restricted to an environment accessible to the senses at a particular point in time). This difference is of great importance in the present context, because, if we apply Wikström and Treiber's analysis to Darren's case, Darren cannot be said to be trying to exercise self-control. (Why not? Because he is not currently tempted when he reaches the agreement with his grandmother; moreover – assuming that the agreement is made by telephone – the setting he is attempting to control (the flats) is not accessible to his senses at the time of the agreement). By contrast, Kennett would be in no doubt that Darren is attempting to exercise self-control, because in setting up the agreement he was aware of a likely future temptation, and was trying to ensure that this temptation would be resisted. (In other words, as required by Kennett's definition, he was trying to bring his actions into line with his all-things-considered moral judgement.) On this point of difference, Kennett's analysis seems to me to be the more persuasive. However, there would also seem to be little difficulty in removing the restriction to contemporaneous settings in Wikström and Treiber's analysis; it is not clear that this restriction serves any truly vital purpose.[9]

Not only does Kennett's definition of self-control allow for cases such as Darren's; she also includes an explicit discussion of this kind of strategy, under the name of *diachronic self-control* (Kennett 2001: 134–135). Diachronic self-control (DSC) has, she suggests, two variants. Using her running example of a woman ('Jane') who is trying to keep her weight down but who loves cream cakes, Kennett argues that one way of exercising DSC ('DSC 1') would involve trying to 'block the onset of the desire', for example by taking an appetite-suppressing pill. But, secondly, and staying with the same example, 'if there is no satisfactory way open to her to prevent the desire occurring, she might instead consider structuring her future circumstances so as to ensure that the desire cannot be acted upon' (p. 134: DSC 2) – perhaps by entering into a bet with her workmates that she will not buy any cream cakes from the works canteen for a whole month.

Although Kennett does not make this point, this distinction between DSC 1 and DSC 2 can be neatly exemplified through the story of Odysseus and the Sirens. Thus, the blocking of the crewmen's ears with beeswax is a successful example of DSC 1, because they never hear the Sirens' song, and therefore never experience the desire; while, by contrast, Odysseus does hear the song, and therefore experiences a strong temptation/desire, but he is saved by having, in advance, 'structured his social circumstances so that the desire cannot be acted upon' (DSC 2).

In the Odysseus story, both of the DSC approaches also come within the category of 'self-applied *situational* harm prevention', because beeswax in ears and being lashed to a mast are clearly situational strategies. It is important to note, however, that DSC strategies are not necessarily situational in character, as the hypothetical discussion of Ryan the habitual shoplifter shows. Here we can also note that Ryan's case was introduced as part of a discussion of Elster's (2000) concept of 'self-binding' or 'pre-commitment'; and we can now see that this concept is in fact identical with Kennett's 'diachronic self-control'. Two analytic conclusions follow from these observations: first, DSC (or self-binding) is a broader concept than is self-applied SCP, because it potentially includes diachronic strategies other than the situational; and, second, as the Odysseus story shows, self-applied SCP strategies can fall within either the DSC 1 or the DSC 2 subcategories.

The discussion in this and the preceding section has suggested that cases such as Darren's need in future to be more carefully considered within mainstream criminology. More specifically, I have argued that, while cases such as Darren's are not congruent with SCP as classically conceived, there would be little difficulty in including such cases if, as recommended by Wortley (2012: 192), SCP theorization is expanded to embrace 'a more sophisticated rendering of the intimate relationship between [potential] offenders and their [putative] crime scenes'. In a very similar manner, if (as in Gottfredson and Hirschi's work) self-control is understood as a bundle of traits cohering into a 'stable construct', then (paradoxically) it will be very difficult to include diachronic self-control tactics within the understanding of self-control. If, however, as seems clearly preferable, we adopt the conceptual framework for the understanding of self-control pioneered by Wikström and Treiber (2007), then it will require only a minor adjustment to include cases of diachronic self-control (including self-applied SCP).

Empirically, however, the discussion so far in this chapter has relied exclusively on Darren's case; it is, therefore, now necessary to consider other empirical evidence on self-applied situational crime prevention, as encountered in a recent study of desistance from crime.

The Sheffield Desistance Study (SDS): General

The Sheffield Desistance Study is a prospective short-term longitudinal research project, undertaken at the University of Sheffield, and directed by Joanna Shapland and myself.[10] The research, for which fieldwork began in 2003, followed a group of 113 mostly persistent male offenders for a period of approximately three years, during which the researchers attempted to interview each member of the sample on four occasions, with each interview lasting approximately 90 minutes. Recontact rates were good, given the nature of the sample; thus, 78 per cent of the original 113 respondents completed the fourth interview, while 86 per cent completed a third or fourth interview. The two principal papers so far published on the results of the research are Bottoms and Shapland (2011) and Shapland and Bottoms (2011).

Selection for the study was deliberately restricted to persons born in three calendar years (1982 to 1984), in order to ensure that sample members were approximately at the peak of the age–crime curve at the first interview (mean age at first interview = 20.7 years). As regards criminal record, the minimum eligibility for entry into the sample was two 'conviction occasions' for a standard list offence.[11] However, because it proved much easier to recruit respondents who were currently in prison than those being supervised by the probation service, in the event the sample was much more recidivistic than might have been expected from the minimum eligibility criterion. Thus, at the time of the first interview the average sample member had eight conviction occasions for a standard list offence, and the aggregate number of conviction occasions in the full sample already exceeded those amassed *by the age of 40* by the subjects in the well-known Cambridge Study in Delinquent Development.[12] When we turn to offending patterns during the 3–4 years of the research study, it is not surprising (given their past history) that no fewer than 80 per cent of the sample were reconvicted during this period; but, much more encouragingly, the frequency of officially recorded offending dropped sharply from 8.2 standard list offences per year at risk in the year before the first interview, to 2.6 in the final period studied, approximately three years later (Bottoms and Shapland 2011: 52). The self-reported criminality data were more complex, but, among those for whom data were available throughout the study, 61 per cent decreased their frequency of offending, while 39 per cent increased it (Bottoms and Shapland 2011: 54).

Three features of the methodology of the SDS are perhaps of particular salience for the present chapter. First, the recruitment of a sample of mostly persistent offenders at the apex of the age–crime curve, coupled with the prospective research design, meant that what was being studied was, in most cases, *the early stages of desistance*. Second, the interviews followed one another at shorter intervals (between 9 and 12 months) than in most longitudinal studies. Third, the research included both a quantitative and a qualitative dimension, with the latter including a special 'qualitative subsample' (to be described more fully below). It is, I believe, the combination of these three features that has enabled the research team to identify the importance of self-applied situational crime prevention among those seriously trying to desist. But, before considering examples of the use of such tactics by offenders in the Sheffield study, it will be beneficial to consider the social–structural context in which these young men found themselves, because this should help to make it clearer why they often turned to self-applied SCP. As will be seen, this social–structural context has some marked resonances with the conceptual analysis of self-control offered independently by Wikström and Treiber (2007) and by Kennett (2001) (see above).

At each interview, the respondents in the Sheffield study were shown a card containing a set of standardized responses about intentions relating to desistance or continued criminality; each interviewee was asked to identify the statement that came closest to his current opinion. At the first interview, no fewer than 56 per cent said they had made a 'definite decision to try to stop'; 37 per cent said they would like to stop but they were not sure whether they could; and only 7 per cent said they were unlikely to stop. While the size of this last category remained constant throughout the study, those saying they had made a 'definite decision to try to stop' (or, in later interviews, that they had stopped) gradually rose, reaching 70 per cent by the fourth interview[13] (Bottoms and Shapland 2011: 57). Other data supported these findings. For example, when asked, in an open-ended question in the first interview, 'what kind of person would you like to become?', the answers given were overwhelmingly conventional; they included 'go straight'; 'be free from a drug/alcohol habit'; 'live a normal life'; 'be a good/responsible person'; and 'be a family man' (Shapland and Bottoms 2011: 362). A principal reason for this kind of response in this sample was, undoubtedly, the age of the respondents: like most 20-year-olds on the threshold of adulthood, they were looking ahead to their future, and wondering what life held in store for them. It is clear from the interview transcripts that many respondents fully understood the likely consequences if they carried on with their criminal activities (i.e. a life spent in and out of prison); and for them this was the 'feared self' that Paternoster and Bushway (2009) have identified as an important incentive for desistance. Additionally, given their age, the offenders were also looking ahead to what the same authors have described as a 'desired self', with the results described above about 'living a normal life' and so on. Sometimes the contrast between an offender's present situation and his desired self could be quite dramatic: for example, one imprisoned 20-year-old with a long criminal record, who was addicted to heroin and crack, had been homeless before his prison sentence and had never held a regular job, said in answer to the question about what kind of person he would like to become: 'Confident; hardworking; trustworthy; a good person to get on with'.

Thus, there is substantial evidence that the majority of the men in the Sheffield sample wanted their lives to change. But there is also substantial evidence that most of the sample thought that, given certain circumstances, they might well offend again – the possibility of committing crimes was by no means yet 'off the agenda'. We have already seen that, during the three years of the follow-up period, over three-quarters were reconvicted, although with less frequency than before; and the great majority of the men also continued to have friends who were active in crime (see further below).[14] Perhaps most tellingly of all, there is strong evidence that, for many men, offending still held a significant emotional attraction. At each interview, we offered each respondent a formal list of 13 'obstacles' to going straight or staying straight, derived from a similar list created by Ros Burnett (1992). With one exception, the top four obstacles remained the same at every interview – and, contrary to expectation, drugs were never one of them. (For the details, see Bottoms and Shapland 2011: 61.) Three of these four 'top obstacles' were concerned in one way or another with a lack of money, or with being offered opportunities for making easy money; clearly, therefore, when money was tight, offending was still seen by many as a way to solve a cash crisis. The fourth item was more unexpected, but very revealing; it was the 'need for excitement or to relieve boredom', which was identified as an obstacle to going straight by 61 per cent of respondents in the first interview, and still by 47 per cent in the fourth interview. (On the emotional 'pull' of offending, too often neglected in academic criminology, see, for example, Katz 1988.)

Hence, we have compelling evidence of two countervailing tendencies. On the one hand, the great majority of men wanted ultimately to go straight and to live normal lives. On the other hand, many of them had become habituated to a lifestyle involving crime; they had many acquaintances who were still offending; they saw acquisitive crime as a potential solution to shortages of cash; they might find it difficult not to get involved in a fight if they got provoked in an altercation; *and* they found that offending continued to have an attraction for them because of the excitement that it generates. In simple language, therefore, while desistance was a desired objective, acts of offending remained a real possibility in certain circumstances of temptation or provocation. As we saw earlier, these are *precisely* the conditions in which we would expect 'weakness of will' to be a problem; that is to say, where a potential desister might find himself, in a particular situation, acting against his all-things-considered moral judgement. As both Kennett (explicitly) and Wikström and Treiber (implicitly) argue, these are also precisely the conditions in which one might expect self-control to be exercised, since 'there is no place for the idea of self-control in a moral psychology which does not admit the possibility of an agent's choosing to act against her better judgement' (Kennett 2001: 5). And, as previously noted, among the possible strategies for planned self-control in such circumstances, self-applied situational crime prevention holds a prominent place.

Of course, SDS is not the first research study on desistance to notice that would-be desisters sometimes plan – as Darren did – to avoid certain places and/or certain people in order to enhance their likelihood of staying out of trouble (for overviews of the desistance literature, see, for example, Farrall et al. 2011; Kazemian 2007; Laub and Sampson 2001; Paternoster and Bushway 2009;). Yet earlier desistance studies, I believe, have not always fully appreciated either the pervasiveness of self-applied SCP among would-be desisters (or, at least, among young adult desisters), or the full significance of such tactics as an important element in their attempts to exercise self-control. These issues will hopefully become clearer as we examine the empirical evidence relating to the use of self-applied SCP by offenders in the Sheffield sample.

Self-applied SCP in the Sheffield Desistance Study

In this section, I shall present evidence relating to both the *extent* and the *nature* of self-applied SCP in the Sheffield Study. Unless otherwise stated, all of the examples given are taken from detailed analyses of the interview transcripts of the 18 cases in the *qualitative sample* within the SDS – a subsample that was selected on the basis of the availability of a full set of interview transcripts.[15]

Since the central topic of this section is 'self-applied SCP', it is important to be clear how this term is being defined. Briefly, 'self-applied SCP' is here understood as *a form of diachronic self-control, intended to be achieved by situational means*. This definition therefore *excludes* two other forms of crime prevention for which there is evidence in the qualitative sample. The first of these consists of attempts to reduce future offending by using tactics that were not specifically situational in character (i.e. not focused on the 'immediate settings in which they [might] occur': Clarke 2010). Such methods included cutting down on alcohol consumption, getting off drugs, taking college or trade courses to improve employability, and so on. By contrast, the cases in the second excluded category were all forms of 'situational crime prevention', yet they are not considered here because the situational crime prevention achieved was in all cases *a by-product of action taken for other reasons*. By way of example, a social housing organization offered one sample member a flat in a different neighbourhood, and he then discovered that this change of location helped him to stay away from 'all the old trouble', as he put it; while several others noticed that, having formed a meaningful partnership with a girlfriend, they gradually saw less of their delinquent friends (on this process see, especially, Laub and Sampson 2003). This is compliance achieved in part by situational means, but it is not deliberate 'self-binding', so it cannot be counted as true 'self-applied SCP'.

However, even using the strict definition of 'self-applied SCP' (see above), no fewer than 14 of the 18 respondents in the qualitative sample mentioned the adoption of such a strategy in at least one of their four interviews.[16] Thus, self-applied SCP was a pervasive, not a marginal, strategy for this group.

Turning to the reasons for adopting such a strategy, the overwhelmingly dominant theme concerned the perceived need to prevent oneself from being adversely influenced by delinquent friends (on the importance of this topic for criminology, especially as regards this age group, see Warr 2002). A commonly mentioned action or intended action was, therefore, a deliberate strategy of *avoiding the company* of such friends – a strategy that was usually stated in general terms, but occasionally by reference to a specific named friend. The purpose of such avoidance strategies, when specifically articulated, was normally said to be to avoid temptations (usually, as regards theft or some other property crime) or provocations (usually, as regards potential involvement in a fight). As Darren's case illustrates, one way of attempting to avoid former friends is not to visit a specific location (see further below); but it should be recorded that eight offenders in the qualitative sample mentioned breaking ties with criminal friends *without* simultaneously avoiding specific locations. One, for example, was particularly concerned to stay away from a group of 'grafters' who lived in his neighbourhood. He said that until recently he would have helped them to commit crimes if they had asked him to, but now he tried to avoid them as much as possible, even though they all lived in the same area.

It should nevertheless be noted that not everyone favoured the strategy of 'planned avoidance of former friends'. For example, one sample member who had stopped offending said: 'I still associate with heroin addicts.... I wouldn't put them down or owt like that, but I'll not go grafting with them.... The other day [they] was going to do a burglary... I says "no, I'm not burgling no house".' In the language of Kennett (2001), this ex-offender's refusal to join in with the burglary was an exercise of *synchronic self-control*; but few felt as confident as this man obviously did about their ability to exercise synchronic self-control in the company of delinquent friends.

As prefigured above, self-applied SCP strategies often included specifically place-based features. There were two main variants of this. The first was again centred on *avoidance strategies*; that is, it involved deliberately avoiding a specific location. The location avoided could, however, vary in size. It might, for example, be a whole district, as was the case for one desister who gave up his flat to go and live with his mother, specifically to avoid the many temptations of the area where his flat was located. But the places to be avoided could also be much more specific: for example, one ex-drug addict refused to go on a drug rehabilitation course because he was afraid that meeting old friends there might actually pull him back to crime. Also, as regards potential provocations to violence, there were frequent references to avoiding specific places such as 'city centre pubs'; 'night clubs'; 'parties' (because of their potential for 'drugtaking and fights'); and so on.

The second type of location-specific SCP strategy was of a slightly different character. It involved, certainly, avoidance of potential 'trouble-spots'; but this was not achieved directly, but instead by deliberately visiting a different location, in a process that might be termed *self-displacement*. So, for example, two members of the qualitative sample mentioned spending a lot of time in the gym, in order to (as one of them said) 'keep myself busy' (and, by implication, away from less desirable pursuits). Various other self-displacement strategies were also found in this sample, including (i) deliberately staying at home a lot of the time; (ii) going to live with, or making frequent visits to, a family member (e.g. girlfriend's grandmother) in order to become involved with the day-to day life of that household, and breaking with normal routines; and (iii) undertaking a displacement activity on a particular occasion (e.g. going fishing one weekend instead of joining his friends on a trip to Blackpool).

I have so far discussed three kinds of self-applied SCP: avoiding criminal friends; avoiding specific places; and self-displacement. There remains one further type of approach evidenced in the qualitative sample; this involved *altering the structure of daily activities* (cf. Kennett 2001: 134). Although only five instances of this were noted, they are of considerable interest, and fall into three subcategories. The first subcategory involved the adoption of different activity patterns when out on the streets – for example, deciding never to go out on the streets alone, but only with trusted friends, in order to avoid being provoked into violence by others. Second, there were two instances of men rethinking their approach to money shortages: one, for example, told us he had adopted a strategy of applying for a crisis loan instead of immediately trying to solve the problem by committing a theft or burglary. Third, there was the interesting case of a man who wanted to break his habit of going out stealing late at night. In a move similar to that of Kennett's 'Jane' and her appetite-suppressing pills, he decided to do this by chemically inducing a different desire – in this case, a desire to sleep. Unfortunately, he chose to do this by taking cannabis each night, and, although he did indeed stop burgling, he became – by his own admission – addicted to cannabis.

This last case illustrates the fact that self-applied SCP was not always a successful strategy. As a further example of that, there was one case that perfectly illustrated the well-known adage of Alcoholics Anonymous (AA) that there are limits to so-called geographic cures, because 'wherever you go, there you are.' (In this case, the offender thought he would solve his problems by moving to a different town, but in fact he soon started to sell drugs in his new location, as he had in his previous area.) Yet not too much should be made of the AA adage in the present context, because the kind of medium-serious property and violent offences mostly committed by members of the Sheffield sample are, in all probability, more susceptible to the situational manipulation involved in self-applied SCP than is alcoholism. Perhaps the clearest example of a proven situational effect as regards the reduction of offences of this kind is found in a rigorous study of the effects of the Hurricane Katrina disaster of 2005: in this research, it was shown that ex-prisoners who were forced by circumstance to move away from their former home neighbourhoods had lower reoffending rates than those who were able to return (Kirk 2009). It would seem, therefore, that, while a change of neighbourhood is no guarantee of success, those who attempt this and other self-applied SCP strategies are indeed acting rationally.[17]

Yet we must finally note a potential problem arising from the use of self-applied SCP, and of diachronic self-control more generally. As Jeanette Kennett (2001: 149) has shrewdly pointed out, if a person takes the exercise of diachronic self-control to extremes, so as to avoid potentially difficult situations, he or she 'is likely to lead a restricted and impoverished existence', because 'too much self-binding reduces the chances of the agent attaining a broader orthonomy.' In discussing self-displacement (see above), I mentioned a member of the qualitative sample who stayed at home a lot of the time; in the broader Sheffield study, we encountered at least one more extreme case, where the ex-offender literally stayed at home all day playing computer games, because he was unable to find employment and he was desperate not to return to offending. As Kennett's comment indicates, cases like this involve choosing an 'impoverished existence' in the service of (in this case) the avoidance of recidivism – a situation that makes many neutral observers morally uneasy, since the desister is clearly not leading a fulfilled life. That case also nicely illustrates the point, which I have no space to elaborate here, that wider social structures (in this case, employment opportunities) are vital to the optimum achievement of desistance outcomes, yet they are largely outwith the influence or control of the person trying to desist (see, further, Farrall et al. 2010).

The evidence presented in this section has shown that even very persistent offenders, in this particular age range, frequently put in place their own strategies of compliance. Since other evidence from the Sheffield study shows that most meetings between probation officers and sample members were of limited duration and scope (Shapland et al. 2012), it is almost certain that most of these self-applied SCP strategies were not being shared by sample members with their supervising probation officers. That seems to be a missed opportunity, to which I shall return in the conclusion.

'Knifing off'

As Maruna and Roy (2007: 105) have observed, the concept of 'knifing off' originated outside criminology, but it has come to occupy an important place in contemporary discussions of desistance from crime. It owes this prominence especially to its utilization by Laub and Sampson (2003) in their seminal long-term follow-up of reform school boys originally studied in the 1940s. The following quotation from Kirk (2011: 245) summarizes their findings:

> According to Laub and Sampson (2003), desistance from crime is made possible by 'knifing off' – '[most] offenders desist in response to structurally induced turning points that serve as a catalyst for sustaining long-term behavioural change' (p. 149). What turning points create are new situations that allow individuals to knife off the past, in part, by changing those routine activity patterns that led to trouble with the law prior to incarceration ... This idea is straightforward ....

The reference here to changes in patterns of routine activities clearly links the concept of 'knifing off' to the discussion in the present chapter. That link is reinforced by the illuminating analysis of the concept of 'knifing off' by Maruna and Roy (2007). These authors show that this concept, as utilized in the criminological literature, has many ambiguities; but in their conclusion they constructively suggest that social scientists should in future 'address the issue of knifing off *opportunities* rather than unspecified concepts such as the past, circumstances, old lives, disadvantage and so forth' (pp. 119–120, emphasis in original). Given that 'opportunities' is perhaps the central concept in SCP theory (see the first sentence of Ron Clarke's (2010) encyclopaedia entry, cited earlier), the potential congruence between 'self-applied SCP' and 'knifing off' becomes very clear.

Yet there are a number of reasons for preferring the terminologies developed in the present chapter to the concept of 'knifing off'. First, as Maruna and Roy have shown, the concept of 'knifing off' is not well defined. Second, as the same authors point out, the implications of using 'a...metaphor involving amputation' is that the listener or reader expects to learn about the 'more extreme structural and social impediments' to achieving one's all-things-considered moral goals (Maruna and Roy 2007: 120). However, the empirical data in this chapter show clearly that self-applied SCP can be, and is, routinely applied by would-be desisters in ways that involve minor adjustments to daily routines, rather than actions akin to amputation.

The third and most important reason for being cautious about the concept of 'knifing off' is more complex. As the quotation from Kirk (2011) above shows, Laub and Sampson (2003) apparently see 'knifing off' as a *supplement* to the 'turning points' (such as military service or marriage) that are central to their theory of desistance. In other words, after a turning point (say, marriage), the would-be desister proceeds to 'knife off' those parts of his/her life that are not compatible with the desired new identity. But the Sheffield study raises significant empirical questions about this picture, arising from the differing methodologies used in the two studies. In brief, Sampson and Laub's qualitative data were derived from interviews with men in their 60s, looking back over criminal careers of varied length, and (in many cases) looking back also over the process of desistance. It was from that vantage point that 'turning points' and 'knifing off activities' were identified. But the concept of a 'turning point' can *only* be identified retrospectively; when one is in the middle of a process of change, it is impossible to know whether what is currently being experienced is really a 'turning point' in one's life, or just another episode. (This is the dilemma famously identified by Kierkegaard: 'It is perfectly true, as philosophers say, that life can only be understood backwards; but they forget the other proposition, that it must be lived forwards' (quoted in Wollheim 1984: 1).) The prospective methodology of the Sheffield study, focused on the early stages of desistance and with shortish intervals between interviews, yielded a different picture. From the perspective of these would-be desisters, 'living life forwards' was a complicated business, typically involving several lifestyle changes, and with no guarantee of a successful outcome. In those circumstances, 'situational self-binding' was a sensible strategy to use. But it was usually deployed alongside other changes, such as trying to get a stable job, drinking less, learning to live on a lower income than their previous offending had accustomed them to, and so on. In this complex situation, self-applied SCP might either precede or follow what the mainstream desistance literature identifies as potential 'turning points', such as marriage or stable employment.[18] In short, and as Joanna Shapland and I expressed the matter in a previous paper, what we observed in the Sheffield study was a group of young adult persistent offenders who were striving to:

> move towards their basic moral views about the person they think they should be. . . . But it was and is a struggle . . . This is partly because of the need to change lifestyles; partly because of the obstacle-strewn path presented by their own lack of human and social capital and by social structures (which tend not to be fundamentally reintegrative: Farrall et al. 2010). So moving towards desistance means accepting the constraints of a non-offending life, for the benefits conveyed by respectable and conventional social bonds – partners, children, relatives. It is hard. It means deliberately avoiding invitations to trouble. This can be portrayed as a maturational theory, but it is an active maturation, animated by the impetus of the offenders themselves.
>
> (Shapland and Bottoms 2011: 276–277)

'Situational self-binding' must be seen as a part – and a not unimportant part – of this wider picture. Crucially, like much else it is usually put in place at 'the impetus of the offenders themselves'. It is not necessarily 'knifing off', and it does not necessarily follow a 'turning point'. But many would-be desisters find it to be a vital element in the process of moving towards their goal.

Conclusion

The scope of this chapter has been wide-ranging. At its heart has been the presentation of fresh empirical evidence about the widespread use of self-applied SCP among young adult would-be desisters, as an aid to their intended compliance with the law. However, in order to do proper justice to this topic, it has been necessary also to consider some much broader issues, such as the understanding within the criminological literature of the key concepts of 'self-control', and, indeed, of 'situational crime prevention' itself.

Among the various contributions to this volume, this chapter is unique in one particular respect: its focus is upon *self-applied* SCP as an aid to compliance, whereas other chapters mainly consider how criminal justice personnel can help offenders to improve their compliance. This difference of focus is, I hope, helpful in the overall context of this volume, in that it draws attention to the fact that many offenders – even persistent offenders – are not only willing to consider compliance, they are also actively putting into effect various compliance strategies of their own making.

As previously indicated, however, the empirical evidence of the Sheffield study appeared to suggest that would-be desisters rarely discussed with their supervising probation officers their attempts at self-applied prevention of offending. This, therefore, seems to have been, for both parties, a largely wasted opportunity for shared consideration of the best ways to achieve a common goal. Hopefully, the juxtaposition within this volume of the evidence in this chapter (from the offender's perspective) and in other chapters (from a criminal justice system perspective) will help to forge a better joint approach to offender compliance in the future.[19]

Notes

1. In Latin, Odysseus's name became 'Ulixes', which in turn became, in English, 'Ulysses'.

2. Two central challenges may be raised to the assertion made in common-sense moral psychology that an agent makes a free choice when s/he succumbs to a temptation to act against his/her all-things considered best judgement. First, perhaps the agent did not really ever subscribe to what he claims is his all-things-considered best judgement – because if he really did subscribe to it, how did he succumb to the temptation so easily? Second, perhaps the agent was in the grip of a strong compulsion (to drink, smoke, eat cream cakes, shoplift, etc.), in which case her act cannot be described as 'weakness of will', because she effectively had no 'will' as regards the action in question. For discussions of the 'weakness of will' literature, see, among others, Mortimore (1971), Kennett (2001) and Stroud and Tappolet (2003).

3. This typology is adapted from the discussion in Bottoms (2002).

4. For a full discussion of the history of SCP, and its current standing and influence, see the recent book of essays in honour of Ronald Clarke, edited by Nick Tilley and Graham Farrell (2012).

5. I have added the words 'potential' and 'putative', because they seem to be necessary if adequate theorization is to include (as it surely must) *successful* SCP initiatives. To explain more fully: if on a given occasion the prevention strategy is fully successful (with no displacement), there will on that occasion be no actual offender and no actual crime-scene.

6. Wikström and Treiber offer a definitional footnote at this point: 'We define a temptation as when an individual connects a desire (or commitment) with an opportunity to fulfil this desire (or commitment); and we define a provocation as when an individual connects a friction with perceived antagonistic intent' (p. 243).

7. For the sake of completeness, it is necessary to add that Wikström and Treiber distinguish between 'self-control', which is an act, and 'ability to exercise self-control', which is a personality characteristic. Although the latter concept (like Gottfredson and Hirschi's theory) draws attention to individual differences, Wikström and Treiber further propose that a given individual will be more likely to exercise self-control in some situational contexts than in others; moreover, self-control itself is an *action within a process of choice*. In a review and reassessment of self-control theory, Gottfredson (2011: 135) describes Wikström and Treiber's article as 'an important recent criticism' of self-control theory (p. 135), but he does not address this central difference between the two approaches.

8. In Kennett's (2001: 132) analysis, an agent is 'strictly orthonomous' when 'she desires and acts in accordance with her beliefs about what she has most reason to do', regardless of whether such beliefs can be rationally defended as 'truly' or objectively desirable.

9. It is also worth noting that Wikström and Treiber's formal definition of 'self-control', quoted earlier, does not specifically include the requirement of occurring in a specific setting. (The definition is: 'the successful inhibition of perceived action alternatives, or interruption of a course of action, that conflict with an individual's morality'.)

10. The Sheffield Desistance Study was funded for five years (2002–2007) by the Economic and Social Research Council as part of a Research Network on the Social Contexts of Pathways in Crime (SCoPiC). My subsequent work on the project has been supported by an Emeritus Fellowship awarded by the Leverhulme Foundation.

11. A 'conviction occasion' is a court appearance at which an offender is convicted of one or more offences. Most offenders accordingly have fewer conviction occasions than convictions. A 'standard list offence' is a technical term that includes offences of violence, sexual offences, robbery, burglary, theft, fraud, criminal damage and most drugs offences but excludes most motoring and administrative offences.

12. In the Cambridge study, 164 males were convicted of a standard list offence by age 40, and between them these men had an aggregate of 686 conviction occasions (Farrington et al. 2006: 17). The 113 males in the Sheffield study had an aggregate of 909 conviction occasions for standard list offences by the time of their first interview.

13. On four key variables (measuring age, self-described ethnic status, lifetime official criminality and early social disadvantage) there were no significant differences between those who completed, and those who did not complete, the fourth interview (Bottoms and Shapland 2011: 50).

14. The importance of this in relation to temptations to offend is considerable. In interviews 2, 3 and 4 of the Sheffield study, we asked respondents the question: 'Since the last interview, has anyone asked you to take part in a crime and you have said no?' Even for these direct requests, the proportions saying 'yes' were high: 43 per cent of respondents at interview 2, 36 per cent at interview 3 and 49 per cent at interview 4 (see Shapland and Bottoms 2011: 272–273).

15. The selection criterion for inclusion in the qualitative sample was simply the availability of complete tape recordings for at least three interviews (not all prisons allowed tape-recording, and, sadly, we also experienced some significant tape malfunctions and recordings of poor quality). Fortunately, however, the qualitative sample does not differ significantly from the remainder of the sample on most key variables, the exception being that there is only one ethnic minority offender in the qualitative sample, as against 22 (19 per cent) in the full SDS sample. Early analyses of the qualitative sample within the SDS were undertaken by Deirdre Healy, and the discussion in this section has benefitted from her careful work.

16. Of the other four, two showed strong evidence of synchronic self-control, and one said that he 'stays in the house mostly', but it was not clear that this was a deliberate self-binding strategy.

17. There is, of course, an important contextual difference between the post-Katrina situation (where a change of residence was forced on ex-prisoners by a climatic disaster) and moving one's area of residence voluntarily as an act of self-applied SCP. Kirk's post-Katrina research is nevertheless relevant, because it demonstrates conclusively that situational crime-reductive effects can follow a change of neighbourhood, and there seems no reason to believe that similar effects could not result from a voluntary move.

18. Cf. also the comment made by McGloin et al. (2011: 372): 'perhaps ironically, the increasing use of more sophisticated [statistical] methods to determine if and to what extent turning points cause desistance ... may have de-emphasized the collection of narrative data, from which much of our insight about desistance is gleaned.'
19. Some of the themes developed in this chapter were more briefly reported in an earlier paper on the SDS: see Shapland and Bottoms (2011), especially the section on 'Temptation and weakness of will' (pp. 272–275). As always in relation to my work on the Sheffield Desistance Study, this paper has benefitted greatly from the wise and constructive comments and the intellectual companionship of Joanna Shapland.

References

Bottoms, A. E. (2002) 'Morality, Crime, Compliance and Public Policy'. in A. E. Bottoms and M. Tonry (Eds) *Ideology, Crime and Criminal Policy: A Symposium in Honour of Sir Leon Radzinowicz*. Cullompton, Devon: Willan Publishing.

Bottoms, A. E. and Shapland, J. M. (2011) 'Steps Towards Desistance Among Male Young Adult Recidivists'. in S. Farrall, M. Hough, S. Maruna and R. Sparks (Eds) *Escape Routes: Contemporary Perspectives on Life After Punishment*. London: Routledge.

Burnett, R. (1992) *The Dynamics of Recidivism*. Oxford: University of Oxford Centre for Criminological Research.

Clarke, R. V. G. (2010) 'Situational Crime Prevention'. in B. S. Fisher and S. P. Lab (Eds) *Encyclopaedia of Victimology and Crime Prevention*. London: Sage.

Cornish, D. B. and Clarke, R. V. G. (Eds) (1986) *The Reasoning Criminal: Rational Choice Perspectives on Offending*. New York: Springer-Verlag.

Cornish, D. B. and Clarke, R. V. G. (2008) 'Rational Choice Perspective'. in R. Wortley and L. Mazerolle (Eds) *Environmental Criminology and Crime Analysis*. Cullompton, Devon: Willan Publishing.

Elster, J. (1984) *Ulysses and the Sirens*, rev. ed. Cambridge: Cambridge University Press.

Elster, J. (2000) *Ulysses Unbound*. Cambridge: Cambridge University Press.

Farrall, S., Bottoms, A. E. and Shapland, J. (2010) 'Social Structures and Desistance from Crime'. *European Journal of Criminology* 7, 546–570.

Farrall, S., Sharpe, G., Hunter, B. and Calverley, A. (2011) 'Theorizing Structural and Individual-Level Processes in Desistance and Persistence: Outlining an Integrated Perspective'. *Australian and New Zealand Journal of Criminology* 44, 212–234.

Farrington, D. P., Coid, J. W., Harnett, L., Jolliffe, D., Soteriou, N., Turner, R. and West, D. J. (2006) *Criminal Careers up to Age 50 and Life Success up to Age 48*, Home Office Research Study No. 299. London: Home Office.

Gottfredson, M. R. (2006) 'The Empirical Status of Control Theory in Criminology'. in F. T. Cullen, J. P. Wright and K. R. Blevins (Eds) *Taking Stock: The Status of Criminological Theory*. New Brunswick, NJ: Transaction Publishers.

Gottfredson, M. R. (2011) 'Sanctions, Situations and Agency in Control Theories of Crime'. *European Journal of Criminology* 8, 128–143.

Gottfredson, M. R. and Hirschi, T. (1990) *A General Theory of Crime*. Stanford, California: Stanford University Press.

Hedström, P. (2005) *Dissecting the Social: On the Principles of Analytic Sociology*. Cambridge: Cambridge University Press.

Homer (1997) *The Odyssey*, translated by Robert Fagles, with introduction and notes by Bernard Knox. London: Penguin Books. (Original c. 700–675 BCE).

Katz, J. (1988) *Seductions of Crime: Moral and Sensual Attractions of Doing Evil*. New York: Basic Books.

Kazemian, L. (2007) 'Desistance from Crime: Theoretical, Empirical, Methodological and Policy Considerations'. *Journal of Contemporary Criminal Justice* 23, 5–27.

Kennett, J. (2001) *Agency and Responsibility: A Common-Sense Moral Psychology*. Oxford: Clarendon Press.

Kirk, D. S. (2009) 'A Natural Experiment on Residential Change and Recidivism: Lessons from Hurricane Katrina'. *American Sociological Review* 74, 484–505.

Kirk, D. S. (2011) 'Causal Inference via Natural Experiments and Instrumental Variables: The effect of "Knifing Off" from the Past'. in J. MacDonald (Ed) *Measuring Crime and Criminality*. New Brunswick, NJ: Transaction Publishers.

Laub, J. H. and Sampson, R. J. (2001) 'Understanding Desistance from Crime'. in M. Tonry (Ed.) *Crime and Justice: A Review of Research*, vol. 28. Chicago: University of Chicago Press.

Laub, J. H. and Sampson, R. J. (2003) *Shared Beginnings, Divergent Lives: Delinquent Boys to Age 70*. Cambridge, MA: Harvard University Press.

McGloin, J. M., Sullivan, C. J., Piquero, A. R., Blokland, A. and Nieuwbeerta, P. (2011) 'Marriage and Offending Specialization: Expanding the Impact of Turning Points and the Process of Desistance'. *European Journal of Criminology* 8, 361–376.

Maruna, S. and Roy, K. (2007) 'Amputation or Reconstruction: Notes on the Concept of "Knifing Off" and Desistance from Crime'. *Journal of Contemporary Criminal Justice* 23, 104–124.

Mortimore, G. (Ed.) (1971) *Weakness of Will*. London: Macmillan.

Paternoster, R. and Bushway, S. (2009) 'Desistance and the "Feared Self": Toward an Identity Theory of Criminal Desistance'. *Journal of Criminal Law and Criminology* 99, 1103–1156.

Shapland, J. and Bottoms, A. E. (2011) 'Reflections on Social Values, Offending and Desistance Among Young Adult Recidivists'. *Punishment and Society* 13, 256–282.

Shapland, J., Bottoms A. E. and Muir, G. (2012) 'Perceptions of the Criminal Justice System Among Young Adult Would-be Desisters'. in F. Lösel, A. E. Bottoms and D. P. Farrington (Eds) *Young Adult Offenders: Lost in Transition?* London: Routledge.

Stroud, S. and Tappolet, C. (Eds) (2003) *Weakness of Will and Practical Irrationality*. Oxford: Clarendon Press.

Tilley, N. and Farrell, G. (Eds) (2012) *The Reasoning Criminologist: Essays in Honour of Ronald V. Clarke*. London: Routledge.

Warr, M. (2002) *Companions in Crime: The Social Aspects of Criminal Conduct*. Cambridge: Cambridge University Press.

Wikström, P.-O. (2006) 'Linking Individual, Setting, and Acts of Crime: Situational Mechanisms and the Explanation of Crime'. in P.-O. Wikstrom and R. J. Sampson (Eds) *The Explanation of Crime: Contexts, Mechanisms and Development*. Cambridge: Cambridge University Press.

Wikström, P.-O., Oberwittler, D., Treiber, K. and Hardie, B. (2012) *Breaking Rules: The Social and Situational Dynamics of Young People's Urban Crime*. Oxford: OUP.

Wikström, P.-O. and Treiber, K. (2007) 'The Role of Self-control in Crime Causation: Beyond Gottfredson and Hirschi's General Theory of Crime'. *European Journal of Criminology* 4, 237–264.

Wollheim, R. (1984) *The Thread of Life*. Cambridge: Cambridge University Press.

Wortley, R. (2012) 'Exploring the Person-Situation Interaction in Situational Crime Prevention'. in N. Tilley and G. Farrell (2012) *The Reasoning Criminal: Essays in Honour of Ronald V. Clarke*. London: Routledge.

6
What and Who Might Enhance Offender Compliance: Situating Responsibilities

Ralph C. Serin, Caleb D. Lloyd, Laura J. Hanby and Marianna Shturman

Recent legislative interest in decarceration (Gartner et al. 2011) and spiralling costs of incarceration have led to community corrections enjoying a kind of renaissance. Indeed, various researchers have implemented empirically informed training and intervention strategies that are changing probation policy and practice. To a large extent, the focus of such training is to give probation staff the necessary skills to better manage their face to face contacts with their clientele beyond a simple check-in and review of supervision conditions. This recent evolution in probation practice has yielded modest but replicable reductions in probation failures (i.e. breaches for technical violations and rates of reoffending (Bonta et al. 2008; Robinson et al. 2011) and has been described as core correctional practice (Dowden and Andrews 2004).

In this chapter, we assert that these improved outcomes could potentially be further enhanced if probationers approach supervision as requiring their cooperation, such that offenders are an active agent in their success. This is consistent with the need for probation officers to be agents of change rather than referral agents, as recently encouraged by Bourgon and Gutierrez (2012). As a backdrop to this position, we integrate research regarding offender change and situate it within a community supervision model. As well, we comment on the philosophical differences apparent in probation supervision, where control and supervision are balanced against offender rehabilitation.

The 'What Works' literature has been well incorporated into community corrections (Bogue et al. 2004) and is reflected in assessments of risk and need with the family of Level of Service Inventory (LSI) instruments (Multi-Health Systems Inc. 2012). This body of work is also incorporated into case planning, with criminogenic needs being targeted in programming and aftercare services. As well, the risk/need/responsivity, a model for correctional programming and intervention, has been utilized to allocate resources (Andrews and

Bonta 2010). In combination and in comparison with prior supervision strategies that ignored criminogenic needs or allocated resources (i.e. frequency of contact, release conditions) based on other factors (e.g. type of crime), probation outcomes are improved. This research has evolved to now consider Core Correctional Practice as a 'best practices' approach to community supervision (Bonta et al. 2010; Lowenkamp et al. 2012). Such curricula Effective Practices in Correctional Settings (EPICS), Strategic Training Initiative in Community Supervision (STICS) and Staff Training Aimed at Reducing Re-arrest (STARR) are the newest generation of training that has at its foundation the issues of risk and need, but earlier examples are present (Taxman 1999) reflecting the iterative nature of advancement in probation curriculum development and practice. Importantly, these approaches incorporate skills training for probation officers and are not interested in a simply didactic approach to training. Coaching and follow-up support in this new training are considered as important as the initial in-class training itself.

With the exception of fleeting emphasis on offender responsivity (Bonta and Andrews 2007), it is possible to review the risk and need literature and incorrectly conclude that the offender is a passive observer in this transition from offender to citizen. Indeed, some might view this new training curriculum as somewhat paternalistic, in that change is expected based solely on this external influence. Intriguingly, only one paper has examined which comes first, external influence that leads to internal change or internal change that predisposes an offender to benefit from external events (LeBel et al. 2008). These authors concluded that subjective states (internal) measured before release have a direct effect on recidivism as well as indirect effects through their impact on social circumstances (external) experienced after release from prison. Admittedly, social circumstances did not reflect the quality of the probation experience per se. Nonetheless, we would be remiss if we did not note that offender change, and by inference offender compliance, are not solely dependent on the actions and attitudes of the probation officer. Consequently, this newer approach in probation practice needs to be situated according to our understanding of offender change. It would seem that change can be influenced by both internal and external factors and that both must be considered in the context of enhancing offender compliance. In a model to be presented shortly, we assert that internal and external factors function synergistically to yield and sustain offender change.

The desistance literature is an obvious and important starting point for understanding offender change and probation success, as it relates to people, situations and factors that are associated with offenders ceasing their criminality. One approach to understanding the importance of factors that enhance offender success is simply to ask them (Healy 2010). This line of enquiry has been illuminating. Notably, the path to desistance eventually ends with a change in the offender's identity, but the journey bridges social and personal forces and involves challenges, adversity and opportunity. As well, the pace of this journey seems to vary by individual, highlighting that desistance must be understood at both the intra-individual and inter-individual levels. At the core of this journey is who or what might be markers of change or function as a change agent. Knowing this could inform resource allocation, case management, programme referral and risk management.

The bulk of this chapter will highlight an ongoing programme of research regarding components of offender change and suggest how this work might be integrated into programme research and inform probation compliance. The first aspect of this research has been an effort to bridge the risk and need research (Andrews and Bonta 2010) with the desistance research. The former seems to focus on crime acquisition with an emphasis on the identification of risk factors, the need to target these criminogenic needs, and the assertion that reoffending will diminish as the rewards for prosocial behaviour increase (Andrews and Bonta 2010). Of note is that criminal behaviour is not expected to decrease through the increase in costs, as from a punishment perspective. From a probation perspective, it is unclear to what extent offenders view conditions from a cost/benefit perspective. Moreover, technical violations are driving up incarceration rates (Travis and Stacey 2010), suggesting that conditions may not be the magic bullet to manage risk in the community, as once believed. As noted earlier, crime desistance is usually a gradual journey to cessation of crime. Importantly, the factors that appear related to crime desistance (i.e. protective factors; see Maruna (2010) for an overview) are not simply the absence of risk factors (Lloyd and Serin 2012). Accordingly, an understanding of both the risk and desistance literature seems preferable in order to inform probation practice.

A model of offender change that bridges the risk and desistance literature is presented in Figure 6.1 (Serin et al. 2010). Against a backdrop of the age–crime curve, it posits that internal and external change factors synergistically combine to influence, augment or capitalize on an offender's commitment to change. Once a threshold of commitment (i.e. readiness or motivation) is met and sustained, crime desistance can proceed, as highlighted by various events and intrapersonal change. This change is not particularly orderly and is marked by hesitation, ambivalence, and degrees of success and failure. This will be expanded on later in the chapter. At present, it is important to note that these recent advances in probation practices tend to reflect the expectation that attending to risk and need, and targeting criminogenic need, will be sufficient to yield offender compliance and change. A theme to be considered in this chapter is the possibility that specifically attending to crime desistance/protective factors and internal change factors might further increase offender change. In our view, such a situation might be more appropriately

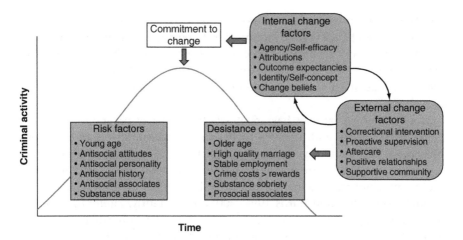

Figure 6.1 Model of offender change

considered offender cooperation, given the prominence of internal change factors. In contrast, compliance seems more influenced by external change factors. Indeed, it seems possible that the acquisition of new skills through cognitive behavioural programming could lead to new behaviours. With practice and repetition, such behaviours could lead to cognitive (i.e. attitudinal) change in terms of expectations, efficacy and identity. Implicit in this model is that both factors influence change and that both are important. In the absence of empirical evidence, it remains speculative which is preferred, or whether internal and external change factors are differentially important among a heterogeneous group of probationers.

It is important to note that we strongly emphasize the importance of and need for assessment and targeting of criminogenic risk factors. We also recognize that both structured correctional programming (Gendreau et al. 1996; Smith et al. 2009) and skilled probation staff (Bourgon and Gutierrez 2012; Skeem et al. 2007) yield improved offender outcomes. Nonetheless, we assert that these gains can be augmented by engaging the offender and empowering him or her to be a change agent. In this manner, they become a driver of change rather than a passive recipient. In a related theme, much has been written regarding offenders being treatment resistant (Serin et al. 2001), so it seems that, if we are to consider offender empowerment, we must begin with an understanding of treatment readiness.

Treatment readiness/engagement

Within the mental health field the notion of treatability has been considered (Heilbrun et al. 1992), but, while efforts to develop a reliable and valid measure have been substantial, success has been modest. This initial work, plus that of Michenbaum and Turk (1987), prompted us to pursue a programme of research regarding treatment readiness, expecting that clarity regarding the conceptualization and measurement of treatment readiness would lead to improved offender cooperation with programming and supervision efforts (Serin et al. 2007, 2010).

Overall, offender samples have relatively high rates of programme attrition (Nunes et al. 2010), and, notably, higher in the community than in prisons (McGuire 2002). Curiously, despite this, effect sizes for programmes are higher in the community than in prisons (Gendreau et al. 1999, 2006), although such findings may not reflect a methodology that includes dropouts with the experimental group (Rice and Harris 1997, 2005). Importantly, failure to complete programmes appears to be associated with higher rates of recidivism (Hanson et al. 2002; Hollin et al. 2008; van Voorhis et al. 2004; Wormith and Olver 2002). Moreover, offenders who fail to complete treatment may be those who most need it (i.e. at highest risk of reoffending). Further, for those probationers for whom programme completion is a condition of probation, such attrition will lead to high rates of technical violations on release. Curiously, despite this situation, there has been relatively little systematic research regarding models and assessment instruments of motivation and/or treatment readiness. A notable exception includes work by Ward and colleagues (Casey et al. 2007; McMurran and Ward 2004).

There appears to be no single or agreed model of offender readiness, although Ward et al.'s (2004) elegant multifactor model of offender readiness (MORM) is perhaps most cited. This model is richer than simple distinctions of motivation and integrates internal (person) and external (context) conditions required for offenders to enter treatment. Such readiness is assumed to enable offenders to minimally function in a therapeutic environment and thereby benefit from treatment. For offenders lacking in readiness, various strategies exist to improve programme engagement (Anstiss et al. 2011; Serin and Preston 2001).

Obviously, even a well-designed programme will have limited efficacy and efficiency if attrition rates are high. For the particular offender, participation in the programme is essential if change is to occur, hence the need to systematically measure and respond to offender readiness. Indeed, researchers have found that lower motivation for treatment is associated with higher rates of drop-out/expulsion across different types of treatment and different types of offenders (Beyko and Wong 2005; Krawczyk et al. 2002; McKenzie et al. 2002; Scott 2004; Wormith and Olver 2002). Both Nunes and Cortoni (2006) and Wormith and Olver (2002) reported that drop-outs/expulsions were higher in risk and lower in motivation for treatment than completers. Getting the probationer to attend treatment is a compliance issue, but getting them to engage in treatment is a cooperation issue. Clearly, an understanding of readiness would augment probation success. Moreover, a failure to consider readiness would certainly exacerbate supervision outcome. Accordingly, routine screening for readiness is something that could help probation staff achieve their goals.

Offender change

Given apparent offender heterogeneity in terms of risk and need profiles, as well as differences in skills and readiness, it is naive to assume all programme completers benefit equally; moreover, effect sizes are modest, rather than perfect. As well, the *process* of change remains unclear and is important if probation officers are to maximize their effectiveness as change agents. With this in mind, our recent work on identifying change constructs may be helpful, as it alludes to an identity change in probationers that resonates with that of an engaged offender and one that is invested in the journey to eventual success.

In order to effectively insert Probation Officers as an agent in the change process, it first is important to understand something about *how* offenders change. Although the treatment evaluation literature convincingly shows that some offenders change with assistance (Lipsey and Cullen 2007), little systematic attention has been paid to which skills these offenders develop that actually instigate remaining crime-free after release (Serin et al. 2010; Serin and Prell 2012). Other offenders appear to change without assistance. Demographic data sources (e.g. sentencing events across the life-span) dependably show that the typical pattern of development in adulthood is a decreasing likelihood for crime (Piquero et al. 2001); however, there is presumably rich psychological meaning involved in this process of ramping up and then removing oneself from criminal activity (e.g. Maruna 2001). Official record data do not provide a window into this, and psychological changes are underexplored.

Drawing on important work that has fleshed out current understanding of cognitive change within the desistance process (Maruna 2001), we set out to design self-report questionnaires that would assess offenders' beliefs about change and desistance (Serin and Lloyd 2009; Lloyd and Serin 2012). Desistance relies on the offender becoming engaged in long-term 'hooks for change' (which can be positive relationships, opportunities for conventional success or any other feature that makes the shift to crime-free living an attractive option for offenders; Giordano et al. 2002), with high-quality prosocial marriages and employment being most cited as having desistance effects (Sampson and Laub 2005). This suggests that the critical features of investment in desistance include a shifting from valuing crime to valuing more conventional living, from using crime as a shortcut when facing challenges to pursuing a new path with a sense of drive and personal agency, and from seeing oneself as embedded in a criminal identity to adopting a non-criminal sense of self. Each of these changes is emphasized as a process, given that building new relationships and transforming identity take both effort and time.

Notably, this work has given initial reason to be optimistic that offenders' beliefs about desistance can be measured reliably (Lloyd and Serin 2012), since offenders' self-reports on a variety of questionnaires reveal an internal logic regarding their readiness to desist. Thus, we argue that supervision practice may be enhanced when probation officers attend to offenders' degree of investment in change, degree of identification as an ex-offender, and availability of opportunities to experience long-term change.

Since the desistance literature emphasizes the human agency of offenders, this serves to encourage probation practice to place some critical importance on offenders driving their own change processes. This especially argues against a paternalistic, compliance-focused approach. Although effective management of risk situations involves the offender complying with the limits placed on their activities, an important goal for probation should become encouraging and setting up opportunities for greater investment in potential for change within the offender's life.

Thus, just as it is important for treatment decisions to be informed by an offender's willingness and readiness to engage in treatment, it is additionally valuable for offender–staff contacts to be informed regarding the offender's degree of investment in maintaining a crime-free life. Although offenders typically report high motivation to remain out of prison (Dhami et al. 2006), some will be more prepared than others to face the challenges of re-entering their communities, rebuilding social ties and resisting returning to previous criminal goals and coping strategies. Although external restrictions have been the standard approach to preventing crime relapse, the offender change literature speaks to there being value added for taking stock of external support systems outside the justice system and internal investment in change. If, ultimately, offenders change through a gradual, increasing commitment to becoming conventional in their identity and lifestyle, probation practice may do well to harness and enhance this process, fitting practice into the offender's natural progression and potential for change.

Offender competencies

Thus far, we have discussed change as a process, but what if certain key attitudes, behaviours and expectations were fundamental to sustained offender change? In an earlier study involving prisoners who completed cognitive behavioural programming, both treatment responsivity and programme completion were predicted by improved inhibitory control using computerized cognitive tasks (Fishbein et al. 2009). This suggests that specific skills or competencies might be identifiable (Serin 2006) which could predict performance. Accordingly, we set out to examine this using an archival offender management system for a sample of offenders ($n = 3374$) for whom programme completion data and post-programme outcome were known (Hanby and Serin 2009). The Offender Competency Index (OCI) is a measure of offender competencies derived from information routinely collected upon intake to a federal institution. An exploratory factor analysis was conducted on 29 items selected from the Offender Management System to represent the core competencies. The following six components were retained (based on parallel analysis), which explained 50.1 per cent of the variance: knowledge acquisition ability, personal accountability and need for change, cognitive flexibility, cognitive awareness, literacy and numeracy, and inhibitory control.

The findings are instructive regarding offender engagement. Treatment completers had significantly higher competency scores than dropouts/expulsions for all of the competencies, with the exception of literacy and numeracy. Treatment completers also had significantly higher competency scores than personal/administrative non-completers for personal accountability and need for change, knowledge acquisition ability and cognitive awareness. Personal/administrative non-completers did not differ significantly from dropouts/expulsions on any of the competency scores. Thus, competency scores did not differentiate between non-completion groups.

The overarching goal of this study was to determine why some offenders are successful while others fail in their attempts to change their behaviour. Offender competencies were found to account for some of the variation in treatment outcome and support was found for the hypothesis that offender competencies predict programme performance. Further, treatment completers had higher competency than non-completers, suggesting that offender competencies may be able to differentiate offenders who are likely to successfully complete treatment from those who fail to complete treatment. Of these competencies, only the literacy and numeracy factor was not significantly correlated with recidivism. Of the remaining five competencies, correlations ranged from –0.09 to –0.19, suggesting that consideration of offender competency might be useful in probation supervision.

While preliminary, these findings suggest that competent offenders are more likely to engage in treatment. Further, offenders lacking the competencies may warrant preparatory interventions before participating in correctional treatment programmes. A pre-treatment primer addressing such competencies may be effective in increasing treatment engagement and improving probationer performance.

Staff competencies

The importance of staff competencies within correctional practice has been highlighted by various authors (Dowden and Andrews 2004; Serin and Shturman 2007). Unsurprisingly, research indicates that the quality and nature of the relationship between probation staff and the offender influence offender outcome (Skeem et al. 2007). Encouragingly, but not surprisingly, skilled probation staff are effective at improving offender outcomes (Bonta et al. 2008; Bourgon et al. 2010a, 2010b; Trotter 1996), demonstrating that probation supervision can be an effective *external* agent of change potentially contributing to resettlement and probation success. As well, and again not surprisingly, caseload size appears to affect outcome (Jalbert et al. 2010), suggesting that quality does count. Recently, the Strategic Training Initiative in Community Supervision (STICS; Bonta et al. 2010) showed that skills-based training for probation officers transfers to real-life client sessions and improves re-entry outcome, even when controlling for risk. However, sessions need to be at least 40 minutes in duration (Bonta et al. 2008). Other research has also noted that offenders' perceptions of the obstacles and utility of their time under supervision influence probation outcomes (Bottoms and Shapland 2011). Finally, correctional managers' orientation also impacts outcome (Friedmann et al. 2007; Taxman et al. 2010).

A growing body of empirical evidence has accumulated pointing to the importance of therapist-related factors. If we view probation officers as agents of change, it seems reasonable that some of this research may, then, be applicable to probation staff. Both general and correctional research has attested that, even in the presence of an optimal client–strategy match, the success of therapy very often depends on factors related to therapists or counsellors, who are the primary agents of change (e.g. Huppert et al. 2001; Marshall 2005; Marshall and Burton 2010; Project MATCH Research Group 1998; Washington State 2004). In fact, in many cases the effects of therapists greatly exceed the effects of treatment techniques in terms of client outcomes (Wampold 2001).

If we accept the importance of therapist contribution to the therapeutic process and outcomes, the question then becomes what makes a therapist effective or what contributes to his/her ability to be an effective agent of change. It seems that the answer to this question lies in therapist intrapersonal and interpersonal relational skills. It has been reported in general literature that the highest percentage of variance (10 per cent) in treatment outcomes, after the client's contribution, can be attributed to the therapeutic relationship, 9 per cent to the therapist, who plays a significant role in establishing the therapeutic relationship, and only 5 per cent to the therapeutic strategies (Norcross and Lambert 2005). Similarly, in correctional literature, Marshall (2005) reported that 32 to 61 per cent of variance in specific indices of change during the intervention with sex offenders can be attributed to a combination of counsellors' relational features.

Andrews and colleagues outlined five principles of core correctional practices (CCP) of community service providers. Their research findings emphasized

the importance of quality of interpersonal relationships along with specific strategies of intervention (e.g. appropriate modelling and reinforcement,
problem-solving and effective use of community resources). As well, Marshall
and colleagues demonstrated that effective therapists working with sex offenders should be warm, empathic, rewarding and directive. They also showed that
a non-confrontational style of interaction (i.e. firm and supportive challenging) with offenders is more effective than a confrontational style of interaction (i.e. harsh, perceived as denigrating challenging) (Dowden and Andrews
2004).

As the first step in a systematic investigation of this topic, we embarked on
research to develop and initially validate a Correctional Counsellor Relational
Competency (CCRC) measure and to present relational profiles of correctional
service providers. Three studies were conducted to achieve these objectives
(Shturman 2011). In the first study, based on the input of experts in the
field of correctional rehabilitation and an extensive literature review, stimulus
materials (vignettes) and the responses to the selected vignettes were developed and then rated by the experts. These vignettes reflect 'learning moments'
when the opportunity is presented whereby a skilled practitioner can promote
change.

Such a vignette is:

> During the first session of substance abuse programme, after the intro-
> ductions a facilitator was just about to move to the topics to be covered
> in the group when she was interrupted by a 28-year-old Aboriginal male
> who has been in and out of prison for initiating fights while intoxicated
> and selling drugs: 'excuse me Miss, what is your background please? Have
> you ever been addicted to something? It does not seem like you have an
> idea of what it is like to be an addict. You have to walk in my shoes to
> understand me.'

The vignettes and responses that demonstrated acceptable content validity
were selected for further validity investigation.

In the second study, 310 correctional programme officers and community
service providers completed the CCRC and a demographic survey to assess initial psychometric properties of the instrument and to compare the relational
profiles of correctional services providers across a number of demographic
factors (e.g. gender, age and ethnicity). As well, 92 participants completed
the CCRC for the second time to assess test–retest reliability. Exploratory
factor analysis revealed a seven-factor structure of the CCRC that included
the following relational factors: confidence, empathy, confrontation, neglect,
blame/criticism, reinforcement of antisocial attitudes and behaviours, and
self-disclosure. The seven scales of the CCRC had high internal consistency

and test–retest reliability. Analysis of repeated measures revealed group differences on a number of demographic factors in the countertransferential scales, blame/criticism and reinforcement of antisocial attitudes/behaviours. Some differences were also found in the confidence, confrontation and self-disclosure scales of the CCRC. Finally, in the third study, 246 correctional programme officers and community service providers completed an on-line package with nine measures selected for construct validation. Encouragingly, the CCRC demonstrated convergent and divergent validity, with empathy predicting group cohesion and confidence and self-disclosure predicting working alliance.

In summary, there is preliminary evidence that, when faced with 'learning moments', staff with a therapeutic focus agree on how to interact with offenders in order to facilitate a working relationship and influence change. For these reasons, employing qualitative and quantitative measures of client perceptions and probation officer skills appears critical to assessing the potential for and obstacles against successful offender resettlement.

Offender support

At the time of our treatment readiness research (Serin et al. 2007), our clinical work informed the need to include something relating to aftercare and support. Some work regarding the importance of prosocial models was available (Andrews and Kiessling 1980), but it is only more recently that its importance in understanding offender success has been demonstrated (LeBel et al. 2008; Maruna 2001; Massoglia and Uggen 2007). Further, recent research in our lab regarding protective factors in dynamic risk assessment of probationers suggests that protective factors are as important as, if not more important than, risk factors in risk management (Serin and Prell 2012). In this pilot research, such factors as accessible social supports, being responsive to advice and connection with prosocial others seem to insulate against risk and were more predictive than traditional risk factors in predicting probation outcome. Moreover, other parallel research has demonstrated that protective factors change over time (Ullrich and Coid 2011), meaning that they need to be systematically measured throughout the period of probation, if risk is to be effectively managed. Given that we have described offender change as a process that requires effort, the degree of support for change by prosocial others would seem an important topic for inclusion within probation sessions. We also believe it is critical to allow the offender to determine who is important to them (preferably family, friends, employer or clergy) and then probe for degree of support by each of them. Change is unlikely to materialize without support. Of note is that enhancing community support underscores the current re-entry initiative in the United States (Burke and Tonry 2006).

Cooperation versus compliance

Various dictionaries define compliance as 'the act of conforming, acquiescing, or yielding' and 'a tendency to yield readily to others, especially in a weak and subservient way'. Cooperation is defined as 'an act or instance of working or acting together for a common purpose or benefit; joint action'. At the risk of seeming paternalistic, this quote by Coloroso (2003) seems apt: 'It's not control or compliance that you are looking for; it's calm and cooperation.' Compliance is someone doing what they are told to do. Even if the request is ultimately in the best interests of the doer, inherent in this situation is an obvious power differential whereby one person can require that another person adhere to their wishes. When the doer fails to fulfil their obligation, the expectation is that punishment or application of sanctions is the next strategy. Cooperation, on the other hand, is when an offender decides or chooses to do that which needs to be done (i.e. meet curfew requirements, avoid intoxicants, avoid procriminal peers, maintain employment). Without threats, bribes, fear or power struggles, cooperation moves everyone in the right direction. One strategy for the probation officer is assisting the offender to evaluate choices, but ultimately they work together toward a solution. Cooperation leads to enhanced self-esteem, the sense of being capable, and, above all, skills to navigate life *after* the end of probation. Cooperation also strengthens the working alliance, although its conceptualization for offender populations remains a work in progress (Ross et al. 2011).

Perhaps, where issues of public safety are paramount, compliance should exceed the need for cooperation. For most other situations, it seems, compliance may be a somewhat short-sighted way of meeting minimal requirements but fails to fully situate probation officers as effective agents of change. Clearly, having sufficiency frequency of contact with clients and having sufficient time for meaningful exchanges during sessions seem essential in order to aim toward cooperation. Nonetheless, probation officers who are mindful of their roles as change agents will be vigilant for those opportunities where they might move the client from simply at-the-moment compliance to the longer-term goal of cooperation.

Summary

The purpose of this chapter has been to note that, despite the recent encouraging evolution in probation practice (i.e. evidence-based), which has led to more systematic assessment of risk and need and appropriate allocation of services, there may be opportunities for further gains. With that in mind, we have highlighted certain work that may not be embedded within mainstream probation research but that, when considered, could lead to augmenting current resettlement and probation success. Like others, we have commented on the importance of crime desistance, but have contextualized it in terms of mechanisms underlying change (i.e. identity, skills) rather than simply events within an offender's life or social capital. We have also asserted that both staff and offender competencies might underscore change, both initiating and sustaining change, but that a greater focus on offender readiness and protective factors is encouraged. We conceded that compliance is clearly an important goal of probation, especially given high rates of technical violations in some jurisdictions (Glaze and Bonczar 2009), but it may be a temporary gain. Hence, we further asserted that a focus on readiness and internal change mechanisms should promote an identity change within the offender which should precede and lead to cooperation with probation services, creating a stronger working relationship between probation officer and probationer and optimally sustained change.

References

Andrews, D. A. and Bonta, J. (2010) *The Psychology of Criminal Conduct.* Third Edition. Cincinnati, OH: Anderson.

Andrews, D. A. and Kiessling, J. J. (1980) 'Program Structure and Effective Correctional Practices: A Summary of CaVI C Research'. in R. R. Ross and P. Gendreau (Eds) *Effective Correctional Treatment.* Toronto, Canada: Butterworth.

Anstiss, A., Polaschek, D. L. L. and Wilson, M. J. (2011) 'A Brief Motivational Interviewing Intervention with Prisoners: When You Lead a Horse to Water, Can It Drink for Itself?' *Psychology, Crime, and Law* 17 (8), 689–710.

Beyko, M. J. and Wong, S. C. P. (2005) 'Predictors of Treatment Attrition as Indicators for Program Improvement Not Offender Shortcomings: A Study of Sex Offender Treatment Attrition'. *Sex Abuse: A Journal of Research and Treatment,* 17(4): 375–89.

Bogue, B. Campbell, N. and Clawson, E. (2004) *Implementing Evidence-Based Practice in Community Corrections.* Washington, DC: National Institute of Corrections.

Bonta, J., & Andrews, D. A. (2007). *Risk-Need-Responsivity Model for Offender Assessment and Rehabilitation (User Report 2007–06).* Ottawa, Ontario: Public Safety Canada.

Bonta, J., Bourgon, G., Rugge, T., Scott, T.-L., Yessine, A. K., Gutierrez, L. and Li, J. (2010) *The Strategic Training Initiative in Community Supervision: Risk–Need–Responsivity in the Real World.* Ottawa, Canada: Public Safety Canada.

Bonta, J., Rugge, T., Scott, T., Bourgon, G. and Yessine, A. (2008) 'Exploring the Black Box of Community Supervision'. *Journal of Offender Rehabilitation* 47, 248–270.

Bottoms, A. E. and Shapland, J. (2011) 'Steps Towards Desistance Among Male Young Adult Recidivists'. in S. Farrall, M. Hough, S. Maruna and R. Sparks (Eds) *Escape Routes: Contemporary Perspectives on Life after Punishment.* London: Routledge, pp. 43–80.

Bourgon, G. and Gutierrez, L. (2012) 'The General Responsivity Principle in Community Supervision: The Importance of Probation Officers Using Cognitive Intervention Techniques and Its Influence on Recidivism'. *Journal of Crime and Justice* 35, 149–166.

Bourgon, G., Bonta, J., Rugge, T. and Gutierrez, L. (2010a) 'Technology Transfer: The Importance of On-Going Clinical Supervision in Translating "What Works" to Everyday Community Supervision'. in F. McNeil, P. Raynor and C. Trotter (Eds) *Offender Supervision: New Directions in Theory, Research and Practice.* Cullompton: Willan.

Bourgon, G., Bonta, J., Rugge, T., Scott, L. and Yessine, A. K. (2010b) 'The Role of Program Design, Implementation, and Evaluation in Evidence-Based "Real World" Community Supervision'. *Federal Probation* 74, 2–15.

Burke, P. and Tonry, M. (2006). *Successful Transition and Reentry for Safer Communities: A Call to Action for Parole*. Silver Spring, MD: Center for Effective Public Policy.

Casey, S., Day, A., Howells, K. and Ward, T. (2007) 'Assessing Suitability for Offender Rehabilitation: Development and Validation of the Treatment Readiness Questionnaire'. *Criminal Justice and Behavior* 34, 1427–1440.

Coloroso., B. (2003) *Kids are Worth It: Raising Resilient, Responsible, Compassionate Kids*. Penguin: Canada.

Dhami, M. K., Mandel, D. R., Loewenstein, G. and Ayton, P. (2006) 'Prisoners' Positive Illusions of Their Post-Release Success'. *Law and Human Behavior* 30, 631–647. doi:10.1007/s10979-006-9040-1

Dowden, C. and Andrews, D. A. (2004) 'The Importance of Staff Practice in Delivering Effective Correctional Treatment: A Meta-Analytic Review of Core Correctional Practice'. *International Journal of Offender Therapy and Comparative Criminology* 48, 203–214.

Fishbein, D., Sheppard, M., Hyde, C., Hubal, R., Newlin, D., Serin, R. C., Chrousos, G. and Alesci, S. (2009) 'Deficits in Behavioural Inhibition Predict Treatment Engagement in Prison Inmates'. *Law and Human Behavior* 33, 419–435.

Friedmann, P. D., Taxman, F. S. and Henderson, C. (2007) 'Evidence-Based Treatment Practices for Drug-Involved Adults in the Criminal Justice System'. *Journal of Substance Abuse Treatment* 32, 267–277.

Gartner, R., Doob, A. N. and Zimring, E. (2011) 'Decarceration in California: The Past as Prologue? Decarceration in California Then and Now'. *Criminology & Public Policy* 10(2), 291–325. DOI:10.1111/j. 1745–9133.2011.00709.x

Gendreau, P., Goggin, C. and Cullen, F. (1999) *The Effects of Prison Sentences on Recidivism*. Ottawa, Canada: Solicitor General of Canada.

Gendreau, P., Little, T. and Goggin, C. (1996) 'A Meta-Analysis of the Predictors of Adult Offender Recidivism: What Works!' *Criminology* 34, 575–607.

Gendreau, P., Goggin, P., French, S. and Smith P. (2006) 'Practicing Psychology in Correctional Settings: "What Works" in Reducing Criminal Behaviour'. in A. K. Hess and I. Weiner (Eds) *The Handbook of Forensic Psychology*. Third Edition. New York, NY: John Wiley & Sons.

Giordano, P. C., Cernkovich, S. A. and Rudolph, J. L. (2002) 'Gender, Crime, and Desistance: Toward a Theory of Cognitive Transformation'. *American Journal of Sociology* 107 (4), 990–1064.

Glaze, L. E., & Bonczar, T. P. (2009) *Probation and Parole in the United States, 2008*. Washington, DC: U.S. Bureau of Justice Statistics.

Hanby, L. J. and Serin, R. C. (2009) *Offender Competencies and Their Relationship to Correctional Program Performance*. Poster session at the Canadian Psychological Association Annual Convention, Montreal, QC, June.

Hanson, R. K., Gordon, A., Harris, A. J. R., Marques, J. K., Murphy, W., Quinsey, V. L. and Seto, M. D. (2002) 'First Report of the Collaborative Outcome Data Project on the Effectiveness of Psychological Treatment for Sex Offenders'. *Sexual Abuse: A Journal of Research and Treatment* 14, 169–194.

Healy, D. (2010) *The Dynamics of Desistance: Charting Pathways Through Change*. Cullompton: Wilan Publishing.

Heilbrun, K. S., Bennett, W. S., Evans, J. H., Offult, R. A., Reiff, H. J. and White, A. J. (1992) 'Assessing Treatability in Mentally Disordered Offenders: Strategies for Improving Reliability'. *Forensic Reports* 5, 85–96.

Hollin, C. R., McGuire, J., Hounsome, J. C., Hatcher, R. M., Bilby, C. A. L. and Palmer, E. J. (2008) 'Cognitive Skills Behavior Programs for Offenders in the Community: A Reconviction Analysis'. *Criminal Justice and Behavior* 35, 269–283.

Huppert, J. D., Bufka, L. F., Barlow, D. H., Gorman, J. M., Shear, M. K. and Woods, S. W. (2001) 'Therapists, Therapist Variables, and Cognitive – Behavioral Therapy Outcomes in a Multicenter Trial for Panic Disorder'. *Journal of Consulting and Clinical Psychology* 69, 747–755.

Jalbert, S., Rhodes, W., Flygare, C. and Kane, M. (2010) 'Testing Probation Outcomes in an Evidence-Based Practice Setting: Reduced Caseload Size and Intensive Supervision Effectiveness'. *Journal of Offender Rehabilitation* 49, 233–253.

Krawczyk, S. C., Witte, T., Gordon, A., Wong, S. and Wormith, J. S. (2002) *Treatment Attrition and Institutional Offending in Violent Offenders*. Poster session presented at the Canadian Psychological Association's 63rd Annual Convention, Vancouver, BC, May.

LeBel, T. P., Burnett, R., Maruna, S. and Bushway, S. (2008) 'The "Chicken and Egg" of Subjective and Social Factors in Desistance from Crime'. *European Journal of Criminology* 5, 131–159.

Lipsey, M. W. and Cullen, F. T. (2007) 'The Effectiveness of Correctional Rehabilitation: A Review of Systematic Reviews'. *Annual Review of Law and Social Science* 3, 297–320. doi:10.1146/annurev.lawsocsci. 3.081806.112833

Lloyd, C. D. and Serin, R. C. (2012) 'Agency and Outcome Expectancies for Crime Desistance: Measuring Offenders' Personal Beliefs About Change'. *Psychology, Crime, and Law* 6, 543–565.

Lowenkamp, C. T., Holsinger, A., Robinson, C.R. and Alexander, M. (2012) 'Diminishing or Durable Treatment Effects of STARR? A Research Note on 24-Month Re-Arrest Rates'. *Journal of Crime and Justice*. 1–9.

Marshall, W. L. (2005) 'Therapist Style in Sexual Offender Treatment: Influence on Indices of Change'. *Sexual Abuse: A Journal of Research and Treatment* 17, 109–116.

Marshall, W. L. and Burton, D. L. (2010) 'The Importance of Group Processes in Offender Treatment'. *Aggression and Violent Behavior* 15, 141–149.

Maruna, S. (2001) *Making Good: How Ex-Convicts Reform and Rebuild Their Lives*. Washington, DC: American Psychological Association. doi: 10.1037/10430–000

Maruna, S. (2010) Understanding Desistance from Crime. http://www.clinks.org/assets/files/PDFs/Desistance.pdf (accessed 12 September 2012).

Massoglia, M. and Uggen, C. (2007). 'Subjective Desistance and the Transition to Adulthood'. *Journal of Contemporary Criminal Justice* 23, 90–103.

McGuire, J. (2002) 'Criminal Sanctions versus Psychologically-Based Interventions with Offenders: A Comparative Empirical Analysis'. *Psychology, Crime and Law* 8, 183–208.

McKenzie, K., Witte, T., Beyko, M., Wong, S., Olver, M. and Wormith, J. S. (2002) *Predictors of Attrition in a Sex Offender Program*. Poster session presented at the Canadian Psychological Association's 63rd Annual Convention, Vancouver, BC, May.

McMurran, M. and Ward, T. (2004) 'Motivating Offenders to Change in Therapy: An Organizing Framework'. *Legal and Criminological Psychology* 9, 295–311.

Michenbaum, D. and Turk, D. C. (1987) *Facilitating Treatment Adherence: A Practitioner's Guidebook*. New York, NY: Plenum.

Multi-Health Systems (2012). http://www.mhs.com/

Norcross and Lambert. (2005) 'The Therapy Relationship'. in J. C. Norcross, L. E. Butler and R. F. Levant (Eds) *Evidence-based Practices in Mental Health: Debate and Dialogue on the Fundamental Questions*. American Psychologial Association.

Nunes, K. L. and Cortoni, F. (2006) *The Heterogeneity of Treatment Non-Completers.* Research Report No. R-176. Ottawa, Canada: Correctional Service Canada.

Nunes, K. L., Cortoni, F. and Serin, R. C. (2010) 'Screening Offenders for Risk of Dropout and Expulsion from Rehabilitation Programs: Enhancing Correctional Outcomes'. *Legal and Criminological Psychology* 15, 341–356.

Piquero, A. R., Blumstein, A., Brame, R., Haapanen, R., Mulvey, E. P. and Nagin, D. S. (2001) 'Assessing the Impact of Exposure Time and Incapacitation on Longitudinal Trajectories of Criminal Offending'. *Journal of Adolescent Research* 16, 54–74. doi:10.1177/0743558401161005.

Project Match Research Group. (1998) 'Matching Alcoholism Treatments to Client Heterogeneity: Project MATCH Three-year Drinking Outcomes'. *Alcoholism: Clinical and Experimental Research* 22(6), 1300–1311.

Rice, M. E. and Harris, G. T. (1997) 'The Treatment of Adult Offenders'. in D. M. Stoff, J. Breiling and J. D. Maser (Eds) *Handbook of Antisocial Behavior.* New York, NY: John Wiley & Sons.

Rice, M. E. and Harris, G. T. (2005) 'Comparing Effect Sizes in Follow-up Studies: ROC Area, Cohen's *d*, and *r*'. *Law and Human Behavior* 29, 615–620.

Robinson, C. R., Vanbenschoten, S., Alexander, M., Lowenkamp, C. T. and Oleson, J.C. (2011) 'A Random Study of Staff Training Aimed at Reducing Re-arrest (STARR): Using Core Correctional Practices in Probation Interactions'. *Journal of Crime & Justice* 35(2), 167–188.

Ross, E. C., Polaschek, D. L. L. and Wilson, M. J. (2011) 'Shifting Perspectives: A Confirmatory Factor Analysis of the Working Alliance Inventory with High-Risk Violent Offenders'. *International Journal of Offender Therapy and Comparative Criminology* 55, 1308–1323.

Sampson, R. J. and Laub, J. H. (2005) 'A Life-Course View of the Development of Crime'. *Annals of the American Academy of Political and Social Science* 602, 12–45. doi: 10.1177/000271620528007

Scott, K. L. (2004) 'Stage of Change as a Predictor of Attrition Among Men in a Batterer Treatment Program'. *Journal of Family Violence,* 19, 37–47.

Serin, R. C. (2006) *Functional Competency Model for Offenders: Programming for Crime Desistance.* Unpublished manuscript, Carleton University, Ottawa, Canada.

Serin, R. C. and Lloyd, C. D. (2009) 'Examining the Process of Offender Change: The Transition to Crime Desistance'. *Psychology, Crime, & Law* 15, 347–364.

Serin, R. C. and Prell, L. (2012) Pathways to Crime Desistance for Probationers. Presentation at the American Psychology-Law Conference, March.

Serin, R. C. and Preston, D. L. (2001) 'Designing, Implementing and Managing Treatment Programs for Violent Offenders'. in G. A. Bernfeld, D. P. Farrington and A. W. Leischied (Eds) *Offender Rehabilitation in Practice: Implementing and Evaluating Effective Programs* (pp. 205–221). Chichester: John Wiley & Sons.

Serin, R. C. and Shturman, M. (2007). Maximizing Correctional Staff's Contribution to Corrections. *Corrections Today, 69(6),* 30–32.

Serin, R. C., Kennedy, S. M., Mailloux, D. L. and Hanby, L. J. (2010) 'The Origins of Treatment Readiness'. in A. Day, S. Casey, T. Ward, K. Howells and J. Vess (Eds) *Transition to Better Lives: Offender Readiness and Rehabilitation.* Devon, UK: Willan Publishing.

Serin, R. C., Mailloux, D. L. and Kennedy, S. M. (2007) 'Development of a Clinical Rating Scale for Offender Readiness: Implications for Assessment and Offender Change'. *Issues in Forensic Psychology* 7, 70–80.

Serin, R. C., Preston, D. L. and Murphy, S. (2001) 'Programming for Persistently Violent Offenders'. *International Community Corrections Association Journal* 10, 19–23.

Shturman, M. (2011). 'Correctional Counsellor Relational Competency Assessment: Development and Validation'. Unpublished doctoral thesis. Carleton University.

Skeem, J. L., Louden, J., Polaschek, D. L. L. and Camp, J. (2007) 'Assessing Relationship Quality in Mandated Community Treatment: Blending Care with Control'. *Psychological Assessment* 19, 397–410.

Smith, P., Gendreau, P. and Swartz, K. (2009) 'Validating the Principles of Effective Intervention: A Systematic Review of the Contributions of Meta-Analysis in the Field of Corrections'. *Victims and Offenders* 4, 148–169.

Taxman, F. S. (1999) 'Proactive Supervision: Supervision as Crime Prevention'. *Journal of Offender Monitoring* 12(2), 25–26.

Taxman, F. S., Henderson, C. and Lerch, J. (2010) 'The Socio-Political Context of Reforms in Probation Agencies: Impact on Adoption of Evidence-Based Practices'. in F. McNeil, P. Raynor and C. Trotter (Eds) *Offender Supervision: New Directions in Theory, Research and Practice.* UK: Willan Publishing.

Travis, L. F. III and Stacey, J. (2010) 'A Half Century of Parole Rules: Conditions of Parole in the United States, 2008'. *Journal of Criminal Justice* 38, 604–608.

Trotter, C. (1996). 'The Impact of Different Supervision Practices in Community Corrections'. *Australian and New Zealand Journal of Criminology* 29, 1–18.

Ullrich, S. and Coid, J. (2011) 'Protective Factors for Violence Among Released Prisoners – Effects Over Time and Interactions with Static Risk'. *Journal of Consulting and Clinical Psychology* 79, 381–390.

van Voorhis, P., Spruance, L. M., Ritchey, P. N., Johnson-Listwan, S. and Seabrook, R. (2004) 'The Georgia Cognitive Skills Experiment: A Replication of Reasoning and Rehabilitation'. *Criminal Justice and Behavior* 31, 282–305.

Wampold, E. (2001). *The Great Psychotherapy Debate: Models, Methods, and Findings.* Mahwah: Lawrence Erlbaum Associates Publishers.

Ward, T., Day, A., Howells, K. and Birgden, A. (2004) 'The Multifactor Offender Readiness Model'. *Aggression and Violent Behavior* 9, 645–673.

Washington State Institute for Public Policy. (2004) Outcome Evaluation of Washington State's Research-Based Programs for Juvenile Offenders. January. http://www.wsipp.wa .gov (accessed September 2012).

Wormith, J. S. and Olver, M. E. (2002) 'Offender Treatment Attrition and Its Relationship with Risk, Responsivity, and Recidivism'. *Criminal Justice and Behavior* 29, 447–471.

7
Compliance through Discussion: The Jersey Experience

Peter Raynor

The background: Compliance, enforcement and toughness

The enforcement of compliance with community sentences has been a topic of vigorous discussion in England and Wales since the early 1990s. A series of studies showed enforcement to be less consistent and less rigorous than a strict interpretation of the law would require (H. M. Inspectorate of Probation 1995; Ellis et al. 1996). Together with a high level of political interest since the 1990s in the processes and outcomes of probation supervision, this led to enforcement becoming a major target (sometimes *the* major target) of the National Probation Service created by amalgamation of over 50 local services in 2001. In the very clear account provided by Robinson and Ugwudike (2012) we see how successive editions of the 'National Standards' for the supervision of offenders from 1992 to 2000 increasingly constrained the discretion of probation officers to accept probationers' reasons for imperfect compliance; this resulted in increases in breach proceedings and the return of probationers to court for more punitive resentencing under the 2003 Criminal Justice Act if as few as two appointments were missed without an acceptable excuse (Home Office 1992, 2000; Ministry of Justice 2011; National Offender Management Service 2007). Targets were set for the proportion of orders to be subject to enforcement action, and, although an additional target for compliance (based on the proportion of orders satisfactorily completed) was introduced in 2004, it is clear that far more thought was given to how to ensure enforcement than to how its presumably intended result, better compliance, might actually be encouraged. Politicians liked to make a lot of noise about enforcement to demonstrate their own toughness (one Home Secretary used to announce 'I am the Enforcer!') and a focus on compliance did not have the same attraction.

Probation managers who wanted their careers to flourish had to pay attention to this new climate, and embraced the enforcement agenda to some degree in order to achieve prescribed targets. However, the driving force behind these developments usually came from politicians and senior civil servants, who often seemed to have a limited grasp of the complexities of supervising disorganized offenders, and of the actual lifestyle of many of the people who found themselves under probation supervision. By way of example, the author was privileged to attend an invited Home Office seminar on enforcement in the late 1990s, at which an exasperated senior official asked in all seriousness 'Why can't they put their appointments in their diaries like normal people do?' With official attitudes driven by this sort of thinking, it is not surprising that many practitioners resorted to rule-bending and turning a blind eye in order to retain what they regarded as a reasonable degree of discretion which allowed them to behave fairly toward the people they were supervising (Ugwudike 2008). The risks entailed by this approach were that rule-bending, if engaged in too obviously, might not be a good prosocial example to people under supervision, and that the perceived legitimacy of the service or the criminal justice system might be weakened if its own staff did not seem to comply with its rules. Strict enforcement, on the other hand, may have been fine in theory, but led in practice to fewer successful completions and more imprisonment, without any convincing evidence that it improved offenders' behaviour (Hearnden and Millie 2004). Nor did it protect the service from more politically driven 'reforms'. Most importantly from the point of view of this chapter, there was no evidence that stricter enforcement generally led to better compliance, and no convincing reason why an approach based mainly on punishment and deterrence would be likely to lead to better compliance by offenders of the kind who typically came under probation supervision.

In the meantime, academic discussion of compliance lent little support to official policy. Readers of this book will be familiar with Bottoms's (2001) typology of four kinds of compliance: instrumental/prudential (to achieve something else which I want, or to avoid something I don't want), normative (because I ought to), constraint-based (because I'm prevented from doing anything else) and habit or routine (because I usually do – I don't really think about it). To these we can add a distinction between formal compliance (sticking to the rules) and substantive compliance (using the Probation Order to make progress toward changed attitudes or behaviour or desired prosocial life goals, and eventually, perhaps, to desistance from offending). Other writers (e.g. Robinson and McNeill 2008) point out that reasons for compliance can be dynamic and change over time. To this we might add that they are non-exclusive and two or more may influence people in combination. It is also argued that over-strict attempts to enforce formal compliance might actually get in the way of substantive compliance, because they cause authorities to appear oppressive and unreasonable. Their expectations and demands have less perceived legitimacy as a result, leading to reductions in normative motivation to comply.

Only a limited amount of research has been carried out to study how these concepts and approaches might operate in the practical business of promoting compliance with community sentences incorporating a supervision requirement (the equivalent of the traditional Probation Order) in England and Wales. Ugwudike's important study of how probation officers try to promote compliance (Ugwudike 2008) shows how probation officers operating in a context of inflexible rules and unhelpful over-regulation make space for the exercise of reasonable discretion by, for example, finding ways round the strict application of the rules. What we still lack, because of the particular history of the issue in England and Wales, are studies showing how policy, management and professional practice might work together to promote compliance. This chapter aims not so much to fill this gap as to show what an appropriate filling might look like. It draws on experience in the Channel Island of Jersey to explore a problem-solving approach to compliance.

The Jersey approach to compliance

The Probation and After-Care Service in Jersey, in the British Channel Islands, is small but highly professional. Jersey is self-governing in most respects, with its own laws (many of them written in a form of mediaeval Norman French) and institutions. Its probation legislation is traditional, dating mainly from the 1930s; its probation officers are mostly qualified in social work, and probation is administered as part of the court system rather than as part of the penal system. (This resembles the situation in England and Wales before the creation of the National Probation Service in 2001 and its absorption into the National Offender Management Service in 2004.) Committed to evidence-based practice and 'What Works', it has been involved in research on probation practice since the mid-1990s (Raynor and Miles 2007) and maintains a good database of information about its activities. The small study which forms the focus of this chapter arose out of a larger research project concerning probation officers' supervision skills (Raynor et al. 2010). It is based on Jersey Probation and After-Care Service (JPACS) policy documents and offender management data, interviews with two probation managers, observation of four compliance-related interviews from the digital video archive collected in the skills study, and, most usefully, interviews with three former probationers who were initially non-compliant and became compliant following specific intervention by JPACS.

The three central building blocks of the Jersey compliance process are guidelines which allow the reasonable use of discretion, a high level of agreement between staff and managers about the right way to treat people, and the use of three-way 'compliance meetings' as a review process before breach action. The guidelines ('Standards and practice issues in relation to Probation supervision', latest version JPACS 2009) cover much the same ground as National Standards in England and Wales, but were produced within the service and discussed with stakeholders such as sentencers, rather than imposed by civil servants or politicians. Two unacceptable missed appointments (which might be appointments with the supervisor or required programme sessions) will trigger a discussion between the supervisor and a senior or assistant chief probation officer about the next step, which could be a warning letter, a compliance meeting with supervisor and manager together, or (exceptionally) breach action straight away. Absences recorded as unacceptable can become acceptable if good reasons are given to and accepted by the probation officer (e.g. uncertified sickness 'where the client's account is believed by the Probation Officer due to the client's encouraging response to supervision' – JPACS 2009). If a warning letter is thought insufficient, or perhaps has already been tried, the probationer will receive a letter from the supervising officer headed 'Notice of Compliance Meeting', which reminds the probationer of the reporting requirement in the Probation Order, states the date and time of the meeting and explains that 'the purpose of the meeting is for you to meet with myself and a manager to discuss ways of improving your progress on probation.' The majority of those who receive this letter attend the meeting, at which the requirements of the Probation Order will be restated and the probationer will be asked to explain any particular difficulties affecting reporting. This also provides an opportunity for the probationer to make a case for continuing the order, and to promise better compliance in future. Finally, the probationer will be told what course of action will follow. This procedure was first adopted in Jersey about ten years ago following the appointment of an officer from Scotland who had experience of a rather similar procedure there, but this bald account does not give the full flavour of the very concrete and realistic discussion, on both sides, which participants describe.

The probation managers' view

One senior manager explained the service's approach to enforcement as follows:

> If we took a different view of probation we could undoubtedly go round now and breach a lot of our clients, but if we did that, within a couple of weeks we would find we had lost our legitimacy with our clients and particularly with the Courts.

In other words, legitimacy in the eyes of both clients (this term is still used for offenders under supervision in Jersey) and sentencers depended on a reasonable exercise of discretion, and the aim is to implement the order fully and, if possible, to achieve its aims and intended effects on and for the probationer: 'The Courts want to know that we have made a real effort before we take anybody back.' The managers who were interviewed in connection with this study were asked to comment particularly on the purpose of the meetings, why they were introduced, how probation policy on matters like enforcement was developed, the process of the meetings and why they were seen as important.

The *purpose* of the meetings was unambiguously to help people to complete their order successfully if at all possible: 'Success is when they complete the work plan, risk is reduced, and they don't re-offend.' 'We wanted to warn people, but also to find out why they were having difficulty, what they might be able to do about it, how we might help. It taught us a lot about the problems in offenders' lives without taking a black-and-white or condemnatory view.'

The *origins* were clearly traced to events some years ago which worried managers: a difficult breach case in the Royal Court (equivalent to a Crown Court in England and Wales) led to the Attorney General asking to review breach cases before they came to Royal Court, and there were also 'concerns in the Magistrates' Court...I wanted to know that we had been fair and reasonable, that there was real legitimacy to the breach, that we had gone the extra mile.' At one time there had been a 'bad atmosphere in the waiting room' and 'some very angry people' due to perceived inconsistency, and 'compliance meetings stopped some breaches which would have been unfair.' Managers were concerned about the possible impact of any perceived unfairness on sentencers and on people likely to come under supervision: 'Most people in compliance meetings are young men with limited stability, limited ability to hold down jobs, limited family support. It's important to be fair because they tend to come back, and they know each other. It's important that the Service is seen to have a reasonable degree of legitimacy.' 'We need to be clear and transparent about what's expected, how much leeway they can be given, and make sure it is followed through.' 'We don't want an offender to say "If I was supervised by another officer this wouldn't have happened".' Although it is up to the supervising officer to judge whether an absence is acceptable, 'differences show up in supervision', and 'with the chaotic users, some will miss one [appointment] but turn up the next day – it may look a bit inconsistent but we try to get them in'. The aim is substantive compliance: 'There has to be some purpose', but lack of substantive compliance is 'harder to evidence' than lack of formal compliance.

Regarding *policy*, it became clear that in Jersey even a significant innovation like compliance meetings was something the service could decide for itself: 'I don't remember the last time there was any question from politicians', 'we are pretty much left alone'. The more important contact was with the courts, through monthly meetings with magistrates, and with other agencies through a variety of inter-agency bodies in which probation managers were very active.

'That's how we find out if something isn't as it should be.' Internal supervision of officers by managers was regular (monthly) and thorough.

The *process* of the meeting normally followed a discussion: 'I would discuss with the officer whether a compliance meeting was needed and what they wanted to come out of it.' 'We could breach after one unacceptable absence but then we wouldn't get people through orders.' Occasionally the meeting can arise from poor behaviour rather than absences (e.g. 'turning up drunk to programme sessions'). In the meeting, 'It works better if I'm not the angry head teacher...we have to look at how to make this order work.' 'I sometimes get out the order and ask them to read it: sometimes we find out about problems with basic skills that way.' The focus is on developing a work plan to make the rest of the order viable. Most people will be offered a compliance meeting before breach (though 'maybe not on a follow-on order' where somebody has already recently breached an order and been given a last chance by the court) and if compliance continues to be unacceptable after a meeting 'the report [to the court] will say there was a meeting'.

The general style in which managers discussed compliance can be illustrated from some of the interviews in the archive of video-recorded interviews collected for the Jersey Supervision Skills Study. For example, a meeting with a young man with a patchy record of missed appointments starts with a reminder of requirements, followed by 'What happened yesterday that you were unable to come in?' This elicits an account of how another family member was assaulted and the resulting problems needed to be dealt with urgently. The interviewer waits for answers, does not lecture and uses open-ended questions. A large part of the interview is devoted to encouraging the probationer to review what he has achieved during the order, with strongly expressed approval for prosocial developments and a very clear explanation of what is compulsory and what is voluntary in the Probation Order. For example, the probationer is involved in a voluntary basic skills project which is not a requirement of the order, but he is finding it useful and likes his volunteer tutor: he needs to be reminded that she is a volunteer and 'if you miss too many sessions you will lose your tutor'. However, where appointments with the probation officer are concerned 'you've got no choice mate. I know X [the supervising officer] hates taking people back to Court but he will' (probationer replies smiling 'Yeah I know'). The interviewer ends by noting with approval that the probationer has not been in trouble ('I hear you are not on the police radar at the moment') and giving written instructions for the next appointment. One of a number of important facts to emerge in this interview is that the probationer has never learned to read a clock face and tell the time, which he is only now getting to grips with in his basic skills course. Clearly there is some way to go before he will be putting the next appointment in his diary as the English civil servant proposed. Throughout the interview there is a positive emphasis on the benefits of probation and on the good progress made so far. The tone is friendly, there is complete clarity about requirements and the probationer does most of the talking.

The probationers' view

Most illuminating of all were the interviews carried out for this study with three probationers who had completed their orders successfully following attendance at compliance meetings and volunteered to come to the probation office to be interviewed. Obviously this is not a representative sample, since they are self-selected from among the successful completers; however, their accounts are interesting and certain themes emerge consistently. They were asked to comment, among other things, on what they thought was the purpose of probation; on why they were regarded at first as non-compliant; on their experience of the compliance meeting itself, which they all remembered; on how they went on to complete their orders successfully; and, finally, on what they thought of the probation service generally. All of them had considerable experience of the penal system, including community sentences and imprisonment. The quotations below are taken from all three, and give a flavour of the range of views as well as the areas of agreement.

The purposes of probation: 'It's to try to help you to find your way out of where you are now.' 'It's to help try to keep you out of trouble – but I don't really think it did that for me . . . I gave yes and no answers so I'd be out quicker.' 'They ask about family and this and that – some people may enjoy these conversations and come to feel they need them.'

Being non-compliant: 'I missed appointments when I was young. You're a bit more all over the place. I genuinely forgot or I was out with the lads.' 'I did intend to comply. I started missing appointments when I realized I could.' 'You say yes in court because it gets you a bit of time. If you say no it's rude and cheeky to the judge . . . you say yes thinking you are going to do it.' 'I had a lot of health problems, very tired, sleeping on the beach, sleeping on floors. I didn't miss the appointments on purpose. One or two times I could have turned up but I was so tired through lack of sleep. Sometimes I turned up when there wasn't anyone to see me. [Question: "Were some of these what they call unacceptable absences?"] Well they thought they was.' 'I was on a course probation put me on, I was up and down, I missed a few. I would come home and fall asleep after work.' 'I was on drugs and drink and all sorts of stuff.'

The compliance meeting: 'We sat down, they said we don't think this is working, you are missing appointments, we are thinking it needs to go back to court. They didn't say prison, but that they would ask for another method. We managed to come to an agreement on one more chance, and I did it.' 'I didn't put it to the test. When you are sitting there with your probation officer and the chief, and they tell you it's your last chance, if you don't turn up to the meeting after that then I think you're finished.' 'I went to the meeting with my probation officer and one of the top people. It was about whether to keep me on probation or take me back to court.' 'When I did the compliance meeting they were going to send me back to court but I gave them a good enough reason not to. They asked me why should we give you another chance. They put me on another course [i.e., programme] and I completed it without missing any.' 'These meetings are a good idea because you can get your point across, explain your reasons. If you go to court you don't get a chance to put your point across. When you're in court you basically shut up.' [What did you say to the probation officers?] 'I met my partner and it's made me realize things I didn't know before, and it's made me change. I want to prove that I will complete the courses and stay out of prison... People come out of prison and they have all that confidence that things will work out, but it doesn't work out and they go back.'

Completing the order successfully: 'My life's more in order.' 'I knew I had to come in because I wanted the job.' 'I got on a course. They put the appointments to different times to fit with the course, and then with the job. You can drop to less frequent if you attend. [They told you that in the meeting?] Yes, which I think is fair.' 'I got a job opportunity – I didn't want to go to prison and miss out.' 'I didn't want to lose my home if I went to prison. Now I'm in college.' 'I started thinking because of the course... if you know you will get a last chance you will push it until you get the last chance.' 'I've got this computer course, I really enjoy it... I think [I started reporting] because they actually got me interested in something – they got me on this computer course.' 'I found the last bit of the Probation Order, when I got focused into the course, it was easier because I got more into a routine.' 'I'd met a girl and it started to change my life. From the age of seven I was always in trouble, it was a life I liked and didn't like, if you know what I mean... now she's expecting.' [Why comply?] 'It keeps you out of trouble and you get a bit of help.'

The Probation Service in general: 'They help you out with lots of things. I can trust [my probation officer]. If you have one you are not keen on, you just come in and talk rubbish and go.' 'They are polite, not rude, not nasty. I've never had them write anything false about me. I think they told me the truth... and you get your chance, or chances.' 'I would say they are fair.'

The outcomes of compliance meetings

From the documents and interviews reviewed above, it appears that the compliance meeting process as practised in Jersey is seen by probation managers, and at least some of the probationers who undergo it, as helpful and useful. It allows discussion, it provides an opportunity for the probation service to restate the purposes of probation and review progress, it allows space for the probationer to state a point of view, and sometimes it helps people to refocus on their own goals and what they hope to achieve. It is particularly striking that probationers feel able, and encouraged, to 'make a case' for another opportunity to make the order work, in contrast with the court situation where 'you basically shut up.' So, given these perceived advantages, is it successful in reducing the need to take probationers back to court for breach of probation and possible resentencing? In particular, how do the results of Jersey's discussion-based approach compare with the more coercive approach to enforcement which has been encouraged on the mainland of England and Wales?

Comparisons between Jersey and the mainland are not straightforward, partly because the recording of probation data is in many respects more thorough and reliable in Jersey. As Robinson and Ugwudike (2012) point out, figures on prosecutions for breach of community sentences have not been published in England and Wales for any year since 2004, for reasons which have never been made entirely clear. In Jersey, on the other hand, we know that, out of 109 Probation Orders terminated in 2011, 72 per cent were satisfactory terminations. The satisfactory completion rate for all community sentences in England and Wales is 67 per cent (Ministry of Justice 2012a). Of the 109 orders terminated in Jersey, 30 had been back to court at some stage for poor compliance, but 17 of these were allowed to continue. The unsatisfactory terminations were 13, who received other sentences after their orders were discharged for non-compliance and 17 whose orders were terminated due to further offences.

If we concentrate on compliance meetings, 24 people were offered compliance meetings on the grounds that their behaviour (usually failure to keep appointments) was putting them at risk of a return to court for breach. (Some of them had already been to court during their probation and their orders had been allowed to continue.) Of the 24, 21 attended their meetings, and 17 of these subsequently complied and completed their orders satisfactorily. Four returned to court and received other sentences, as did the three who did not attend their meetings. Although the numbers are small, it may be helpful to think in percentage terms: 81 per cent of those who attended compliance interviews completed satisfactorily. It should be noted that this is not a lenient system which condones non-compliance: indeed, the threshold for attending a compliance meeting in Jersey may well be lower in practice than the threshold for breach action in England and Wales, where less drastic options are not available and we know that rule-bending occurs. In Jersey quite frequent reporting is required and unacceptable failures are not ignored, but the system is geared to achieving substantive compliance and dealing constructively with non-compliance. The problem-solving approach to compliance is also reflected in the behaviour of the Jersey courts: 28 per cent of the Probation Orders terminated in 2011 had been involved in breach proceedings in court at some point, with a report from the probation service, but fewer than half of these actually resulted in discharge of the order and substitution of a more severe sentence. In England and Wales a 37 per cent breach rate was recorded in 2004, and sentencers were obliged by the 2003 Criminal Justice Act to respond to any breach with a more severe sentence.

Although no figures are now published, it is likely that punitive enforcement of community sentences has passed its peak in England and Wales. In contrast to the 'two strikes and you're out' position adopted in the 2000 National Standards (which were rumoured to have been subject to a politician's personal input at the drafting stage) and the requirement that all absences are unacceptable until proved otherwise, the 2007 National Standards allowed the 'offender manager' to 'form a view' about the reasonableness of the supervised person's explanation or 'excuse'. The most recent National Standards issued in 2011 completely avoid prescribing how the sentence should be enforced, though this may be an invitation for Probation Trusts and other supervising agencies to develop their own guidelines rather than a blank cheque for unlimited practitioner discretion. It is not clear yet what results this will have, or, indeed, how we will find out what the results are. Meanwhile, politicians are still addicted to demonstrations of 'toughness' in their handling of probation, but the latest proposals shift the emphasis from tough enforcement to the inclusion of punitive content within every community sentence (Ministry of Justice 2012b).

Conclusion: Tough or fair?

The Jersey model offers an alternative to the traditional dichotomy of prescribed toughness versus unfettered and inconsistent practitioner discretion. Responses to non-compliance are reasonably consistent, leading in most cases to discussion and restatement of the probation contract and a return to compliance. This seems clearly preferable to a wasteful proliferation of prosecutions and failed community sentences, or to turning a blind eye to practitioners' continuing use of discretion. It also has the advantage of presenting the probation service to non-compliant probationers as a reasonable, fair and responsive authority that is interested in what they have to say. Now that punitive enforcement is no longer a strict requirement in England and Wales, this kind of approach might help to promote compliance.

In relation to the theoretical models summarized at the beginning of this chapter, this small-scale study shows probation staff making a clear distinction between formal and substantive compliance, and regarding the latter as more important. They clearly also take the view that over-rigorous enforcement of formal compliance would obstruct substantive compliance by reducing the proportion of completed orders and reducing the perceived legitimacy of the service in the eyes of both courts and offenders. This, they thought, could happen quite rapidly: as everyone said, 'It's a small island.' From the probationers' point of view, compliance was mainly presented as instrumental, sometimes becoming habit or routine. The cost of non-compliance would be damage to valued relationships or opportunities, much as proposed by control theories (Hirschi 1969), and compliance meetings sometimes provided an opportunity to think about these costs and to decide not to risk them. Positive goals were important, and it could be worth the (considerable) effort of complying in order to achieve them. In some cases it appeared that the probation service had been involved in creating or facilitating some of these valued opportunities.

The interviewed probationers also knew the difference between formal compliance ('just turning up') and substantive compliance: they knew the Probation Order was there to help them to 'sort out' their lives, and were prepared to engage with this if they got on well with their probation officer, and if they believed they needed that kind of help. They complied when compliance had a purpose. In general, probation officers were seen as truthful, reasonable, polite and 'fair', and as genuinely trying to help, although some problems were seen as too big for their help to be effective. Overall, everybody mentioned fairness: according to the probation managers, trigger-happy enforcement was 'unfair' because it failed to take into account the difficulties which led to people being on probation in the first place. From both a moral and an instrumental point of view, the pursuit of fairness and the solution of problems were seen as preferable to a display of toughness, and the results tend to support this choice.

References

Bottoms, A. E. (2001) 'Compliance with Community Penalties'. in A. E. Bottoms, L. Gelsthorpe and S. Rex (Eds) *Community Penalties: Change and Challenges*. Cullompton: Willan.

Ellis, T., Hedderman, C. and Mortimer, E. (1996) *Enforcing Community Sentences*. Home Office Research Study 158. London: Home Office.

Hearnden, I. and Millie, A. (2004) 'Does Tougher Enforcement Lead to Lower Reconviction?' *Probation Journal* 51(1), 48–58.

Her Majesty's Inspectorate of Probation (1995) *Dealing with Dangerous People: The Probation Service and Public Protection*. London: Home Office.

Hirschi, T. (1969) *Causes of Delinquency*. Berkeley and Los Angeles: University of California Press.

Home Office. (1992) *National Standards for the Supervision of Offenders in the Community*. London: Home Office.

Home Office. (2000) *National Standards for the Supervision of Offenders in the Community*. London: Home Office.

Jersey Probation and After-Care Service. (2009) *Standards and Practice Issues Relating to Probation Supervision*. St Helier: JPACS.

Ministry of Justice. (2011) *National Standards for the Management of Offenders*. London: Ministry of Justice.

Ministry of Justice. (2012a) *Offender Management Statistics (Quarterly) April-June 2012*. London: Ministry of Justice.

Ministry of Justice. (2012b) *Punishment and Reform: Effective Community Sentences*. Consultation Paper CP8/2012; Cm 8334. London: The Stationery Office.

National Offender Management Service. (2007) *National Standards for the Management of Offenders*. London: National Offender Management Service.

Raynor, P. and Miles, H. (2007) 'Evidence-Based Probation in a Microstate: The British Channel Island of Jersey'. *European Journal of Criminology* 4(3), 299–313.

Raynor, P., Ugwudike, P. and Vanstone, M. (2010) 'Skills and Strategies in Probation Supervision: The Jersey Study'. in F. McNeill, P. Raynor and C. Trotter (Eds) *Offender Supervision: New Directions in Theory, Research and Practice* (pp. 113–129). Abingdon: Willan.

Robinson, G. and McNeill, F. (2008) 'Exploring the Dynamics of Compliance with Community Penalties'. *Theoretical Criminology* 12(4), 431–449.

Robinson, G. and Ugwudike, P. (2012) 'Investing in "Toughness": Probation, Enforcement and Legitimacy'. *Howard Journal of Criminal Justice* 51(3), 300–316.

Ugwudike, P. (2008) 'Developing an Effective Mechanism for Encouraging Compliance with Community Penalties', unpublished PhD thesis, Swansea University.

8
Compliance in Prisons

Ben Crewe

Discussions of compliance often take for granted that it is something desirable. But we do not need to spend much time consuming prison film and literature to sense a deep ambivalence about rule-abidance and rule-breaking, and an intuitive concern that compliance within prison might bear little relationship to psychological health or future prospects. Some of our most celebrated cinematic heroes – for example, McMurphy in *One Flew Over the Cuckoo's Nest*, and Andy Dufresne in *The Shawshank Redemption* – are men who have railed against authority in the name of justice, or have escaped institutions of confinement either in spirit or in person. Just as tellingly, in both films, we see the perils of total compliance, in the form of characters whose absolute submission to the demands and rituals of institutional life makes them unable to function outside the boundaries of their confinement (or, at least, fearful of this possibility). As McNeill and Robinson suggest (above), there is no straightforward relationship between short-term institutional compliance – which I will argue, in the prison, is often equated with 'obedience' – and longer-term legal compliance (or 'desistance'), which can at best be a subject of informed conjecture during the period of imprisonment.

In the first sections of this chapter, I briefly detail recent theoretical explorations of compliance, and provide some comment on how these accounts bear relevance to the prison. I then go on to provide an empirical typology of prisoner compliance, derived from a study of a medium security prison in England and Wales, which draws on and fleshes out the conceptual distinctions outlined in the earlier section.

Theorizing compliance

Nellis (2013: 166) defines compliance as the 'willing alignment of one's behaviour, however begrudging, with the prohibitions of a penal or civic authority', and, in recent years, a number of frameworks have been offered for thinking about the nature and dynamics of compliance (e.g. Bottoms 2001; McNeill and Robinson 2013; Nellis 2006). Although different in their details, these frameworks share some basic properties. First, they distinguish between different forms of compliance, noting that compliant behaviour may be underpinned by very different attitudes and motivations. It may be *normative*, based on moral acceptance of, or commitment to, the institutions or regulations at stake, or on a sense of allegiance or attachment to individuals who represent the authorities or are 'significant others' in our lives. It may also be based on recognizing the right of those in power to exercise their authority (legitimacy). An alternative form of compliance is *instrumental*, based on incentives and rewards or disincentives and deterrents. Compliance can also be *habitual* or *fatalistic*, based on routines or conventions, or a sense that there is no alternative but to 'do things this way'. Finally, it may be *constraint-based* or *coercive*, based on physical control, surveillance, restriction or fear. Thus, a citizen might drive below the motorway speed limit for a range of underlying reasons: because they are committed to the laws of the land or think that 70 miles per hour constitutes a sensible threshold (normative); because their wife, whom they love, or their probation officer, whom they trust, does not want them to speed (normative (significant other)); or because, despite their personal view that the limit should be 80, they accept that the state has the moral right to set it at a lower point – a view that is reinforced when those in authority are fair and respectful in their normal dealings with the public (normative (legitimacy)); because they cannot afford a speeding fine, do not want points on their licence, or have been promised ten pounds by their passenger if they remain within the law (instrumental); because they are used to driving at this speed or just accept that everyone else does too (habitual/fatalistic); or because their car has been disabled from going above the limit, because the amount of traffic prevents them from going any faster, because they are aware of a patrol car in their wing mirror, or because they live in terror of going too fast and/or being stopped by the police (constraint-based/coercive).

In practice, these mechanisms inter-relate in complex ways, so that – for example – rewards may be used to 'train' people into habitual compliance, and people may be both committed to and scared of their partner at the same time. More important for current purposes is that this range of mechanisms highlights the potential inconsistency between attitudes and behaviour. People who criticize and complain about the authorities may be no less compliant in practice, or, indeed, in their general disposition to underlying norms, than those who do not. Meanwhile, formally compliant behaviour may conceal attitudes that are cynical and hostile, as well as backstage activities that are highly deceptive or non-compliant (Braithwaite 2003; Crewe 2009). Here, the important distinction is between *formal* and *substantive* compliance, the former denoting behaviour which meets official criteria of compliance in a superficial or merely technical sense (e.g. simply turning up to specified probation appointments), and the latter suggesting an active and sincere engagement with the true purposes of the sanction (e.g. turning up to specified appointments with a genuine will to make amends and move one's life forwards). Whereas formal compliance is more likely to last for only as long as the sanction or sentence is being enforced, substantive compliance (what might be called 'commitment') is more likely to generate *longer-term* compliance with social and legal norms (see Bottoms 2001).

Formal compliance is relatively easy to measure, but, as Crawford (2013: 192) notes, it is 'an output indicator rather than a social outcome, as it is defined more by the exigencies of the regulatory regime rather than by the activities, conduct or values of the subjects of regulation'. Thus, formal compliance is not a stable entity, but is defined as such by those with the power to label action. Much of the work of criminal justice practitioners involves precisely this kind of discretionary judgement: the evaluation and ongoing negotiation of whether certain activities merit official attention and sanction. In the United Kingdom, the apparent non-compliance of female prisoners, as measured by disciplinary charges, may say more about how this group is policed than about its behaviour or underlying attitudes. Meanwhile, the same behaviour can be judged as compliant or non-compliant, or can be deemed as actionable or ignorable, in different contexts as well as by different personnel (Robinson and McNeill 2008). Thus, in apartheid era prisons in South Africa, the pursuit of education was considered highly subversive (Buntman 2003), while in contemporary prisons in the United Kingdom it is more likely to be viewed as a mark of commitment to institutional ends. In sum, then, compliance cannot be understood outside the wider context in which behaviour is defined and policed.

Compliance and the prison

Most of the recent theoretical reflection and empirical research on compliance has occurred outside the domain of prison studies. Tyler's body of work is primarily focused on interactions between free citizens and police or courts, while, in the United Kingdom, considerations of compliance have mainly been grounded in studies of community penalties (Bottoms 2001; McNeill and Robinson 2013; although see Bottoms 2003). Sparks et al.'s (1996) *Prisons and the Problem of Order* offers a sophisticated analysis of legitimacy and order within prisons, but the focus here is collective order rather than individual compliance; likewise, Liebling's (2004) work on 'moral performance' advances our understanding of what constitutes a legitimate prison, but does not specifically address questions of how institutional conditions might generate differential responses among individual prisoners. These studies build on an established

sociological literature which demonstrates that such things as prisoner violence are shaped by regime factors, rather than being the simple reflection
of disruptive or violent personalities (see Cooke 1991 and Bottoms 1999 for
summaries; and also DiLulio 1990; Reisig 1998). And, while a number of studies have been conducted on forms of prisoner resistance (e.g. Bosworth 1999;
McEvoy 2001; Buntman 2003; and see Crewe 2009), far less has been written
on the dynamics of prisoner compliance. It is important, therefore, to think
through the ways that prisons differ from other criminal justice contexts in
regard to these issues.

First, the mechanisms of compliance noted in the previous section have different forms and meanings than in community settings. In some very obvious
ways, prisons can make much greater use of constraint-based forms of compliance. Thus, while McNeill and Robinson (2013: 132) note that there is no
'definable form of architecture' in community sanctions, prisons are specifically
designed to locate individuals in particular spaces and prevent their movement
beyond them. In addition, prisons can make use of a host of direct constraints –
control and restraint techniques, segregation, or transfer to another establishment – in order to ensure certain basic forms of compliance. In the super-max
prison in the United States, one finds the exemplary form of situational and
coercive control. Prisoners are almost completely isolated from each other, and
can only leave their cells while cuffed and shackled in various ways (King 2005).
Coercive measures of this kind are generally a provocative, expensive and inefficient means of running a complex institution, and their impact on prisoners
is egregious (Haney 2005). However, as a 'final persuader' (Wrong 2002: 26),
coercion can be a powerful threat ('you can walk yourself to the segregation
unit, or we can walk you there . . . '). Indeed, warnings about the possible uses of
power – the potential for evening association to be cancelled 'if we get any more
litter out of the windows', or for informal perks to be removed 'if you don't
clear this mess up *now*' – are routinely used in prisons to enforce compliant
behaviour.

The potency of incentives and disincentives is also shaped by the institutional context. In his classic treatise on prison order, Sykes (1958) questioned
the idea that rewards and punishments were effective means of inducing
inmate compliance. Few meaningful rewards were available, he argued, while
little could be done to worsen the prisoner's circumstances. Rational-choice
models of prisoner behaviour are flawed for other reasons. The very fact that
incentives and disincentives have an official status may undermine or invert
their intended impact: being punished can become a badge of honour, while
being rewarded by the institution can draw stigma. This is all the more likely
in prisons than in other contexts, because of the way that anti-authority values
circulate among prisoners and are embedded in the 'inmate code'. Meanwhile,
rewards may have limited influence because (some) prisoners seek to avoid

becoming dependent on them or because they regard them with suspicion (Crawford 2013; Ericson 1975), as suggested in the following descriptions of the prison's incentives and earned privileges scheme:

> [The prison's] saying to you, 'we'll give you that but you've got to do this for us'. [...] They give you so much now, but they only give you things which they can take back off you. [...] All this 'enhanced', 'standard', 'basic', it's a good thing in the long run because prison did need this change, where they gave you a bit more. But the prison system will only give you stuff which they can take away from you.
>
> (Carter)

> These tellies, these associations, the bit of canteen they do give you: experience has taught me not to let them use it as a tool to influence me.
>
> (Tommy)

As Emery (1970) notes, measures that the prison authorities regard as 'improvements', worthy of better behaviour, may be seen by prisoners as only a partial remedy for poor conditions, and therefore hardly grounds for grateful compliance. Some of the other reasons why incentives and disincentives may not work as intended reflect problems with the rational-choice paradigm (see Liebling et al. 1997; Bottoms 2003), which assumes that people are self-interested calculators of personal utility. Yet, as Crawford (2013) highlights, compliance requires certain kinds of competences, which many people do not possess. Due to mental health problems, learning difficulties or cognitive limitations, for example, prisoners may not understand incentive schemes or may just find it difficult to conform to their demands, however much they wish to. Even prisoners who have no such problems often find that, given the stresses and strains of prison life, it can be difficult to conform to basic norms of conduct (see below). Others may be more influenced by religious beliefs or family commitments than by material enticements – hence, apparently irrational actions like hunger strikes and dirty protests (McEvoy 2001). The degree to which incentives have 'bite' is thus highly dependent on a range of factors that cannot easily be explained within a simple, rational-choice framework.

At the same time, it is easy to see why – because of the particularities of the environment – incentives and disincentives can matter enormously in determining prisoner compliance. Since prisoners are deprived of many conventional forms of status and comfort, items and opportunities that are of minor importance in the outside world – an extra pouch of tobacco, the chance to wear one's own clothes, the promise of a paintbrush or magazine – can become major preoccupations (Mathiesen 1965). Here, one prisoner explains the importance to him of having in-cell television, while another describes the way that imprisonment magnifies the significance of 'small things':

> [TV] makes a phenomenal difference. Phenomenal. [...] Yeah, it helps the time go, it eases the time. [...] it eases the tension out of the brain. [...] It matters very much. It's very important, because it makes my time easier, it takes me off an aggression mood.
>
> (Colin)

> You play cards and that, you play for Mars Bars. You get excited, 'oh yes, I'm owed five Mars Bars!' It's pathetic really, but it's just the way it is. If you were on the out, five Mars Bars is nothing. It's like the littlest things mean a lot more to you. It's like – £2.50 – if you dropped £2.50 it wouldn't bother you. But in jail, £2.50 is a packet of burn [tobacco]. Small things become really important.
>
> (Rhys)

As Goffman (1961) notes, these are the levers around which the institution reshapes inmate identity and behaviour. Incentives which entail a taste or glimpse of freedom are all the more potent, as I discuss further below.

Given the rarity and difficulty of escape, the sense that one is powerless to alter one's general predicament is almost completely realistic (Carrabine 2005). Fatalism is, therefore, a component of almost every prisoner's reasons for certain forms of compliance. Most prisoners do not bother to check whether the locks, bolts and bars of their cells are unyielding; they are simply resigned to the unbreachable nature of their surroundings. This sense of fatalism is reinforced by a range of symbolic reminders of the relative powerlessness of the prisoner relative to the institution, from the ritual degradation of reception procedures (Garfinkel 1956; Goffman 1961) to the ongoing presence of surveillance cameras, drug dogs and high, stark walls. The term 'institutionalization' and its more specific form 'prisonization' (Clemmer 1940) highlight the way in which the daily customs and routines of prison life may, in the end, become completely internalized. This certainly does not mean that prisoners do not engage in all kinds of forms of minor dissent and resistance – indeed, it may be the case that they do so all the more because of the need to claw back some sense of power and control – or that some do not attempt much more radical challenges to penal power and logic, in the form of escape attempts and riots. What it emphasizes is the distinctive role of habit and resignation in prison, both in limiting the frequency of full-frontal assaults on institutional power and in the daily and complex reproduction of penal order (see Carrabine 2005; Sparks et al. 1996).

It is easy to assume that normative factors play little role in securing prisoner compliance. Sykes, for example, argued that prisoners lacked any 'inner moral compulsion to obey' (1958: 48), and it seems improbable that prisoners will willingly assent to being locked up. As I suggest below, however, such assumptions underestimate the degree to which some prisoners feel deep shame about their crimes and behaviour, so that, although very few truly wish to be in prison, a good number express a form of moral or ideological commitment toward the aims of the institution. Likewise, while critical penologists have emphasized the structural features of imprisonment, such as its profoundly undemocratic character, which make legitimacy almost impossible to achieve (Scraton et al. 1991), it is equally clear that prisoners regard some prisons as more legitimate than others. Where prisoners feel that their treatment is humane and respectful, and where the regime is considered legal, decent and consistent, for example, they are more likely to accept the demands of the institution, even when these clash with their personal wishes (see Liebling 2004; Sparks et al. 1996). Despite the gulf that is typically found between the norms and preferences of the institution and those it holds, there is generally a shared moral framework to which both parties can agree – albeit tentatively and conditionally. The commonly heard expression, among both prisoners and staff, that 'if you treat them with respect, they treat you with respect' bears witness to this possibility.

A second, salient way in which prisons differ from other criminal justice context relates to their fundamental concern with matters of order and security. Rehabilitation may be one of the primary purposes of sentencing, and one of the main aims of imprisonment, yet alongside this is a more fundamental need for the prison to maintain and reproduce itself as a total institution (i.e. an institution in which all aspects of life are lived; Goffman 1961). As a result, prison officers, in particular, operate with a daily time horizon (Liebling et al. 2011), in which such matters as making sure that prisoners are fed, maintaining a clean and tidy wing, and ensuring that prisoners are in the right places at the right times are of paramount importance. Accordingly, uniformed staff tend to define non-compliance in relation to forms of behaviour which threaten either the smooth accomplishment of everyday tasks (what we might label 'disruption') or the underlying basis of staff authority (what we might call 'challenge'). Thus, a prisoner who is always late getting up in the morning or who repeatedly fails to submit her meal slip on time is non-compliant in a different way from a prisoner who deliberately sets off a fire alarm or ignores an order to go to his cell at the end of the prison day. Officers may recognize that there is a difference between such behaviours in terms of levels of wilfulness and defiance, but they may nonetheless bracket together both kinds of prisoner as 'difficult' or 'non-compliant' because each is a threat to the underlying stability of the institution.

Yet prisoners do not need to represent a threat to the *overall* order of the prison in order to be considered non-compliant. As Bosworth (1996: 8) notes,

'Women's prisons are rarely perceived to be disordered; yet, female prisoners often seem to be far from compliant.' Most non-compliance in prisons appears relatively minor, taking form in assertions about such issues as food, personal appearance and identity (Bosworth 1999; Bosworth and Carrabine 2001), or in attempts to prevent incursions of power against self-identity and personal dignity (Ugelvik 2011; Rowe 2011). In women's prisons especially, the preoccupation among prison staff with matters such as the cleanliness of cells and personal hygiene may reflect the policing and imposition of certain versions of feminine propriety. But the potential for such apparently trivial issues to become battlegrounds between prisoners and staff also points to their symbolic, moral and practical significance. Even when non-compliance of this kind poses no risk to collective order, it is laden with meaning about who holds power and who controls the environment. And, because order in prisons is always fragile – staff are outnumbered by prisoners, and prisons may drift in and out of states that are somewhat precarious (Carrabine 2005) – it is never clear which events might puncture the fabric of stability. It takes little, therefore, for prisoners and staff to find themselves in mutually reinforcing relations of non-compliance.

In order to be seen by uniformed staff as compliant, then, prisoners need to be, at the very least, *obedient*. Yet, as indicated above, obedience to the daily demands of institutional life may have little relation to either *substantive* or *long-term* compliance. This is partly to say that adjustment to prison life may be dysfunctional in many ways for life after release (see Maruna and Toch 2005). Learning to be passive, subservient or accepting the status of being 'an offender' may weaken the capacity to go straight (see Maruna and LeBel 2003), whereas having a strong sense of agency, optimism and self-worth – with all that goes with it, in terms of defiance of petty rules and illegitimate treatment – may strengthen it. The appeal of the prison rebel comes not from their resistance, as such, but from their strength and spirit in the face of institutional might and injustice. Here, Goodstein's (1979: 265–266) conclusion is worth quoting at length:

> It appears that the prison, like the traditional mental hospital, does not prepare inmates for a successful transition to freedom through its routine administration of rewards and punishments. It is ironic that institutionalized inmates who accepted the basic structure of the prison, who were well adjusted to the routine, and who held more desirable prison jobs – in essence, those whom some might call model prisoners – had most difficulty adjusting to the outside world. Even more ironic is the fact that inmates who might have been called the troublemakers in prison seemed to have the fewest problems after release. . . . In the process of rewarding acquiescent and compliant behaviour, the prison may, in fact, be reinforcing institutional

dependence [while] it is possible that the rebellious inmates, the group scoring highest on the prisonization scale, adapted more easily to the outside world because they had maintained their autonomy and decision-making ability throughout their prison terms.

Goodstein's findings have been corroborated in several other studies (see Ditchfield 1990: 43–44 for a summary). Ward (1987: 94), for example, found that 'inmates with a moderate number of disciplinary reports... are more likely to succeed [post-release] than inmates with under five reports or those with more than ten reports.' Maruna and Mann (2006), writing about offence denial, note that various forms of non-compliance with the demands of treatment regimes might be positive indicators of the potential for desistance. There are all kinds of defensible and rational reasons why prisoners might reject the discourse of cognitive–behavioural therapy, while excuse-making is normal, often accurate (in that there generally are mitigating factors for offending), and may be beneficial for future outcomes, in helping offenders to relieve anxiety, maintain self-esteem and protect themselves from damaging forms of shame and stigma. Whether or not desistance from crime occurs *to spite* the authorities, it can certainly occur *in spite* of in-prison behaviour which is considered non-compliant.

Third, then, it is worth noting the sheer difficulty of measuring compliance in prison in a meaningful way. It goes without saying that, in relation to *long-term* compliance (or future desistance), it is logically impossible to do anything more than develop actuarial models which predict future behaviour. In terms of *short-term* compliance, though, the 'total' nature of the environment means that it is harder to know how to specify a unit measure of compliance. Whereas, in the community, metrics such as hours of 'community payback' work or attendance at supervisor meetings serve as rudimentary indicators of compliance, such measures of 'presence' are even less meaningful in prisons, where absence is more or less impossible. Mandatory drug tests provide a measure of compliance that is somewhat similar, since they are based on a specific moment in time, but, in most respects, compliance in prison is a matter that is ongoing and all-encompassing. As explained by a prisoner in the following quotation, all aspects of conduct are consequential for prisoners' privilege level and, therefore, their quality of life:

> ...it's all tied in. Like there's a notice out there, 'don't fill a bucket from the hot water tap or you get a strike.' You get three strikes, you're knocked down a level, you might lose your TV, [or] a couple of visits. Right down to the slightest little thing, it's all tied in to your behaviour. So right down to the sort of tiniest sort of forms of behaviour, it's all monitored; it's all tied in to your future.

For prisoners who need to demonstrate that they are addressing their offending behaviour or reducing their level of risk in order to be granted some form of early, temporary or eventual release (which excludes only those serving short sentences), the task is not only to keep to the rules, but, in effect, to demonstrate through *current* behaviour the likelihood of substantive compliance *in the future*. Thus, there is an expectation of compliance at multiple levels and to multiple institutional audiences: everyday obedience to the daily rules and regulations, policed primarily by uniformed staff; and an imperative to project to wing staff and forensic psychologists (the practitioners who undertake risk assessments and contribute significantly to prisoner reports) a certain kind of prospective persona. As prisoners describe, this compliance mechanism functions rather like a panoptical gaze (Foucault 1977):

> You might not think you're even being watched, but y'know, they watch and reports are written about you, and you don't even realize they're being written about you and if you're up for parole and whatever, they'll keep a special watch on you to see how you are on the wing, how you are with other prisoners, how you are with staff [...] there's reports written about you all the time.
>
> (Danny)

Such a description is redolent of Nellis's (2006: 104) definition of surveillance-based compliance as something which instils:[1]

> an awareness of immediate, here-and-now regulation as a result of being perpetually or intermittently watched, close up or at a distance, with one's trails and traces retrievable from databases.

As I have described elsewhere (see Crewe 2009, 2011a, 2011b), for prisoners, this expectation both of current obedience and of compliance to a nebulously defined projection of a future desisting self is highly demanding. In most social situations, 'ordinary' behaviour tends to elicit neither positive nor negative sanctions (Ellickson 1991), yet, given the deprivations and antagonisms of the environment, it could be argued that prisoners should be rewarded simply for managing to get through the day *without* breaking rules or losing their heads. Instead, as prisoners often note, prisons tend to be environments where negatives (or 'deficits') are picked up on more quickly than positives (or 'strengths'), and where 'proving' change can be extremely difficult:

> They might, in a year, say 'his attitude's changed.' But they'll still have the bad comments [in your file]. [And] what real good can you do in here? You turn up to work on time, you're polite, tidy, your cell's clean. Little things

like that aren't on your file. But 'he spoke to me out of hand at the servery,' they'll pick up on that. Then when you go for a home leave, or [recategorization], or even a good job, they'll pull this magic file out with all the bad comments in it.

(Tyler)

You have one minor incident and they'll go write it in the file. That's gonna catch up with you in two or three years' time: a silly little incident, every few months, a minor indiscretion. But you add them all together and they show a pattern of something that's not really there. What do they expect? That you're gonna get up every morning smiling and happy? You're in prison. You've just got the hump, or you've slept badly.

(Alexis)

Fifth, it is relevant that the prison is a place where people live, semi-permanently, both watching and under the watch of the authorities. Tyler (2013: 19) notes, in relation to policing, that 'every contact socializes people because it communicates information about the legitimacy of the law and legal authorities. This is true both of personal encounters and of indirect experiences that occur when people learn about police behaviour from friends, family or the media.' But, while citizens have only fleeting and occasional contact with the police, or have only regular contact with probation staff, their contact with officers on their residential units is intimate and sustained (Liebling 2000) – more fully 'relational' than in any other criminal justice context. The nature of imprisonment thus amplifies the importance of these interactions and relationships. Information about how others are treated travels quickly, which makes issues of fairness particularly significant (see Bottoms 1999); and, when staff are perceived to be using their power unfairly or disrespectfully, the fact that prisoners remain subject to their authority exacerbates the impact of substandard treatment on legitimacy and, thus, compliance.

Meanwhile, prisoners are forced to live alongside each other, which impacts on their behaviour in ways that are different from most other criminal justice settings. They posture and perform to their peers, as well as to the authorities, meaning that that there are two fairly immediate audiences for (and therefore determinants of) compliant or non-compliant behaviour. They have a distinctive collective stake in, and influence upon, each other's conduct, because the behaviour of their fellow prisoners has such a significant impact on their own quality of life and behaviour. If a prisoner's neighbour is non-compliant by playing his or her music at excessive volume, s/he is an irritation; if s/he is non-compliant by fighting on the landings, his or her behaviour risks drawing the attention of staff to prisoners' semi-private zones, which may have negative consequences for other prisoners who are themselves in breach of the rules (e.g. smoking drugs or gambling);[2] if s/he is so committed to full compliance that s/he is liable to inform staff of violations by his or her fellow prisoners, then – again – this constitutes a risk to a wide group of prisoners; and, if s/he has sufficient clout or charisma, then it may be difficult to avoid complying with his or her will, whether that will is directed at keeping to or breaking the rules. Thus, prisoners are regulated not only by those with formal power, but by their immediate peer group, through both direct interventions and the tenets of the inmate code.

A typology of compliance

In this section, I draw on a typology of prisoner adaptation that I have elaborated in more detail elsewhere (see Crewe 2009), in order to bring into relief the different mechanisms of compliance that I have already outlined. The typology derives from a study of a medium security men's training prison in the United Kingdom (HMP Wellingborough), conducted in the early 2000s. It may not be generalizable to all prison populations, and there is good reason to believe that it would need considerable amendment to apply to contemporary high security prisons in England and Wales (see Liebling et al. 2012). Nonetheless, I am confident that it presents a framework for thinking about penal compliance that is somewhat transferable, and which, above all, demonstrates the complex nature of prisoner compliance, in particular when taking into account the distinctions between formal, substantive and long-term compliance.

Enthusiasts were generally prisoners who had been serious drug or alcohol addicts prior to their imprisonment, and were ashamed of the offences they had committed. Central to their narratives was the sense that their behaviour and identity while drinking or taking drugs did not represent their true self. Imprisonment thus offered them the opportunity not only to turn their lives around, but to reconstruct themselves as morally righteous and respectable. In this regard, they were substantively compliant, in that they shared the aims of the prison and were committed to going straight on release. More than other prisoners, they appreciated opportunities to learn skills and actively engage with the regime, both in order to prepare themselves for post-release life and to demonstrate to those around them their prosocial identities. They submitted enthusiastically to mandatory drug testing, because they were keen to demonstrate their abstinence. Their strong sense of personal morality was reinforced by institutional rewards: being on the 'enhanced' privilege level, for example, proved the benefits of compliance and differentiated them from prisoners who cared less about personal development.

However, this committed form of substantive compliance did not mean that *enthusiasts* were always formally compliant. While, in principle, they respected the job that officers did and the prison's rehabilitative opportunities,[3] the strength of their moral drive and their sense of themselves as ethical arbiters meant that they could be rather challenging, particularly when they felt that the prison – or its staff – was not living up to their expectations (e.g. by responding slowly to official communications, or by providing forms of work, education and rehabilitative resources that they deemed substandard). Likewise, in asserting their moral integrity, *enthusiasts* could be resistant to the imposition of institutional power. For, although their aims were aligned with official objectives, it was important to them to feel that their change was self-generated rather than imposed, and that they were agents rather than objects of power. This determination to honour their 'true selves', and to engage with the prison without duress, could conflict with systemic prescriptions, particularly if they were obliged to undertake offending behaviour courses that they did not welcome or respect:

> I won't go on a course unless I think it's going to benefit me. [...] I would like to show that I have looked at that area within myself, without being told to do it. [...] I can't not be me. When I go for my parole, I'm going to tell them straight. And if they don't give me it they don't give me it. It isn't going to make the slightest difference to me, because the development I've made personally within myself, is so great, from what I came into prison to what I am now. [...] My idea [for parole] was not to do all their courses, but the ones that I felt was beneficial to me. Not what they told me to do, because of their statistics. When I tried to do ETS [Enhanced Thinking Skills], [my dissatisfaction] was a lot to do with the other people on the course. They were there for the sake of doing the course, not because they wanted to gain anything from it. They were just making up the numbers.
>
> (Luke)

Any suggestion that they were compliant, committed and generally respectful because of institutional impulsion was fiercely disputed. Luke's comments typified this attitude of moral voluntarism: 'even if they opened the front gate now and said "go down the road, get a loaf of bread and come back" I would do it – I would go down the road, get a loaf of bread and come back.' In sum, then, personal morality trumped constraint, and other mechanisms of compliance, in determining the behaviour of this set of prisoners.

In contrast to *enthusiasts*, *pragmatists* complied primarily for reasons of personal need, or out of feelings of resignation and powerlessness. For these prisoners, who were often young, repeat offenders, serving relatively short sentences, there was little question that power lay in the hands of the institution:

> I just get on with it. That's all you can do. [...] They're always going to win. [...] [Officers] think they're higher than you, which I suppose they are. They're the bosses, we're the inmates.
>
> (Connor)

> The screws have got the power. The screws have got the keys and we're behind the doors at night; what they say goes.
>
> (Cameron)

Such views were indicative of the sense among *pragmatists* that there was little they could do but comply with institutional demands. Sentiments of fatalism were expressed in mundane descriptions of doing time: 'I don't make no fuss or nothing,' declared Ellis, 'I've just plodded along with the sentence.' *Pragmatists* were highly aware (and somewhat fearful) of the prison's coercive potential – for example, being transferred to establishments where visits might be harder to receive, or being segregated from other prisoners. Resistance was, therefore, perceived as highly counterproductive:

> If you fight against it, you don't get nothing. You lose no matter what. The only way you'll beat it is if you just go with the flow. You've just got to keep your head down basically. Just do your time and just get out, and don't let it get you down. [...] The best thing you can do is just do what they say. And no matter how much they annoy you, just grit your teeth and move on. [...] No matter what you do, you're still going to lose aren't you. You can't beat the system. The only time you beat it is when you get out. And you just play by their book.
>
> (Chris)

Meanwhile, these prisoners were unusually motivated by material incentives and concerns about everyday living conditions. Often, they struggled to cope with the daily demands and deprivations of prison life. In-cell television, visits and access to the prison gym were therefore vital means of coping psychologically with the sentence, while opportunities to spend private cash on trainers, clothing and grooming products enabled displays of status that they prized. Compliance, then, was secured to a significant degree by instrumental means: 'I'm not content, I'm never gonna be content,' Colin clarified, 'but the last thing I wanna do is to make any trouble for myself. Cos that means getting canteen wiped off, which then would make it harder on me. So basically, yeah, I'm quite compliant.'

Generally, *pragmatists* sought to develop positive relationships with staff, both because they saw them as 'normal people', just 'doing a job', and because they relied upon their discretionary power. 'There's some, obviously, that I won't like. But I'll try and get on with every officer. Mainly to make my life easier so he don't get on my back' (Cameron). Often, they attended offending behaviour courses in order to gain personal insight into their criminal behaviour. Here, their compliance was loosely substantive, in that they were open to interventions and willing to engage positively with the institution. The attendance of anger management, alcohol awareness and other such courses was also seen as a way of improving relationships with loved ones. Indeed, the yearning to be reunited with children and partners was a significant motivation for these prisoners, not least because they found imprisonment hard to bear. Emotional (normative) attachments thus reinforced, and sometimes trumped, other mechanisms of compliance.

At the same time, these prisoners were often deemed non-compliant by staff, largely as an outcome of their vulnerabilities and inadequacies rather than through any conscious desire to make trouble. Some *pragmatists* were immature and boisterous, and were therefore penalized for making excessive noise or mess; others struggled to control their emotions and frustrations, and were disciplined for outbursts against staff when post went missing or decisions were delayed (for example); some found it hard to follow the regime, or relied on informal trade in order to survive the sentence – as Callum noted, 'keeping your head down is actually a lot harder than it sounds'; others were easily lured or coerced into illicit activity, through economic need, naivety or fear of the consequences of refusing. Thus, a set of prisoners who were, in spirit, relatively committed to formal compliance, and potentially committed to substantive compliance, were often the most visible non-compliers in the eyes of uniformed staff.

Stoics – who were generally long-term prisoners, coming toward the end of their sentences – also complied for reasons of pragmatism and resignation, but this disposition was determined primarily by the yearning for release, and the dread of doing anything that might delay it, rather than the drive to enhance everyday comforts. Compared with pragmatists, they were more motivated by longer-term goals than by immediate conditions and short-term objectives. Sticking to the rules was more important as a way of demonstrating 'good character', and maintaining a positive 'file', than as a means of obtaining privileges. Most *stoics* had endured imprisonment in a more austere era, considered current conditions to be reasonable, and did not have any particular fear of coping without televisions or other such perks (although they certainly appreciated having them, in order to make their lives more comfortable). Indeed, they tended to resent a privilege scheme which they saw as a manipulative, and somewhat coercive, tool of control and a means of transforming rights into removable privileges: 'There's no carrots,' said Nathan, 'it's all stick.'

Stoics were often highly disillusioned with aspects of the prison system, in particular, what they saw as an impersonal, inefficient, inconsistent and ineffective bureaucracy, and an oppressive and illegitimate system of psychological assessment. However, they saw little point in trying to alter their general predicament, and considerable risk in expressing dissent or resisting the system.

> So how do you make your voices heard about issues?

> I don't. I just accept them. I don't let them walk over me, but I never let the little things bother me. Time and experience have taught me that if I complain about it, I'm labelled as a kick-off merchant or a ringleader or an inciter. [...] I just accept it. I don't like it, but I just accept it for what it is.
>
> (Tommy)

This kind of fatalistic language was common among *stoics*: 'There's nothing you can do about it and to resist it will just cause you problems' (George). Most sought to bite their tongues, 'keep their heads down', and suppress their frustrations, without engaging in an unduly enthusiastic way with the institution. As Nathan argued, striking this balance between compliance and engagement was tricky: 'I wanna get out, but at the same time I'm not gonna compromise my integrity *to* get out. So it has been a careful balancing act between the two things.' They were thus formally compliant, and genuinely committed to long-term compliance, post-release, but they were not what would be considered fully or substantively compliant within (or by) the prison, in part because they did not see its rehabilitative provisions as the basis of their own rehabilitation: in their eyes, any reform occurred despite rather than because of the system. Similarly, *stoics* attended offending behaviour programmes with little enthusiasm, often having taken the same courses many times, but aware that they had to 'tick the right boxes' in order to ensure speedy release. In their interactions with staff, they developed relationships that were courteous yet detached, saving their complaints about illegitimate treatment for private conversations, but also acknowledging those officers who were fair and respectful in their dealings. *Stoics* caused staff few problems, challenging them only when necessary, with caution and through official channels, to ensure that they could not be accused of non-compliance, disobedience or 'trouble-making'.

Disengaged prisoners were generally pragmatists gone awry: men who were normally or potentially compliant on the basis of incentives and disincentives, but for whom these levers had become irrelevant or ineffective. Some had no private income, or were too far from home to receive visits, and were therefore unconcerned by the benefits of being 'enhanced' or the threat of being transferred further afield:

I said to them, 'well, you can't send me no further from home, so you might as well take me today if you want. I'm not fucking bothered. Take me straight to [the Isle of Wight]'. Because the damage has been done for me. They don't give me parole. They've told me basically I'm not getting home leave. They can't hurt me any more than what they've already done.

(Carter)

As suggested here, others had been turned down for parole, due to poor behaviour, or were ineligible for early release because they had no permanent address at which they could be 'tagged'. As a result, or simply because they anticipated negative institutional decisions, they felt that they had few meaningful goals, and disengaged from the normal grip of the institution:

I've been turned down for parole Ben, I feel that my chances for home leave are very limited, and to [get a] move to a different prison is going to be a struggle because of my previous record. What do you think you can really offer me in HMP Wellingborough? What goals have I got? What am I really supposed to do? I feel I'm locked in a very negative society.

(Tyler)

Some deliberately detached themselves from institutional mechanisms in order to evade the burdens of impression-management and avoid feelings of dependence, choosing an existence that was somewhat ascetic but meant that they did not have to 'depend on [not] fucking upsetting some member of staff' (Marcus). As with stoics, then, the drive to maintain some sense of personal dignity could clash with the effort required to meet institutional demands. But, while stoics were resigned to the prison's coercive potential, the semi-detached compliance of this group of prisoners related to the failings of the prison's incentive structure to correspond with their current needs or predicaments.

For another set of prisoners – *retreatists* – compliance was equally divorced from institutional mechanisms, but this was as a result of life circumstances and a deeply fatalistic attitude toward the self, rather than to the dominance of the institution, as such. *Retreatists* were long-term drug addicts outside prison, who felt significant guilt about the crimes they had committed and their general behaviour prior to their sentence. Unlike *enthusiasts*, though, they had little support in the community (and thus no audience to whom they could prove their moral worth) and little confidence that they would ever fully escape the grip of their addictions: 'If I could stop taking drugs, stop drinking, I'd be fine, but I can't honestly sit here and say to you I think I could. I don't think I could stop taking drugs and drinking' (Alfie). Their hopes for the future were modest – 'a bedsit ... a couple of posters on the wall, my bed made, my telly in the corner. I'll probably make my bedsit into a cell because I'm quite happy with that' (Noah) – but they were generally pessimistic about the prospect of long-term compliance, even though they had no actual desire to reoffend. Within the prison, they were relatively content, because the conditions under which they lived were preferable to those they experienced when using drugs outside:

> It sounds crazy, but my quality of life at the moment is better. I'm eating. I'm sleeping in a clean bed. I'm getting clean clothes every day. And I've got some kind of order in my life.
>
> (Noah)

As suggested here, within the prison, their aspirations were simple: self-renewal rather than radical transformation, and inner peace rather than external validation. Imprisonment was an opportunity to regenerate, and the main priority was to develop an ordinary existence and a comfortable routine: 'I keep it simple, one day at a time. I don't even work for one day at a time. I work for meals. From dinner to tea. From tea till bedtime' (Noah). In some regards, *retreatists* were non-compliant, in that they were prepared to dabble in illicit activity in order to make ends meet, but this was done with little resistant intent. *Retreatists* felt little bitterness toward either the institution or its staff ('they're just doing their job'), and saw little cause for anti-institutional sentiment. They were well liked by officers, because they were courteous, compliant and undemanding: 'I just get my head down. I try and cause as little upset and unhappiness to people. I go with the flow' (Alfie).

Compliance, then, was to a large degree internally driven. *Retreatists* were neither seduced nor subdued by the prison's mechanisms of power. They attended offending behaviour courses out of curiosity, rather than enthusiasm or obligation, and had little interest in the trimmings of 'enhanced' status. In effect, they were compliant *beyond* the system. They sidestepped the grip and objectives of the prison, doing little to 'prove' themselves to the institution, because they were in no particular rush to leave it and did not want to disturb their psychological equilibrium:

> I'm not really trying to reduce my sentence in any way. [...] I'm not trying to – in a way – get out of jail. I just want to do my full sentence, and hopefully come out a better person. [...] Sort my head out. Get myself back to how I used to be before I got really badly into the drugs.
>
> (Rhys)

> At the moment I'm on course: I've got my little bit of burn, I've got my little job, and I've got my little room. [...] I'm not going to bang my head on the wall for stuff that I'm not interested in, and don't want anyway. [...]. If I'm not expecting anything then my happiness is in myself and what I've built round [me].
>
> (Noah)

Overall, then, these prisoners were aligned with, but disengaged from, the official discourses of the institution, neither substantively compliant nor confident about their likely desistance, and yet, on the whole, obedient and formally compliant.

In contrast, *players* feigned compliance, while masking attitudes and behaviour that were resentful and resistant. Generally career criminals, with defiant anti-authority views, they had little intention of desisting from crime when released, and were normatively opposed to the institution – that is, substantively non-compliant. However, they were formally compliant in many respects as part of a highly self-conscious performance of both obedience and future desistance. They recognized that they were, in certain respects, powerless, that the rules were defined from above and had to be seen to be followed. At the same time, they saw opportunities to manipulate the system in their favour through the use of hidden and creative tactics. Surface compliance was thus combined with backstage rule-breaking:

> You're cleaning, mopping, sweeping, doing whatever they say. You finish your work you then start doing what you're doing: double bubble [trading tobacco], selling drugs whatever. You show them that you're willing to do the work and you're polite, whatever else you do in your own time is nothing to do with them.
>
> (Paul)

In their performances, then, *players* often appeared more enthusiastic than most other prisoners, acting out the desired institutional script of committed engagement. They attended offending behaviour courses resentfully, and with cynicism, but spoke the language that was necessary in order to obtain the kinds of reports that would hasten their release.

> The first thing they put down about me are 'polite' and 'compliant', two important words, and that's what matters. I might walk away and say 'wanker', but as long as they don't hear it, then there's no harm done. [...] A weapon that staff can use against you is that they'll smile and talk and call you by your first name, and then they'll go into the office and write something bad about you. Once I learned that, I never give them the opportunity to do that to me. Even though they might be sat behind their desk, knowing that I just disabled the windows or whatever.
>
> (Stephen)

Often, *players* deliberately cultivated good relationships with officers in order to advance their interests through positive reports or minor perks: 'The more screws on my side the better it is for me' (Wilson). They also recognized the need to shape their performances to different staff audiences:

> It's like juggling. With a psychologist, perhaps, you might want to come across as being a bit weak and timid. But on the wing, if you come across like that, the screws don't like you very much. [...] They look at your file and if you're in for a violent offence, they expect you to be pretty solid. [...] They don't like you to be violent, but in a conversation they wouldn't expect you to be talking about flowers and bumble-bees.
>
> (Stephen)

In their private attitudes and hidden transactions, however, they were more hostile and resistant than other prisoners to the institution and its staff. They consistently expressed contempt and disdain for their captors, bracketing them all as representatives of a despised state authority and deriding their masculinity: 'I don't class them as men,' said Ashley. 'I mean, who wants a job opening doors for arseholes all fucking day long? They're weak. They are weak.' Whereas *stoics* were resigned to their own resignation, and *retreatists* were reluctantly non-compliant when engaging in low-level trade, *players* were dedicated to 'beating the system' through illicit activity (e.g. drug use and dealing; stealing from kitchens), active subversion (e.g. setting off fire alarms and buzzers) and off-stage contempt. 'I know there's nothing I can do to change my routine each day,' said Pierce, 'but give me half the chance to do something I shouldn't and get away with it, and I'll do it.' Such resistant activities, and minor acts of dissent, were relished as symbolic triumphs:

> I get my victories by selling drugs. They pay me £11 a week. I live well above that. I can have what I want. [...] When a screw comes in my pad and sees my pad overflowing with food and tobacco and just everything, that's good enough for me. Just to let them know 'you can't stop me.'
>
> (Ashley)

Discussion and conclusions

One of the weaknesses of typologies is that they inevitably imply that people are one thing or another: static 'types' rather than people whose orientations may shift over time. In fact, prisoners may comply for different reasons at different stages of their sentence, and changes in their attitudes may be determined by factors such as ageing, relationships with external parties and shifts in institutional treatment. These dynamics of personal change within prison, while documented in some celebrated prisoner autobiographies (e.g. Boyle 1977), have rarely been the focus of academic research, or have attributed little agency or dynamism to prisoners or prisons (e.g. Wheeler 1961). Yet many prisoners are highly conscious of the need to wean themselves off illicit activity as their sentence goes on, in order not to jeopardize their release date, and the complex interplay between individual motivation and institutional behaviour surely merits further exploration. *Pragmatists* whose compliance is initially secured through incentives may find themselves normatively persuaded of the benefits of compliance, if the rewards that they receive are perceived as forms of positive feedback and personal encouragement.[4] *Players* who begin by feigning compliance may find themselves converted by their own performances:

> I was pretending, and then after pretending for so long I sort of drilled it into my own head. They started throwing more trust towards me, and I thought: 'I'm onto a winner [laugh], this is a good thing.' Before, they'd only give me jobs like in the packing workshop – they started giving me more trustworthy jobs. Before, I'd be like Jekyll and Hyde, two different people. Now I'm just me, I find it better.
>
> (Kyle)

The language of trust is significant here, for many prisoners find themselves highly ambivalent about compliance and change, and require considerable support for both to be possible. Often, they lack conviction that they can be a different kind of person – 'as much as I feel I've changed while I've been in here, there will always be a part of me that's programmed to [have a] criminal side' (Fin) – or feel more ontologically secure in resistant identities than in the unknown terrain of change:

> There's a battle going on inside me. I do generally wanna sort myself out. I'm trying to get help, and when I can't get that help it's frustrating. Sometimes I think to myself 'would I better if I went back to where I was and what I was?', but then I think of my family.
>
> (Alexis)

Prisoners facing such dilemmas want the prison to recognize their internal struggles and need reassurance that they are taking the right steps toward change. Poor, indifferent and suspicious treatment can easily encourage them back into less compliant orientations. Meanwhile, the need to maintain some sense of dignity, reputation and agency means that, if regulated too closely – forced rather than enabled into compliance – they may be induced merely into hollow performances of compliance rather than the harder task of substantive change. To use Scott's (1990: 3) terms, 'the more menacing the power, the thicker the mask.'

In his study of offenders on parole, Werth (2012) identifies a similar issue. The highly demanding nature of parole conditions can be counterproductive, creating subversion and hostility and generating game-playing, even among offenders who are committed to going straight. Such offenders are normatively aligned with the spirit of the law, but struggle to be formally compliant or law-abiding because their commitment to such things as work, family life and personal autonomy put them in conflict with the tight regulations that govern them. As Werth notes, then, the question is not just why people obey laws that they do not believe in, but why they break legal norms to which they are, in broad principle, committed. The formal compliance of parolees, he argues, is thus a highly misleading measure of 'conformity to the larger goal of going straight' (Werth 2012: 14). The same is the case in prisons, where the relationship between formal, substantive and long-term compliance is little understood by either prison scholars or administrators.

Notes

1. Here, we are also reminded of literary depictions of surveillance-based control systems: The smallest thing could give you away. A nervous tic, an unconscious look, a habit of muttering to yourself – anything that carried with it the suggestion of abnormality, of having something to hide (Orwell 1949:79).
2. 'You can't have a fight in prison, because there's that much noise made, with the concrete floors being the way they are: it makes a hell of a racket. So the officers hear it' (Danny)
3. For example: 'I've got a lot of time and respect for officers and police officers, believe it or not. . . . I could not do their job, not a fucking prayer. I could not come to work, put up with the shit that the inmates give the officers in here' (Kyle).
4. That is, as McNeill and Robinson (2013) note, instrumental mechanisms may serve as an 'initial step or building block' toward psychological legitimacy.

References

Bosworth, M. (1996) 'Resistance and Compliance in Women's Prisons: Towards a Critique of Legitimacy'. *Critical Criminology* 7(2), 5–19.

Bosworth, M. (1999) *Engendering Resistance: Agency and Power in Women's Prisons*. Aldershot: Dartmouth.

Bosworth, M. and Carrabine, E. (2001) 'Reassessing Resistance: Race, Gender and Sexuality in Prison'. *Punishment and Society* 3(4), 501–515.

Bottoms, A. (1999) 'Interpersonal Violence and Social Order in Prisons'. *Crime and Justice: A Review of Research*. 26, 205–281.

Bottoms, A. (2001) 'Compliance with Community Penalties'. in A. Bottoms, L. Gelsthorpe and S. Rex (Eds) *Community Penalties: Change and Challenges*. Cullompton: Willan.

Bottoms, A. (2003) 'Theoretical Reflections on the Evaluation of a Penal Policy'. in L. Zedner and A. Ashworth (Eds) *The Criminological Foundations of Penal Policy: Essays in Honour of Roger Hood*. Clarendon: Oxford.

Bosworth, M. and Carrabine, E. (2001) 'Reassessing Resistance'. *Punishment and Society* 3(4), 501–515.

Boyle, J. (1977) *A Taste of Freedom*. London: Pan Books.

Braithwaite, Valerie (2003) 'Dancing with Tax Authorities: Motivational Postures and Non-compliant Actions'. in Valerie Braithwaite (Ed.) *Taxing Democracy: Understanding Tax Avoidance and Evasion*. Aldershot: Ashgate.

Buntman, F. L. (2003) *Robben Island and Prisoner Resistance to Apartheid*. Cambridge: Cambridge University Press.

Carrabine, E., (2005) 'Prison Riots, Social Order and the Problem of Legitimacy'. *British Journal of Criminology* 45 (6), 896–913.

Clemmer, D. (1940; Second Edition 1958) *The Prison Community*. New York: Holt, Rinehart and Winston.

Cooke, D. (1991) 'Violence in Prisons: The Influence of Regime Factors'. *The Howard Journal of Criminal Justice* 30(2), 95–109.

Crawford, A. (2013) 'Sticks and Carrots . . . and Sermons: Some Thoughts on Compliance and Legitimacy in the Regulation of Youth Anti-Social behaviour'. in A. Crawford and A. Hucklesby (Eds) *Legitimacy and Compliance in Criminal Justice*. Oxon: Routledge.

Crewe, B. (2009) *The Prisoner Society: Power, Adaptation and Social Life in an English Prison*. Oxford: Clarendon.

Crewe, B. (2011a) 'Depth, Weight, Tightness: Revisiting the Pains of Imprisonment'. *Punishment and Society* 13(5), 509–529.

Crewe, B. (2011b) 'Soft Power in Prison: Implications for Staff-Prisoner Relationships, Liberty and Legitimacy'. *European Journal of Criminology* 8(6), 455–468.

DiLulio, J. (1990) *Governing Prisons: A Comparative Study of Correctional Management*. New York: The Free Press.

Ditchfield, J. (1990) *Control in Prisons: A Review of the Literature*. Home Office Research Study 118. London: HMSO.

Ellickson, R. (1991) *Order Without Law: How Neighbours Settle Disputes*. Cambridge, MA: Harvard University Press.

Emery, F. (1970) *Freedom and Justice Within Walls: The Bristol Prison Experiment*. London: Tavistock Publications.

Ericson, R. B. (1975) Criminal Reactions: The Labelling Perspective. Farnborough, Hants: Saxon House Publishing.

Foucault, M. (1977) *Discipline and Punish: The Birth of the Prison*. Harmondsworth: Penguin.

Garfinkel, H. (1956) 'Conditions of Successful Degradation Ceremonies'. *American Journal of Sociology* 61, 420–424.

Goffman, E. (1961) *Asylums: Essays on the Social Situation of Mental Patients and Other Inmates*. Harmondsworth: Penguin.

Goodstein, L. (1979) 'Inmate Adjustment to Prison and the Transition to Community Life'. in R. Cater, D. Glaser and L. Wilkins (Eds) *Correctional Institutions*. New York: Harper and Row.

King, R. (2005) 'The Effects of Supermax Custody', in A. Liebling and S. Maruna (Eds) *The Effects of Imprisonment*. Cullompton: Willan.

Liebling, A. (2000). 'Prison Officers, Policing and the Use of Discretion'. *Theoretical Criminology* 4(3), 333–357.

Liebling, A. and assisted by Arnold, H. (2004) *Prisons and Their Moral Performance: A Study of Values, Quality, and Prison Life*. Oxford: Clarendon Press.

Liebling, A., Muir, G., Rose, G. and Bottoms, A. (1997) *An Evaluation of Earned Priviledges: Final Report to the Prison Service*. Cambridge: Institute of Criminology

Liebling, A., Price, D. and Shefer, G. (2011) *The Prison Officer*. Second Edition. New York, NY: Willan Publishing.

Liebling, A., Arnold, H. and Straub, C. (2012) *An Exploration of Staff – Prisoner Relationships at HMP Whitemoor: 12 Years On*. London: Ministry of Justice.

Maruna, S. and LeBel, T. (2003) 'Welcome Home-Examining the Reentry Court Concept from a Strengths-Based Perspective'. *Western Criminology Review* 4(2), 91–107.

Maruna, S. and Toch, H. (2005) 'The Impact of Imprisonment on the Desistance Process'. in J. Travis and C. Visher (Eds) *Prisoner Reentry and Crime in America*. Cambridge: CUP.

Maruna, S. and Mann, R. (2006) 'A Fundamental Attribution Error? Rethinking Cognitive Distortions'. *Legal and Criminological Psychology* 11(2), 155–177.

Mathiesen, T. (1965).*The Defences of the Weak: A Sociological Study of a Norwegian Correctional Institution*. London: Tavistock.

McEvoy, K. (2001) *Paramilitary Imprisonment in Northern Ireland*. Oxford: Clarendon Press.

McNeill, F. and Robinson, G. (2013) 'Liquid Legitimacy and Community Sanctions'. in A. Crawford and A. Hucklesby (Eds) *Legitimacy and Compliance in Criminal Justice*. Oxon: Routledge.

Nellis, M. (2006) 'Surveillance, Rehabilitation and Electronic Monitoring: Getting the Issues Clear'. *Criminology and Public Policy* 5(1), 401–407.

Nellis, M. (2013) 'Implant Technology and the Electronic Monitoring of Offenders: Old and New Questions about Compliance, Control and Legitimacy'. in A. Crawford and A. Hucklesby (Eds) *Legitimacy and Compliance in Criminal Justice*. Oxon: Routledge.

Orwell, G. (1949) *Nineteen Eighty-Four*. 31st Edition. Harmondsworth: Penguin.

Reisig, M. (1998) 'Rates of Disorder in Higher-Custody State Prisons: A Comparative Analysis of Managerial Practices'. *Crime and Delinquency* 44(2), 229–244.

Robinson, G. and McNeill, F. (2008) 'Exploring the Dynamics of Compliance with Community Penalties'. *Theoretical Criminology* 12(4), 431–449.

Rowe, A. (2011) 'Narratives of Self and Identity in Women's Prisons: Stigma and the Struggle for Self-definition in Penal Regimes'. *Punishment and Society* 13(5) 571–591.

Scott, J. (1990) *Domination and the Arts of resistance*: Hidden Transcripts. New Haven and London. London: Yale University Press.

Scraton, P., Sim, J. and Skidmore, P. (1991) *Prisons Under Protest*. Milton Keynes: Open University Press.

Sparks, R., Bottoms, A. and Hay, W. (1996) *Prisons and the Problem of Order*. Oxford: Clarendon.

Sykes, G. (1958) *The Society of Captives: A Study of a Maximum-Security Prison*. Princeton, NJ: Princeton University Press.

Tyler, T. (2013) 'Legitimacy and Compliance: The Virtues of Self-Regulation'. in A. Crawford and A. Hucklesby (Eds) *Legitimacy and Compliance in Criminal Justice*. Oxon: Routledge.

Ugelvik, T. (2011) 'The Hidden Food: Mealtime Resistance and Identity Work in a Norwegian Prison'. *Punishment and Society* 13(1), s 47–63

Werth, R. (2012) 'I Do What I'm Told, Sort Of: Reformed Subjects, Irresponsible Citizens, and Parole.' *Theoretical Criminology* 16 (3) 329–346.

Ward, D. (1987) 'Control Strategies for Problem Prisoners in American Penal Systems'. in A. Bottoms and R. Light (Eds) *Problems of Long-Term Imprisonment*. Aldershot: Gower.

Wheeler, S. (1961) 'Socialization in Correctional Communities'. *American Sociological Review* 26, 697–712.

Wrong, D. H. (2002) *Power: Its Forms, Bases and Uses*. New Jersey: Transaction Publishers.

9
Surveillance-Based Compliance using Electronic Monitoring

Mike Nellis

Introduction

Electronic monitoring (EM) is a generic term for a number of remote surveillance technologies – radio frequency (RF) curfew checking at single locations, biometric voice verification at single or multiple locations, remote alcohol monitoring (home-based breathalysers or mobile sobriety bracelets which measure the presence of alcohol transdermally) and Global Positioning System (GPS) satellite tracking which monitors mobility and/or the perimeter of specified exclusion zones – which have been used to extend the range of spatial and temporal (and to some degree behavioural) regulations that can be imposed on offenders under supervision in the community. One or other of the technologies can be used at the pre-trial, sentence or post-release phase of the criminal justice process, sometimes with a view to achieving reductions in the use and cost of imprisonment. They can be applied to a wide range of offenders or suspects, as a stand-alone measure for low-risk people, or as a component of an intensive supervision programme for higher-risk people. Singly or in combination – EM curfews/home detention predominate – they have been used in approximately 40 countries around the world, beginning in the United States in the early 1980s, spreading to Canada, Australia and Europe, and most recently to Korea, Latin America and Saudi Arabia. They have been embedded in many different legal, administrative and discursive frameworks, reflecting different penal cultures and traditions, which have variously inflected EM as a new tough punishment, as an aid to rehabilitation or, more neutrally, as an additional layer of control which can serve either punitive or rehabilitative ends (Nellis et al. 2012).

Because of these diverse purposes and contexts of use, there can be no single 'effect' or 'outcome' of EM measures; they might be judged by their impact (singly or in conjunction with other services) on recidivism, on prison populations, on cost savings – or simply on compliance with specified requirements.

EM, furthermore, has in itself no particular 'punitive intensity': it can be imposed to monitor night-time curfews, leaving the offender free during the day, or to monitor 24-hour home lockdowns, or any prescribed interval in between, while the painfulness (or otherwise) of the experience can be affected by the spaciousness of the accommodation and the composition of the household in which one is 'confined' (Martinovic 2002). The onerousness of an EM measure can be eased or intensified according to whether and how it is integrated with other services. The duration of such a measure is usually governed by a legislative maximum, but it can be imposed for short periods of time – a matter of weeks and months – or for several years: some states in the United States have actually legislated for the lifetime GPS tracking of sex offenders released from prison, although police forces are not enamoured of having sole responsibility for this, and the strategy may founder (Bishop 2010).

The question of what EM can contribute to compliance, and of what it means to comply with EM, have gradually become of interest to policy makers, service providers, theorists and researchers. Within the context of his compliance typology, Bottoms (2001) rightly characterized EM as a form of 'constraint-based compliance', but said little about the very distinct form of constraint that it represents. By combining Bottoms's reflections on 'compliance' with Lawrence Lessig's (1999) reflections on the control 'architecture' (the socio-technological infrastructure) which makes remote monitoring possible, Jones (2006) improved on this, but more could still be said about the precise regulatory mechanisms that different modalities of EM entail, or make possible. Hucklesby's (2008, 2009, 2011) rich and nuanced empirical research on offender compliance with largely stand-alone EM curfews in England suggests deterrence – fear of detection and a worse penalty if they are shown to have violated regulations – is the predominant reason for compliance with EM. While this may be true, and indeed intended – as with many forms of community supervision – focusing on 'fear of future consequences' can obscure the distinct and specific ways in which EM requires offenders to 'perform compliance' in the here and now: to wear (and, in the case of GPS, charge) equipment, regulate their schedules, tolerate the proximity of others while under curfew, avoid certain areas and routes, and manage public (and potentially stigmatizing) perceptions of the bracelet. The routines (and pains) of complying with EM are rather different from other community penalties, and, depending on the offender's motivation to desist and perception of the measure's legitimacy, may be more or less bearable than other measures. They require discernment as to when and how they are used. Offenders on EM are 'surveilled subjects' to a far greater degree than offenders on other forms of community supervision, and are required to orient themselves not only to the requirements of a court of law and its professional agents, but also, at root, to an 'automated socio-technical system' (Lianos and Douglas 2000). EM is thus best characterized as a form of 'surveillance-based compliance', a term which signifies more precisely than 'constraint' or 'deterrence' the nature of the regime – namely, the real-time remote monitoring of their schedules and locations – with which offenders have to contend.

This chapter will focus exclusively, and somewhat schematically, on the theoretical and practical aspects of compliance (and non-compliance) with EM, ignoring broader debates about its history, development and effectiveness, while using selected (and mostly new) international evidence to highlight the complex questions that EM raises. EM-based measures can, indeed, be extremely constraining, but the mere wearing of a traceable ankle tag is not physically incapacitative in the manner of locks, bolts and bars. A tag, in the mind's eye of an offender, may prohibit, but it does not literally inhibit. Tagged offenders can, of course, choose to disregard their requirements and risk the consequences, or offend while wearing the bracelet, or even cut off their tags (which are mostly made of tough plastic, with fibre optics in the strap). Contemporary EM penalties only function if offenders learn how they work and cooperate with imposed requirements – they are, as Satellite Tracking of People (STOP), an American GPS tracking provider, calls them, 'participant dependent' (advertisement, *Journal of Offender Monitoring* 19, 2). 'Participant dependence' has typically been understood as a design weakness, a technological limitation to be overcome, an impediment to complete control over an offender – STOP marketed its one-piece tracking unit as 'the least participant dependent device available today' (idem), but from an 'offender management' perspective the fact that participants have the leeway to reject monitoring, and are deliberately trusted to do otherwise (or threatened), lies at the heart of what compliance, as an active, willed process, means. EM 'responsibilizes' offenders, makes them (rather literally) 'accountable', creating precise, retrievable, time-stamped digital records of presence or absence, or their whereabouts more generally, against which, and for which, they can be held to account. It vividly exemplifies what Adam Crawford (2003) has elsewhere called a mode of 'contractual governance – regulated self-regulation', because it requires offenders to cooperate with the socio-technical system in which, to use the term favoured by the commercial monitoring companies in Britain, they have been 'enrolled'.

EM Curfew Regimes

While a curfew requirement is the core of what electronically monitored offenders have to comply with, they must also submit to a routine of collateral activities – a regime – the rigour and perceived legitimacy of which may also affect compliance (Hucklesby 2009). In England and Wales offenders on court-ordered EM curfews are not legally required to consent, although the householders with whom they reside are, and can withdraw consent, in effect rendering the offender non-compliant. Prisoners deemed eligible for EM early release are required to consent, and some prisoners refuse, preferring the sanctuary and status of incarceration rather than tolerating the irksomeness of electronic surveillance (and the isolation if they live alone). Early release on EM can be anticipated weeks in advance, and installations of equipment and 'enrolment' of the offender onto the database can be planned for the afternoon of the release day, giving the offender time to travel from prison to home. Requests for court-ordered EM curfew requirements are usually notified (by fax or email) to monitoring centres late on the working day they are made, with installation and enrolment undertaken at night. Once the system is operative, monitoring centre staff tend to experience a 'busy period' from 7 pm (when most curfews are set to begin), when their screens register *en bloc* who has arrived home on time and who has not, and the process of phoning the absentees and logging violations begins (Hucklesby 2011; Jones 2005; Paterson 2007).

Compliance begins in the first instance with instructions to be available for enrolment. If monitoring officers are denied entry to an offender's home, or if the offender is not there, they photograph the house (to avoid accusations of mistaking the address) and return the following day. Once the tag is fitted to an offender's ankle, monitoring officers check whether the home base unit registers its presence from all points within the home, and calibrate its range so that it does not reach beyond the curtilage of the house or flat (although in practice it might). This usually bars offenders from using gardens or backyards to do chores or play with their children, although courts sometimes authorize more flexible arrangements:

> The monitoring provider will only monitor internal areas of the curfew address unless otherwise stated on the court notification. Gardens should only be included if there is a definite reason for the subject to use them during the curfew hours. If gardens are to be included specific areas should be specified and it is preferable to monitor the back garden only. It may be necessary to limit the area defined to enable it to be effectively monitored by the EM equipment.
>
> (Serco 2010, p. 6)

A precise timekeeping regime is created when monitoring officers synchronize the LED-displayed time on the home base unit with the monitoring centre computer: offenders must synchronize their phones and watches with this. 'Enforcement thresholds' in respect of requirements in a community order are explained to the offender, namely, that brief absences or late arrivals home are tolerated until, over time, two hours' worth have been accumulated, while missing a whole curfew period constitutes a violation in its own right. They are told what constitutes 'technical violations' (e.g. tampering with the tag or base unit, failing to register changes of circumstance, verbally abusing staff), as well as how to get orders officially altered (e.g. to do overtime at work), and the occasions when permission to leave home during curfew hours can be requested (weddings, funerals, job interviews, court appearances, medical emergencies), offer freephone numbers for contacting the monitoring centre (whose location they do not divulge) and leave easy-to-read brochures which repeat all this information.

In England and Wales, curfews can be made for a 12-hour maximum in any given day (which imminent legislation will likely increase to 16 hours). Most are of this length, and most are made overnight from 7 pm to 7 am. Murray Melbin (1987: 44) long ago noted that 'night-time has a popular image as a period of anarchy and risk, crime-ridden and outside of social control', and curfews are a simple means of sequestering people from risky times and places, disrupting incipient nocturnal criminality. They are also a way of requiring offenders to adopt the conventional habit of sleeping at home at night, which some of them may have done anyway. It can be purely retributive, punitively depriving someone of their evening leisure time, or, as has happened more recently, it can be imposed 'constructively' to ensure an offender is awake and refreshed enough to undertake unpaid work the following day – using EM to foster compliance with other elements of a sentence. Spontaneous decisions to spend an evening with friends (unless they come to your home) or to sleep elsewhere are ruled out. Compliance with an EM curfew may well be harder on warm summer evenings than cold winter ones (Herzog-Evans 2012).

Curfews can be used more flexibly, during the day, splitting the 12 hours into blocks, tailoring them to specific patterns of offending. One of the monitoring companies describes 'a curfew imposed on a dealer found guilty of selling drugs [which] requires him to be housebound daily at the start of the school day, at lunchtimes, and again at the end of the school day; football hooligans [who] have curfews imposed on them that coincide with their team's match days and at weekends; and a prolific shoplifter … given two curfew periods a day from 9am to 2pm and from 4pm to 9pm, to keep her away from the shops as much as possible. The free periods allow her to take her children to and from school' (G4S International 2009: 36–37). These are interestingly imaginative uses of EM, although G4S does not say whether they were stand-alone or linked to interventions designed to address offending. Such cases are not easily identifiable in EM statistics and have figured little in research. The Criminal Justice Joint Inspection (2008: 7) noted only 'a small number of cases' of this kind, but recommended more.

The Joint Inspection also noted that offenders were confused by the 'enforcement thresholds' to which they were subject, largely because cumulative data about their brief absences was withheld from them, meaning they never knew how close they were to being 'in violation'. It was assumed by the monitoring company that uncertainty would make them err on the side of caution, and thereby reduce breach rates. In practice, this proved 'problematic in that whilst the impression was created that curfewed offenders were given very little rope, they were formally allowed a surprising amount' (Criminal Justice Joint Inspection 2008: para 1.27). The Inspectorate recommended an overhaul of enforcement and compliance practice, and the establishment of a 'smart' approach that was both stricter and more transparent to offenders, but which allowed offender managers considerable discretion regarding a breach decision in individual cases. A follow-up report found insufficient change four years later (Criminal Justice Joint Inspection 2012).

GPS satellite tracking regimes

The integrated use of GPS satellites and cellphone networks to monitor offenders' movements was piloted in the United States in 1997 and became more widespread after 2005, especially in respect of released sex offenders (Nellis 2012). Tracking technologies can, potentially, trail and trace offenders wherever they go, replicate curfews (inclusion zones) and permit the creation of exclusion zones (around former victims' homes or in areas of previous offending) from which offenders are prohibited entry. There are different types of technology (one-piece units, two-piece units) and different types of regime (active/continuous real-time monitoring or passive/retrospective checking of movements, and hybrid – a mix of the two), which, between them, vastly extend the scope of surveillance beyond a single location. Mapping software can display both patterns of movement, over a day, a week or a month, and speed of movement (from which mode of transport can be inferred). Tracking systems can trigger alerts if exclusion zone perimeters are approached, or if two or more tracked offenders who have been forbidden to meet (e.g. criminal associates or rival gang members) come within close proximity of each other. Some programmes can tally offender movements alongside known (and time-stamped) crime incidents stored on police computers, placing individuals at or near the scene, or (as usefully) exonerating them. Tracking devices require more powerful batteries than presence-monitoring devices, and the offender may need to set aside time each day to charge the equipment; clip-on batteries are reducing the need for offenders wearing one-piece units to sit for two hours with the unit plugged into an electrical socket. A tracked, mobile offender can be informed by an LED and/or mild vibration of his tag that the battery needs charging, that he has 'lost signal' and must move to a space where GPS can again pick him up, or that he is suspiciously close to an exclusion zone (Martinovic and Schluter 2012). Some United States companies advise monitoring staff to make active use of these contact capabilities, particularly at the onset of tracking, in order to remind the offender of their constant, remote presence in his life:

> Let your offender know that you are watching. Even if they are not generating a notification send them occasional messages, ie 'slow down' if they are exceeding the speed limit. An offender who continuously generates notifications should be called into the office and reinstructed, if not reincarcerated. Offenders who know that they will experience this inconvenience will begin to comply with the system. Offender behavior modification requires responding to offender violations as soon as possible. It is the key to reducing man-hours and running an effective programme. Most successful programmes are those which are strict with the offender.
>
> (iSECUREtrac 2006: 19)

Proven successes in EM have been hard to find (Renzema and Mayo-Wilson 2005) but are now appearing (Renzema 2012). Padgett et al.'s (2006) statistical analysis of 75,661 offenders who experienced EM home detention or GPS tracking in Florida between 1998 and 2002 convincingly demonstrated a crime suppression effect (reduced reoffending, absconding and technical violations), even with serious offenders, for the duration of the surveillance period, but not necessarily afterwards. Bales et al.'s (2010: x) follow-up study, which gathered more qualitative data, confirmed that EM significantly 'reduces the likelihood of failure under supervision (p. x) with GPS being more effective at controlling offender behavior than RF' (p. 153). It noted some 'unintended detrimental consequences' (p. 154) of EM – a sense of shame among wearers and reduced employment opportunities – and, as other studies have done, frequent false alerts and potential information overload for supervisors, but considered these remediable (some with better technology) and recommended expansion of the programme.

California runs the largest programme of GPS sex offender monitoring in the United States (6968 people, as of August 2011), three times larger than Florida. A recent study comparing 516 offenders who were either given 'traditional parole' or 'parole and GPS combined' concluded that 'the subjects in the GPS group demonstrate significantly better outcomes for both compliance and recidivism... [the likelihood of] both a parole revocation and a return-to-custody custody event... are about 38 per cent higher among the subjects who received GPS supervision' (Geis et al. 2012: vii). Compliance was understood here not only in relation to spatial and temporal restrictions (although exclusion zones were little used), but also with 'specialized treatment and supervision conditions'. Particular attention was paid to time to first violation and/or revocation, with GPS 'increasing the time until these events' occur (idem: xvii). California erred toward 'zero tolerance' (rapid return to prison) in response to parole violations, including GPS violations, which Geis et al. (2012: xviii) considered neither proportionate nor necessary for public safety, recommending instead a 'graduated sanctions system' for dealing with such violations (starting with a home curfew, where one was not already imposed). They also recommended greater use of inclusion and exclusion zones.

Manitoba police and youth probation services created an intensive post-custody supervision programme targeted at high-risk juvenile car thieves in 2005, adding (under political pressure) GPS monitoring to improve compliance with requirements and further reduce recidivism in 2008 (for never more than 20 offenders at any given time). Offenders are tracked for an initial three-month period, but probation officers have discretion to subsequently reimpose and remove tracking devices at any point in the supervision process, for variable periods of time, according to perceived risk and need. Participants were also given free mobile phones to facilitate contact with their workers (including agreed 'reporting-in' times). Forty-five of the 57 young people tracked between 2008 and 2011 were evaluated alongside an appropriate comparison group, 15 more than once. The evaluation concluded that, while GPS was not devoid of technical problems, it helped 'compliance with conditions'. Workers were immediately notified, via laptop or phone/text, of alerts and violations, including tampering with or removal of devices, and immediately phoned the offender to coach them back into compliance, or, failing that, ordered their arrest. Enforcement was not necessarily of the 'zero tolerance' kind: the programme permitted both strict and flexible responses to violations, depending on circumstance (Pearson 2012).

Claims that GPS tracking is an inherently superior 'upgrade' which will finally deliver the promise that anachronistic RH technologies failed to do (Doffing 2009; Geohegan 2012) are premature. GPS has found a (usually small and reasonable) niche in a number of European jurisdictions, and is still expanding, but EM home detention still serves a useful purpose. In the United States GPS has inevitably fallen short of the overhyped, techno-utopian expectations that policy makers have often bestowed on new forms of EM there (Lilly and Nellis 2012). Unsurprisingly, some offenders have, in fact, evaded its reach or committed serious crimes while being tracked: Myers (2011: 60) observed, of a tracked offender who killed a 13-year-old girl, that 'although the girl's location was not known until later, the offender's tracking device had been transmitting his location throughout the assault.' Media furore about such spectacular failures, fateful as it can be for policy making, should not obscure the far greater incidence of mundane compliance on GPS, or the high rates of verified non-compliance, or the manifest consensus that has grown, even among technology manufacturers themselves, about the importance of embedding tracking schemes in supportive social programmes, not only as 'good practice' but also, more cynically perhaps, to spread blame if and when serious violations occur:

[GPS] technology is highly effective, but it is not a replacement for in-person interaction between supervising agents/officers and enrollees. In fact, no technology can replace the critical person-to-person meetings, phone calls and visits. These interactions between supervising agents/officers and enrollees provide much needed information that isn't available by simply looking at a map of tracks.

(Satellite Tracking of People 2012)

The importance of this always seems to have been understood in England and Wales, where tracking, when it has been used, has (unlike most stand-alone EM curfews) been seen as an element of an intensive, integrated supervision programme, often jointly managed by police and probation officers. In the tracking pilots in 2004–2006 it was used in this way over a three-month period with sex offenders and persistent and prolific offenders (often drug-using burglars) who had been released on licence from prison, and with juveniles as part of Intensive Supervision and Surveillance Programmes. Offenders were not required to consent, but it was pitched to them as something which would be helpful, in so far as their location data could potentially exonerate them from future crimes of which, given past form, they would otherwise be suspected. Some resented it as an unduly intrusive follow-up to an already completed prison sentence: others accepted it with varying degrees of legitimacy. With the drug-using burglars, in particular, enforced exclusion from the zones in which they had previously offended (near or around where they, their family and friends lived) proved to be a highly effective way of gaining compliance with all aspects of their supervision (reporting to a police station, accepting home visits, participation in programmes, random drug testing). Full compliance with exclusion for a month earned them a day per week in the zone during the second month and longer periods in the third month; any non-compliance with any measure lost them this privilege (Nellis 2009a).

An enterprising new technology company called Buddi helped reintroduce GPS tracking in England and Wales, in two 'private arrangements' outside the auspices of the Ministry of Justice, one in a South London Health Service Trust psychiatric secure unit (monitoring offenders for short absences or periods of temporary home leave) and one in Hertfordshire Police (monitoring persistent and prolific offenders (PPOs) which made creative use of crime scene correlation technology. In the latter case, GPS tracking was grafted into a pre-existing intensive supervision programme as a matter of local policy, and, as such, could only be used with offenders who voluntarily consented to wear tracking devices. What had merely been motivational in the GPS pilots – location data that would potentially exonerate them – here became the centrepiece of a programme which purposefully gave offenders the opportunity to 'demonstrate desistance', with the additional incentives of (a) avoiding relentless 'stop-and search' demands from the police and (b) not being regularly arrested as 'a usual suspect' whenever a typical PPO offence occurred. Unlike the GPS pilots, exclusion zones were little used. Tracked offenders who, over time, were deemed 'desisting' were treated more discriminatingly by the police and spared intrusive attention, thereby increasing programme efficiency and saving time and money. 'Participant dependence' has been reduced in Buddi GPS schemes by the use of straps with steel bands inside them; they can be cut with industrial bolt cutters (which can take 20 minutes, assuming an offender has access to them). The police prefer them because they are not as easily removable as the more widely used plastic straps, although they may pose 'health and safety' risks. Although the Hertfordshire programme has not been properly evaluated, the officer-in-charge has reported that a significant proportion of PPOs have welcomed the voluntary wearing of GPS trackers, experiencing it as both an incentive and an aid to going straight, and welcoming the freedom from the intrusive 'police attention' that they would otherwise have received (Murray and Campfield 2011). The programme played a part in renewing Ministry of Justice interest in GPS tracking, and at the time of writing 27 police forces, probation areas and Youth Offending Teams are showing interest in emulating such programmes (personal communication from Alexandra Vogel, Buddi, November 2012). What is intriguing about the Hertfordshire model is that it uses GPS tracking to go beyond mere compliance with specified conditions – though that remains an important element of the programme, including a general condition 'not to offend' – toward empowering persistent offenders to show that they have changed and to affect the way agencies understand and act towards them.

Offender responses to electronic monitoring

Studies of offenders' and families' experiences of EM measures (Gainey and Payne 2000; Richardson 2002; King and Gibbs 2003; Martinovic 2007; Martin et al. 2009; Payne and Gainey 1998, 2004; Roberts 2004; Staples 2005; Vanhaelemeesch and Vander Beken 2012) have shed much useful light on compliant and non-compliant responses. Given the variable 'punitive intensity' of EM programmes both within and between countries, it should be borne in mind that offenders are always speaking of EM in context, of *their* particular experience, of specific timekeeping regimes and variable responses to enforcement, not of a universal, timeless 'effect of remote monitoring' (Nellis 2009b). While little is known of the ways cultures and subcultures affect perceptions of being monitored and shape the vocabularies used to make sense of it, there is, internationally, a research consensus that EM is experienced by offenders as something more punitive and more psychologically demanding than the general public believe it to be, but is still, in the main, thought preferable to imprisonment because of the relative 'quality of life' it permits.

Even stand-alone EM can foster short-term prudence in offenders, encouraging them to think twice and enabling them to break bad habits such as association with other known offenders (Hucklesby 2009). There is evidence in several studies that offenders do use EM to resist peer pressure; indeed, with GPS there is evidence that a tracked offender may actually be shunned by his peers, lest *their* location be inferred by the authorities by dint of their usual association with him. In a manner suggested by routine activities theory, EM can function as a 'mobile guardian', demotivating offending by countering impulsivity and restricting opportunity. The presence of a bracelet on the ankle, or the base unit at home, can act as a prop, a tangible reminder to resist temptation. Furthermore, as Bonta et al.'s (1999) research suggested, the routines it fosters can stabilize some offenders – 'the bracelet helped change my life – it helped slow me down drastically,' a youth told Pearson (2012, p. 75) in Winnipeg. A curfewed offender told Vanhaelemeesch and Vander Beker (2012, p. 89) that 'In the beginning it is hard to become used to living on the hour ... just to go outside on certain hours ... I was used to going outside whenever I wanted.' Another person in the same study said:

> If I am at home, I can cut off the bracelet and can go away. In prison you cannot say, 'I will open this door and leave' ... Now you have more urge ... to go outside ... I feel a lot of pressure to go outside. Then I always have to look at the box and think 'I may not go outside'.
>
> (idem)

GPS tracking permits 'going outside', but has its own constraints and can create its own resentments. 'Giving me the bracelet made me want to steal cars,' said a youth in Winnipeg. 'It was them versus me, they were trying to put me back in the system with that bracelet. Regular probation means being checked on a few times a week. I like that freedom more. No-one is watching over you then ....' (quoted in Pearson 2012: 72). Offenders may find ways of performing 'partial compliance' with GPS, toeing some lines while reoffending in a spirit of insouciance or nihilism: 'I only complied with some of my conditions,' said one, 'I partied a lot with friends and stole cars a couple of times with the bracelet. I went joyriding in three cars, which is way less than normal in a two-week time span. But I did not breach my curfew.' Another youth did things the other way round: 'I missed curfews and would get arrested for being out after curfew. I would also forget to charge my bracelet and my phone. I did commit other crimes with it on, but I didn't steal cars' (quoted in Pearson 2012: 72–73). Some found the tag unbearable, ridiculous or shaming and cut it off. One of the Winnipeg youngsters who compared stealing cars to taking drugs, however, indirectly affirmed the logic of the Hertfordshire police's 'demonstrating desistance' model of EM, by saying 'the bracelet does not help or make them want to quit – unless they are ready to do so' (quoted in Pearson 2012: 76).

Given offender propensities for non-compliance, technical means of detecting it have had to be designed in to monitoring systems, and foolproof strategies for countering plausible offender excuses devised. Breathalyser-based remote alcohol monitoring uses voice verification, photography or pre-programmed facial recognition technology to ensure that the person breathing into it is the convicted person, and not a sober proxy. Sobriety bracelets can allegedly be spoofed by slipping luncheon meat, tape or paper between the sensor and the skin, or pouring ice-cold water on the foot to prevent perspiration, although the device has sensors which can tell if this occurs (McKnight et al. 2012). GPS jamming devices are illegal but can be bought on the open market. It is not clear whether these are being used by offenders, but Satellite Tracking of People's (STOP) BluTag tracker can notify the monitoring centre of attempts being made to jam it. Some tags contain motion sensors or heat sensors. The standard-use plastic strap cannot be pulled off accidentally (e.g. by bike pedals) – it has a breaking strain of between 35 and 40 kg – and cannot be stretched sufficiently to slip it off by heating it with a hair dryer: 'if pulled using fingers telltale impressions will be left in the fabric of the strap' (Serco 2010: 13). If it is cut or tampered with in the vicinity of the base unit the monitoring centre detects this. Some offenders will claim in court that they have been wrongly breached on the grounds that 'the monitoring company came and changed the kit, because it wasn't working,' to which Serco has responded:

> Those monitored frequently challenge or test the system by denying short absences or refusing to answer telephone calls. They often test the boundaries by walking very slowly away from the curfew address, when the phone rings they run into the house and answer it pretending that they have been in the address all along, claiming 'your kit doesn't work'. As a response we will call to check the calibration and replace the equipment. This is not because the equipment is faulty, but to prove when it happens again that both sets of equipment were operating properly.
>
> (Serco 2010: 13)

Tagged offenders can and have taken advantage of technical or administrative errors. If the base unit is calibrated wrongly – say at medium rather than short range – the data sent to the monitoring centre will indicate that the offender is indoors when he is not. When EM-curfewed Callum Evans committed murder a few yards from his front door, using a machete and an axe which he kept under his mattress, he was still in range of his base unit, which fooled the monitoring centre into believing that he was indoors at the time. Only because the two-minute attack was captured on a nearby CCTV camera did investigators examine the base unit, and discover that its range had been wrongly calibrated, giving Evans leeway to move beyond the curtilage of his house (*The Scotsman* 18 May 2006). Organizational inefficiencies can have similarly fateful consequences. For example, on the night when he murdered another teenager, Kieran Wright should have been sequestered under an EM curfew: he had had a tag imposed for a previous offence removed just two days before, but, because the court had given the monitoring company the wrong date for a new tag (for an new offence) to be fitted, he was inadvertently given the small window of opportunity in which the killing occurred (*The Daily Mail* 18 December 2007).

The dubious concept of 'Assisted Compliance'

In Sweden, Norway, Denmark, Belgium and Germany, EM home detention is only ever used as part of an integrated rehabilitation programme. EM fulfils a control function in such programmes, and may well be subjectively experienced as a punishment, but is, nonetheless, formally subordinated to a larger rehabilitative purpose. All participants have social workers or probation officers, part of whose task is to help, where necessary, with the stresses and strains that may be occasioned in families by the imposition of EM on one of their members. In England and Wales, where EM curfews have largely been stand-alone measures, without social work input, the concept of 'assisted compliance' has latterly developed, understood as measures to help offenders complete their periods on EM. It emerged collaboratively from both government and the commercial providers, drawing on accumulated evidence about patterns of non-compliance gathered by G4S, and Hucklesby's (2009) pioneering research. Most violations occurred, for example, in the first few days of an order: 73 per cent of those in the *first two* days related to no-shows for installation. Most violations were not premeditated, and reflected disorderly lifestyles: 69 per cent of them were for time violations. G4S responded with an experimental Compliance Project in South Yorkshire in 2011, to help offenders comply with the requirements of stand-alone EM. It aimed to foster increased completion of orders by reducing breaches and returns to custody, to make more efficient use of G4S resources and to meet national targets on order completion. It began by texting offenders a reminder to be at home when the installers called, and included making 'customer welfare calls' within seven days of the order commencing. These sought to check whether offenders understood both their curfew requirements and the way the equipment worked, to identify and resolve difficulties the offender may have been having with managing their curfew, and to 'show that we are here to help the offender successfully compete their curfew' (personal communication from Claire Sims, G4S, November 2011).

When violations occur, G4S will call the offender and invite explanations of why they missed their curfew start, or left home during it, and offer 'appropriate advice'. In line with the Criminal Justice Joint Inspection (2008) recommendation on transparency of time violations, G4S reiterate information about the cumulative two-hour threshold, advise how many minutes they have left before violation, warn them of consequences and 'offer our support to prevent escalation'. Where a pattern of lateness becomes apparent, G4S may start sending offenders a daily text, for seven days, one hour ahead of their curfew start – 'this is to help the offender get into a routine of getting home on time.' When these initial efforts at assisted compliance have failed, and breach initiated, the project has also texted reminders to offenders to attend court promptly for their hearings, which increases the likelihood of sentencers allowing an EM requirement to continue, as well as preventing wasted journeys to court by G4S personnel. An evaluation of the Compliance Project is awaited.

In an Australian context, Marietta Martinovic has suggested another form of assisted compliance, proposing a short-term (one month maximum) intensive support programme 'to get detainees who have committed repeat technical violations [of stand-alone EM] "back on track" in order to complete their EM-sentence' (Martinovic 2010: 422). It entails a somewhat stronger social work element than G4S's Compliance Project, in so far as it requires 'uncovering the reason/s behind the detainees lack of compliance' and 'working with an offender in a holistic manner' (idem). This is the reverse of the approach legislated in Scotland, where an EM curfew can be imposed as a punitive alternative to custody for breach of a Community Payback Order managed by social workers, allowing the original order and its putative benefits to continue to completion.

Conceptually, 'assisted compliance' seems to acknowledge an awareness of the limitations of stand-alone EM, acceptance that the unruly lifestyles and dispositions of many offenders are simply not amenable to meticulous regulation without additional social support, but it is not the equivalent of properly integrating EM in probation and subordinating it to broader rehabilitative aims (as in the aforementioned mainland European countries). On the contrary, 'assisted compliance' discursively, symbolically and practically (if subtly) affirms EM as the primary penalty, and compliance as the primary goal, and then seeks the addition of a means to accomplish this. Martinovic's version promotes task-centred social work, while G4S uses other components of the electronic communication infrastructure (mobile phones and texting) and some human contact to provide brief counselling. But compliance, as Robinson and McNeil (2008) have cogently argued, is inadequate as an over-riding aim in community supervision, and in the jurisdictions where 'assisted compliance' is catching on – compliance as an end in itself, rather than the further pursuit of offender change and desistance – it may well be signalling the insidious diminishment of former penal and social work sensibilities by burgeoning technological capacities (Franko Aas 2004; Parton 2008).

Control architecture and electronic monitoring

Much of the compliance-with-community-penalties literature, including that relating to EM, focuses on individuals. Negligible attention has been paid to the fact that EM constitutes an 'automated socio-technical system' which monitors the compliance of hundreds (and in some countries thousands) of offenders simultaneously. The hardware and software of EM systems – the tags and base units, the monitoring centres, the computer programmes and the code which underpins them, alongside the skills, routines and protocols of the workforce which operates them – constitute a distinct 'architecture' which is relatively new in penal practice, opening up to governments new possibilities in the control of offenders, and new experiences of constraint for offenders themselves (Jones 2006). EM architecture does not – could not – exist in isolation from the broader affordances of what Castells (2000) calls 'the network society' – cellular radio systems, GPS satellites, the internet – and represents a specifically surveillant way in which those globally available affordances can be honed and customized for penal purposes in particular nations. EM entails, at root, a simple form of autonomic computing which registers the presence or absence of large numbers of offenders at or from designated locations, at certain times of the day or night, or, in the case of GPS tracking, their mobility more generally. EM systems relentlessly correlate the proximity of tag and base unit, or triangulate specific locations, simultaneously, for thousands of offenders. Arrival at home for a curfewed individual becomes, simultaneously, entrance into digital space. EM converts the digital trace of someone's material presence at – or absence from – home into a sign on a screen in a monitoring centre, renders it actionable and inscribes a retrievable record of it into a database. In the monitoring centre, the offender becomes a 'datavidual', an attenuated telepresence, whose compliance or not with imposed requirements can be confirmed and responded to in real time (although limited resources and sometimes deliberate policy choices can dilute the near-immediacy which technology permits, and slow down response times). Typically, the offender does not self-identify – the tag signals his identity (and in some instances the staff 'know' offenders only by encrypted numberstrings, not by their names).

There are undeniably elements of immaterial, virtual oversight here, but the material architecture of EM systems must also be acknowledged as a necessary penal investment if this form of control is to be effected (Braidotti 2003). Operationally, current EM systems require a human workforce to interact with offenders, but it is a 'monitoring machine' with nationwide reach, embedded within existing information and telecommunication networks, that makes the remote surveillance of offenders' mobility possible, rendering enforceable the legal and administrative requirements with which they are expected to comply. Some monitoring arrangements are, in fact, cross-national: sex offenders in an Irish GPS pilot in 2010 were tracked from G4S's monitoring centre in Salford, England, while young offenders in Winnipeg are tracked at OmniLink's monitoring centre near Alpharetta, Georgia, over a thousand miles south in the United States. The many component parts of the 'monitoring machine' – GPS signals in particular – are prone to occasional meteorological and environmental interference, and technical malfunctions, which can affect the continuity and quality of the surveillance to which offenders are subject, though not to the extent of rendering the use of the systems untenable (Royal Academy of Engineers 2011).

In conceiving EM as a form of surveillance-based compliance, ocular metaphors cannot be pressed too far. EM does not 'see' in the way that CCTV surveillance does, and, given that it works by remotely monitoring a wearable device, it (skin-sensitive sobriety bracelets in particular) may well be better thought of as 'informated touch' (Bogard 1996: 77) – but it nonetheless creates 'regimes of visibility and intelligibility' (Rouvroy 2011: 122) that have no real precedent in the more humanistic forms of offender supervision. In so far as it utilizes a computerized database of offender locations, which in some jurisdictions can be linked to other police databases, it resembles Poster's (1996) 'superpanopticon', while in sequestering offenders at home, and using GPS tracking to enforce exclusion from designated areas of public space, it also exemplifies what Bigo (2006) has aptly called the 'ban-opticon'. None of this would be feasible, on a vast scale, in real time, without computers into which the code-equivalent of correctional goals has been programmed. It is code that generates the signals (lateness, tampering) to which human monitors respond (by phone) in dealing with monitorees, or which go direct to the artefacts carried or worn by offenders (e.g. alerts about low battery strength or proximity to a forbidden perimeter). Code mediates human–machine interaction, or, to use a more technical term, it *entrains* – signals certain courses of action (instructions or suggestions) to people who are engaged with it (the monitors) or enrolled in it (the offenders). 'Just as code is at once a language system and an agent commanding the computer's performances,' writes Hayles (2006 – cited in Rouvroy 2011: 137), 'so it interacts with and influences human agency.' The inalienable reflexive element in *entrainment* makes it the equivalent, conceptually, of Crawford's (2003) 'regulated self-regulation'. It is only in terms of what encoded regulatory mechanisms actually require an offender to do, the way they attempt to entrain his/her performance, that the distinct nature of compliance with EM – of what is being complied with – can be fully understood (Jones 2006).

EM systems are a form of mass monitoring from one or several centres, which *individuates*, but rarely *personalizes* its approach. Nationwide (in Britain), thousands of 7pm curfews are enforced simultaneously, using only a handful of monitoring officers working shifts 24/7, to appraise data, communicate with offenders deviating from their schedules, troubleshoot domestic problems and notify the relevant authorities of the non-compliant. Each individual offender relates to a schedule that has been programmed into a machine, compliance with which, for the duration of the period of surveillance, is measured and recorded in seconds, a level of techno-managerial precision which evokes Rouvroy's (2011: 134) fears about 'the annihilation of contingency'. In this sense, the emergence of 'electronic tracking', as Gilles Deleuze (1990, 1995) dubbed EM generally, may well be illustrative of a shift from 'disciplinary societies' in which individuals were required to internalize certain norms of law-abidingness via discrete social interventions, which (notionally) built character and had lasting effects, to 'control societies' in which individuals are required to obey rules generated by 'expert systems', without any necessary expectation that they will internalize norms, acquire character or improve their self-control in the longer term. Deleuze's contrast between 'governing the soul' (cultivating intrinsic self-discipline) and 'modulating mobility' (imposing extrinsic control) may be unduly polarized, but he correctly sensed that EM, while having disciplinary elements, was not disciplinary in quite the manner of earlier, more humanistic, forms of community supervision (Binkley 2009; Bogard 2010). Manifest differences of control architecture apart, imposing EM is akin to imposing a fine, where the simple binary of paid/not paid is the criterion of compliance (see Bottoms 1983): the equivalent binary in EM's case is presence/absence. In essence, all that EM measures require is the positioning of one's tagged body within a matrix of designated schedules and locations. Sobriety bracelets extend this, requiring behavioural compliance as well – refraining from alcohol use – but, under most prevailing forms of EM, it is *where one is*, rather than one's normative commitments or broader behavioural choices, that shapes the operation of the penalty: location, not demeanour, is what is monitored. The fact that EM alone may not effect lasting behavioural change beyond the duration of the order itself may be irrelevant to its champions: rather than investing now in support and treatment which may possibly improve future behaviour, why not, they may ask, simply reimpose further successive periods of electronic control?

Conclusion

Monitoring compliance (or its absence) with specified requirements is what EM is designed and intended to do. It can and does achieve it, not perfectly, not without collateral consequences, but sufficiently well to render the continuing appeal of EM to penal policy makers intelligible. Spatial and temporal restrictions were placed on offenders in the community in the pre-EM era, and unpunctual timekeeping at probation appointments and community service sites was previously penalized, but EM has vastly increased the range and precision of schedules and location requirements with which offenders can be instructed to comply, the span of time per day over which they can practically be held accountable. While commendable effort has been devoted in many mainland European EM schemes to integrating EM with probation-based support and treatment programmes, the swift, efficient and effective identification of violations, rather than any contribution it makes to rehabilitation and desistance, may be a more attractive feature of EM to some policy makers. Verifying failure to comply is as much 'success' in EM as desistance, and more intrinsic to its nature and purpose – it is evidence that the technical, computer-programmed aspect of the monitoring system works. EM's steady ascendancy is perhaps better understood as an expression of a deepening techno-managerial culture in criminal justice than as a wholly rational, properly considered and obviously better means of supervising offenders than what prevailed hitherto (Fionda 2000; Nellis 2009c). It is not that EM cannot or could not be used well in practice, parsimoniously, alongside other constructive measures: it can – the question is whether it will be. Centre-right scenarios in which there might be 140,000 tagged and tracked offenders per day in England and Wales in five or six years (Geohegan 2012: 18) – up from 25,000 per day at present, already the largest scheme in Europe – would utterly transform understanding of what 'community supervision' means, and not for the better. Although no one knows for certain what the vectors and timescales of techno-correctional change might be, it is tempting to suggest, especially when one looks at the fading fortunes of the probation service in England and Wales and the continuing growth of the private sector in criminal justice, that something new and sinister is growing in the ruins of the old (Collett 2013).

The concept of 'compliance' now informs several United States EM companies' self-description. BI Incorporated describes its suite of EM systems as 'compliance technologies that help monitor individuals released to community supervision'. iSECUREtrac's advertising tagline is 'monitoring compliance, modifying behavior'. Sentinel offers a full service of 'curfew compliance, location compliance, behavioral compliance [and] fiscal compliance' (the latter relating to offenders' means-tested rental of EM equipment). The danger here is that compliance is becoming a 'penal endpoint' in itself simply because systems can easily be customized from existing telecommunications infrastructures to monitor it, and that more humanistic, relational means of effecting further change in offenders, focused on desistance and reintegration, will come to seem idealistic, anachronistic, costly or unnecessary. We may, in Sherry Turkle's (2011) bleak words, come to 'expect more from technology than we do of each other'. The affordances of 'the network society' undoubtedly create new options for penal policy makers, different from traditional forms of community supervision. They can and should be embedded within older agencies and practices, but may, instead, acquire momentum and authority of their own. Electronic connectivity is now ubiquitous and widely desired for a range of commercial, governmental and recreational purposes; there is also widespread citizen acceptance of personal locatability for both convenience and pleasure. In a world in which 'mobile phones [have become] the technical foundation of the presumption of constant accessibility and availability' (Bauman 2011: 35) the state's (or its commercial proxies') capacity to pinpoint the whereabouts of a curfewed offender at night, or a tracked offender 24/7, is hardly, nowadays, the fearful spectre it would have appeared to George Orwell in the mid-20th century; it is simply a point toward the coercive end of a continuum of locatability. In a networked world where pinpointing is becoming easy and cheap, and in a hedonistic, consumerist culture, even one tainted by austerity, where social inducements to internalize self-control may be losing both credence and traction, the question that arises is less 'why would the state want to remotely monitor and manage offenders' locations?' and more 'why would it not?'

Notes

1. Sophisticated 'Plug and Play' EM technology, in which offenders are fitted with a tag before leaving court or prison, and given a base unit which they carry home and self-install, obviates the need for installation visits by monitoring officers, and reduces the opportunity for this particular kind of non-compliance, although it creates others.

References

Bales, W., Mann, K., Blomberg, T., Gaes, G., Barrick, K., Dhungana, K. and McManus, B. (2010) *A Qualitative and Quantitative Assessment of Electronic Monitoring*. Report for the National Institute of Justice. Miami: Florida State University.

Bauman, Z. (2011) 'Strange Adventures of Privacy (3)'. in Z. Bauman (Ed.) *44 Letters from the Liquid Modern World*. Cambridge: Polity Press.

Bigo, D. (2006) 'Security, Exception, Ban and Surveillance'. in D. Lyon (Ed.) *Theorising Surveillance: the Panopticon and Beyond*. Cullompton: Willan.

Binkley, S. (2009) 'Governmentality, Temporality and Practice: From the Individualization of Risk to the "Contradictory Movements Of The Soul" '. *Time and Society* 18(1), 86–105.

Bishop, L. (2010) 'The Challenges of GPS and Sex Offender Management'. *Federal Probation* 74(2), 35–41.

Bogard, W. (1996) *The Simulation of Surveillance: Hypercontrol in Telematic Societies*. Cambridge: Cambridge University Press.

Bogard, W. (2010) 'Deleuze and Machines: A Politics of Technology?' in M. Poster and D. Savat (Eds) *Deleuze and New Technology*. Edinburgh: Edinburgh University Press.

Bonta, J., Rooney, J. and Wallace-Capreta, S. (1999) *Electronic Monitoring in Canada*. Canada: Public Works and Government Services.

Bottoms, A. E. (1983) 'Neglected Features of Contemporary Penal Systems'. in D. Garland and P. Young (Eds) *The Power to Punish: Contemporary Penalty and Social Analysis*. London: Heinemann.

Bottoms, A. E. (2001) 'Compliance and Community Penalties'. in A. E. Bottoms, L. Gelsthorpe and S. Rex (Eds) *Community Penalties; Change and Challenges*. Cullompton: Willan.

Braidotti, R. (2003) 'The Material Foundations of Virtual Subjectivity'. in G. Kreutzer and H. Schelowe (Eds) *Agents of Change: Virtuality, Gender and the Challenge to the Traditional University*. Opladen: Leske and Budrich.

Castells, M. (2000) *The Rise of the Network Society*. Oxford: Blackwell.

Collett, S. (2013) 'Riots, Rehabilitation and Revolution'. *Howard Journal of Criminal Justice* (forthcoming).

Crawford, A. (2003) 'Contractual Governance of Deviant Behaviour'. *Journal of Law and Society* 30(4), 479–505.

Criminal Justice Joint Inspection. (2008) *A Complicated Business: A Joint Inspection of Electronically Monitored Curfew Requirements, Orders and Licences*. London: HMI Probation; HMI Court Administration and HMI Constabulary.

Criminal Justice Joint Inspection. (2012) *It's Complicated: The Management of Electronically Monitored Curfews*. London: HMI Probation; HMI Court Administration and HMI Constabulary.

Deleuze, G. (1990) 'Postscript on Control Societies'. *L'Autre Journal* 1 May 1990.

Deleuze, G. (1995) 'Control and Becoming: Conversation with Tony Negri'. in *Negotiations*. New York: Columbia University Press.

Fionda, J. (2000) 'New Managerialism, Credibility and the Sanitisation of Criminal Justice'. in P. Green and A. Rutherford (Eds) *Criminal Policy in Transition*. Oxford: Hart Publishing.

Franko Aas, K. (2004) 'From Narrative to Database: Technological Change and Penal Culture'. *Punishment and Society* 6(4), 379–393.

G4S International. (2009) 'Using Curfews to Change Behaviour'. *Monitoring Matters* 3, 35–37.

Gainey, R. R. and Payne, B. K. (2000) 'Understanding the Experience of House Arrest with Electronic Monitoring: An Analysis of Quantitative and Qualitative Data'. *International Journal of Offender Therapy and Comparative Criminology* 44(1), 84–96.

Geis, S. V., Gainey, R., Cohen, M. I., Healy, E., Duplantier, D., Yeide, M., Bekelman, A., Bobnis, A. and Hopps, M. (2012) *Monitoring High Risk Offenders with GPS Technology: An Evaluation of the California Supervision Programme*. Final Report. Washington: National Institute of Justice.

Doffing, D. (2009) 'Is There a Future for RF in a GPS World?' *Journal of Offender Monitoring*. 22 (1) 12–15.

Geohegan, R. (2012) *Future of Corrections: Exploring the Use of Electronic Monitoring*. London: Policy Exchange.

Herzog-Evans, M. (2012) 'The Six Month Limit to Community Measures "Under Prison Registry": A Study of Professional Perception'. *European Journal of Probation* 4(2), 23–45.

Hucklesby, A. (2008) 'Vehicles of Desistance? The Impact of Electronically Monitored Curfew Orders'. *Criminology and Criminal Justice* 8, 51–71.

Hucklesby, A. (2009) 'Understanding Offender's Compliance: A Case Study of Electronically Monitored Curfew Orders. *Journal of Law and Society*. 36(2), 48–71.

Hucklesby, A. (2011) 'The Working Life of Electronic Monitoring Officers'. *Criminology and Criminal Justice* 11(1), 1–18.

Jones, A. (2005) 'A Tagging Tale: The Work of the Monitoring Officer: Electronically Monitoring Offenders in England and Wales'. *Surveillance & Society* 2(4), 581–588.

Jones, R. (2006) 'Architecture, Criminal Justice and Control', in S. Armstrong and L. McAra (Eds) *Perspectives on Punishment: The Contours of Control*. Oxford: Oxford University Press.

King, D. and Gibbs, A. (2003) 'Is Home Detention in New Zealand Disadvantaging Women and Children?' *Probation Journal* 50, 115–126.

Lessig, L. (1999) *Code and Other Laws of Cyberspace*. New York: Basic Books.

Lianos, M. and Douglas, M. (2000) 'Dangerisation and the End of Deviance: The Institutional Environment'. in D. Garland and R. Sparks (Eds) *Criminology and Social Theory*. Oxford: Clarendon Press.

Lilly, J. R. and Nellis, M. (2012) 'The Limits of Technoutopianism: Electronic Monitoring in The United States of America'. in M. Nellis, K. Beyens and D. Kaminski (Eds) *Electronically Monitored Punishment: International and Critical Perspectives*. London: Routledge.

Martin, J. S., Hanrahan, K. and Bowers, J. H. (2009). 'Offenders' Perceptions of House Arrest and Electronic Monitoring'. *Journal of Offender Rehabilitation* 48, 547–570.

Martinovic, M. (2002) *The Punitiveness of Electronically Monitored Community-Based Programmes*. Paper presented at the Making the Community Safer Conference, Perth, 23–24 September 2002.

Martinovic, M. (2007) 'Home Detention; Issues, Dilemmas and Impacts for Detainees Co-Residing Family Members'. *Current Issues in Criminal Justice* 19(1), 90–105.

Martinovic, M. (2010) 'Increasing Compliance on Home Detention-Based Sanctions Through Utilization of an Intensive Intervention Support Programme'. *Current Issues in Criminal Justice* 21(3), 413–435.

Martinovic, M. and Schluter, P. (2012) 'A Researcher's Experience of Wearing a GPS-EM Device'. *Current Issues in Criminal Justice* 23(3), 413–432.

McKnight, A. S., Fell, J. C. and Auld-Owens, A. (2012) *Transdermal Alcohol Monitoring: Case Studies*. Washington, DC: National Highway Traffic Safety Administration.

Melbin, M. (1987) *Night as Frontier: Colonizing the World after Dark*. New York: The Free Press.

Murray, S. and Campfield, S. (2011) *GPS Tracking of Persistent and Prolific Offenders in Hertfordshire*. Workshop Presentation at 7th CEP Electronic Monitoring Conference, Evora, Portugal. May 2011.

Myers, R. (2011) 'Monitoring Sex Offenders by GPS III'. *Sex Offender Law Report* 12(4), 60–63.

Nellis, M. (2009a) 'Mobility, Locatability and the Satellite Tracking of Offenders'. in K. Franco Aas, H. O. Gundus and H. M. Lommell (Eds) *Technologies of Insecurity: The Surveillance of Everyday Life*. London: Routledge.

Nellis, M. (2009b) 'Surveillance and Confinement: Understanding Offender Experiences of Electronically Monitored Curfews'. *European Journal of Probation* 1(1), 41–65.

Nellis, M. (2009c) 'Electronic Monitoring and Penal Control in a Telematic Society'. in J. Doakes, P. Knepper and J. Shapland (Eds) *Urban Crime Prevention, Surveillance and Restorative Justice: Effects of Social Technologies*. Boca Raton, FL: CRC Press.

Nellis, M. (2012) 'The GPS Satellite Tracking of Sex Offenders in the USA'. in J. Brayford, F. Cowe and J. Deering (Eds) *Sex Offenders: Punish, Help, Change or Control*. London: Routledge.

Nellis, M., Beyens, K. and Kaminski, D. (Eds) (2012) *Electronically Monitored Punishment: International and Critical Perspectives.* London: Routledge.

Padgett, K., Bales, W. and Blomberg, T. (2006) 'Under Surveillance: An Empirical Test of the Effectiveness and Consequences of Electronic Monitoring'. *Criminology and Public Policy* 5(1), 103–108.

Parton, N. (2008) 'Changes in the Form of Social Work Knowledge in Social Work: From the Social to the Informational?' *British Journal of Social Work* 38, 253–269.

Paterson, C. (2007) 'Street-Level Surveillance: Human Agency and the Electronic Monitoring of Offenders'. *Surveillance and Society* 4(2–3), 314–328.

Payne, B. K. and Gainey, R. R. (1998) 'A Qualitative Assessment of the Pains Experienced on Electronic Monitoring'. *International Journal of Offender Therapy and Comparative Criminology* 42(2), 149–163.

Payne, B. K. and Gainey, R. R. (2004) 'The Electronic Monitoring of Offenders Released from Jail or Prison: Safety, Control and Comparisons to the Incarceration Experience'. *The Prison Journal* 84(4), 413–435.

Pearson, A. (2012) *An Evaluation of Winnipeg's Electronic Monitoring Pilot Project for Youth Auto Theft Offenders*, MA thesis, Winnipeg: University of Manitoba.

Poster, M. (1996) 'Databases as Discourse; or, Electronic Interpellations'. in D. Lyon and E. Zureik (Eds) *Computers, Surveillance and Privacy.* Minneapolis: University of Minnesota Press.

Renzema, M. (2012) 'Evaluative Research on Electronic Monitoring'. in M. Nellis, K. Beyens and D. Kaminski (Eds) *Electronically Monitored Punishment: International and Critical Perspectives.* London: Routledge.

Renzema, M. and Mayo-Wilson, E. (2005) 'Can Electronic Monitoring Reduce Crime for Medium to High Risk Offenders?' *Journal of Experimental Criminology* 1(2), 215–237.

Richardson, F. (2002) 'A Personal Experience of Tagging'. *Prison Service Journal* 142, 39–42.

Roberts, J. V. (2004) *The Virtual Prison: Community Custody and the Evolution of Imprisonment.* Cambridge: University Press.

Robinson, G. and McNeil, F. (2008) 'Exploring the Dynamics of Compliance with Community Supervision'. *Theoretical Criminology* 12(4), 431–450.

Rouvroy, A. (2011) 'Technology, Virtuality and Utopia: Govermentality in an Age of Autonomic Computing'. in M. Hildebrandt and A. Rouvroy (Eds) *Law, Human Agency and Autonomic Computing: The Philosophy of Law Meeets the Philosophy of Technology.* London: Routledge.

Royal Academy of Engineers (2011) *Global Navigation Space Systems: Reliance and Vulnerabilities.* London: Royal Academy of Engineers.

Serco (2010) *Electronically Monitored Offenders: A Guide for the Judiciary.* Norwich: Serco.

Staples, W. G. (2005) 'The Everyday World of House Arrest: Collateral Consequences for Families and Others'. in C. Mele and T. Miller (Eds) *Civil Penalties, Social Consequences* (pp. 139–159). New York: Routledge.

Turkle, S. (2011) *Alone Together: Why We Expect More from Technology than We Do of Each Other.* New York: Basic Books.

Vanhaelemeesch, D. and Vander Beken, T. (2012). 'Electronic Monitoring: Convicts' Experiences in Belgium'. in *Social Conflicts, Citizens and Policing.* Antwerp: Government of Security Research Paper Series (GofS) Series 6.

10
Compliance with Community Orders: Front-line Perspectives and Evidence-Based Practices

Pamela Ugwudike

Introduction

Studies and official statistics consistently show that many people serving community orders in England and Wales fail to complete their orders for negative reasons. According to the most recent official statistics, of the number of community orders terminated in the quarter ending December 2011, approximately 34 per cent of those serving community orders did not complete their orders successfully. Similarly, a significant proportion of those released on licence and placed under probation supervision were recalled to prison for breaching the conditions of their licence (Ministry of Justice 2012). Other studies have found that many people fail to complete offender behaviour programmes (Hollin et al. 2008; Kemshall et al. 2002; Palmer et al. 2007). Despite these findings, little is known about the strategies front-line practitioners employ to encourage compliance and how they deploy these strategies within ever-changing policy contexts. Equally, although there are now useful developments in the field of compliance theory (Bottoms 2001; Robinson and McNeill 2008) and evidence-based compliance strategies (Andrews and Bonta 2010), insufficient attention has been paid to the views of front-line practitioners regarding the strategies they employ. Consequently, very little is known about front-line practices and how these parallel or diverge from emerging theoretical perspectives on compliance and evidence-based practices. There is a need to examine these issues in order to find out how best to ensure that theoretical understandings and the relevant evidence base can inform policy and practice.

Conceptualizing compliance: Recent theoretical explanations

A commonly cited theoretical framework for understanding compliance is the one put forward by Bottoms (2001). Several chapters in this volume refer to this framework. As such, only a brief summarization of the framework is presented here. According to the framework, compliance may be the product of the singular or interactive effect of four mechanisms. Constraint-based mechanisms operate through physical constraints such as electronic monitoring and other surveillance devices that aim to control the offender and reduce opportunities for non-compliance. Habit or routine compliance mechanisms are habits that encourage conventional behaviour. Normative compliance mechanisms are internalized obligations to obey because the offender has formed a positive bond with a person in authority or with others in society, or because the offender believes that the probation officer metes out fair treatment and, as such, exercises their power legitimately.

Instrumental mechanisms of compliance operate as incentives that encourage compliance or disincentives (such as severe sanctions) that may discourage non-compliance.

Robinson and McNeill (2008; McNeill and Robinson 2013) develop Bottoms's framework further by providing insights into additional dimensions of compliance – formal and substantive compliance. Formal compliance involves complying with the basic legal requirements of a court order. It may involve simply attending statutory appointments without engaging with the change process. By contrast, substantive compliance involves the 'active engagement and co-operation of the offender with the requirements of his or her order' (McNeill and Robinson 2013; Robinson and McNeill 2008: 434).

Evidence-based compliance mechanisms

Added to the conceptual work on compliance developed by Bottoms (2001) and by Robinson and McNeill (2008), an emergent body of empirical work has drawn attention to specific skills practitioners can employ to encourage compliance during and after community-based supervision. These skills are described as Core Correctional Practices (CCPs) (Andrews and Kiessling 1980; Andrews and Bonta 2010; Bourgon and Lowenkamp, this volume; Alexander et al. this volume) and they can be summarized as follows:

- Effective use of authority
- Appropriate modelling and reinforcement
- Problem-solving
- Use of community resources – Brokerage/Advocacy
- Quality of interpersonal relationships

Effective use of authority involves using a 'firm but fair' approach (Dowden and Andrews 2004: 204). Being 'firm but fair' entails clarifying relevant formal rules and promoting compliance using positive reinforcements rather than controlling or abusive approaches. Appropriate modelling and reinforcement involve modelling prosocial behaviour that the probationers can emulate, such as being respectful and polite. It involves showing approval when clients exhibit desired behaviours and showing disapproval when clients exhibit undesirable behaviour. The clients should also be informed of the reasons why their behaviour was desirable or undesirable. According to Dowden and Andrews (2004), the primary objective of prosocial modelling and reinforcements is to ensure that probationers develop prosocial attitudes and prosocial behavioural patterns through their interactions with practitioners.

Problem-solving practices involve helping probationers learn how to resolve the problems that contribute to non-compliance. It entails helping probationers learn how to identify problems, implement plans of action, clarify goals, evaluate options, discuss alternatives and evaluate the entire problem-solving plan (Dowden and Andrews 2004). Advocacy and brokerage takes the form of referring clients to agencies that can help address their welfare needs such as employment, health and educational needs. The CCP 'quality of interpersonal relationships' involves displaying warmth, a sense of humour, enthusiasm, self-confidence, respect, flexibility and commitment to providing help. It also involves good communication skills that engage the clients, for example, communication that is 'non-blaming' but solution-focused. Several studies employing a variety of methods which include meta-analysis (Dowden and Andrews 2004) and observation methods (Raynor et al. 2010; Trotter 1996, 2006, this volume) demonstrate that the CCPs can help encourage compliance.

How do the conceptual frameworks and strategies described above translate in practice? To answer this question, this chapter draws on data that were generated from 19 main-grade probation officers based in several probation offices in Wales. Interviews with the probation officers explored (among several other issues) the strategies they employ to encourage compliance. Compared with the wider population of probation areas, the study sample has several distinctive features. The probation offices visited were located in predominantly rural areas with low rates of recorded crime compared with other probation areas. There is also a high rate of socioeconomic deprivation in the area. Other distinctive features include: the small population density and the large landmass, which poses transportation problems; the small size of the probation area in terms of its revenue budget and staffing levels; and also the under-representation of ethnic minorities, although the latter is reflective of the wider population of Wales in general. Alongside these disparities, there are consistencies between the study sample and the national average. Chief among these are the average lengths of service reported by the officers (eight years), which means that most of the participating officers were trained under the new training arrangements for probation officers that were introduced in 1997/1998.

Conceptualizing compliance: Front-line perspectives

Before I explore whether theoretical understandings of compliance and evidence-based compliance strategies inform front-line practice, it is perhaps useful to describe how the practitioners who participated in the study tended to define compliance. As Robinson (this volume) points out, compliance is not a static concept. Policy priorities and practice contingencies are just two of several factors that may shape constructions of compliance (see also Ugwudike 2008). Like several existing studies, the current study found that most of the participating practitioners tended to define compliance and non-compliance in terms of attendance and non-attendance (see, for example, Ellis et al. 1996). Asked to describe what constitutes compliance, the officers below stated:

> ...the standard failure to attend and that can have all different kinds of reasons to it acceptable or not...

> ...not attending appointments without good reason and without providing evidence for that.... Often it's the non-attendance that ends up in court but that's not the only thing...

The officers below also describe the form of behaviour (non-compliance) that would typically result in breach action:

> Failing to turn up obviously and not getting in touch with me and telling me why you haven't turned up.

> ...what's normally resulted in me breaching people is people not just bothering to turn up for their appointments...the main reason I breach people is basically just for a lack of contact. They've not bothered to come in and see me.

Other studies have observed this tendency to focus on a one-dimensional conceptualization of compliance and non-compliance (Ellis et al. 1996; Mair and May 1997). Robinson (this volume) traces the general view of compliance as attendance to prevailing policy priorities in the period she describes as 'the era of standardisation (the 1990s)'. In that era, attending statutory appointments became the prevailing definition of compliance, at least at policy level. Robinson (this volume) rightly notes that this conceptualization of compliance persisted during the 'era of enforcement' (the late 1990s to 2004), when policy attention came to focus on improving 'compliance levels'. Under current policy arrangements, in the era that Robinson describes as the 'era of pragmatism', there has been a shift toward 'offender engagement' (Ministry of Justice 2012). Greater attention is being paid to the importance of encouraging not only attendance but the active engagement of the offender in the change process. Robinson (this volume) addresses some of the policy and practice developments that have been linked to the shift toward offender engagement.

Meanwhile, it is worth noting that the study presented here was conducted in the 'era of enforcement'. Probation areas (as they then were) were required to achieve target enforcement rates (Home Office 2000). In contexts where practitioners are expected to produce quantifiable 'results' in the form of rates of enforcement action for non-compliance, there may be a tendency to focus on absenteeism as the main form of non-compliance. Attendance, being as it is a readily quantifiable 'result', may become the primary definition of compliance. Therefore, the reductionist view of compliance as attendance may have also been attributable to the difficulty of providing evidence to support qualitative forms of non-compliance, such as the refusal to engage in the change process. A difficulty posed by this one-dimensional definition is that the probationers may internalize this definition of compliance (and non-compliance) and come to define compliance as routine attendance even where such attendance amounts to nothing more than formal compliance as described by Robinson and McNeill (2008). A key implication of formal compliance is that, as Robinson and McNeill observe, it may become difficult to ascertain the offender's level of motivation and to adapt the change process accordingly. In addition, probationers who are more committed to the objectives of the order, but who are for genuine reasons unable to meet routine attendance requirements, may be unfairly penalized (Robinson and McNeill 2008).

Practitioner-defined compliance mechanisms

Interviews with the participating officers addressed two key areas that can affect compliance, namely:

- How the practitioners encourage compliance during supervision.
- How the practitioners respond to non-compliance during supervision.

The second aspect of practice was quite relevant at the time of the study, not least from a policy perspective. Enforcement action was at the time the primary compliance mechanism prescribed by the relevant policy (Ministry of Justice 2007; National Probation Service 2005).[1]

Encouraging compliance

Most of the participating practitioners reported that, to encourage compliance, it is important to address potential and actual obstacles to compliance. They identified several key obstacles, which may be categorized as structural problems (such as a lack of suitable accommodation, unemployment and literacy problems). The officers also identified non-criminogenic obstacles to compliance, and these include employment commitments. There are practical obstacles such as travel difficulties, and lifestyle-related obstacles such as substance use. The officers reported that, to encourage compliance, it is important to address these obstacles:

> ...I mean the whole point, the reason people get into trouble is that they have, well one of the reasons is the difficulties in their lives and so to reduce the risk of reoffending you've got to look at those areas and work on them...you've got to take things a stage at a time and look at the priorities but you can't expect people to do huge amounts of work while they've got lots of practical difficulties that are really worrying them...

> ...we acknowledge, like the Offender Manager side, that individuals have lives of stress and you're sort of trying to understand where that person is in their lives. Especially if they're homeless. Probation might not feel a priority for them when they're like trying to find somewhere to sleep. It's like trying to get the right balance which is hard but you sort of do it...you've got guidelines but you're sort of flexible according to the individual's needs...PO19F

Most of the participating officers also reported that they try to address the non-criminogenic routines that affect compliance (mainly employment commitments) by offering more flexible reporting arrangements. They try to address literacy deficiencies that may affect compliance by referring the offenders to appropriate agencies. Indeed, most of the officers identified poor literary skills as an important obstacle to compliance. Asked what the main obstacles to compliance are, the officers below state:

> Literacy if we don't acknowledge that..., I just think it's one we need to acknowledge and we need to ensure that our correspondence is easy to understand for those varying needs...

> Huge problem, huge problem. I couldn't believe until I started this job how big an issue literacy is in this area ...When you do a PSR you do the self assessment form. I had one guy filling it in asking me how to spell need and...you know, really bad. You know they were putting 'no' down as 'know'...And the way the warning letter and a lot of written information

here, the way they are it's almost as if they expect people to have very high basic skills levels. But you find that most, not most but many probationers will probably struggle with some correspondence.

To address this problem the practitioners try to ensure that they effectively communicate formal enforcement rules to the probationers:

It [the enforcement rules] is always explained to them verbally, you never just give them a piece of paper particularly in cases where you either know there are literacy difficulties or if you don't know whether there are or not, then you have to assume that they might not be able to.... PO3F

Indeed, all the participating officers reported that proactive rule clarification is another compliance strategy they employ. At the beginning of an order, the officers define the boundaries of expected behaviour when they inform the probationers of the formal rules:

At what stage do you tell them [the probationers] what would happen if they fail to comply?

Well they'll be told at the stage prior before them going to court because most offenders come to us for a PSR. So we will discuss the disposal and if it's going to be a Community Order then we would have explained to them what the circumstances will be of breaching that order. What the consequences might be for them so they know.

Studies reveal that rule clarification is an important compliance strategy (Trotter 2006). It is also a dimension of the CCP 'effective use of authority' (Dowden and Andrews 2004). Some officers identified travel difficulties as a key obstacle to compliance. The probation area visited has several offices that are spread across wide geographic areas with unstable public transport facilities. In some cases, probationers are unable to attend appointments because of the financial costs of travelling to the probation offices. Some of the officers reported that they make home visits to address this problem:

Travel is a biggy round here as well. I mean people from ... which must be 20 miles ... 30 miles away, and the bus service is not very regular here. So you will take into account ... People live out in the countryside and if they don't drive, or they are banned from driving you can't force them to. So you know you drive out, home visits ...

Substance misuse was identified as a problem that can fuel a chaotic lifestyle and make routine attendance (compliance) extremely difficult. Most of the participating officers reported that they respond to non-compliance in such cases by making home visits, offering reminders and offering flexible appointments:

> ...we try to arrange appointments...time of day that is best for them. So if people have to take medication maybe first thing in the morning, we arrange it for later on. Some people just can't function in the morning whereas other people would rather come in before they start drinking...P2F

Other officers rejected the use of these strategies. They tended to adopt a responsibilizing stance that allocates responsibility for compliance to the probationer:

> I wouldn't normally phone because at the end of the day any order made between the court and the offender is between them. We don't make the order, we stand back and we supervise it. So it's actually the offender's responsibility to comply...

Added to the effort to address the difficulties that can affect compliance, another key compliance strategy identified by several participating officers is the effort to build a positive relationship with the probationer. This approach was perceived to be more effective in encouraging compliance than strict enforcement action:

> ...I don't want to breach people unless I have to breach people because I don't think it's very useful ...I just like to try to sort of get some sort of relationship going with people and try and help them make the changes that they need and so there's not that many that I've had to sort of breach really.

Here the objective of this practitioner's approach is to develop bonds with the probationer in order to facilitate compliance. Below another officer emphasizes the importance of developing relationships in order to secure compliance:

> *How do you encourage compliance...?*
>
> ...it's about trying to develop a good working relationship with them from the very beginning so that they feel that there's actually some point to them coming here. PO3M

The relationship may be characterized by respect, empathy and flexibility:

If you treat them with respect all the time you get respect back. If you're gonna be this sort of robotic probation officer then I think you're gonna be breaching a lot of people.... So I think it's about respect really. You respect people and they respect you back. That's how it works.

There were opportunities to observe several supervision interviews, and it was clear that the practitioners try to engage the probationers with what may be described as 'open, warm, and enthusiastic communication' and that there is 'mutual respect and liking' between the probationers and practitioners (Dowden and Andrews 2004: 205). According to Dowden and Andrews, and several studies mentioned above, these relationship factors are aspects of the CCP 'good quality interpersonal relationships between both parties', which can help encourage compliance.

Responding to non-compliance

In responding to non-compliance, most of the participating officers appeared to prefer client-centred approaches that are similar to the strategies they use to encourage compliance. Most of the officers reported that they employ individualized responses to non-compliance. There was a generalized view that a flexible approach that is responsive to the needs of the probationer is a more productive approach to enforcement than strict enforcement:

I really do believe if you take a very authoritarian approach to people quite often you're gonna to come to a brick wall.

That's why I am wondering about the current enforcement framework you know two strikes and you're out, I don't know how that would work with probationers ... whether that's an effective deterrent if at all?

I don't think there's anything to show that it is, do you see what I mean? I think all that does is just basically mask the problem up. There's only so long that can go on for anyway, everyone is gonna be locked up you know? PO13F

The enforcement policy operative at the time of the study required practitioners to commence breach action following two unacceptable absences within any 12-month period[2] (Ministry of Justice 2007; National Probation Service 2005). These provisions were perceived by most of the practitioners to be counterproductive. Strict enforcement in the form of breach action in court tended to be reserved for cases involving persistent absenteeism where no effort has been made to notify the practitioner of the reason or reasons for absence.

The findings regarding the use of welfarist compliance strategies, such as being responsive to obstacles to compliance and adopting individualized enforcement strategies, were consistent even among practitioners who qualified after the introduction of the 'tough' enforcement policies of the mid-1990s onwards (see also Deering 2010). Indeed, most of the participating officers were trained under the training arrangements that were introduced in the late 1990s.

Encouraging compliance in contemporary policy contexts

While most of the participating officers reported that they try to adopt compliance strategies that are individualized and responsive to the needs of the people they supervise, they did identify several policy developments that undermine their ability to work effectively to implement these strategies. Although the current government has revealed that it intends to decentralize probation policy (Ministry of Justice 2010a, 2011a, 2011b), managerialist strategies such as centralized performance targets may incentivize performance-focused practices. For example, as mentioned earlier, practitioners may find themselves under perceived or real pressure to focus on practices that produce quantifiable results.

Another development that has reconfigured probation policy and which may also impact on front-line compliance strategies is the discourse of 'risk management' and its corollary 'public protection'. Several commentators have extensively theorized the emergence of 'risk' as a key penal discourse (see Feeley and Simon 1992). In community-based supervision contexts public protection became an important feature of probation policy, particularly following the provisions of the Criminal Justice Act (CJA) 1991, which allocated the service greater responsibility for supervising groups who are assessed as posing a high risk of reoffending or a high risk of harming others (National Probation Service 2005). In addition, the 2005 National Standards introduced a system of allocating probationers to interventions that match their levels of assessed risk. Some may argue that the 'what works' approach, which emphasizes the importance of allocating and treating probationers according their levels of assessed risk, may have contributed to the risk-focused discourse in penal supervision. Nevertheless, the proponents of the approach do clearly state that risk assessment practices should be applied to the more productive aim of ensuring that interventions are adequately tailored to suit probationers' treatment needs (Bonta and Andrews 2007). According to the relevant evidence base, tailoring interventions in this way can help reduce reoffending (Andrews and Bonta 2010; McGuire 2007). Despite the advent of risk as a key penal discourse, several participating officers reported that they employ flexible enforcement strategies in response to non-compliance even in cases involving probationers assessed as 'high' risk:

With [a certain probationer] particularly, I mean he has an incredibly chaotic lifestyle... He's assessed as high risk so he's on twice weekly reporting in any event. It's his lifestyle; his alcohol use which he very much goes through ups and downs with it and personal issues. He has an on and off relationship that causes tremendous difficulties. So in a two month period, he'll be incredibly compliant turning up nearly every day and then he'll go through a two week period when he's drinking, when she's back in his life. With your highly chaotic offenders, when they are in a difficult patch the last thing they actually need is to be dragged before the court again for enforcement.

Here, it appears that individualized practices are deemed to be more productive than adopting rigid enforcement practices even in the case of an offender who has been assessed as high-risk. The officer uses her professional judgement to assess the case and to make an informed decision as to whether enforcement action will be productive in the given case.

Inter-agency working is another contemporary policy development that poses implications for the use of compliance strategies. The probation service now has a statutory duty to work collaboratively with external agencies drawn from the private, voluntary and other sectors. The advent of inter-agency working arrangements has heralded a rise in fragmentary supervision processes. The officers expressed mixed views about the implications of inter-agency working for compliance. Some officers endorsed inter-agency working because, in their view, it offers probationers access to a broader range of services that can help address obstacles to compliance:

> ...with the drive towards partnership agencies we've actually got a lot of ways in which we can deal with that [obstacles to compliance]. Whereas if we had to do it all yourself there simply won't be time... But if you've got somebody who's got alcohol and accommodation and employment [problems] we've got partnership agencies that we can refer to address that as well as us.

Other officers rejected the increasing requirement to delegate what they perceived to be the traditional role of the probation officer to external agencies, pointing out that delegation can create discontinuity. It can, as such, reduce opportunities to develop the working relationships they felt were crucial for encouraging compliance:

> ...I wonder as well with compliance,...I do wonder, I know what I would prefer, seeing the same person...I think in the end you won't wanna talk you just say yep, no...Cos it's always a stranger you see when you come in,

isn't it? . . . But I would imagine that if it was me that would be an issue with compliance . . .

How do you feel that affects motivation to comply where probationers have, see different (people)?

Very very badly. I think that's where we lose a lot of people to be quite honest. Because we're telling people, you've got to comply with this order, this is important, that's important. So important that you won't see the same person every week and you'll be asked exactly the same questions. . . . Unlike a lot of my colleagues, and I am not putting people down. I see all my own cases myself the majority of the time unless I am off ill, sick, training whatever. But if I'm training and I know I'm gonna be training, then I'll rearrange so that my cases will see me on another day. And I found that by taking that approach even though it's very stressful, it's paid dividends in terms of building a relationship with people. Because I know that I will very much resent somebody telling me what I need to do with my life and how I need to change it particularly if I have only met them three times.

As the views above suggest, discontinuity can undermine the relational element of supervision, which is now increasingly linked not only to short-term engagement during penal supervision, but also to longer-term compliance (Burnett and McNeill 2005). Burnett and her colleagues (2007: 230) observe that the fragmented supervision model 'distances staff from opportunities to relate to probationers as individuals', furthering the 'depersonalisation' of probation supervision.

The current study found that, even in a policy climate of 'tough' enforcement, most of the participating practitioners employed discretionary, individualized and welfarist compliance strategies. This finding is not surprising. It is quite consistent with several studies which show that front-line practitioners do not necessarily translate even the most rigid policy provisions in any straightforward manner. Practitioners may exercise their autonomy even where prescriptive policies exist (see, for example, Cheliotis 2006; Evans and Harris 2004; Lynch 1998). Reinforcing this finding, other studies reveal that welfarist values still exist within the punitive policy agenda (Bailey 2007). It is widely acknowledged that these values still inform front-line practice (Burnett et al. 2007). Commentators acknowledge that 'the practical tasks' (Mair 1997: 203) or 'the model of practice for working with probationers remains almost unchanged since 1907' (Burnett et al. 2007: 210). It is, however, important to recognize that, although many front-line practitioners may not translate policy provisions in a straightforward manner, preferring, instead, more welfare-oriented compliance strategies, policy developments can steer practices in particular directions. The one-dimensional definition of compliance described above demonstrates this (see also Phillips 2011; Robinson, this volume). In addition, the increase in officially recorded enforcement rates since the introduction of 'tough' enforcement policies also demonstrates the possible impact of policy developments (Ministry of Justice 2010b).

Discussion and conclusion

If we apply Bottoms's typology to the findings of the study presented here, it is quite possible to state that the responsive compliance strategies most of the practitioners employ could encourage normative compliance during penal supervision based on perceived fairness, which could in turn enhance the perceived legitimacy of authority and encourage compliance (Murphy 2005; Tyler (1990). It is also quite possible that the responsive approach, which, according to the participating officers, involves efforts to help the probationers address the problems that affect their lives, could act as an instrumental mechanism of compliance where the probationers view the help they receive as an incentive to comply. Here, two different mechanisms could operate simultaneously to encourage compliance. Equally, it is possible that building relationships may promote normative compliance based on bonds with people in authority. As Bottoms (2001) suggests, such bonds or attachments may trigger a willingness to comply with the directives of people in authority. Indeed, studies of community-based supervision show that relationships between probationers and their officers characterized by 'support and encouragement' may also be crucial for ensuring normative compliance (Rex 1999: 379). Such relationships could engender a sense of loyalty and a sense of obligation. Where loyalty and obligation are internalized, compliance is the likely outcome. Officers are, therefore, able to exert a 'positive moral influence over probationers' (Rex 1999: 380). Consequently, normative compliance based on the positive influence of bonds with people in authority may be achieved.

Apart from normative and instrumental mechanisms, Bottoms describes other mechanisms of compliance. While constraint-based mechanisms involving the use of devices to physically restrain people who are under penal supervision may not be directly relevant in probation supervision contexts, Bottoms's framework draws direct attention to habit mechanisms of compliance. As noted above, in Bottoms's (2001) typology of compliance mechanisms, habitual compliance 'occurs unthinkingly', more so than the other types of compliance. In the light of this brief description of habit compliance, it is clear that, although the practitioners' efforts to address obstacles may promote normative compliance which is based on attachments and perceived legitimacy, and although welfarist practices may serve as incentives to comply, such compliance does not necessarily 'occur unthinkingly'. Moreover, it is based on events that occur during supervision, such as bonds formed during supervision, perceived incentives on offer during supervision and the use of authority during supervision. What happens when bonds are severed at the end of the order? Can the feelings of attachment and perceptions of legitimacy transcend the immediate contexts of supervision and stimulate longer- term compliance? In addition, where compliance stems from perceived benefits such as the welfarist provisions available during supervision, what happens after the order ends and the perceived incentives to comply are no longer on offer? Perhaps these questions direct attention to the importance of ensuring that front-line practices incorporate habit compliance mechanisms (as described by Bottoms). Habit compliance, being as it is a phenomenon that triggers automatic compliance with conventional habits and routines (Bottoms 2001), is perhaps more likely to persist beyond the specific contexts from which it emerges. This is not to categorically state that normative mechanisms, such as building relationships based on mutual respect, remaining responsive to difficulties and adopting other strategies that are likely to be construed as legitimate use of authority, cannot promote long-term normative compliance, but to draw attention to the importance of helping people serving community orders to address the dispositions, routines and behaviours that have been empirically shown to underlie non-compliance.

Fortunately, in discussing possible mechanisms of habit compliance, Bottoms (2001) does draw attention to the cognitive behavioural approach[3] that now dominates supervision policy in England and Wales. The cognitive behavioural approach is also the dominant approach to offender rehabilitation in several North American and Western jurisdictions (Andrews and Bonta 2010). Broadly, in practical terms, the approach involves helping offenders learn how to replace antisocial attitudes and behaviours with prosocial alternatives. Several chapters in this book refer to the approach (see, in particular, Chapters 13 and 15). The approach incorporates the relationship principle, which involves developing good-quality working relationships with offenders. The cognitive behavioural approach also incorporates the structuring principle, which involves using relevant CCPs (described earlier in the chapter) to help offenders learn how to develop prosocial attitudes and behaviours (Dowden and Andrews 2004). In sum, the approach focuses on helping offenders address not only overt behaviours but also mental dispositions that may encourage offending behaviour.

Of the four CCPs, the participating officers did describe practices that fit in well with the CCP 'effective use of authority' and 'use of community resources'. In terms of the 'effective use of authority', efforts to communicate enforcement rules and individualized approaches to responding to non-compliance are consistent with a 'firm but fair' approach that underpins the CCP 'effective use of authority'. The practitioners also described practices that demonstrate that they 'use community resources effectively'. They refer the probationers to relevant agencies that can address the welfare needs that impede compliance. In addition, the effort to develop good-quality relationships was evident in the practitioners' accounts and in my observations of supervision interviews. Studies suggest that the remaining dimensions of the CCPs are also necessary for encouraging compliance. These dimensions are, as described above, appropriate modelling and reinforcement, and problem-solving (Dowden and Andrews 2004; Raynor et al. 2010; Raynor et al. forthcoming). While it is, of course, possible that the participating officers do implement both CCPs, they did not emerge as key themes or from my observations.

In sum, the strategies that most of the participating officers employ are responsive to the needs of individual probationers. Studies conducted by desistance theorists (Maruna and LeBel 2010; Ward and Maruna 2007) and by psychologists (Andrews and Bonta 2010), reveal that being responsive to offenders' needs, including their social, economic, practical and other needs, is very useful for achieving not only short-term compliance during supervision but also longer-term compliance with the law. But there are policy constraints that pose implications for the degree to which probation practitioners can remain responsive to these needs. In addition, given the emerging evidence base which points to the impact of CCPs on outcomes, it has perhaps become necessary to develop insights into how best to align front-line practices with the dimensions of the CCPs.

Notes

1. In current policy arrangements, there has been a shift away from the use of enforcement as the primary compliance mechanism. There are now measures in place that could effectively formalize the greater use of individualized compliance strategies that are based on professional judgement (see, for example, Ministry of Justice 2011a, 2011b; Rex 2012). What can explain the emerging official interest in compliance? One explanation might be that, quite apart from its human cost implications, an enforcement-focused approach to encouraging compliance can produce high rates of breach action in court. Custodial sentencing for non-compliance, which subsequently inflates prison numbers (Ministry of Justice 2010a), can also increase the fiscal costs of imprisonment. In addition, frequent recourse to court breaches can be costly and at odds with managerialist concerns of cost-effective offender management. Added to the ideals of improving efficiency and cost-effectiveness, there may be yet another pragmatic reason for the growing interest in compliance – securing compliance or 'offender engagement' now represents an important element in the drive for public and judicial credibility, just as enforcement has been in the recent past (Robinson and Ugwudike 2012).
2. The current enforcement standards have removed these requirements. They permit greater use of discretion during enforcement decision making (Ministry of Justice 2011a, 2011b).

3. The cognitive behavioural approach to offender rehabilitation underpins supervision policy and practice in England and Wales, and in several Western jurisdictions. Broadly, in practical terms, the approach involves helping offenders learn how to replace antisocial attitudes and behaviours with prosocial alternatives. Several chapters in this book refer to the approach. See for example, Chapters 13 and 15.

References

Andrews, D. A. and Kiessling, J. J. (1980) 'Program Structure and Effective Correctional Practices: A Summary of the CaVic Research'. in R. R. Ross and P. Gendreau (Eds) *Effective Correctional Treatment*. Toronto: Butterworth.

Andrews, D. A. and Bonta, J. (2010) *The Psychology of Criminal Conduct* Fifth Edition, Cincinnati, OH: Anderson.

Bailey, R. (2007) 'The English Probation Service up to 1972', in L. Gelsthorpe and R. Morgan (Eds) *Handbook of Probation*. London: Willan

Bonta, J. and Andrews, D. A. (2007) *Risk-Need-Responsivity Model for Offender Assessment and Rehabilitation*. http://securitepubliquecanada.gc.ca/res/cor/rep/_fl/Risk_Need_2007-06_e.pdf (accessed 10 March 2009)

Bottoms, A. E. (2001) 'Compliance and Community Penalties', in A. Bottoms, L. Gelsthorpe and S. Rex (Eds) *Community Penalties: Change and Challenges*. Devon: Willan.

Burnett, C., Baker, K. and Roberts, R. (2007) 'Assessment, Supervision and Intervention: Fundamental Practice in Probation'. in L. Gelsthorpe and R. Morgan (Eds) *Handbook of Probation*. London: Willan.

Burnett, R. and McNeill, F. (2005) 'The Place of Officer-Offender Relationship in Assisting Offenders to Desist from Crime'. *Probation Journal* 52(3), 221–242.

Cheliotis, L. (2006 'How Iron Is the Iron Cage of New Penology? The Role of Human Agency in the Implementation of Criminal Justice Policy'. *Punishment and Society* 8(3), 313–340.

Deering, J. (2010) *Probation Practice and the New Penology: Practitioner Reflections*. Farnham: Ashgate.

Dowden, C. and Andrews, D. A. (2004) 'The Importance of Staff Practice in Delivering Effective Correctional Treatment: A Meta-Analytic Review of Core Correctional Practice'. *International Journal of Offender Therapy and Comparative Criminology* 48(2), 203–214.

Ellis, C., Mortimer, E. and Hedderman, C. (1996) *Enforcing Community Sentences: Supervisors' Perspectives on Ensuring Compliance and Dealing with Breach*. London: Home Office.

Evans, T. and Harris, J. (2004) 'Street-Level Bureaucracy, Social Work and the (Exaggerated) Death of Discretion'. *British Journal of Social Work* 34(6), 871–895.

Feeley, M. and Simon, J. (1992) 'The New Penology: Notes on the Emerging Strategy of Corrections and its Implications'. *Criminology* 30, 449–474.

Hollin, C. R., McGuire, J., Hounsome, J. C., Hatcher, R. M., Bilby, C. A. L. and Palmer, E. J. (2008) 'Cognitive Skills Behaviour Programs for Offenders in the Community: A Reconviction Analysis'. *Criminal Justice and Behavior* 35, 269–283.

Home Office (2000) *The Use of Information by the Probation Services: A Thematic Inspection in 4 Parts, Part 1: Making National Standards Work: A Study by HMIP of Enforcement Practice in Community Penalties*. London: Home Office.

Kemshall, H., Canton, R., Bailey, R., Dominey, J., Simpkin, B. and Yates, S. (2002) *The Effective Management of Programme Attrition: A Report for the National Probation Service*. Leicester: De Montfort University.

Lynch, M. (1998) 'Waste Managers? The New Penology, Crime Fighting and Parole Agent Identity'. *Law and Society Review* 32(4), 839–870.

Mair, G. (1997) *Evaluating the Effectiveness of Community Penalties*, Aldershot, Avebury.

Maruna, S. and LeBel, T. (2010) 'The Desistance Paradigm in Correctional Practice: From Programmes to Lives'. in F. McNeil, P. Raynor and C. Trotter (Eds) *Offender Supervision: New Directions in Theory, Research and Practice* (pp. 41–64). New York, NY: Willan.

McGuire, J., Bilby, C. A. L., Hatcher, R. M., Hollin, C. R., Hounsome, J. and Palmer, E. J. (2008) 'Evaluation of Structured Cognitive-Behavioural Treatment Programmes in Reducing Criminal Recidivism'. *Journal of Experimental Criminology* 4, 21–40.

McNeill, F. and Robinson, G. (2013) 'Liquid Legitimacy and Community Sanctions'. in A. Crawford and A. Hucklesby (Eds) *Legitimacy and Compliance in Criminal Justice* (pp. 116–137). NY, London: Routledge.

Ministry of Justice (2007) *National Standards for the Management of Offenders: Standards and Implementation Guidance*. London: NOMS, Ministry of Justice.

Ministry of Justice (2010a) *Breaking the Cycle: Effective Punishment, Rehabilitation and Sentencing of Offenders*. http://webarchive.nationalarchives.gov.uk/20120119200607/http:/www.justice.gov.uk/consultations/docs/breaking-the-cycle.pdf (accessed June 2011).

Ministry of Justice (2010b) *Offender Management Caseload Statistics 2009*. Ministry of Justice Statistics Bulletin. https://www.gov.uk/government/uploads/system/uploads/attachment_data/file/163023/omcs-2009-complete-210710a.pdf.pdf (accessed June 2011)

Ministry of Justice (2011a) *National Standards for the Management of Offenders in England and Wales*. https://www.gov.uk/government/uploads/system/uploads/attachment_data/file/162202/national-standards-management-offenders-2011.pdf (accessed October 2011).

Ministry of Justice (2011b) *Breaking the Cycle: Government Response https://www.gov.uk/government/uploads/system/uploads/attachment_data/file/186345/breaking-the-cycle-government-response.pdf (accessed June 2011)*.

Murphy, K. (2005) 'Regulating more Effectively: the Relationship Between Procedural Justice, Legitimacy, and Tax Non-Compliance'. *Journal of Law and Society* 32(4), 562–589.

National Probation Service (2005) *National Standards*. London: National Probation Directorate.

Palmer, E. J., McGuire, J., Hounsome, J. C., Hatcher, R. M., Bilby, C. A. L. and Hollin, C. R. (2007) 'Offending Behaviour Programmes in the Community: The Effects on Reconviction of Three Programmes with Adult Male Offenders'. *Legal and Criminological Psychology* 12, 251–264.

Phillips, J. (2011) 'The Exercise of Discretion in the Probation Service and Bottoms' Model of Compliance'. *Howard League for Penal Reform, Early Career Academics Network Bulletin*, October 2011.

Raynor, P., Ugwudike, P. and Vanstone, M. (2010) 'Skills and Strategies in Probation Supervision: The Jersey Study'. in F. McNeill, P. Raynor and C. Trotter (Eds) *Offender Supervision: New Directions in Theory, Research and Practice*. Cullompton: Willan.

Raynor, P., Ugwudike, P. and Vanstone, M. (forthcoming) 'The impact of skills in probation work: A reconviction study.' *Criminology and Criminal Justice*.

Rex, S. (1999) 'Desistance from Offending: Experiences of Probation'. *The Howard Journal* 38(4), 366–383.

Robinson, G. and Ugwudike, P. (2012) 'Investing in "Toughness": Probation, Enforcement and Legitimacy'. *Howard Journal of Criminal Justice* 51(3), 300–316.

Trotter, C. (2006) *Working with Involuntary Clients: A Guide to Practice.* Second Edition. London: Sage.

Tyler, T. R. (1990) *Why People Obey the Law.* New Haven, CT: Yale University Press.

Ward, T. and Maruna, S. (2007) *Rehabilitation: Beyond the Risk Paradigm.* London: Routledge.

Section III

Evidence-Led Compliance Mechanisms: Recent Developments in International Research

11

Offender Recall for Non-Compliance in France and Fairness: An Analysis of 'Sentences Implementation Courts' Practices

Martine Herzog-Evans

In France, sanctions for non-compliance with community sentences and early release measures are imposed by special courts devoted to the implementation of sentences: the *Juge de l'application des peines* (JAP) and, for more serious cases, a three JAP court, the *Tribunal de l'application des peines* (TAP). Given that France is a written law country and not a common law country, courts are not allowed to create legal rules, laws or decrees that dictate what they can and cannot do. As a result, legal provisions expressly prescribe what constitutes non-compliance. Nevertheless, the special courts devoted to the implementation of sentences have considerable discretion. Previous research has shown that, in practice, these courts are very desistance and rehabilitation oriented. Therefore, they tend to be reluctant to activate the recall process except in cases involving serious non-compliance (such as reoffending, escape or repeat violations). The courts also tailor their reaction to the personal circumstances of the offender. To provide insights into the nature and impact of the compliance strategies employed by JAPs, the present chapter will draw, on the one hand, upon a large-scale research study that explored the professional culture of JAPs and, on the other hand, upon a smaller-scale research study that examined JAPs' practices of recall.

Introduction

Enforcement action in court for non-compliance during supervision seems to raise three questions. First, has the offender been given his day in court, and has the court listened to what he had to say, respected him and observed all the procedural features of a real court? Second, has the judge really tried to determine with all the rigour and caution of a court of law whether the offender is innocent or guilty of non-compliance? Third, if a sanction for

185

non-compliance is imposed, is it fair and proportionate with the offence and with the individual's circumstances?

In France, sanctions for non-compliance with a community sentence or measure are pronounced by special courts: the *Juge de l'application des peines* (JAP) and, for the most serious cases, a three JAP court – the *Tribunal de l'application des peines* (TAP). France being a written law country, what constitutes non-compliance is laid down in legal provisions. It nonetheless allows the courts some discretion.

Discretion can be defined as 'the freedom, power, authority, decision or leeway of an official, organization or individual to decide, discern or determine to make a judgement, choice or decision, about alternative courses of action or inaction' (Gelsthorpe and Padfield 2003: 3). This definition raises significant fairness issues. It suggests that the use of discretion may lead to discrimination or to significant, yet unjustifiable, differences between offenders placed in the same situation, and this has, particularly in the Anglophone world, fuelled the sentencing guidelines movement (Blumstein et al. 1983; Tarling 1979; Tonry 1996). In Europe, this movement had been promoted by the transparency in sentencing recommendation (No. R (92) 17, adopted by the Committee of Ministers of the Council of Europe on 19 October 1992), which, interestingly, has been totally ignored in France, where an individualized approach to sentencing that is based on the use of discretion prevails.

Indeed, French law permits the courts the use of considerable discretion. Although both article 132–24 of the French Penal Code and article 707 of the Penal Procedure Code (PPC) provide that sentences and their implementation must aim at and facilitate 'the reintegration of convicted persons as well as the prevention of recidivism, whilst respecting the interests of society and the rights of victims', article 132–124 section 1 adds ample reference to the principle of individualization of sentences, which has been cardinal in the French penal system since Saleilles (1898). Combined, these principles encourage French scholars and practitioners to believe that discretion is necessary in order to adapt the sentence, both at the time of sentencing and during its execution as the person and his circumstances change.[1] Thus, under French law, substantial fairness implies that the decision is discretionary and based on the offender's personality and circumstances, not on prescriptive sentencing guidelines.

It is acknowledged that the use of discretion also raises issues of procedural fairness. In France, since the enactment of two important laws in 2000 and 2004 (Herzog-Evans 2009) (art. 712–715 to 712–716 of the PPC), fair trial standards have regulated offender release, sanctions for non-compliance and other important supervision decisions (e.g. changing the conditions of the community sentence or measure). If, however, further reforms, particularly in 2009, have dejudicialized part of JAPs' decisions, the judge remains solely responsible for recalling offenders.

A discretionary approach based on individual circumstances is more likely to evoke perceptions of fair treatment than a rigid approach. The concept of fair treatment has been extensively explored in the legitimacy of justice literature. The literature suggests that compliance, which includes compliance with sentences (Collins 2007) and their implementation (Belenko 2011; McIvor 2010; Padfield et al. 2012), is increased when courts are fair.

Indeed, the legitimacy of justice literature has shown that people's satisfaction with courts is first and foremost based on the fairness with which they have been treated (Tyler 2006; Tyler and Huo 2002). Such fairness is supported by due process principles such as the right to a hearing, to counsel, to appeal and to access to the file, but it is also a matter of behaviour, respect and attitude toward people, as the therapeutic jurisprudence (TJ)[2] movement suggests (Burke and Leben 2007).

This chapter will explore the key themes described above. It will examine how offenders who have been accused of non-compliance during community-based supervision are treated by the French JAPs. To achieve its objectives, it will draw on a study that explored the activities of the JAPs in responding to cases of non-compliance, the views of other practitioners involved in prosecuting probationers for non-compliance and the factors that may affect decision making in such cases. The chapter will also describe the implications of the study's findings for offender compliance.

The study: Methodology

The study commenced in 2010 (Herzog-Evans, forthcoming a) and was ongoing when this article was written. It was conducted by the author, assisted by a team of students. It sought to ascertain whether French JAPs had a desistance compass when they ruled and met offenders, that is, whether they had an understanding of the desistance process and acted with the ultimate goal of encouraging desistance.

Our objectives were three-fold. First, we wanted to know what JAPs said and thought about their practice. We interviewed 72 JAPs (of the 387 existing JAPs, that is, nearly 20 per cent of all JAPs). Second, we compared JAPs' points of view with other practitioners' perceptions. Therefore, at the time this article was written, we had interviewed 38 probation officers, five trainee probation officers, 14 probation chiefs, 19 solicitors and 11 prosecutors. Third, in order to compare interviews with actual practice, we attended 45 hearings which dealt with a total number of 525 offenders. In the same vein, we collected 1300 court rulings, 292 of which concerned sanctions.

In order to cover a large variety of regions, the field work and the interviews were done by the author (who interviewed most JAPs) and fifth-year law students[3] situated in the three universities where the author teaches (Nantes, on the West coast; Reims, in the North East; Agen, in the South West). From our interviews, hearing attendance and observations of rulings, we covered most French regions. All interviews were based on semi-structured questionnaires; they were recorded and then transcribed verbatim. During the hearings we noted everything that was said, but also the tone of voice, the ambiance, the facial expression of both the judge and the probationer, and so on. All hearings and rulings were coded by the author.

An evident limitation of this study is, however, that no offender was interviewed (compare Digard 2010). In France it is extremely difficult to gain access to offenders for various reasons explained elsewhere (Herzog-Evans 2011). These include the duty of professional secrecy (art. 226–13, Penal Code) and the extremely powerful principle of privacy (Jacobs and Larrauri 2012). Given the extent of our research, it would have been simply impossible to generate a comparable sample of offenders in all the regions where we investigated. Also, I decided earlier on that I would not submit my students to the worry of seeing the term pass without being able to collect such a sample. Still, I have not abandoned such a project for the upcoming years. Moreover, as mentioned above, in order to try and counterbalance this serious limitation, I also compared JAPs' points of view with the perceptions of other practitioners.

Below I describe our key findings regarding JAPs' approach to dealing with cases of non-compliance during supervision.

Prosecuting breach in JAP courts: Does procedural fairness matter?

In France, most cases of non-compliance are dealt with in the course of a hearing which is very similar to that of a Drug Court.[4] Since the consequence of a recall is that the person may return to prison (Digard 2010), fairness matters (Liebling 2007) just as much as it does in a sentencing court, which is the court that imposes the initial order. There should, therefore, be no difference as to the burden of proof, the principle of innocence and the need for a fair trial, between such cases and sentencing cases. What this research has shown is that JAP hearings are rehabilitative, fair, intimate and collaborative rituals where offenders can defend themselves. However, both the law and practitioners have not given sufficient thought to the issues of presumption of innocence and burden of proof.

A limitation of JAP courts: Undermining the presumption of innocence and the procedural rules regarding the burden of proof in criminal cases

The most prominent weak point of JAP breach hearings is a lack of concern for the presumption of innocence, which is hardly compensated by an obsession with demanding that the probationers being prosecuted for breach should bear the burden of proof by providing relevant documents to support their claims. As we argued earlier, the courts should have an equally open mind as to the person's guilt. Likewise, solicitors should be attentive to the possibility that their client is innocent and, when in doubt, should opt for an adversarial stance. In other words, the collaborative *'auxiliaire de justice'* (justice auxiliary) attitude should be halted in the presence of a reasonable doubt.

In practice, however, we observed that at best the offender or his solicitor might present a document showing he has actually complied with the obligation; for instance, that he has looked for a job, started treatment, paid damages or the day-fine, or has not received notification of the meeting. However, from the legal viewpoint, this is arguably wrong: why should the offender give documented proof that he is 'innocent'? Should there not be a strong burden of proof for the prosecutor to establish, beyond reasonable doubt, that the offender has committed the litigious breach?

For the most part, JAPs are oblivious to the fact that they may be recalling innocents. They only concede that there may be an issue of presumption of innocence in instances when the breach consists in a new offence. In such a case, a minority of JAPs wait until the person has actually been sentenced before they examine the breach. However, the law does support this direction, which mentions that conditional release (PPC, art. 733) and other measures (PPC, art. D 49–24) can be withdrawn if the person has displayed 'notorious misconduct' or 'bad behaviour', respectively. This is understood by most JAPs as allowing them to revoke a release measure when an individual has been charged with an offence by the prosecutor, but has not yet been sentenced.

Moreover, when the offender is imprisoned and the issue at stake is whether the JAP should revoke remission for a prison disciplinary offence, the French legal system is far from inspired. There, the law states that the offender should not be heard, that there should be no counsel, that the JAP has to decide during a 'CAP' (for *commission de l'application des peines*) meeting – not a hearing – situated in the prison, surrounded by prison staff (the governor, guards and probation officers) and the prosecutor (PPC, art. 712–5). The procedure is thus neither adversarial nor even fair. It is plain that, for example, in view of the European Court of Human Rights rulings in Ezeh and Connors v. United Kingdom, 15 July 2001, 39665 and 40086/98, France would be held in violation of article 6.[5] Another issue is that during CAP meetings it is very difficult for the JAP to resist the pressure of the prison service. It is clear that CAP procedures constitute an anomaly that needs to be eliminated.

Also, numerous JAPs mentioned in the course of their interviews that they were ill at ease with the fact that they were legally entitled to self-seizure. French JAPs share with Youth Judges the possibility to self-seize, that is, to decide to rule on a case, whereas with most courts only the parties or the prosecutor can refer a case to a court or judge (PPC. art. 412–4). *'Autosaisine'*, as it is called by French law, is justified, as with Youth Judges, by the fact that JAPs are perceived as good courts, who have the offender's best – desistance – interests in mind. However, this finds, in our opinion, its limit with breach cases. In order to get round this difficulty, JAPs told us that when informed of non-compliance[6] by the probation service they send the file to the prosecutor who, in turn, apprises them of the case. Yet the total number of all sanctions drew a result of 63.70 per cent *autosaisines*. This reveals that, despite what some JAPs say, in practice most do use *autosaisine*, probably because it takes less time. They also expect offenders to give documented proof of compliance.

Practitioners, JAPs, prosecutors and even probation officers (POs) live in a 'culture of paperwork' where probationers must give evidence of their circumstances and reinsertion efforts. If offenders work, this is taken into consideration only if they can provide documented proof; it they argue that they are ill or are complying with their treatment obligation, a medical certificate is required; if they are looking for a job, they need to prove it; if the offender says he does not drink or take drugs anymore, the judge will ask for blood analysis. Public opinion and the media would have a field day if the judge merely took the offender's word for it. Documented proof is part and parcel of any French legal procedure. It is thus vested with the apparel of rationality and legality.

Conversely, it also is completely at odds with most probationers' habits. Most of them have serious reading and writing issues (Ministry of Justice, Prison Services, *Les chiffres Clefs de l'Administration pénitentiaire*, January 2012, p. 9). A lot of these offenders may have thus developed an avoidance pattern whereby they try to ignore paperwork. Despite being aware of this, since it is an unavoidable judicial demand, most JAPs patiently try to enforce it, by explaining again and again and saying something akin to this: 'I function based on paperwork. If you don't give me documented proof of what you tell me, it equals not doing it at all as far as the law is concerned' (JAP 46).

Unfortunately, in numerous cases, the offender has complied, but has forgotten to give evidence to the probation service or the JAP. In other cases, the probation service forgot to transfer such evidence to the JAP. In some regions, in particular in the Paris and Provence-Alpes-Côte d'Azur[7] regions, the focus on documented proof has generated organized paperwork trafficking. A lot of these difficulties would be avoided if the probation service had the time to investigate offenders' circumstances. This would also allow more sustainable substantive fairness.

Collaborative hearings in JAP courts: Another potential limitation

Another procedural concern is the collaborative nature of the activities of the key practitioners involved in prosecuting breach in JAP courts. In the context of an adversarial legal system (which operates in some Western jurisdictions, including the United States and England and Wales), the very fact that an attorney might work in a collaborative (Daicoff 2009) manner with a judge, a prosecutor and the offender in order to support the desistance process is difficult to fathom. Indeed, on the European continent, procedures are not fully adversarial; the French word *'contradictoire'* conveys a notion of balance and proportion, where each party has his say and where a common goal is to be achieved (truth, communication, reinsertion...). As Arie Freiberg has hypothesized, such legal systems may be more receptive to problem-solving approaches (Freiberg 2011). In this context, counsels are also called *'auxiliaires de justice'*, that is, auxiliaries of the judiciary. This does not mean that they cannot intensively defend their clients. What it means is that, like the JAP, they usually have an ulterior objective in mind: their client's desistance and rehabilitation.[8]

In the case of breach hearings, one might argue that the collaborative stance adopted by all parties ill serves the best interests of offenders and is pushed a little too far. For instance, even though this is legally possible, JAPs hardly ever call in witnesses, and the very fact that the offender has breached the terms of his supervision is hardly ever disputed; solicitors usually try to avoid recall to prison by drawing on the person's positive actions (e.g. having started treatment) and by explaining how detrimental to his tentative progress or to his family recall would be. However, attorneys are quite capable of shifting from one role to another.

During one of JAP 13's hearings, the counsel first disputed each one of the details of the probation service report, which accused his client of having had an argument with the victim. Since the argument occurred in part over a dispute about the offender's visitation rights and in part as a result of having been drunk, the JAP then moved to sorting the visitation issue and addressing the alcohol addiction. At this point, the attorney followed his cue and discussed what progress had been made with the family judge, on the one hand, and what his client had endeavoured to do with regard to his addiction, on the other. In doing so, the attorney showed remarkable in-depth knowledge of the case. For instance, he supplied the JAP with the name of his client's phone company without even looking at his notes.

Some counsels push the collaborative approach to yet another level. These counsels start preparing a release plan the minute the person is sentenced, work with the family, constantly contact the probation service in order to obtain compulsory documents, and interact with the JAP and sometimes even the prosecutor. All these occur weeks or months before the hearing. When confronted with breach cases, they are thus able to present a comprehensive picture of the offender's personality and explain, in context, what his current 'regression' signifies and how it can be addressed. As suggested by alternative legal movements (Daicoff 2006), they reinvent what being a solicitor entails and incidentally, as a result, show a remarkable lack of the classic criminal lawyers' stress (Benjamin et al. 1990; Kneusé 2003; Enkaoua 2012).

As solicitor two put it: 'I get the immense satisfaction of emptying the sea with a teaspoon.'

The study found that offenders chose to be assisted by an attorney in only 2.53 per cent of the breach cases, compared with 41.91 per cent of the other cases. In 55.07 per cent of the breach cases, the offender was present at the hearing without an attorney (compared with 4.91 per cent for other cases). Lastly, in 48.55 per cent of the breach cases, the offender was not present at all (compared with 0.29 per cent of the other cases). Interestingly, in the breach cases, when a solicitor was present, in 42.59 per cent of them, the offender was fully recalled; in 27.77 per cent he benefitted from one form of leniency or another (when that applied); in 29.62 per cent there was no sanction at all. When the offender was present but without a solicitor, he was fully recalled in 34.73 per cent of cases, he benefitted from a lenient sanction in 36.84 per cent, and he was not sanctioned in 28.42 per cent of the cases. When neither a solicitor nor the offender was present,[9] the offender was fully recalled in 84.09 per cent of cases, benefitted from a lenient sanction in 7.5 per cent, and was not sanctioned in 8.3 per cent of the cases.

The first patent indication from these statistics is that what is more important is whether the offender is present or not. When he is absent, he stands little chance of being treated with leniency. Two reasons might explain this. On the one hand, an offender who is not present cannot present any form of evidence that might explain his breach. The judge is thus left with nothing but the file and, clearly, the file points to recall. Another reason might be that JAPs are irritated when a person does not make the effort to attend the hearing. One must also remember that offenders who do not show up for a hearing are also often those who have fewer mitigating circumstances and have usually absconded or been consistently non-compliant.

Leaving cases of absconding aside, the study's most surprising finding is that offenders seem to do better in JAP courts if they do not have a solicitor. Nothing in the files allowed us to think that the cases where a solicitor intervened were more serious than the others. Could it be that JAPs are more likely to pity offenders who have no solicitor? Or, conversely, that they have not fully realized that offenders should be assisted in their hearings, just like in sentencing courts? It could also reveal that, despite our general impression, most attorneys are not very good, or very dedicated. Whatever the explanation, the research shows that not being present and not being assisted constitute signs of 'regression', as Spanish law puts it (Cid and Tebar 2012), as in not living in the future tense, but only in the here and now, and as in not holding the reins of one's life.

JAPs as good courts

Notwithstanding the limitations described above, JAP hearings are, for the most part, 'Good Courts' in the therapeutic jurisprudence sense (Berman and

Feinblatt). The first feature that one notices is that most JAPs really do listen to offenders. They typically start their breach hearings with a stern admonition of the offender, where they clearly set the boundaries and remind the individual of his obligations, but they subsequently switch to a therapeutic, rehabilitative and problem-solving stance where they change the tone of their voice.

The study found that, typically, offenders enter the judge's office with either a provocative or a disillusioned attitude, slump in their seat and look at their feet, but progressively sit up, and leave the court with a smile, a 'thank you Mr/Madame the Judge' and sometimes even a handshake. Such was the case with a participating JAP court (JAP 47) hearing. The female offender involved had not attended several meetings with her probation officer (hereafter PO) and she did not fulfil the obligation to seek employment. She was not recalled to prison or otherwise sanctioned but sternly reminded of the law and her obligations; such a practice, called *'recadrage'* (i.e. 'straightening out'), albeit not being provided for by the law, is used by all JAPs.[10] Her excuses and denials were confronted one by one. Thereafter, the JAP discussed with the offender her complex circumstances: she lived in a rural area, four kilometres away from the first bus stop, and had to be home at lunch for her children as she could not pay for them to have their meals at the school canteen. JAP47 and the offender tried to find very practical solutions so that she could nonetheless attend the meetings. The probationer then explained that she did not like her PO, who treated her 'like a criminal' and spoke to her contemptuously, and that she only wanted to 'speak to my judge'. The JAP reminded her several times: 'you *are* not a criminal. You *have* committed an offence.' The JAP added that he knew the PO very well, and that he would be very surprised if she actually harboured such feelings. He gently told her that perhaps she was the one feeling debased by the penal process, or perhaps because, as she conceded herself, she had a temper, so that the PO might have spoken to her a little harshly in response. He suggested that she might try to sit on her pride and try a little harder; that everyone around her wanted to help and understood her circumstances, but that she had no choice but to submit to the order. This case illustrates the dual position JAPs appear to occupy. Where appropriate, they may combine a reprimand with a responsive stance that takes into account the probationer's circumstances.

Whenever the offender is clearly exaggerating, though, JAPs keep their stern tone of voice and do not tolerate any unacceptable attitude until the end of the hearing. This was evident in the case of another offender, a chronic alcoholic who kept giving the PO and the JAP involved wrong addresses, arrived fully drunk for the hearing, was not making much sense when he spoke, made unacceptable excuses for not complying with anything, and was stooping and putting his elbow on the judge's desk, at which the JAP sternly made him take it off.

Most JAPs also try to explain to offenders exactly what their order entails. They systematically ask 'do you understand this?' If the offender answers that he does not or looks puzzled, they patiently try again, using more simple words. This makes for a collaborative, problem-solving intimate hearing.

Causes of recall and non-recall: Decision making in JAP courts

In the present section we shall draw upon the analysis of the 292 sanction ruling sample. The reader must bear in mind that, in all of these cases, the offender had first benefitted from a '*recadrage*' and sometimes less taxing sanctions. The sample thus only concerned cases where everything else had failed.

With this in mind, statistics do show that JAPs are rather lenient. Although they pronounced a full recall sanction in 69.1 per cent of all cases, they had previously imposed a more lenient sanction in 8.95 per cent of all these cases[11] and no sanction at all in 21.95 per cent of them.

Why do JAPs choose one alternative over another? During their interviews, they said that they would be more inclined to recall for the following reasons, none of which automatically led to recall:

– The offender had committed a new offence during his order;
– There was an immediate risk for the victim, in particular the spouse or children;
– The offender had violated his restraining order/obligation;
– The offender was notoriously dangerous (e.g. was a sexual offender or a very violent offender);
– The offender had systematically disregarded his obligations;
– The offender was not present at his hearing or adopted an aggressive, carefree attitude.

The analysis of the hearings showed that JAPs did, indeed, sometimes recall based on several of these items. They mentioned the risk of reoffending in 24.87 per cent of all their decisions to sanction (and in 30.35 per cent of the probation and parole recall decisions). This was particularly apparent with sexual offenders and domestic violence offenders.

Reading the cases, it was also clear that, in most instances, the JAP based his/her decision to fully recall on a repetition of violations. In virtually all the cases, there had first been a *recadrage* after the PO had attempted to address the issue him/herself. In other words, by the time the JAP was notified of the breach, the situation had already escalated.

JAPs were also correct in saying that they took the person's behaviour into consideration. Notwithstanding the repeat violations, we found that the attitude that the offender had displayed with his PO or the judge, his patent disingenuous attitude, and so on was mentioned in 27.6 per cent of the cases.

In the interviews, many JAPs had mentioned that they would recall if the measure 'lost all meaning'. Coherently with this, 61.34 per cent of all decisions to recall or sanction made an express reference to this. The rulings typically concluded that the measure had no sense anymore given the offender's behaviour and, therefore, needed to be withdrawn. Conversely, not a single decision referred to the need to punish the probationer's behaviour. In other words, JAPs do keep in mind article 707's reinsertion compass. When this fails, and repeatedly so, they sadly conclude that nothing more can be done at this point; their hope clearly remains that that the next time around will be the right one.

In fact, one particular type of 'lenient' measure consists in prolonging the probation order. In these cases, as argued elsewhere (Herzog-Evans 2012a), it is plain that JAPs hope that by prolonging the order the person will be given the opportunity to comply with his obligations. JAPs are thus keeping focused on compliance and on reinsertion. In 95.23 per cent of these prolongation decisions, the JAP expressly mentioned the need to make the person comply with the order.

The rulings similarly refer to the need to give the offender yet another chance in 25 per cent of all cases. Equally, 21.59 per cent of them mention that the offender produced documented proof that he had at long last complied with the obligation (often the previous day or the very day of the hearing) or at least showed a first attempt at doing so. JAPs also weigh up the pros and cons of the entire file and decide, in 25 per cent of cases, that the offender has also made efforts to comply. It is likewise clear that JAPs consider that an individual's desistance process would be more compromised by sending the person back to prison. This is mentioned expressly in 19.44 per cent of all cases. However, JAPs also seem to consider that prison would be an easier solution in cases involving offenders who want to disregard their obligations.

In 52.77 per cent of the decisions not to sanction, this was explained by various legal reasons, such as some legal technicality or the fact that the person had been expelled from the country, had died, had proved that he/she could not pay (only with non-payment of day-fine). In 11.11 per cent of the no-sanction decisions the court decided not to recall based on the fact that the offender had already been sanctioned by a penal court of law as his breach consisted of another offence. In 5.5 per cent of all these cases, the JAP did not sanction the offender where he/she observed that it was the whole penal system's fault if he had not complied: for instance, if the probation service had not done anything to help with his reinsertion or had not even set up a single meeting.

To sum up, JAPs are particularly lenient, as they remain focused on the offender's rehabilitation (McNeill 2010). This can partly be explained by what happens during the breach hearings.

The JAP court: a forum for intimate hearings

Unlike the sentencing courts (which pass the original sentence), JAPs' hearings are not public.[12] There are several reasons why JAPs' hearings are generally not held in public (Herzog-Evans 2012b). First, it is felt that a JAP hearing is not an appropriate forum for imposing punishments. Its key aim is to work toward the individual's reinsertion. As such, when it comes to imposing a sanction for breach, punishment is not the first option. What JAPs consider is that the measure has failed, that the person needs to address issues, that it is time to try alternative measures. Whether they grant a release or impose a sanction to offenders who are in breach, JAP have to abide by the aforementioned principles of article 707 PPC; that is, they must aim, inter alia, at reinsertion, which is the French legal term describing the desired outcome of probation and supervision, that is, desistance and rehabilitation. Besides, JAPs are not interested in formal or instrumental compliance (Bottoms 2001; Robinson and McNeill 2010); they want substantive compliance.[13] Their hearings are also not public because this would be detrimental to the person's reinsertion (e.g. would make employment or housing more difficult). Lastly, it is also conducive to intimate hearings, where the offender can feel secure enough to confide in the JAP and reveal important circumstances or states of mind.

The hearings take place for those in the community, at the tribunal, in the JAP's office; for inmates, in a prison meeting room (PPC, art. 712–6). The judge, the prosecutor and the offender attend the hearing. The offender can be assisted by a solicitor. In some courts, a probation officer, a court clerk, an intern or a trainee judge may also be present. On rare occasions, when relevant or needed, there can also be a translator, a nurse and a curator.

The therapeutic jurisprudence attitude that JAPs display during the hearings, along with the intimate setting where they take place, allows offenders to be very forthright. For instance, during a hearing the offender was asked how much he drank each day. He replied: 'Two Pastis!' 'Two glasses?' asked the JAP. 'No two bottles!' replied the offender.

The research raised the issue of whether JAPs should wear their judges' robes. Contrary to most problem-solving courts, JAPs do not wear the robes, even during formal hearings. On the one hand, this is probably conducive to the intimacy that characterizes JAP hearings. On the other hand, especially in breach cases, it might be argued that it does not allow the judge to be taken seriously enough. As JAP 3 told us: 'I do think that the robe has numerous symbolic advantages: it makes everyone aware of the spatial-temporal judicial context: neither a bar, nor super social-work, and not the X factor.... It is a hearing, a moment which is laden with meaning.'

The simplicity of the JAP along with his/her humanitarian attitude can generate very positive surprises in offenders used to harsher treatment from the courts. As Charles Amrheim, PsyDClinical Director of the Bronx Mental Health Court, emailed the author (see Herzog-Evans forthcoming b):

> in problem-solving courts, the fact that the judge will connect with the participant in spite of the unequal relationship, has been shown in the procedural justice literature to have meaningful impact.

> In psychology we might call this a 'violation of expectations,' in this case the expectation of unfair treatment is violated by the surprising experience that one's case has been heard and recognised with respect...

> And surprise itself, despite a lack of comment in the empirical literature, has long been held as a critical element of psychotherapeutic treatment in the theoretical literature.

Factors that affect substantive fairness: Time and means

The first and most striking feature of breach procedures is that, despite the focus on what practitioners call the 'meaning of the measure' – that is, the end result of supervision: rehabilitation, reinsertion and desistance – a considerable amount of time often separates, on the one hand, the moment when the sentence is passed and the moment when the offender is actually taken charge of by the JAP and probation service; and, on the other hand, the moment when the breach occurs and the moment when a judicial response by the JAP is given to it. In both cases it can lead to a feeling of impunity, which both JAPs and other practitioners often commented upon. It also leaves offenders unsupported and uncontrolled, which, unsurprisingly, leads to more violations. The reason for such delays lies in the excessive caseload of POs and JAPs. A PO officially has about 100 files, but in some services it can go up to as many as 180 and usually averages 120–130. In our sample, JAPs had between 900 and 1400 opened files at any given time.

Reading the rulings, we realized that a typical case was that of an offender sentenced in 2008 for something he had done in 2007, who missed appointments in 2009 and was recalled in 2010. If this is for the most part the product of high caseloads and a terrible lack of resources (see below), it is also in some small part nurtured by the sheer leniency of practitioners: the POs who wait until things get seriously bad before they notify the JAPs; the JAPs who first do a *recadrage*, then, in some cases, explore other options. Whether practitioners are good or bad people thus bears little weight compared with this total lack of supervision, care and support of offenders in need, particularly those with addictions and mental illness issues, the lack of care and support being reinforced by a punitive shift that has marked recent probation policy (Herzog-Evans 2012b).

Granted, both probation services and JAPs' offices have to operate in a context of extremely limited material resources. In such dire circumstances, when an offender suddenly leaves his residence without notifying the JAP or his PO, unless he is a very dangerous or high-profile offender, very little is done to investigate his whereabouts. If offenders are eventually found, it is because they make a mistake, draw the police's attention to themselves (e.g. a very young man driving a very expensive car) or commit another offence. Equally, when offenders are addicted to a drug or alcohol, the penal system cannot finance reliable tests; JAPs ask the offender to provide evidence of a recent ordinary laboratory test, which is the easiest thing to forge or obtain fraudulently (e.g. by sending another person). There is, therefore, no doubt that most violations go unnoticed.

Other agencies' poverty or lack of dedication can also affect offenders and how their violations are dealt with. For example, an increasing number of letters written to offenders are misplaced; the postmen are not committed – and do not have the time – to really try to find the relevant recipients. Consequently, a lot of offenders are found in breach as a result of the dysfunctional mail service.

There is a similar issue with the Parisian Treasury: it does not allow offenders to pay their day-fine[14] by instalments; it is all or nothing, despite the fact that most offenders are unable to pay it all at once. JAPs are aware of this and do provide offenders with a longer period to make the payment than they should, thereby nurturing a feeling of impunity in some of them.

JAPs' substantive fairness as seen by other practitioners

As mentioned above, the study presented here also compared JAPs' points of view with the perceptions of other practitioners. All the participating prosecutors and solicitors (apart from two solicitors) depicted a picture of JAPs as being good and humane judges. The two solicitors who painted a more contrasting portrait were based in Paris, a jurisdiction where JAPs have to rule in most cases without a hearing. It is, however, important to note that these 'no hearings' procedures do not apply to sanctions and recall: they only apply to release decisions granted by the JAP, and only when both the prosecutor and the offender agree. In line with this, we had to apply considerable effort and ruse to try and find the names of 'bad Japs', that is, JAPs who were unaware of what the desisting process was, who did not seem to care about the offenders, and who behaved harshly with them. Applying these considerable efforts, and bearing in mind that we managed to interview nearly 20 per cent of all JAPs we only managed to find two of these 'bad JAPs'. However, interviewing POs yielded more contrasting views. For this reason, and also because it illustrates the complexity of the current situation between JAPs and probation services, we shall focus on these interviews.

Since 2008, the probation service's central administration has launched a systematic feud against the JAPs, with the patent objective of replacing them entirely with probation staff (Herzog-Evans 2011, 2012b). For this reason, one might have expected that POs would have been quite critical of JAPs. Quite the opposite, most POs had a very positive opinion of their JAPs:

> I rarely disagree with their decisions. I find the local practice [of the four JAPs] very coherent. They only recall as a last resort...when every single other options has been tried and failed, or when the risk that the person is causing to public security or to the victim is too important. I find them very fair.
>
> (PO 2)

Other POs are happy that JAPs are responsive to their needs, and there is effective communication between JAPs and the probation service:

> What I really appreciate with this JAP is that she is available and trusts PO. Here, magistrates are really very available to the point where we have their direct line and do not need to go through their clerk or need any authorization of any sort. It is very pleasant. Truthfully for a judge who is fresh out of the judge's school, she has done an incredible amount of good work here.
>
> (PO 30)

> This is a true collaborative work; information is really shared. When I am in doubt I can call her. There is true professional trust between us. It is a very serene type of work.
>
> (Chief 1)

Some POs do not feel they can have a say in whatever the JAP does, as they perceive him/her as an authority rather than as a person.

> Well I don't have any demands with regards to magistrates. The magistrate is both the judge of legality and of incidents. He/she is independent and I have to respect this independence. Who am I to judge them? Things are fair just the way they are.
>
> (PO 20)

Other POs were, indeed, critical of JAPs. Still, only one in our entire sample (PO 4) strongly challenged JAP and judiciary intervention in supervision.

An interesting finding was that a significant number of POs (25 per cent) mentioned that they occasionally disagreed with the JAP's leniency, thereby giving a hint of the more punitive professional culture that POs display:

> sometimes there is a clear lack of severity such as in cases where there has been a huge number of lenient sentences such as two probation orders, two community work sentences, a day-fine and why the hell not, a tag! After a while I think that imprisonment cannot be avoided.
>
> (PO 5)

There is another reason why POs appeared to be dissatisfied with JAPs' leniency. As we described earlier, by the time they notify the JAP of an offender's misbehaviour, things have already escalated. They usually have tried to chastise the offender themselves. Using a parental metaphor, a PO is like a worn-out mother who has told her children several times 'just you wait, I'm going to tell Dad,' whereas the JAP, being the Dad in this metaphor, actually does nothing when he comes back at night. Mum/PO thus feels rather disowned and ridiculed.

> Duh, hang on Ms Such and Such, you say that you are making an effort to pay the damages based on your means, but you could definitely pay more than 15 euros a month! Then perhaps the prosecutor will say 'oh poor little thing' or something like that. But I say 'hey wait a minute, she chain smokes fags and she does not care about the victim, and I as a PO look like a complete moron.'
>
> (PO 3)

The POs who criticize JAPs' leniency would like the JAP to act very fast based on their breach report.

> Well to be honest your typical PO is rather egotistical. When we write a breach report for the JAP, we want an immediate reaction when she probably receives ten on a given day and cannot in all likelihood react that very same day.
>
> (PO 28)

It is often simply a matter of disagreeing with the outcome. Clearly some POs expect the JAP to simply follow their cue.

> Well she is a rather peculiar person in the sense that she does not always follow our advice.
>
> (PO 4)

In this vein, PO 31 candidly said that a good JAP decision was a decision that followed through with her suggestion.

Clearly there is an issue of individual maturity here and of rapport with authority. For, indeed, other POs display a more balanced and mature view of JAPs' decisions:

> some colleagues may have a different perception of judicial mandate and judicial authority than I. But here I do think that they have all integrated what the law entails.
>
> (PO 9)

Essential to some POs' criticism of JAPs' leniency – and, more rarely, harshness – is that they perceive JAPs' practice as being incoherent, diverse and dependent on who the JAP is.

> Well here we have three JAP. We have nice and kind JAP; moderate JAP and I really like working with her; then we have 'crushator'.
>
> (PO 3)

But, when they are asked to illustrate the differences between their JAPs, what POs actually describe are differences in personalities, whether a JAP listens to them, whether he or she communicates easily with them. They do not describe drastically different practices.

For, indeed, these perceptions – which are in clear opposition to our own findings, based on the interviews, hearings and rulings which, conversely, show a remarkable consistency in JAPs' practices – may be explained by the fact that POs do not have all the information that JAPs have, or take into account the same factors. Indeed, several sources of misunderstanding can explain this disagreement. One example is that JAPs, being courts of law, need to base their decisions on precise, actual facts and not on interpretations, possibilities or hearsay. They need to be precise; they need to pay attention to details and, as we have seen, they need documented proof. Several JAPs whom we interviewed lamented that some POs were too loose, not cautious enough in what they wrote in their reports. In some jurisdictions, in particular in the Paris region, they did not even ask POs for reports, as they felt they would not learn anything new and could not trust their content. Another source of misunderstanding is that POs are not present during the hearing. They thus miss important facts, evidence and attitudes. A third and crucial source of misunderstanding is that, for POs, public opinion is never in their mind. In fact, in the course of their interview, they unanimously and strongly affirmed that they 'could not care less' about public opinion. By contrast, fewer than 20 per cent of the JAPs said they were not concerned about public opinion. To be sure, whenever a high-profile offender on parole or a similar measure commits an offence, JAPs typically take all the blame, while probation services are, for the most part, blissfully ignored by the media. Similarly, JAPs are in direct contact with victims, whereas POs do not deal with victims.

However, investigating more deeply into the reasons why some POs disagreed with JAPs' leniency, or, more rarely, with the harshness of 'their' JAP, it appeared that they expected the JAP to render absolutely identical decisions in spite of the offender's circumstances.

> Sometimes there is a young adult and the judge will say 'yeah but you must understand that he's young, what he needs is community *educative* supervision'. But on the other hand another offender who would do exactly the same thing would get it in the neck.
>
> (PO 4)

In saying this POs are quite right: JAPs do rule differently according to individual circumstances. This is the essence of the principle of individualization laid down by the law.

There is a clear paradox in this delusional expectation of absolute uniformity, given that POs themselves show extremely diverse practices when they are asked what violations they would not reveal to the JAP and which ones they would immediately report. For instance, one of the participating POs – PO 8 – explained that she would tell the JAP if the person who had been a drug addict drank three beers every night, but not if he smoked one joint! PO 18 explained she was more vigilant with treatment and damages payment obligations. PO 6 systematically informed the JAP ... when *he* thought things were going wrong. Some said they were more reactive where the measure at stake was a sentence management measure as opposed to a community sentence; others were more reactive with general control measures as opposed to individual obligations.[15] PO 7 explained that he did not tell the JAP if a person sentenced for the offence of Driving Under the Influence drank and drove all over again 'because there are so many of them', whereas PO 6 said precisely that he systematically did because drink-driving was so dangerous. Some POs immediately informed the JAP if the offender did not attend a meeting; others waited until it had happened twice, others until it had happened three times. PO 11 said she waited a little bit when she heard there was a problem before telling the JAP, just to see 'what would happen next'. Clearly, POs want discretion for themselves but would like the JAP not to have any. This is not capricious delusion. As we said above, by the time POs inform the JAP, the POs would have tried to resolve several incidents. As a result, they expect the JAP to follow their cue. When he does not, they obviously feel he/she is too soft. However, from the JAP's point of view, this is a 'first' occurrence as he was not informed before. Clearly the problem here is that JAPs should be notified of every single incident so that they have a clearer view of a case beforehand. In fact, many JAPs did tell us that they regretted that they were kept in the dark by POs.

Despite these misunderstandings, virtually none of the POs (but one: PO 4), along with all their chiefs, said that they would not want to be in charge of sanctioning probationers. Many POs are lawyers and have integrated the notion that an offender should have a proper trial.

> We cannot be judge and party.
>
> (PO 3)

> Our role is to assist judicial decision-making. We are not those who decide. It has to be a judge, equivalent to the one who sentenced the person, who revokes.
>
> (PO 7)

> Because of my background, I think that only a judge should decide; a judge guarantees individual liberties ....
>
> (PO 9)

If, by all accord, most JAPs are generally good judges who exercise fair and legitimate justice, there are serious substantive flaws in the recall system.

Conclusion

French JAPs have existed for 67 years. They are problem-solving courts which use a wide range of tools to consistently keep a reinsertion compass in mind when they deal with issues regarding offenders who have breached their community sentence or measure. In their view it is not about sanctioning breach, it is about making sure that the roots of non-compliance (which they view as a 'regression') are addressed so that the person will continue to be supported through the desistance process. In doing so, the JAPs exercise a level of discretion which might be mistaken for leniency. In fact, the relationship between POs and JAPs is sometimes slightly tarnished by the POs' misunderstanding of JAPs' immediate response to repeat non-compliance, while claiming discretion in their own (the POs') practice.

Rather than fuelling a sterile and counterproductive war between probation services and JAPs, the government and prison authorities would be better inspired to encourage these practitioners to learn to work together as they used to in the past, given that they still share, for the most part, a common reinsertion and rehabilitation culture.

For, indeed, JAPs are also fair courts, which display most of the legitimacy of justice traits listed by the legitimacy of justice literature. However, the

French sanction system presents several important flaws: insufficient attention to issues of presumption of innocence, confusion between proof and paperwork, excessive caseloads and lack of adequate means resulting in monumental delays before a breach is eventually addressed.

Notes

1. Interestingly, the virtues of professional discretion in supervision are now being rediscovered in English and Welsh probation (Deering 2011).
2. TJ is the study of the effect of the law and the legal system on people, their well-being, their emotions and health. It thus encourages courts to take into consideration the end result of their decisions and the impact these may have on well-being. It is linked to the problem-solving court movement and the collaborative law movement (Daicoff 2011).
3. Clémentine Danet, Brice Peigné, Marceline Bobinet, Marlène Brouca, Lucie Benoist, Cécile Bigayon, Aurélie Bruyant, Jeremy Chené, Habib Benmed Jamed.
4. Drug Courts were created in the United States as part of a 'problem-solving courts' movement which originated in Miami in 1989. Their founding principles are: judiciary supervision; collaboration of all actors and agencies with the ultimate goal of reinsertion and abstinence; presence of all useful services (treatment, housing and benefit agencies, AA, and so on) on site; a problem-solving approach; specialization (Drug Courts, domestic violence courts, mental health courts, etc.). There are about 3000 problem-solving courts in the United States today and they have been exported to Canada, Australia, England, Scotland and Belgium (Berman and Feinblatt 2005; Nolan 2009).
5. Article 96 states that in matters of civil rights and obligations or criminal charges a person shall be entitled to a fair trial, that is, a public hearing, counsel, time to prepare his/her defence, to be notified of the charges and to examine and have witnesses examined, to have the assistance of an interpreter whenever needed, and to be presumed innocent.
6. When the breach consists of a new offence, it is always the prosecutor who is informed first and thus seizes the JAP.
7. Provence-Alpes-Côte d'Azur.
8. Even prosecutors behave in most cases in a collaborative way. Everyone is concerned for the person's 'regression', to quote the Spanish recall system (Cid and Tebar 2012), as opposed to onward progress, and tries to suggest ways of doing things better. Indeed, some prosecutors are harsher, but in most cases those who work in sentence implementation are much less punitive than regular prosecutors.
9. A solicitor cannot be present without his client.
10. This customary procedure is not provided for by the law, but has nonetheless developed to the point of being systematic, thereby refuting an author (Mouhanna 2011) who thought he had perceived vast differences in JAPs' practices – but he had not specifically studied sanctions, or any hearing or ruling.
11. Bearing in mind that such a sanction only applied in 231/246 of all cases.
12. Parisian JAPs are different in this respect; they cannot hold their hearings in their offices, but at the central tribunal, 20 minutes away by car. The only available chamber is the courtroom of the 12th Correctional Tribunal. As a result, the breach hearings resemble those of a sentencing court.

13. 'Formal compliance denotes behaviour which technically meets the minimum specified requirements of a community sanction ... Substantive compliance implies active engagement of offenders with the (productive) purposes of the sanction' (McNeill and Robinson 2013, p. 120).
14. A day-fine is a sentence passed by the penal court or a measure imposed by the JAP (in this case the JAP transforms a custody sentence of up to six months into day-fines) whereby the offender has to pay a fine related to a specified number of days, for example, 60 days at 5 euros, which means the person has to pay 300 euros.
15. General control measures as listed in aforementioned article 132–44 of the Penal Code are mandatory in all cases. The obligations to attend meetings and to notify the JAP of a change of address are general obligations. Individual obligations are laid out in article 132–45 of the penal code. They are optional and only apply if the JAP actually decides to impose them. Examples are the obligation to work or seek employment, to get treatment or to pay damages.

References

Belenko, S. (2011) *Research on Drug Courts: A Critical Review 2000 Update*. New York: National Center on Addiction and Substance Abuse at Columbia University.

Benjamin, G. A. H., Darling, E. J. and Sales, B. (1990) 'The Prevalence of Depression, Alcohol Abuse, and Cocaine Abuse Among United-States Lawyers'. *International Journal of Law and Psychiatry* (13), 233–246.

Berman, G. and Feinblatt, J. (2005) *Good Courts. The Case for Problem-Solving Justice*. New York: The New Press.

Blumstein, A., Cohen, J., Martin, S. and Tonry, M. (Eds) (1983) *Research on Sentencing: The Search for Reform*. 2 volumes. Washington: National Academy Press.

Bottoms, A. (2001) 'Compliance with Community Penalties'. in A. Bottoms, L. Gelsthorpe and S. Rex (Eds) *Community Penalties: Change and Challenge* (pp. 87–116). Cullompton: Willan Publishing.

Burke, K. and Leben, S. (2007) *Procedural Fairness: A Key Ingredient in Public Satisfaction: A White Paper of the American Judges Association*. http://aja.ncsc.dni.us/htdocs/AJAWhitePaper9-26-07.pdf (accessed 2 July 2012).

Cid, J. and Tebar, B. (2012) 'Revoking Early Conditional Release Measures in Spain'. *European Journal of Probation* 4(1), 112–124.

Collins, H. (2007) 'A Consideration of Discretion, Offender Attributes and the Process of Recall'. in N. Padfield (Ed.) *Who to Release, Parole Fairness and Criminal Justice* (pp. 159–172). Cullompton: Willan Publishing.

Daicoff,S. (2011) 'The Future of the Legal Profession'. *Monash University Law Review* 37(1), 7–32.

Daicoff, S. (2009) 'Collaborative Law: A New Tool for the Lawyer's Toolkit', *Florida Journal of Law and Public Policy* 20, 113–140.

Daicoff, S. (2006) *Lawyer Know Thyself. A Psychological Analysis of Personality Strengths and Weaknesses*. Washington: American Psychological Association.

Deering, J. (2011) *Probation Practice and the New Penology. Practitioner Reflections*. Farnham: Ashgate.

Digard, L. (2010) 'When Legitimacy Is Denied: Offender Perceptions of the Prison Recall System'. *Probation Journal* 57(1), 43–61.

Enkaoua, C. (2012) 'Le barreau de Paris lève le tabou du stress des avocats'. *Gazette du Palais*, 4–6 Mars, 9–11.

Freiberg, A. (2011) 'Post-Adversarial and Post-Inquisitorial Justice: Transcending Traditional Penological Paradigms'. *European Journal of Criminology* 7, 77–93.

Gelsthorpe, L. and Padfield, N. (2003) 'Introduction'. in L. Gelsthorpe and N. Padfield (Eds) *Exercising Discretion. Decision-Making in the Criminal Justice System and Beyond.* Cullompton: Willan Publishing.

Herzog-Evans, M. (2009) 'French Post-Custody Law (2000–2009): From Equitable Trial to the Religion of Control'. *EJprob* 1(2), 97–109.

Herzog-Evans, M. (2011) 'Desisting in France: What Probation Officers Know and Do. A First Approach'. *EJprob* 3(2), 29–46.

Herzog-Evans, M. (2012a) 'Non-Compliance: A Human Approach and a Hair Splitting Legal System'., *EJprob*, n° 4(1),: 45–61.

Herzog-Evans, M. (2012) *Droit de l'exécution des peines.*, Fourth Edition. Paris: Dalloz.

Herzog-Evans (forthcoming a) 'To Robe or not to Robe: Discussion Internationale informelle autour du port de la robe par les magistrats et les avocats'., *Actualité Juridique pénal.*

Herzog-Evans (forthcoming b) 'The Importance of the Professional Culture: The Example of a Desistance, Reinsertion aAnd Rehabilitation French Reentry Court'., in Herzog-Evans (Ed.), *'How to Release? The Role of Courts and the Use of Discretion in Sentences' Implementation and Reentry.* Nijmegen: Wolf Legal Publishers.

Jacobs, J. B. and Larrauri, E. (2012) 'Are Criminal Convictions a Public Matter? The USA and Spain'. *Punishment and Society* 14(1), 3–28.

Kneusé, E. (2003) 'Sous le strass, le stress'. *Le Bulletin du Barreau de Paris, Ordre des avocats à la Cour de paris* 18(39).

Liebling, A. (2007) 'Why Fairness Matters in Criminal Justice'. in N. Padfield (Ed.) *Who to Release. Parole, Fairness and Criminal Justice* (pp. 63–71). Cullompton: Willan Publishing.

McNeill, F. (2010) 'La désistance: What Works et les peines en milieu ouvert en Ecosse'. *Ajpénal*, September, 376–380.

McNeill, F. and Robinson, G. (2013) 'Liquid Legitimacy and Community Sanctions'. in A. Crawford and A. Hucklesby (Eds) *Legitimacy and Compliance in Criminal Justice* (pp. 116–137). Abingdon: Routledge.

McIvor, G. (2010) 'Beyond Supervision: Judicial Involvement in Offender Management'. in F. McNeill, P. Raynor and C. Trotter (Eds) *Offender Supervision. New Directions in Theory, Research and Practice* (pp. 215–238). Cullompton: Willan Publishing.

Mouhanna, C. (2011) *La coordination des politiques judiciaires et penitentiaries. Une analyse des relations entre monde judiciaire et administration pénitentiaire*, CNRS-CESDIP, June.

Nolan, J. L. (2009) *Legal Accents, Legal Borrowing. The International Problem-Solving Court Movement.* Princeton: Princeton University Press.

Padfield, N., Morgan, R. and Maguire M. (2012) 'Out of Court, Out of Sight? Criminal Sanctions and Non-Judicial Decision-Making'. in M. Maguire, R. Morgan and R. Reiner (Eds) *The Oxford Handbook of Criminology* (pp. 955–985). Oxford University Press.

Robinson, G. and McNeill, F. (2010) 'The Dynamics of Compliance with Offender Supervision'. in F. McNeill, P. Raynor and C. Trotter (Eds) *Offender Supervision. New Directions in Theory, Research and Practice* (pp. 367–383). Cullompton: Willan Publishing.

Saleilles, R. (1898) *L'individualisation de la peine. Étude de criminalité sociale.* Paris: Germer Baillière et Cie, Félix Alcan (in English *The Individualization of Punishment*, Bibliobazaar, reedited 2009).

Tarling R (1979) *Sentencing Practice in Magistrates' Courts*. Home Office Research Study No. 56, London: HMSO.

Tonry, M. (1996) *Sentencing Matters*. New York: Oxford University Press.

Tyler, T. R. (2006) *Why People Obey the Law*. Second Edition. New Haven, CT: Yale University Press.

Tyler, T. R. and Huo, Y. T. (2002) *Trust in the Law: Encouraging Public Co-operation with the Police and Courts*. New York: Russell Sage Foundation.

12
Compliance Dynamics: A Multidisciplinary Review and Exploration of Compliance Processes in the Belgian Context

Stef Decoene and Kristel Beyens

Systematic empirical criminological research on compliance is still relatively scarce, and this is also the case for Belgium. However, with the growing use of community sanctions the topic is becoming more important in a political landscape in no small part governed by a media logic of fear and calls for repressive control. Compliance can be studied from different angles: from the perspective of the person being put under supervision, from the standpoint of the supervisor and from the standpoint of the institution that has to take formal decisions in cases of non-compliance or breach of conditions or requirements. In this chapter, we mainly focus on the first perspective. We briefly discuss Bottoms's (2001) analysis of compliance and present the relevant Belgian research known to us. More importantly, we try to make an effort at placing compliance within an interdisciplinary context.

Bottoms's typology of compliance processes

In studying the mechanisms of compliance from the perspective of the person under supervision, the conceptual framework of Bottoms (2001) has become influential (see also McNeill and Robinson 2013; Robinson and McNeill 2008). Bottoms (2001) distinguishes two types of compliance with community sanctions. When an offender complies with the specifically defined legal conditions, there is 'short-term requirement compliance'. 'Longer-term compliance' refers to a more fundamental compliance with the law. Bottoms also distinguishes four principal mechanisms underpinning compliant behaviour: instrumental/prudential compliance, normative compliance, constraint-based compliance and compliance based on habit/routine. Compliance is instrumental when it is based on self-serving calculation of costs–benefits, normative when based on a felt moral obligation, commitment or attachment (i.e. based on some form of moral appraisal or reasoning), constraint-based when following from some sort of limitation of freedom, and habitual when following from an automatic, learned response (Bottoms 2001: 90–94). Robinson and McNeill (2008, 2013) subsequently argued that 'short-term requirement compliance' should be divided into formal and substantive compliance, to differentiate the 'pro forma' following of conditions from a more engaged (internalized) acceptance of imposed constraints. Formal compliance was defined as 'behavior which technically meets the minimum specified requirements of the order and is a necessary component of short-term requirement compliance' (Robinson and McNeill 2008: 434), while substantive compliance is considered to involve 'the active engagement and co-operation of the offender with the requirements of his or her order' (p. 434). The literature draws attention to the importance of the relationship between the supervisor and the supervised in both the desistance (Burnett and McNeill 2008) and the risk management process (Andrews and Bonta 2010), and compliance research has focused on the dynamics of the interaction between both parties. Also, offenders under supervision may have already interacted with actors or representatives of the penal system in previous phases, which could influence their perception of the criminal justice system in general and also their relationship with the supervisor in the implementation phase. Consequently, the perceived legitimacy of the penal system by the person under supervision has been identified by Bottoms (2001), Robinson and McNeill (2008) and McNeill and Robinson (2013) as an important factor in the process of both short-term and longer-term compliance.

While influential, Bottoms's typology and its elaboration should be seen as a first approximation of the compliance process. There is not much empirical research available. With the exception of Hucklesby's research (2009, 2013a, 2013b) on compliance with electronic monitoring and Ugwudike's (2010) research with probation staff and people serving probation orders on compliance with probation orders in England and Wales, no empirical studies are known to us that have used this framework in the context of conditional release or other community sanctions. Of course, the risk management literature (Andrews and Bonta 2010; Conroy and Murrie 2007) is large and addresses the recidivism process, which is one specific form of non-compliance, but is not well integrated into the penological analysis of non-compliance (see also below).

Moreover, Bottoms's typology is not as conceptually transparent as it should be. For example, Robinson and McNeill (2008) proposed a subtyping of short-term requirement compliance, suggesting that, when an order is still in place, only two compliance processes can be at work (instrumental or normative). To us, there seems to be a mixing of compliance duration and compliance phases (e.g. with or without an active order) with the underlying dynamics of compliance. This potential problem can also be seen in McNeill and Robinson (2013), where long-term compliance is explicitly described as being based on (psychological) legitimacy, generating the question of whether only long-term compliance could be based on perceived legitimacy.

The difference between normative and habit-based compliance is also a difficult one. Normative compliance as defined by Bottoms implies an active thinking-through or moral reasoning. There is, however, little research in moral psychology to support the idea that most people function on this explicit moral reasoning level, or habitually make conscious norm-based decisions (Appiah 2009; Flanagan 1991; Gibbard 1990; Haidt 2007). Also, Bottoms et al. (2004) only touch upon the question of how, for example, desistance should be integrated into his typology. They suggest that desistance may be motivated by all four processes mentioned above and emphasize the need to understand the social mechanisms underlying the desistance process. But then again, if all processes can be present at any given time, the supposed relationship between processes and duration becomes more difficult to visualize. In fact, from a theoretical point of view it would seem more logical to focus on mechanisms and processes, irrespective of duration, and to test empirically over the course of ex-offenders' lives how and when processes interact, reinforce or weaken one another, and depending on which factors (e.g. an active order).

Nevertheless, the typology offered by Bottoms and its elaboration by Robinson and McNeill (2008) and McNeill and Robinson (2013) is conceptually important, and is inspiring much-needed research on when and how ex-prisoners or other offenders under supervision try to comply with imposed conditions. In this chapter we will, therefore, also look at how compliance research could benefit from insights from other disciplines, such as medicine and psychology, which have a large literature of empirical and theoretical work on this issue. We will also highlight important suggestions for criminological research. Understanding offenders' compliance is, however, very much linked to the study of the interactions of the offender with the penal system and the reaction of this system to different forms and levels of non-compliance. As little is known about this aspect in a Belgian context, we begin this chapter with some insights into the institutional processing of non-compliance.

Institutional processing of non-compliance

Although their application is increasing, to date, the implementation of community sanctions in Belgium is still heavily understudied. This is even more the case for topics such as compliance, breach and recalls. Belgian law does not provide clear standards or criteria to define the reasons for breach or revocation of community sanctions such as probation, working penalties, conditional release or electronic monitoring. However, it can be relevant to have an idea of the success rates of supervisory sentences and the decision-making processes behind these outcomes.

With the growing use of the so-called working penalty,[1] we know that its completion rate has slightly decreased since its introduction in 2002 to about 80 per cent (Beyens 2010). However, this can still be considered as a rather high success rate. Research from Luypaert et al. (2007) and Dantinne et al. (2009) shows that there is room for discretion and negotiation between the offenders and the supervisors at the different levels of the implementation process before non-compliance is reported to the Probation Commission, which has to decide whether to refer a non-compliant case to the public prosecutor in order to start the implementation of the substitute sentence (prison sentence or fine). The Probation Commission can also give a warning, or a 'second chance' as it is called, which implies that the supervisors at the different levels of the implementation of the work penalty[2] have to look for a solution for the non-compliant offender to continue his sentence. In focus group meetings it is pointed out that, when offenders have to return to the same work place after a warning for non-compliance, the supervisors on the floor perceive this as weakening of their authority and that it impedes their hierarchical working relationship with the offender. Luypaert et al.'s (2007) research also shows that there is a lack of transparency, and sometimes large differences in the decision-making processes with regard to compliance requirements between the different districts, also due to the lack of clear regulations.

In 2007, National Standards on 'offender guidance' were developed by the Houses of Justice,[3] which cover all aspects of ensuring offender compliance and the breach process, aiming to standardize all work practices and curb the discretion of the supervisors. Because they are developed as minimum procedural guidelines of practice, they do not always provide ready-made or instant solutions to the dilemmas practitioners face on a daily basis. The standards still leave room for an individualized approach toward each compliance case, because it is stated that the offender's social and personal contexts have to be taken into account in the decision-making process (Bauwens et al. 2012). The standards also state that any failure to comply with a condition or a requirement must be followed up. Professional discretion has always been highly valued in Belgian supervisory practice and there has been resistance from the justice assistants who have worked in the 'old' system before the introduction of the standards, because they consider them as a vehicle for curbing their professional social skills in favour of uniformization and standardization (Claus and Schoofs 2011).

With regard to non-compliance with conditional release requirements, the justice assistant[4] responsible for the daily follow-up of the case is required to write a 'warning report' for the Sentence Implementation Court,[5] which can decide to recall the offender to prison. We see that the success rate of conditional release is considerably lower than that of the work penalty. In 2010, 57 per cent of conditional release orders were successfully completed (Bauwens et al. 2012) and 86 per cent of the breach cases were referred back to the Sentence Implementation Courts for violating one or more conditions of release. In only 5.5 per cent of the cases was referral to the Sentence Implementation Court induced by having committed a new offence while being under conditions (Devos 2011). These figures illustrate the importance of technical violations with regard to recalls under conditional release orders. To date, there is no systematic research into decision making with regard to recall or breach in Belgium, and so it is not clear whether these high violation figures are due to a strict recall policy or related to other mechanisms. A case study of recalls in one Belgian district in 2009 (Van Cutsem 2009–2010) confirms these general breach figures and shows that recalls are mostly due to non-compliance with more than one condition.[6] Van Cutsem also found that 61 per cent of the recalls take place during the first year of the conditional release period and 23 per cent even within the first three months after release from prison, which suggests that the first period of release and supervision is crucial with regard to compliance.

As mentioned above, in the case of non-compliance with the conditions the justice assistant is required to write a 'warning report' for the Sentence Implementation Court. Research by Bauwens (2011) at the Houses of Justice points at tensions between the Sentence Implementation Courts, which take the decision to revoke, and the justice assistants, who mainly have a better knowledge of the non-compliant offender's situation, needs and demands. The more holistic, client-centred social work approach of the latter is not always compatible with what they consider as the more controlling and public protection-inspired approach of the Sentence Implementation Courts.

Although more systematic research with all parties involved in this process of decision making in case of non-compliance in different districts is needed, these findings suggest that quantitative compliance or non-compliance rates are the result of a decision-making process that is subjected to power relations and the struggle for the 'ownership' of the decision. This is not only the case for conditional release, but for all decision making in this regard.[7] The registration of compliance or breach rates (e.g. Digard 2010) is, therefore, only a first step. It is more important to understand the production of these figures as the result of an interaction between the different penal and supervisory actors involved in the decision-making process and between the supervisor or the justice assistant and the person being put under supervision.

Compliance research in Belgium

In recent years the authors have run small-scale studies touching on various aspects of compliance with conditions and the underlying dynamics. Verrydt and Zwartebroeck (2003) carried out an exploratory study of conditional release failure, focusing on factors predicting failure (both reoffending and infractions of conditions leading to a new detention, making the predicted outcome more inclusive that just recidivism), and on how probation officers view and experience their success-inducing interventions. All non-compliance files from one district for the period 1989–2000 (to allow at least two years of follow-up) were used to code Historical-Clinical-Risk Management-20 (HCR-20) and Level of Supervision Inventory-Revised (LSI-R). Eighteen files were found, and supplemented by 30 successfully terminated conditional release files. Using logistic regression (using LSI-R and HCR-20 items and scales), conditional release failure could be predicted with self-control, financial status and (less clearly) having a job (with a 88 to 95 per cent correct prediction score). Using a semi-structured interview and a small vignette study, the three probation officers stressed that their role involves providing a humane service, trying to manage, with the ex-prisoner, his work, time management, social and familial context, and possible substance abuse. Although they considered the personality of the ex-prisoner important as such, they focused more on trying to use their working relationship as an instrument for and an indicator of going straight.

Brants et al. (2006) selected, for the period 1999–2005, all conditional release failures recorded in three districts and then selected matched conditional release successes. Sixty-six failures versus 69 successes were included in the study. Brants and colleagues assessed a number of risk assessment measures (LSI-R, HCR-20, Violence Risk Assessment Guide (VRAG) and the Historisch-Klinisch-Toekomst-30-lijst (HKT-30).[8] The quantitative analyses focused not only on predicting success/failure, but also on predicting time before failure. Failure/success was most successfully predicted using criminal history, financial problems, substance abuse problems, antisocial attitudes (thoughts, feelings and beliefs that are supportive of criminal conduct[9]) and criminogenic personality characteristics (with low self-control and callousness the most prominent). Time before failure was best predicted by criminal history, financial problems, substance abuse problems and criminogenic personality characteristics (with antisocial cognitions disappearing from the prediction models). Eight justice assistants were interviewed using semi-structured interview methods and a self-selected real-life 'prototypical' failure case. While all justice assistants used mostly dynamic predictors – such as impulsivity, drug use or antisocial attitudes – resembling these from the quantitative analyses, the most interesting observations were that they could be subdivided into three broad categories: assistants mainly focusing on control of conditions imposed, assistants focusing on a cognitive transformation of the ex-prisoner, and assistants focusing on how ex-prisoners felt. The second group were the most complex, as they integrated 'condition' management with motivation for and stimulation of identity change. The activities of the second group closely resembled the activities of the eight justice assistants interviewed in Verrydt and Zwartebroeck's (2003) study. Their activities provide clearer insights into the importance of a well-defined but constructive working relationship.

We did not receive permission to match the justice assistants' classification with sanction success/failure rates, but informal results suggested that the emotion-focused justice assistants did somewhat worse than the others, and that condition-oriented justice assistants had as a time frame for their case management a more short-term perspective than the transformation-focused justice assistants. Finally, the three groups of justice assistants had clear preferences concerning their preferred collaboration with the three commissions for conditional release and tried to select their own caseload as much as possible in concordance with the decision making style of the commission of their preference. The condition-focused justice assistants preferred the commission that simply checked conditions and did not stimulate nuanced decision making when something went wrong during a conditional release period. The more person-oriented justice assistants preferred working with the commissions that valued individualized and contextualized decision making. These findings are in tune with those of Bauwens et al. (2012), pointing at the tensions between the justice assistants and the Sentencing Implementation Courts which were introduced in 2007.

Wetzels (2008–2009) studied compliance with electronic monitoring from a broader perspective of the lived experiences of persons being put under electronic monitoring and of family members, using semi-structured interviews. The purposive sample of 16 respondents comprised five 'compliant' offenders who were serving their electronic monitoring and whose electronic monitoring period was between three and seven months, six non-compliant offenders who were recalled to prison due to breach and who had served between two weeks and 13 months of electronic monitoring, and six family members. It should be noted that all the offenders in the sample had already had a prison experience. Therefore it is not possible to identify the possible influence of previous detentions on the propensity for compliance with electronic monitoring. The offenders stressed, however, the fear of being recalled to prison as the most important reason to comply with the daily schedule and the conditions imposed. This points at the importance of considerations of possible incentives or disincentives in compliance (see also threat-based, instrumental compliance). It is also emphasized that adequate information about the requirements of the sentence (respecting the time schedule and the conditions to be fulfilled) to the offenders as well as to the family members was crucial in order to be able to comply with the conditions.[10] In tune with Hucklesby's findings, the interviewees mention the role of EM in structuring the life of the offender, not only through the electronic control, but also due to the obligation of having to perform 'meaningful' activities, such as having or looking for a job. Through the imposition of obligations and a daily EM schedule, the life of the offender becomes more structured, which points at compliance through habit and routine. Mediated by a bonding process with the family members due to the regular presence at home, this change of lifestyle seemingly facilitates the road toward long-term compliance. Interesting in this research is the enquiry into the involvement or the role of the family members in the compliance process. The EM measure also influences family life, for the good and the better. Most family members do play a role in ensuring compliance with the time schedule and the conditions, and thus increase formal compliance. With regard to formal compliance with minimum requirements, this research also shows that flexibility and negotiation in the case of minor violations, such as being a few minutes too late, for example, has a positive influence on the offender's perception of procedural justice. Being flexible and understanding from the controlling side thus also has a positive impact on global long-term compliance, which is in tune with Ugwudike's (2010) findings pointing at the importance of understanding and managing structural, situational and practical contradictions in order to foster compliance.

The studies are what they are: small-scale. They nevertheless show a potentially fruitful linkage between risk management literature, the broader concept of compliance, and professional issues such as working style and effectiveness. In fact, this was the starting point of Bottoms's 2001 article: studying effectiveness implies studying compliance, and the way compliance is defined sets the goal by which the effectiveness question is defined.

First, although recidivism studies, and the risk assessment literature in general, may seem far off from the field of compliance research, the issue they address is a specific kind of compliance – recidivism is a form of non-compliance. Mirroring Bottoms's typology of non-compliance, reoffending could at first sight be considered a form of normative or substantive non-compliance and a violation of imposed conditions – constraint-based non-compliance. The fact that this translation is tenuous (reoffending can also be a form of habitual non-compliance, as the impact of low self-control on non-compliance implies, for example) in our view again suggests that the categories in Bottoms's framework are as yet insufficiently demarcated from one another. Second, the qualitative results underscore the relational aspects of supervision resulting in different forms of compliance, but also show that good case management builds on criminogenic factor management (a humane service supervision focusing on factors functionally predictive of (re)offending) – stressing the need for a more explicit integration of compliance, risk management and desistance research (De Smaele and Decoene 2011).

Both observations reveal how seemingly different but really similar the perspectives of compliance, risk assessment and, of course, desistance are. What appears to be lacking is an interdisciplinary study of compliance.

Compliance research as an interdisciplinary enterprise

It is clear to us that interdisciplinary research on compliance needs both a common language (compliance or non-compliance versus risk assessment, for example) and scientific border-crossing into other disciplines that basically address the same problem. We want to underscore these points by showing how other disciplines could help to (re)focus criminological compliance studies. We do not aim at a systematic review, but simply want to pinpoint interesting elements to be found in these domains. Robinson and McNeill (2008) already pointed at relevant research within economics and political science. We expand this a little with medical research. But, more importantly, we want to highlight the social-psychological research on persuasion as a more general framework within which penological research on compliance might find inspiration.

Compliance: Medical perspectives

The problem of treatment adherence is a major one in medical research and practice, both practically and theoretically (Osterberg and Blaschke 2005; van Dulmen et al. 2007; Vermeire et al. 2001). Patients routinely fail to comply with clear prescriptions – a failure with sometimes life-threatening consequences, often high costs for society, and further deterioration of health. Also, much research is directed at finding effective interventions for improving compliance (e.g. Haynes et al. 2006).

Jin et al. (2008) reviewed 102 articles related to medical non-compliance. They noted that it was estimated that the compliance rate of long-term medication therapies was between 40 per cent and 50 per cent. The rate of compliance for short-term therapy was much higher at between 70 per cent and 80 per cent, while the long-term compliance with lifestyle changes was the lowest at 20 per cent to 30 per cent. They reviewed a large number of interacting factors associated with lower compliance, dividing these into hard (direct) versus soft (complex, interacting) factors. Therapy-related factors (such as treatment complexity, duration of treatment, side effects, degree of behavioural change required), healthcare system problems (such as accessibility, client satisfaction orientation), disease characteristics (such as chronic versus acute disease, fluctuation of symptoms) and healthcare costs appeared as hard, clear-cut factors affecting compliance. Psycho-social factors (such as beliefs and attitudes toward illness and healthcare, therapy motivation, relationship and communication style/quality, gender, age) showed complex interactions with one another and with the hard factors.

In another review, Krueger et al. (2005) also stressed the often very high non-adherence rates, and found that factors similar to those identified by Jin and colleagues affect non-compliance. They found that one of the most important healthcare system factors affecting adherence is 'the relationship that providers establish with patients. In ten of the 12 studies that included an evaluation of this factor, investigators found that a trusting, supportive relationship increased adherence' (p. 331). They mentioned, among others, the following principles:

- respect patients' perspective of the illness and its treatment;
- do not use therapy as an expedient way of satisfying a patient;
- provide patients with a rationale for the diagnosis and treatment;
- negotiate a plan, and expect problems;
- share experience in a way that is useful to a patient;
- ensure that communication has cognitive and emotional significance;
- monitor adherence in a non-judgemental and non-threatening manner;
- when non-adherence is observed, use a collaborative approach involving the patient in the decision-making process and in the selection of a solution.

Other authors (e.g. Gray et al. 2002) also note the difficulty in defining when compliance is observed, and the importance of choosing the best concept (Blackwell 1996). The medical literature uses compliance, adherence and, more recently, concordance to describe problems in following medical instructions and requests (Aronson 2007; Horne et al. 2005). The concept of concordance is used to stress patient rights, the need for information and the importance of two-way communication and decision-making. In contrast to the compliance model, a concordance model suggests that 'patients have the right to make decisions (such as stopping medication) even if clinicians do not agree with the decision' (Gray et al. 2002: 278). Adherence is sometimes preferred as a term because it views rule-following as active, instead of passive, stressing that patients need to actively regulate different goals and therefore have to invest in choosing to follow the medication regimen (Aronson 2007; Osterberg and Blaschke 2005). However short this section, these results should be quite familiar if we substitute medication for sanction-related conditions. Clearly, it is not so much (ex-)prisoners who often fail to comply, but people in general, even when we could expect that for many patients compliance would be the preferred (and voluntary) course of action. People are simply not very good at consistent rule-following! Individual factors associated with non-compliance are quite similar; suggestions for more effective compliance-gaining interventions abound, but all stress relationship characteristics. Also, medical research stresses the need for concepts that are fine-tuned to the actual processes studied – witness the discussion over whether, for example, compliance or concordance should be used. And, importantly, the medical literature shows that it is not just patients who fail to follow instructions, but also medical service providers (e.g. Harris and Nicolai 2010)!

Compliance: Social-psychological perspectives

Criminology is well acquainted with the pioneering social-psychological studies of Milgram (1974), Asch (1951) and Zimbardo (2007, for a research synthesis). Deservedly famous, these studies are, however, not the end point of a research tradition but the start of a vigorous and ever-growing investigation of how people influence and persuade one another (or resist and counter influences and requests) (see, e.g. Cialdini 2001 for a textbook introduction). It is an intriguing question why this more recent research has not yet found its way into criminological compliance theory, keeping in mind that both Allport's and Zimbardo's research is founded in concerns that are also criminology's concerns.

There is, in fact, an enormous amount of knowledge on the various forms of social influence with respect to: variables concerning the recipients of social influence processes and tactics; and variables concerning social actor variables and concerning the what, when and how of various influence tactics and processes, including the ethics of it all (Brock and Green 2005; Forgas and Williams 2001; Gass and Seiter 2011; Kelman 2001; Pratkanis 2007). Important underlying themes of this research are that persuasion is heavily situationally dependent, and that influence processes should be attuned to core social motives (see, especially, Fiske 2010 and Cialdini 2001 for further examination of the link between influence and motives).

It is beyond the scope of this chapter to review all this research, or to discuss the various, often competing, models that try to explain influence. Instead, we focus on some broader insights and their implications for the criminological research on 'compliance' with conditions. First of all, social psychology defines compliance as acting in conformity with a request. It involves doing what is asked, thus changing a behaviour, but without aiming at or necessarily involving internal (attitudinal) change. Different processes underlie behavioural change versus attitude change (Cialdini 2001; Kelman 2006). Bringing social psychology in tune with the framework developed by Bottoms, and Robinson and McNeill, the implication would be that the typology does not distinguish compliance clearly enough from attitude (and, ultimately, identity) change, and could be elaborated and fine-tuned with respect to the processes generating behavioural or attitude change. From this point of view, it would be better to restrict the concept of 'compliance' to the phenomenon Bottoms labels requirement compliance and prudentially based legal compliance, and to differentiate it more clearly from kinds of change that are based on internal (attitudinal, self- or identity-related, including norm-based) processes.[11] Maruna's concept of 'identity transformation', for example, could be used to differentiate the two kinds of change.

Second, a crucial insight is that persuasion works (or doesn't) through the way it helps to fulfil the social motives of the influence recipient. Authors differ on the number of core social motives. Fiske (2010), for example, identifies belonging, understanding, controlling, enhancing self, and trusting (but notes that some would delete 'trusting'). Cialdini (2001; Cialdini and Goldstein 2004) structure their view on compliance using affiliation, accuracy and maintaining a positive self-concept (see also Pittman and Zeigler 2007). Both the amount of change allowed by the recipient target and the effectiveness of the tactics used by a social actor to influence depend on the fit between the actor's influence tactic and the recipient's dominant social motive(s) in the here-and-now situation.

The social motive perspective is explicit in the famous Kelman model of social influence (1958, 1974, 2006). Early on, trying to differentiate between public 'behavioural' conformity versus private (internalized) acceptance (attitude change) of a position advocated in an influencing communication, he distinguished compliance, identification and internalization. Kelman's (2006) definition of these three kinds of social influence processes is as follows:

> very briefly, compliance can be said to occur when an individual accepts influence from another person or a group in order to attain a favourable reaction from the other – either to gain a specific reward or to avoid a specific punishment controlled by the other, or to gain approval or avoid disapproval from the other. Identification can be said to occur when an individual accepts influence from another person or a group in order to establish or maintain a satisfying self-defining relationship with the other. The relationship may be based on reciprocity, where the person seeks to meet the other's expectations for his or her own role, which stands in a reciprocal relationship to the other's role. Alternatively, the relationship may be based on modelling, as in classical identification, where the person vicariously seeks to take on the role (or part of the role) of the other – to be like or actually to be the other person. Finally, internalization can be said to occur when an individual accepts influence from another in order to maintain the congruence of actions and beliefs with his or her own value system. Value congruence may take either the form of cognitive consistency, where the induced behaviour is perceived as conducive to the maximization of the person's own values, or the form of affective appropriateness, where the induced behaviour is perceived as continuous with the person's self-concept.
>
> (2006: 3–4)

Even more briefly: 'we can speak of P's compliance with O's demands, P's identification with O's expectations, and P's internalization of O's ideas' (Kelman 2006: 7). Kelman explicitly links motives/goals with interaction of persons in a social system, noting that compliance is the acceptance of behavioural requirements set for group members to gain reward and avoid punishment (adherence to rules); that identification entails meeting the expectations of their group roles (thus maintaining a desired relationship with the group and a self-concept embedded in these roles (involvement in group roles); and internalization means that the person lives up to the implications of the shared values, maintaining the integrity of their personal value framework (sharing the group values) (Kelman 2006: 11–12). Kinds of influence depend on what the target finds important (or is willing to accept), the strategies the actor is willing or able to use, and the broader social organization of the group within which the influencing occurs. It is of note that Kelman (2006) applies his framework to authority relationships, legitimacy issues and inter-group dynamics, making it potentially quite fruitful for criminology.

When this classification is compared with that of Bottoms, legal compliance seems equivalent to Kelman's description of compliance when based on instrumental motives or habit. In addition, legal compliance is similar to identification when based on attachment, or internalization when based on norm acceptance.

Third, compliance, and influencing in general, is basically an in-group process. Asking why a person doesn't comply with a condition or does not feel persuaded by a message or tactic only makes sense if one can assume that the person considers him/herself to belong to the same group as the person asking for compliance. In this light, the set of processes that in criminological–psychological research are subsumed under terms such as anti-sociality and antisocial attitudes necessarily entails the question of which ex-offenders consider themselves (and are considered as such by society) as members of the in-group, and should therefore be taken into account in the research of ethically informed requests to change (both behaviourally and/or attitudinally). While it may be tempting to reduce this issue to a question of objective social inclusion/exclusion, the social-psychologically important lesson here is that the crucial variable is perceived/interpreted/felt inclusion/exclusion. Defining the actions of an ex-offender as more or less compliant only makes sense if the compliance-seeking actor considers the offender part of his group, and if the ex-offender feels himself (or wants to be) a member of the compliance-seeking actor's group. Otherwise, the question is not one of compliance, but of psychological obedience and/or submission. We should not blindly assume that any given ex-prisoner accepts either the authority or the norms that are applied to him, and which he is asked to accept (at least behaviourally). Again, with respect to Bottoms's typology, this could imply that goals of obedience and submission (and their constituting processes) should be included in the nomological network – and, as a consequence, the ethical question of whether (or when, why and how) obedience and submission tactics should be considered legitimate, made clearer.

Another important point is that the social-psychological research has also given attention to processes such as psychological reactance – the process of not yielding to social influences following the actual or threatened loss of decisional freedom (Brehm 1966; Brehm and Brehm 1981; Wicklund 1974; see also Sagarin and Wood 2007 and Knowles and Riner 2007). Non- compliance, in this context, may not be an aberrant phenomenon. People are more or less influenced by messages and requests made by others. Reactance toward some kinds of influences is psychologically normal, much as is resistance to tactics aimed at obedience or submission – especially when the realization of core social motives, such as autonomy, is threatened. In the light of the previous points, much will depend on situation, the social motives activated in a given situation for a given person, the relationship between target and actor (in-group versus out-group, subordinate versus authority) and the broader socioeconomic, cultural context.

Applied to compliance with community sanctions, this suggests that 'condition-following' by ex-prisoners will need to be fine-tuned to their individual functioning in order to find ways to overcome reactance (or defence, when the individual defines himself as out-group). As complying with imposed constraints accompanying a community sanction is by definition an, at least subjective, loss of freedom, reactance is normative instead of aberrant, and should be treated as such.

Finally, the social-psychological research integrates the two points of view present in the problem of compliance with conditions: on the one hand, the person requesting compliance in order to influence/change; on the other hand, the person (not) complying or accepting change. Social-psychological research has investigated in some depth many possible influencing tactics which are effective depending on situational constraints and the social motives driving the target (Pratkanis 2007). These tactics offer interesting ways to change and improve communication with ex-offenders. Again, individualization seems to be the message here, and closer attention to the perceived relationship between the person trying to influence and his recipient.

Conclusion

Starting from the model developed by Bottoms (2001), we briefly presented exploratory compliance research within the Belgian context, with respect to both the processing of breaches and how the Belgian penal system tries to deal with them, and with the processes involved in individual non-compliance. It is pointed out that non-compliance with conditions and its formalization in official breach should be studied in a context of previous and ongoing experiences of the offender with the penal and para-penal system. We have shown that the formalization of non-compliance is the result of a negotiated process between supervisors and decision makers that is characterized by power relationships and struggles for ownership of the decision to take.

We argue, moreover, that penological research on compliance should become much more interdisciplinary, as many scientific disciplines confront equivalent issues. We illustrated this with medical research on treatment concordance, and by highlighting how social-psychological research could offer valuable insights for the development of a conceptually rich model of compliance. We have shown that models explaining compliance with supervisory measures can benefit from insights from other disciplines when investigating when, why and how to influence (ex-)offenders to take up requests or to change, and when investigating how best to reach them, will involve a sustained effort at multidisciplinarity. Many domains of applied science try to tackle various forms of absence of 'rule-following' or taking up requests to follow rules. More fundamentally, penology could benefit from a renewed friendship with social psychology, which harbours an enormous amount of knowledge directly relevant to the question of how to reach ex- offenders so that they feel really invited to (re)turn to their in-group.

Notes

1. In Belgium, community service or unpaid work is called 'work penalty'.
2. This can be the justice assistant, the dispatching service or the work place in the community.
3. Belgian National Standards are essentially procedural documents aimed at raising minimum guidelines of practice. They do not in themselves provide detailed guidance on the methods and approaches that might be adopted in offender supervision (Bauwens 2010: 154).
4. In Belgium, the follow-up of conditional release measures, probation orders, community service and training orders is organized by the so-called 'Houses of Justice'. The daily follow-up is done by 'justice assistants', who can be compared to probation officers. Until 2007, justice assistants were called probation officers in Belgium.
5. In Belgium, Sentence Implementation Courts decide about the imposition and recall of conditional release. Justice assistants have to report on the progress and compliance with the conditions at these Sentence Implementation Courts.
6. The number of imposed conditions to comply with can diverge enormously: in one district the number of conditions varies between seven and nine, in another the number varies between 13 and 18 (Van Cutsem 2009–2012).
7. The question of 'professional ownership' is already described in the context of the use of pre-sentence reports (Tata et al. 2008; Beyens and Scheirs 2010).
8. Two well-known risk assessment instruments (see Conroy and Murray 2007 for a description).
9. For example: 'real men are allowed to hit their wife'; 'children are sexually seductive'; 'justice is for the rich'.
10. It has to be mentioned that the practical organization of electronic monitoring is very complex (Beyens and Kaminski 2013) and that offenders and housemates may

not always realize or understand what the real expectations or requirements of an electronic monitoring measure are. Non-compliance can thus also be the result of lack of knowledge of obligations.

11. From this social-psychological perspective, routine-based compliance is complex, as it is basically behavioural, but presupposes at least acceptance of roles/values, and should maybe not be understood as compliance strictu senso.

References

Andrews, D. and Bonta, J. (2010) *The Psychology of Criminal Conduct.* New Jersey: LexisNexis.

Appiah, K. A. (2009) *Experiments in Ethics.* Cambridge: Harvard University Press.

Aronson, J. (2007) 'Compliance, Concordance, Adherence'. *British Journal of Clinical Pharmacology* 63, 383–384.

Asch, S. (1951) 'Effects of Group Pressure Upon Modification and Distortion of Judgment'. in H. Guetzkow (Ed.) *Group Leadership and Men* (pp. 177–190). Pittsburgh: Carnegie Press.

Bauwens, A. (2011) 'The Transformation of Offender Rehabilitation?' Unpublished PhD Thesis, Criminology Department, Vrije Universiteit Brussel, Brussels.

Bauwens, A., Robert, L. and Snacken, S. (2012) 'Conditional Release in Belgium: How Reforms Have Impacted Recall'. *European Journal of Probation* 4(1), 19–33.

Beyens, K. (2010) 'From "Community Service" to "Autonomous Work Penalty" in Belgium. What's in a Name?' *European Journal of Probation* 2(1), 4–21.

Beyens, K. and Kaminski, D. (2013) 'Is the Sky the Limit? Eagerness for Electronic Monitoring in Belgium'. in M. Nellis, K. Beyens and D. Kaminski (Eds) *Electronically Monitored Punishment. Critical and Comparative Perspectives* (pp. 150–171). NY, London: Routledge.

Beyens, K. and Scheirs, V. (2010) 'Encounters of a Different Kind. Social Enquiry and Sentencing in Belgium'. *Punishment and Society* 2(3), 309–328.

Blackwell, B. (1996) 'From Compliance to Alliance: A Quarter Century of Research'. *Netherlands Journal of Medicine* 48, 140–149.

Bottoms, A. (2001) 'Compliance and Community Sanctions'. in A. Bottoms, L. Gelsthorpe and S. Rex (Eds) *Community Penalties. Changes and Challenges* (pp. 87–116). Cullompton: Willan.

Bottoms, A., Shapland, J., Costello, A., Holmes, D. and Muir, G. (2004) 'Towards Desistance: Theoretical Underpinnings for an Empirical Study'. *Howard Journal of Criminal Justice* 43(4): 368–89.

Brants, E., Soons, M. and Vanhauwere, J. (2006) *Inschatting van risico op herval bij voorwaardelijk in vrijheid gestelden.* K.U.Leuven: Departement Psychologie.

Brehm, J. (1966) *A Theory of Psychological Reactance.* New York: Academic Press.

Brehm, S. and Brehm, J. (1981) *Psychological Reactance.* New York: Academic Press.

Brock, T. and Green, M. (Eds) (2005) *Persuasion. Psychological Insights and Perspectives.* Thousand Oaks: Sage.

Burnett, R. and McNeil, F. (2005) 'The Place of the Officer-Offender Relationship in Assisting Offenders to Desist from Crime'. *Probation Journal* 52(3), 221–242.

Cialdini, R. (2001) *Influence: Science and Practice.* Fourth Edition. Boston: Allyn & Bacon.

Cialdini, R. and Goldstein, N. (2004) 'Social Influence: Compliance and Conformity'. *Annual Review of Psychology* 55, 591–621.

Claus, V. and Schoofs, A. (2011) 'Justitieassistent in het verleden tot nu. Ervaringen binnen een organisatie in evolutie'. in Federale Overheidsdienst Justitie (Ed.) *10 jaar Justitiehuizen. Balans & perspectieven* (pp. 51–58). Brussel: FOD Justitie.

Conroy, M. and Murrie, D. (2007) *Forensic Assessment of Violence Risk. A Guide for Risk Assessment and Risk Management.* Hoboken, New Jersey: Wiley.

Dantinne, M., Duchêne, J., Lauwaert, K., Aertsen, I., Bogaerts, S., Goethals, J. and Vlaemynck, M. (2009) 'Peine de travail et vécu du condamné. Beleving van de veroordeelde tot een werkstraf', Unpublished report, Liège, Leuven: Université de Liège; Katholieke Universiteit Leuven.

De Smaele, G. and Decoene, S. (2011) 'Desistance and Risk-Need-Responsivity Thinking. Finding Ways Towards Conceptual and Empirical Integration'. Presentation during Panel Session with Prof. Shadd Maruna, V.U.Brussel.

Devos, A. (2011) 'Voorwaardelijke invrijheidstelling heeft zijn nut bewezen'. *De Morgen,* 21 June 2011.

Digard, L. (2010) 'When Legitimacy Is Denied. Offender Perceptions of the Prison Recall System'. *Probation Journal* 57, 43–61.

Fiske, S. (2010) *Social Beings. Core Motives in Social Psychology.* Second Edition. New Jersey: Wiley.

Flanagan, O. (1991) *Varieties of Moral Personality. Ethics and Psychological Realism.* Cambridge: Harvard University Press.

Forgas, J. and Williams, K. (Eds) (2001) *Social Influence: Direct and Indirect Processes.* Philadelphia: Psychology Press.

Gass, R. and Seiter, J. (2011) *Persuasion, Social Influence, and Compliance Gaining.* Fourth Edition. Boston: Allyn & Bacon.

Gibbard, A. (1990) *Wise Choices, Apt Feelings. A Theory of Normative Judgment.* Oxford: Oxford University Press.

Gray, R., Wykes, C. and Gournay, C. (2002) 'From Compliance to Concordance: A Review of the Literature on Interventions to Enhance Compliance with Antipsychotic Medication'. *Journal of Psychiatric and Mental Health Nursing* 9, 277–284.

Haidt, J. (2007) 'The New Synthesis in Moral Psychology'. *Science* 316, 998–1002.

Harris, S. and Nicolai, L. (2010) 'Occupational Exposures in Emergency Medical Service Providers and Knowledge of and Compliance with Universal Precautions'. *American Journal of Infection Control* 38, 86–94.

Haynes, R. B., Ackloo, E., Sohota, N., McDonald, H. P., Yao, X. (2008) 'Interventions for Enhancing Medication Adherence'. Cochrane Database of Systematic Reviews, Issue 2. Art. No. CD000011. DOI: 10.1002/14651858.CD000011.pub3.

Horne, R., Weinman, J., Barber, N., Elliott, R. and Morgan, M. (2005) *Concordance, Adherence and Compliance in Medicine Taking.* Report for the National Co-ordinating Center for NHS Service Delivery and Organisation.

Hucklesby, A. (2009) 'Understanding Offenders' Compliance: A Case Study of Electronically Monitored Curfew Order'. *Journal of Law and Society* 36(2), 248–217.

Hucklesby, A. (2013a) 'Compliance with Electronically Monitored Curfew Orders: Some Empirical Findings'. in A. Crawford and A. Hucklesby (Eds) *Legitimacy and Compliance in Criminal Justice* (pp. 138–158). London, NY: Routledge.

Hucklesby, A. (2013b) 'Insiders' Views: Offenders' and Staff's Experiences of Electronically Monitored Curfews'. in M. Nellis, K. Beyens and D. Kaminski (Eds) *Electronically Monitored Punishment. International and Critical Perspectives* (pp. 228–246). London, NY: Routledge.

Jin, J., Sklar, G. E. and Li S. C. (2008) 'Factors affecting therapeutic compliance: A Review from the Patient's Perspective'. *Therapeutics and Clinical Risk Management* 4 (1) 269–286.

Kelman, H. (1974) 'Social Influence and Linkages Between the Individual and the Social System: Further Thoughts on the Processes of Compliance, Identification, and Internalization'. in J. Tedeschi (Ed.) *Perspectives on Social Power* (pp. 125–171). Chicago: Aldine.

Kelman, H. (2001) 'Ethical Limits on the Use of Influence in Hierarchical Relationships'. in J. Darley, D. Messick and T. Tyler (Eds) *Social Influences on Ethical Behavior in Organizations* (pp. 11–20). London: Erlbaum.

Kelman, H. (2006) 'Interests, Relationships, Identities: Three Central Issues for Individuals and Groups in Negotiating Their Social Environment'. *Annual Review of Psychology* 57, 1–26.

Kelman, J. (1958) 'Compliance, Identification, and Internalization: Three Processes of Attitude Change'. *Journal of Conflict Resolution* 2, 51–60.

Knowles, E. and Riner, D. (2007) 'Omega Approaches to Persuasion: Overcoming Resistance'. in A. Pratkanis (Ed.) *The Science of Social Influence* (pp. 83–114). Philadelphia: Psychology Press.

Krueger, K., Berger, B. and Felkey, B. (2005) 'Medication Adherence and Persistence: A Comprehensive Review'. *Advances in Therapy* 22, 313–356.

Luypaert, H., Beyens, K., Françoise, C., Kaminski, D. and Janssens, C. (2007) *Werken en leren als straf. Le travail et al formation comme peines*. Brussel: VUBPress.

McNeill, F. and Robinson, G. (2013) 'Liquid Legitimacy and Community Sanctions'. in A. Crawford and A. Hucklesby (Eds) *Legitimacy and Compliance in Criminal Justice* (pp. 116–137). NY, London: Routledge.

Milgram, S. (1974) *Obedience to Authority*. New York: Harper.

Osterberg, L. and Blaschke, T. (2005) 'Adherence to Medication'. *The New England Journal of Medicine* 353, 487–497.

Pittman, T. and Zeigler, K. (2007) 'Basic Human Needs'. in A. Kruglanski (Ed.) *Social Psychology: Handbook of Basic Processes*. Second Edition. New York: Guilford Press.

Pratkanis, A. (Ed) (2007) *The Science of Social Influence*. Philadelphia: Psychology Press.

Robinson, G. and McNeill, F. (2008) 'Exploring the Dynamics of Compliance with Community Penalties'. *Theoretical Criminology* 12(4), 431–449.

Sagarin, B. and Wood, S. (2007) 'Resistance to Influence'. in A. Pratkanis (Ed.) *The Science of Social Influence* (pp. 321–340). Philadelphia: Psychology Press.

Tata, C., Burns, N., Halliday, S., Hutton, N. and McNeill, F. (2008) 'Assisting and Advising The Sentencing Decision Process: The Pursuit of "Quality" In Pre-Sentence Reports'. *British Journal of Criminology* 48(6), 435–455.

Ugwudike, P. (2010) 'Compliance with Community Penalties: The Importance of Interactional Dynamics'. in F. McNeill, P. Raynor and C. Trotter (Eds) *Offender Supervision. New Directions in Theory, Research and Practice* (pp. 325–343). Oxon, NY: Willan.

Van Cutsem, N. (2009–2010) *Voorwaardelijke invrijheidstelling: een onderzoek naar de herroeping ervan*. Brussel: Vrije Universiteit Brussel.

Van Dulmen, S., Sluij, E., van Dijk, L., de Ridder, D., Heerdink, R. and Bensing, J. (2007) 'Patient Adherence to Medical Treatment: A Review of Reviews'. *BMC Health Services Research* 7, 55.

Vermeire, E., Hearnshaw, H., Van Royen, P. and Denekens, J. (2001) 'Patient Adherence to Treatment: Three Decades of Research. A Comprehensive Review'. *Journal of Clinical Pharmacy and Therapeutics* 26, 331–342.

Verrydt, G. and Zwartenbroeckx, K. (2003) *Dynamische risicotaxatie van recidive bij voorwaardelijk invrijheid gestelden*. K.U. Leuven: Departement psychologie.

Wetzels, A. (2008–2009). *Elektronisch toezicht: een onderzoek naar de beleving van de effecten en de gevolgen op de onder toezicht gestelden en hun huisgenoten*. Brussels: Vrije Universiteit Brussel.

Wicklund, R. (1974) *Freedom and Reactance*. New York: Wiley.

Zimbardo, P. (2007) *The Lucifer Effect*. New York: Random House.

13
Effective Supervision of Young Offenders

Christopher Trotter

Introduction

A lot has been written about what works in interventions with offenders (e.g. Andrews and Bonta 2008; McIvor and Raynor 2008; McNeill et al. 2010). In recent years there have also been a small number of studies focusing on what works in the routine supervision of offenders on probation. This is the focus of this chapter, which draws on the findings of a study that was conducted in New South Wales, Australia. The terminology for 'probation' and who delivers probation supervision varies. The term probation is used in this article to refer to community-based supervision whether it relates to probation orders, parole orders, supervised bonds or other legal community-based orders which involve supervision. Similarly, the term 'probation officer' is used to refer to probation officers, community corrections officers, parole officers, juvenile justice workers or counsellors, or others who supervise offenders in the community under court orders.

Knowledge about the effectiveness of community-based supervision is important for several reasons. It is one of the most, if not the most used disposition for criminal offences in Western countries, and most persistent offenders experience probation or other community-based orders at some stage in their lives. According to the United States Bureau of Justice Statistics (BJS), as many as 5 million people were on probation or parole at the end of 2009 – about 3 per cent of adults in the United States resident population. In Australia during 2008–2009, an average of 56,972 offenders were serving community corrections orders on any given day. This is a rate of 338 per 100,000 adults (562 per 100,000 adult males and 121 per 100,000 adult females) (AIC 2010).

Probation represents the primary form of intervention with young offenders in many parts of the world. In Australia (AIHW 2011), for example, around 7200 young people were under juvenile justice supervision on any given day in 2008–2009. Most (90 per cent) were under community-based supervision, with the remainder in detention. In NSW during 2009–2010, 4521 young offenders were under the supervision of the NSW Department of Juvenile Justice on community-based orders (NSW Government 2010). Aboriginal and Torres Strait Islander young people continue to be over-represented, in community supervision as well as in detention (AIHW 2011).

Some studies have found that certain supervision skills offered by supervisors can lead to reduced levels of reoffending (Bonta et al. 2011; Dowden and Andrews 2004; Robinson et al. 2011; Trotter 1996). These studies have been predominantly undertaken with adult offenders.

This chapter reports on a study which aimed to examine the relationship between the use of these practice skills by supervisors in juvenile justice in NSW and reoffending rates by their clients (those under their supervision). Reoffending during and after supervision can be described as key measures of compliance. Reoffending demonstrates a failure to comply with the central objective of supervision, which is to reduce recidivism. It was hypothesized that it would be possible to identify the extent to which supervisors used particular practice skills through the direct observation of interviews by trained research officers. It was also hypothesized that the more the effective practice skills highlighted in earlier research were used, the less frequently the offenders under supervision would reoffend. The study also considered whether or not high-risk offenders would benefit more from their workers' use of effective practice skills than low-risk offenders, and whether the more offenders were engaged in the supervision process, the more they would benefit from the skills offered by their workers.

Literature review

A review of research (Trotter 2006) suggests that the following worker skills are related to reduced offending by those under supervision: (1) The worker is clear about their role. This includes helping the client to understand the dual social control and helping aims of supervision and other issues such as confidentiality and what is expected of the client. (2) The worker models and reinforces prosocial values and actions and makes appropriate use of challenging or confrontation. In other words, the worker is reliable and fair and questions rationalizations for offending. (3) The worker helps offenders with problems which are identified by the client rather than the worker. (4) The worker encourages clients to focus on problems or issues which are related to the person's offending (e.g. drugs, peers, employment, family). (5) The worker helps clients to develop strategies to address these issues. These strategies focus on practical issues and may include cognitive–behavioural and/or relapse prevention strategies. (6) The worker takes a holistic approach to client issues rather than focusing on just one or two specific problems or symptoms. (7) The worker develops a therapeutic alliance. In other words, they work in a collaborative, friendly, optimistic way so that the client develops trust in the worker as someone who can genuinely help them with their problems.

These principles are consistent with the best practices principles enunciated and researched by others in the field (e.g. Dowden and Andrews 2004; Raynor et al. 2010; Robinson et al. 2011). This is not to say that there is universal agreement on best practice principles in offender supervision. Bonta and Andrews (2007, 2010) have spent many years developing the 'Risk/Needs/Responsivity' model, which incorporates most of the principles outlined above but places particular emphasis on focusing on high-risk offenders, on using actuarial tools to assess levels of offender risk and needs, and on the use of predominantly cognitive–behavioural approaches to assist offenders to address their risk-related needs. Ward et al. (2007), on the other hand, have argued that the focus on risk and risk assessment has been at the expense of opportunities for offenders to develop 'good lives' on their own terms. They and others (e.g. McNeill et al. 2005) have emphasized the importance of therapeutic alliance and the worker/client relationship, which they argue may be compromised by a focus on risk factors which may be defined by workers rather than clients.

Several studies have specifically examined the relationship between worker skills and reoffending rates of clients. Some of these studies have also examined the extent to which training has influenced the use of the skills by workers. One study also looked at the relationship between use of the skills and education in social work and welfare and further offending. These studies are briefly reviewed below.

Andrews et al. (1979) published a seminal study conducted in probation in Ontario, Canada, which focused on the use of skills in the routine community supervision of offenders. They found that probation officers who made use of prosocial modelling and reinforcement and problem-solving and who had high levels of empathy had clients with significantly lower recidivism.

A further study undertaken in Victoria (Trotter 1996) offered training to 12 community corrections officers (community supervisors of adult offenders on court and parole board orders) in role clarification, problem-solving, prosocial modelling and relationship skills. Those who received training were significantly more likely to make use of skills (as determined by examination of file notes) and had significantly lower reoffence rates at 18-month and four-year follow-up in comparison to a control group of clients of officers who had not received training. There were a total of 261 clients in the study, and the differences in recidivism between the two groups were between 20 and 45 per cent depending on the recidivism measure used. In a further study using the same population (Trotter 2000) it was found that supervisors who had academic qualifications in social work or welfare made more use of the effective practice skills and their clients had lower recidivism rates at statistically significant levels compared with the clients of workers without training or trained in other disciplines.

A study undertaken in adult probation in Canada (Bonta et al. 2011) followed up 143 clients, supervised either by one of 33 supervisors who had undertaken training in effective practice skills or by one of 19 supervisors who had not undertaken such training. The training course followed collaboration with staff involved in the earlier Australian study (Trotter 1996) and included similar content, although the Canadian training placed greater emphasis on cognitive–behavioural interventions. The workers who volunteered for the project then provided tape recordings of worker/client interviews which were analysed by researchers using a detailed coding manual to assess the skills of the workers. They reported high levels of inter-rater reliability and they found that those who had received training made more use of each of the practice skills of structuring, relationship, behavioural techniques and cognitive techniques. They also found that those under the supervision of the trained officers had significantly lower rates of recidivism after controlling for client risk levels. Thirty-three per cent in the non-trained control group committed a further offence within two years compared with 24 per cent of clients of those who were trained. The clients of those officers who made maximum use of ongoing clinical supervision had a recidivism rate of only 15 per cent. They found that the most influential skills in terms of reduced offending were those relating to cognitive–behavioural principles, in contrast to relationship and other skills, which were not significantly related to recidivism.

A larger study with similar aims was conducted by Robinson et al. (2011) with United States courts and Middle District of North Carolina. They used a sample of 41 officers in the trained experimental group and 26 in the control group and a total of more than 1000 pre-trial and post-conviction adult clients. When tapes of interviews were analysed, they found that those in the experimental group who undertook three and a half days' training in effective supervision skills were more likely to use the effective practice skills. The researchers used a coding manual developed following consultation with researchers in the earlier studies. The training and the training manual focused on:

> Active Listening, Role Clarification, Effective Use of Authority, Effective Disapproval, Effective Reinforcement, Effective Punishment, Problem Solving, and Teaching, Applying, and Reviewing the Cognitive Model.
>
> (Robinson et al. 2012: 6)

The offenders supervised by officers in the experimental group had a reoffence rate of 26 per cent in the experimental group compared with 34 in the control group for moderate to high-risk clients. This study, like the earlier ones, was conducted with volunteers and experienced some methodological problems in terms of drop-outs; however, the experimental and control groups showed no significant differences in terms of demographics or risk levels.

The evidence is mounting, therefore, that the skills offered by supervisors to offenders sentenced to community supervision make a difference to the reoffending rates of the offenders. The studies undertaken to date have focused on adult offenders in Australia, the United States and Canada. No studies of this type have focused specifically on young offenders in Australia or elsewhere. Also, the studies to date have used analysis of file notes or coding of audio-tapes of interviews to determine the nature of skills used by workers. None have observed interviews in person, a method which might provide information about non-verbal interactions. The various studies have also used different definitions of skills. Further, none of the studies have considered the relationship with levels of education of staff in counselling skills or their specific designated role as a counsellor versus worker. There is also some uncertainty as to which aspects of the effective practice principles have the most impact, with one earlier Australian study (Trotter 1996) pointing to prosocial modelling and reinforcement as most strongly related to positive outcomes, in contrast to the Canadian study (Bonta et al. 2011), which found the use of cognitive techniques to be the most influential. Some of these issues are addressed in this study.

A substantial literature has pointed to the value of focusing correctional interventions on high-risk offenders. It is argued that high-risk offenders are likely to benefit from intensive interventions and that low-risk offenders are likely to show minimal, if any, benefit. This has been argued in relation to correctional interventions in general (Andrews and Bonta 2008) and in relation to supervision of offenders on probation and parole (Lowenkamp et al. 2006). One recent United States study, however, found that officers who had been trained in and made use of effective practice skills had a positive impact on low and moderate-risk offenders but less impact on high-risk clients. A similar outcome was found in an Australian study, albeit some years ago (Trotter 1994).

Much of the literature on correctional interventions emphasizes the importance of the worker/client relationship. It is argued that workers who have good interpersonal skills and who develop a working alliance with those they supervise will have clients with lower recidivism rates (Andrews and Bonta 2008; Trotter 2012; Ward 2010). On the other hand, some studies examining probation supervision found that worker empathy was unrelated to offender recidivism (Andrews et al. 1979; Trotter 1990, 1996). The extent to which the effective skills can be effective regardless of the worker/client alliance is not clear from the research in probation settings. It may be that skills such as role clarification and prosocial modelling may be effective with offenders who are not engaged in the supervision process.

Methodology

Aims

- To examine the relationship between the use of effective practice skills by supervisors in Juvenile Justice NSW and reoffence rates by clients
- To consider which of the skills, if any, have the most impact on reoffending rates
- To consider whether high-risk offenders benefit more from effective practice skills than low-risk offenders
- To consider whether offenders who are engaged in the supervision process are more likely to benefit from effective practice skills.

Sample

After receiving university and Department of Juvenile Justice ethics approval, juvenile justice staff with responsibility for direct supervision of young offenders were invited to be involved in the project. Forty-eight staff members initially volunteered. For each worker, the next five clients allocated to them became eligible for the study. Interviews between the staff members and young people were then observed within three months of the young person receiving their court order. In total 117 interviews were observed over a period of four years, 39 in a pilot project and the remainder as part of a project funded through the Australian Criminology Research Council. Five interviews could not be observed for each worker due to staff and client turnover.

Coding

A coding manual was developed following collaboration with other researchers on similar projects (Bonta et al. 2011; Raynor et al. 2010), although it was different in some respects from the coding manuals used on those projects. The manual reflected the effective practice skills referred to in the literature review and outlined in Trotter (2006). The manual aimed to define the skills and assist in the accuracy and reliability of the estimates of the extent to which the skills were used in interviews. It was divided into 15 sections, including: set-up of the interview; structure of the interview; role clarification; needs analysis; problem-solving; developing strategies; relapse prevention/cognitive–behavioural techniques; prosocial modelling and reinforcement; nature of the relationship; empathy; confrontation; termination; use of referral/community resources; non-verbal cues; and incidental conversations. Each of the 15 sections contained a number of items which could be rated on a five-point scale. For example, the problem-solving section included: problem survey; problem ranking; problem exploration; setting goals; time frame; review; developing a contract; developing strategies; ongoing monitoring; and time spent conducting problem-solving.

For the skill to be rated highly it needed to be implemented in a way which was consistent with the research about good practice referred to in the literature review. For example, problem-solving would be rated highly if the worker frequently helped clients to identify their own problems and goals and to identify strategies themselves to address them. It would be rated low if the worker identified problems with minimal input from the client and then set goals and strategies for the client.

Each of the interviews was coded either by the researcher who observed the interview or subsequently by another researcher from an audio-tape of the interview. When the coding was undertaken from an audio-tape, the coder also had access to a non-verbal check list which was completed by the observer following each interview. The non-verbal check list provided information about the body language and non-verbal interactions between the workers/counsellors and the clients.

Inter-rater reliability

Three research officers conducted field observations. Ninety-seven observations were completed by the first research officer, who was employed continuously on the project for a period of four years. Sixteen observations were completed by an Aboriginal research officer and four were completed by another research officer.

The coding was undertaken by three coders. The second and third coders did not observe the interviews but coded from the tapes and the non-verbal cues checklist. Each of the coders was trained in using the coding manual and cross-coded a number of interviews using the audio-tapes of the interviews prior to doing the final coding of the interviews. Detailed discussions were undertaken ensuring that each of the coders had consistent interpretations of the wording in the coding manual.

Twenty of the interviews were coded by the research officer who observed the interview and subsequently cross-coded by another research officer using the audio-tapes and the non-verbal check list. There was a high degree of consistency in the ratings. For example, the correlation on the overall global skill score between first and second coders was 0.741 (sig 0.000), on time spent discussing role clarification it was 0.548 (sig 0.006), on time spent on problem solving it was 0.626 (sig 0.002) and on prosocial modelling 0.561 (sig 0.005).

Recidivism

The recidivism measure reported in this paper is any further offence within two years taken from police records. While there are obvious limitations in using only one measure, there was a significant correlation between this measure and other recidivism measures used in the study – for example, placement in detention or prison within two years (r 0.351, sig 0.000).

Results

Use of skills by workers and client recidivism

The global skills score was rated out of ten by the researchers based on the overall use of skills by the worker. A score of one indicated that 'The worker did not utilize any of the effective practice principles' whereas a score of ten indicated that 'the worker deliberately used the effective practice principles in an efficient and successful manner'. Table 13.1 shows that the workers with high global skill scores (six or above) had clients with lower rates of reoffending after two years (after receiving the original order) compared with those with low global scores. The differences are, however, not within conventional levels of significance.

There is, however, a statistically significant association between the recidivism rates of clients and particularly low global scores of supervisors. As shown in Table 13.2, if the probation officers were allocated a score of less than five their clients offended more often than the clients of other probation officers. To look at this another way, those supervised by workers with more skills survived two years without reoffending at almost twice the rate of those who displayed fewer skills.

This significant difference is also evident when a regression analysis is undertaken in Statistical Product and Service Solutions (SPSS) taking account of the Youth Level of Service Inventory (YLSI) (the standard risk assessment measure used in NSW Juvenile Justice). In other words, the differences cannot be explained by the risk levels of the clients as shown in Table 13.3.

Table 13.1   Overall use of skills by workers (scored 6 or more and 5 or less) by any further offence in 24 months by clients

Reoffended in two years	
Skills score 5 or less	74% (39/53)
Skills score 6 or more	62.5% (40/64)

Table 13.2   Overall use of skills by workers (scored 5 or more and 4 or less) by any further offence in 24 months by young people

Reoffended in two years	
Skills score 4 or less	81% (26/32)
Skills score 5 or more	62% (52/85)
One-tailed Fischer's exact test	

$p = < 0.04$

Table 13.3 Logistic regression analysis of overall use of skills by workers (scored 5 or more and 4 or less) by any further offence in 24 months by clients, including client risk levels

Variables in the Equation

		B	S.E.	Wald	df	Sig.	Exp(B)
Step 1[a]	Skill Score	−1.088	0.553	3.869	1	0.049	0.337
	YLSI	0.116	0.029	15.690	1	0.000	1.123
	Constant	0.642	1.056	0.370	1	0.543	1.901

[a] Variable(s) entered on step 1: gs4, FR.YLSI_score

The use of other skills and client recidivism

Most of the skills coded during the observations were related to lower reoffending by clients. In most cases, however, this did not reach statistically significant levels. For example, the more time workers were involved with clients undertaking problem-solving, the lower the recidivism rates of the clients. When strategies were developed in the sessions to address problems, this was related to reduced offending, particularly when the young people developed the strategies rather than the worker. In each instance when the workers used cognitive–behavioural skills and relapse prevention skills, the clients had lower rates of recidivism. Workers who used prosocial modelling and relationship skills also had clients with lower reoffending. Workers who scored as open and honest, non-blaming, optimistic and enthusiastic, used appropriate self-disclosure and were friendly all had clients with lower reoffending.

None of these measures, however, reached conventional levels of statistical significance. The two worker skills which were most strongly related to reduced offending were the use of rewards by the worker and a non-blaming approach. Fifty-five per cent (27/49) of the young people reoffended when the use of rewards by the worker was scored three or more on the five-point scale, compared with 76 per cent (52/68) when use of rewards was scored two or less. This was significant at the 0.05 level on a chi square analysis, although it was just outside the 0.10 level when the YLSI was included in a regression analysis. Those who scored above two on the five-point scale for the non-blaming measure had a recidivism rate of 61 per cent (40/66) compared with those who scored two or below (76.5 per cent (39/51)). The level of significance was 0.052 (0.056 when the YLSI was included in a regression analysis).

Staff role and qualifications

Juvenile justice workers may be employed as juvenile justice counsellors or as juvenile justice officers. Counsellors are appointed by the organization to

Table 13.4 Regression analysis of staff position (juvenile justice officer or juvenile justice counsellor), client risk level and any further offence in two years

Variables in the Equation

		B	S.E.	Wald	df	Sig.	Exp(B)
Step 1[a]	FR.YLSI_score	0.126	0.030	17.354	1	0.000	1.134
	Staff_position	−1.269	0.501	6.403	1	0.011	0.281
	Constant	0.205	0.726	0.080	1	0.778	1.227

[a] Variable(s) entered on step 1: FR.YLSI_score, Staff_position.

undertake a more active counselling role than other staff and are required to be qualified as either social workers or psychologists. Thirty-two of the interviews which were observed were conducted by counsellors, with the remainder conducted by officers. The counsellors made more use of the effective practice skills. In fact, they were twice as likely to be rated above five on the global score (45 per cent (38/84) for workers and 80 per cent (26/33) for counsellors (p <0.01)).

They also had clients with lower recidivism (54.5 per cent (18/33) for counsellors compared with 73 per cent (61/84) for officers). They also supervised clients who were higher-risk, in other words, who scored higher on the risk assessment tool used in NSW Juvenile Justice (the Level of Service Inventory - Revised (LSI-R). These differences were statistically significant at the 0.01 level after taking risk levels into account through the regression analysis as shown in Table 13.4.

Impact on high and low-risk offenders

It was pointed out earlier that a number of studies have found that medium and high-risk offenders are more likely to benefit from correctional interventions than low-risk offenders. Most of this work has, however, examined correctional interventionism in general rather than the delivery of evidence-based supervision to offenders under community supervision. Three studies referred to earlier (Robinson et al. 2011; Trotter 1990, 1994) found, on the other hand, that, when effective supervision practices were offered to offenders, low-risk offenders were as likely to benefit from them as high-risk offenders. This was the case in this study, as shown in Tables 13.5 and 13.6. The numbers are relatively small and do not show statistically significant associations; nevertheless, for both high-risk and low-risk cases reoffending was lower when offenders were offered effective supervision. The low-risk offenders in particular have lower rates of reoffending when exposed to evidence-based supervision.

Table 13.5   Worker global scores by reoffending for high-risk offenders (LSI >20)

| | | | Global score low(1) high(2) | | Total |
			1.00	2.00	
Reoffended within 24 months total	No	Count	1	6	7
		Per cent within gs 1 to 4	6.3%	17.1%	13.7%
	Yes	Count	15	29	44
		Per cent within gs 1 to 4	93.8%	82.9%	86.3%
Total		Count	16	35	51
		Per cent within gs 1 to 4	100.0%	100.0%	100.0%

Table 13.6   Worker global scores by reoffending for low-risk offenders (LSI <21)

| | | | Global score low(1) high(2) | | Total |
			1.00	2.00	
Reoffended within 24 months total	No	Count	5	26	31
		Per cent within gs 1 to 4	31.3%	52.0%	47.0%
	Yes	Count	11	24	35
		Per cent within gs 1 to 4	68.8%	48.0%	53.0%
Total		Count	16	50	66
		Per cent within gs 1 to 4	100.0%	100.0%	100.0%

Were offenders engaged in the supervision process?

Reference was made earlier to the importance of the worker/client alliance. It might be anticipated that if workers were engaged in the interview process and engaged with their workers this would lead to lower reoffending. The observers of the interviews estimated the extent to which the client was engaged in the overall process of supervision. This was done independently of the assessment of the worker's skill. While there was a correlation between workers' skills and client engagement, there were often occasions, particularly with high-risk clients, when the worker demonstrated good skills but the client displayed minimal engagement. Previous studies on probation (Trotter 1996) have suggested that the evidence-based practices of workers may be independent of the levels of workers' empathy.

Table 13.7   Worker global scores by reoffending for offenders who were engaged overall

| | | | Global score low(1) high(2) | | Total |
			1.00	2.00	
Reoffended within 24 months Total	No	Count	2	18	20
		Per cent within gs 1 to 4	28.6%	34.6%	33.9%
	Yes	Count	5	34	39
		Per cent within gs 1 to 4	71.4%	65.4%	66.1%
Total		Count	7	52	59
		Per cent within gs 1 to 4	100.0%	100.0%	100.0%

Table 13.8   Worker global scores by reoffending for offenders who were not engaged overall

| | | | Global score low(1) high(2) | | Total |
			1.00	2.00	
Reoffended within 24 months total	No	Count	4	14	18
		Per cent within gs 1 to 4	16.0%	42.4%	31.0%
	Yes	Count	21	19	40
		Per cent within gs 1 to 4	84.0%	57.6%	69.0%
Total		Count	25	33	58
		Per cent within gs 1 to 4	100.0%	100.0%	100.0%

$p = <0.05$

It was evident that the skills of the worker are related to reduced reoffending regardless of levels of engagement of the offenders under supervision. However, this was only at statistically significant levels for offenders who were less engaged in the supervision process, as shown in Tables 13.7 and 13.8. The reoffending rate for the offenders who were less engaged in the process was 57.6 per cent where their workers were rated as having good skills, compared with 84 per cent where the workers did not display good skills.

Discussion

A growing body of studies have indicated that correctional interventions characterized by certain features lead to reduced levels of recidivism. A small group of studies has also found that the nature of the skills used by supervisors in the routine supervision of offenders on community-based orders relates to the recidivism of offenders under supervision (Bonta et al. 2011; Robinson et al. 2011; Trotter 1996). These studies have also shown that supervisors are more likely to use these skills if they have received specific training and supervision based on the skills. One study (Trotter 2000) also found that supervisors who had completed social work and welfare qualifications (courses in which these skills are commonly taught) were more likely to use the skills and more likely to have clients with lower recidivism. There is some doubt, however, about the precise nature of the effective practice skills, with some studies supporting the importance of cognitive behavioural skills and others placing more emphasis on relationship skills (Bonta et al. 2011; Trotter 1996; Ward 2010). The studies to date have also focused on adult offenders rather than young offenders, and they have used various methods to assess the use of skills.

This study aimed to examine the relationship between the use of skills in youth justice and client recidivism, which can be described as a form of non-compliance. The study used observation of interviews and a detailed coding manual. It found that when the observers rated the workers as having good skills the clients had fewer further offences in the two-year follow-up period – although this only reached statistically significant levels when the clients of workers who were rated as making minimal use of the skills were compared with the clients of other workers. The workers with few skills seemed to be particularly ineffective.

The study found particular associations between the use of rewards and low reoffending, consistently with earlier research on prosocial modelling and reinforcement (Trotter 1996). It also provides support for a non-blaming approach. These findings relating to individual skills need, however, to be considered cautiously, given that they were not quite within statistical levels of significance. More work is needed with larger samples to tease out the impact of different skills with different offender populations.

The study also found that the skills were effective regardless of the risk levels of the clients and regardless of the extent to which the client was engaged in the supervision process. While many studies have pointed to the value of focusing on medium to high-risk offenders, these studies have not examined the extent to which low-risk offenders might benefit from supervision which is characterized by good skills. It could be that low-risk offenders may not benefit, or may even be harmed by intensive supervision programmes which are not characterized by effective practices. They may be drawn into the system and stigmatized or labelled, with consequent increased criminality. It seems, however, that if the supervision offered is characterized by good worker skills then low-risk offenders may benefit from supervision. The results of this study suggest, when considered alongside the previous research, that it may be particularly important not to offer poor-quality interventions to low-risk offenders, but that all offenders can benefit from high-quality interventions.

The results of this study also suggest that it is particularly important to use effective practice skills with disengaged clients. Disengaged clients, those who don't appear to be responding to the worker and participating in supervision, seem to benefit from being exposed to effective supervision skills. It is hard to argue that workers should not attempt to engage clients in the supervision process, however; for clients who are inarticulate, unmotivated and seemingly disinterested in supervision, it seems that if their workers continue to use skills of role clarification, prosocial modelling and problem-solving their clients will do better than if they do not use these skills.

What can be concluded from this study? When it is considered alongside the earlier research, this study does support the hypothesis that workers with certain skills will have clients with lower recidivism, and that the extent to which those skills are used by individual workers can be determined through a process of observation. It also provides support for the view that workers who have qualifications in social work or psychology and who are given a counselling role are likely to make more use of effective practice skills and have clients with lower recidivism. The study also suggests that workers with good skills are likely to be effective regardless of the levels of risk of their clients and regardless of the extent to which their clients are engaged in the supervision process. These findings have implications for selection, training and the role of youth justice staff.

References

AIC Australian Institute of Criminology. (2010) *Australian crime: Facts & figures 2010* Available at: http://www.aic.gov.au/publications/current%20series/facts/1-20/2010/6_ corrections.aspx

AIHW. (2011) *Juvenile Justice in Australia 2008–2009*. Juvenile justice series no. 7. Cat. no. JUV 7. Available at: http://www.aihw.gov.au/publication-detail/?id= 10737418606&tab= 2 (Accessed 2012).

Andrews, D. A. and Bonta, J. (2008) *The Psychology of Criminal Conduct*. Cincinnati: Anderson Publishing.

Andrews, D. A., Keissling, J. J., Russell, R. J. and Grant, B. A. (1979) *Volunteers and the One-to-One Supervision of Adult Probationers*. Toronto: Ontario Ministry of Correctional Services.

United States Bureau of Justice Statistics. (2010) Probation and Parole in the United States, 2009 http://www.bjs.gov/index.cfm?ty= pbdetail&iid= 2233 (accessed 7 July 2011).

Bonta, J. and Andrews, D. A. (2007) Risk-need-responsivity model for offender assessment and rehabilitation. Public Safety Canada. http://www.publicsafety.gc.ca/res/cor/rep/_fl/ Risk_Need_2007-06_e.pdf

Bonta, J. and Andrews, D. (2010) 'Viewing Offender Assessment and Rehabilitation Through the Lens of the Risk-Needs-Responsivity Model'. in F. McNeil, P. Raynor and

C. Trotter (Eds) *Offender Supervision: New Directions in Theory, Research and Practice.* Devon: Willan Publishers.

Bonta, J., Bourgon, G., Rugge, T., Scott, T.-L., Yessine, A. K., Gutierrez, L. and Li, J. (2011). 'An Experimental Demonstration of Training Probation Officers in Evidence-Based Community Supervision'. *Criminal Justice and Behaviour* 38, 1127–1148.

Dowden, C. and Andrews, D. A. (2004) 'The Importance of Staff Practice in Delivering Effective Correctional Treatment: A Meta-Analytic Review of the Literature'. *International Journal of Offender Therapy and Comparative Criminology* 48(2), 203–214.

Lowenkamp, C., Pealer, J., Smith, P. and Latessa, E. (2006) 'Adhering to the Risk and Need Principles: Does it Matter for Supervision-Based Programs?' *Federal Probation* 70(3), 3–8.

McIvor, G. and Raynor, P. (Eds) (2008) *Developments in Social Work with Offenders.* London: Jessica Kingsley.

McNeil F., Raynor, P. and Trotter, C. (Eds) (2010) *Offender Supervision: New Directions in Theory, Research and Practice.* Devon: Willan Publishers.

McNeill, F., Batchelor, S., Burnett, R. and Knox, J. (2005) *21st Century Social Work: Reducing Re-Offending: Key Practice Skills.* Edinburgh: Scottish Executive.

NSW Government Human Services: Juvenile Justice. (2009/10) Annual Report Statistics 2009/10. http://www.djj.nsw.gov.au/publications.htm

Raynor, P., Ugwudike, P. and Vanstone, M. (2010) 'Skills and Strategies in Probation Supervision: The Jersey Study'. in F. McNeil, P. Raynor and C. Trotter (Eds) *Offender Supervision: New Directions in Theory, Research and Practice.* Devon: Willan Publishers.

Robinson, C., Vanbenschoten, S., Alexander, M. and Lowenkamp, C. (2011) 'A Random (almost) Study of Staff Training Aimed at Reducing Re-arrest (Reducing recidivism through intentional design'. *Federal Probation* 75, 2. http://www.uscourts.gov/viewer .aspx?doc= /uscourts/FederalCourts/PPS/Fedprob/2011-09/index.html

Robinson, C. R., Lowenkamp, C. T., VanBenschoten, S., Alexander, M., Holsinger, A. M. and Oleson, J. C. (2012). 'A random study of Staff Training Aimed at Reducing Rearrest (STARR): Using Core Correctional Practices in Probation Interactions'. *Journal of Crime & Justice* 1–22.

Trotter, C. (1990) 'Probation Can Work: A Research Study using Volunteers'. Australian Journal of Socila Work 43 (2), 13–18

Trotter, C. (1994) *Effective Supervision of Offenders,* PhD Thesis, LaTrobe University, Melbourne.

Trotter, C. (1996) 'The Impact of Different Supervision Practices in Community Corrections'. *Australian and New Zealand Journal of Criminology* 29(1), 29–46.

Trotter, C. (2000) 'Social Work Education, Pro-Social Orientation and Effective Probation Practice'. *Probation Journal* 47, 256–261.

Trotter, C. (2006) *Working with Involuntary Clients.* Sydney: Allen & Unwin.

Trotter, C. J., 2012, Effective community-based supervision of young offenders, *Trends & Issues in Crime and Criminal Justice [P],* vol 448, Australian Institute of Criminology, Australia, pp. 1–7.

Ward, T. (2010) 'The Good Lives Model of Offender Rehabilitation'. in F. McNeil, P. Raynor and C. Trotter (Eds) *Offender Supervision: New Directions in Theory, Research and Practice.* Devon: Willan Publishers.

Ward, T., Melser, J. and Yates, P. M. (2007). 'Reconstructing the Risk-Need-Responsivity Model: A Theoretical Elaboration and Evaluation'. *Aggression and Violent Behavior* 12, 208–228.

14

A Tale of Two Innovations: Motivational Interviewing and Core Correctional Practices in United States Probation

Melissa Alexander, Christopher T. Lowenkamp and
Charles R. Robinson

The recent past in community supervision has witnessed the introduction of a number of new innovations intended to improve offender outcomes. While many of these innovations have focused on various 'programs', more recently the focus has shifted to officer supervision skills and their impact on outcomes. This chapter focuses on two broad officer skill sets, motivational interviewing and what has come to be known as core correctional practices. The chapter discusses the efforts of the United States probation system in implementing these skill sets, with a focus on how the implementation process may impact fidelity to the intervention and subsequent offender outcomes. Over a three-year period several hundred probation officers were trained in motivational interviewing (MI). While initial training was fairly standard, there was considerable variability in follow-up training, coaching and implementation practices. Scores based on the Motivational Interviewing Treatment Integrity (MITI) manual were collected from a sample of trained officers. The MITI revealed that very few officers were actually proficient in MI. Further, the outcomes of the trained officers' caseloads before and after training were compared with the outcomes of caseloads belonging to officers who were not trained in MI. This comparison showed no significant differences in client success. A couple of years later, probation officers were trained in core correctional practices. Officers were provided with initial training and then several structured booster sessions to ensure that they were correctly using the skills. A randomized trial of the training revealed that trained officers were more likely to demonstrate the core correctional skills, and their post-training caseloads had significantly lower (25 to 50 per cent) recidivism rates than the control group officers. The

242

differences in the training and implementation approaches and the outcomes of the two attempts at innovation diffusion are discussed.

Historical context

Community supervision in the United States is one of the most widely imposed criminal sanctions, with approximately 5,018,900, or 69 per cent, of the correctional population being under supervision (Glaze 2010). Community supervision has gone through vast changes in approach over the years, from various rehabilitation approaches to a more monitoring/law enforcement focus, and back again. This pendulum shift has been driven by philosophical differences in the purpose of community supervision and the lack of research on effective approaches. The end of a rehabilitation era in the 1970s was partially driven by the now infamous research review of Martinson, who concluded: 'with few and isolated exceptions, the rehabilitative efforts that have been reported so far have had no appreciable effect on recidivism' (1974: 25). The shift to more law enforcement approaches produced similarly disappointing results. For example, Taxman (2002) reviewed studies of intensive supervision and caseload size and concluded that mere supervision did not reduce recidivism: 'unless the contacts are more than check-ins it is unlikely that they will impact outcomes' (p. 17). Most recently, Bonta et al. (2008) reviewed studies from 1980 to 2006 and found supervision had little to no impact on recidivism rates.

Despite this disappointing history, recent approaches to supervision practices have shown great promise. These tactics focus on adhering to the Risk/Need/Responsivity principles (Andrews and Bonta 2010; Dowden and Andrews 2004) and teach officers specific skills for utilizing cognitive–behavioural and other research-based approaches in supervision, which have come to be known as core correctional practices. Andrews and Kiessling (1980) defined these correctional practices as: (1) use of authority, (2) role modelling/reinforcement, (3) problem-solving strategies, (4) use of community resources and (5) relationship factors. Dowden and Andrews (2004) provided a meta-analytic review of the core correctional practices, indicating that the use of authority, disapproval, reinforcement, modelling, teaching problem-solving skills and structured learning are all related to the effectiveness of correctional services. While much of the research reviewed by Dowden and Andrews focused on treatment programmes, other research has examined the use of these skills in community supervision settings (Taxman et al. 2006; Trotter 1996, 1999). Several studies have demonstrated favourable results for these approaches (e.g. Bonta et al. 2010; Robinson et al. 2012), with decreases in recidivism ranging from 25 to almost 50 per cent lower than traditional supervision.

The United States probation system is charged with supervising offenders who have been convicted of federal offences and spans 94 probation districts spread across the country. Collectively, the agency supervises over 130,000 individuals on probation or parole. Since 2002, the system has focused on strategic use of resources by focusing on and expanding the use of evidence-based practices. In particular, the system has attempted to transform basic supervision practices through the implementation of two innovative practices, Motivational Interviewing (MI) and Staff Training Aimed at Reducing Rearrest (STARR). This chapter outlines the implementation process and the results of these implementation efforts.

Motivational Interviewing

Motivational Interviewing (MI; Miller and Rollnick 2002), a strategy first developed for addressing alcohol use, has exploded since its first publication in 1992. Over the past 20 years MI has evolved and is now seen as 'a form of collaborative conversation for strengthening a person's own motivation and commitment to change. It is a person-centered counseling style for addressing the common problem of ambivalence about change by paying particular attention to the language of change' (www.motivationalinterviewing .org). MI focuses on a 'spirit' of collaboration, respect of the individual's right to choose about his/her behaviour, and evocation from the client of potential reasons for/against change. Specific strategies used within MI include a focus on reflections rather than questions, specific strategies to encourage discussion about reasons for change, and decreasing 'MI non-adherent' strategies such as directly confronting the client or telling him/her what to do (i.e. 'you need to go to AA').

Since its success with multiple problem behaviours (see meta-analyses by Hettema et al. 2005 and Rubak et al. 2005) a number of practitioners have attempted to translate the strategy to criminal justice populations and interventions. A recent bibliography of criminal justice-related publications notes 40 articles related to the use of MI within criminal justice (National Institute of Corrections 2011). However, there are relatively few systematic research studies on the impact of MI within correctional populations. A meta-analysis by McMurran (2009) found only 19 studies that attempted to determine effectiveness, with only ten of those being randomized controlled trials. As such, she concluded that 'no overall definitive conclusion about the effectiveness of MI with offenders can be drawn' (p. 95). Since that time additional results have been conflicting, with some studies showing MI interventions can reduce reconviction rates for male offenders (Anstiss et al. 2011) while others have found no effect on probationer outcome (Walters et al. 2010).

It is important to note that in many of these studies there was little to no evaluation of the quality of the MI intervention. Thus, it is difficult to determine the fidelity of the intervention, which is critical to the evaluation of its impact.

Core correctional practices

Andrews and Kiessling (1980) introduced an image of the effective correctional supervision professional and the practices designed to increase the therapeutic value of rehabilitation programmes for clients. The five dimensions of effectiveness include effective use of authority, demonstration or modelling of prosocial attitude, values and beliefs, the use of reinforcement, problem-solving, the use of community resources and the quality of the relationship between the professional and the client. Largely based on social learning theory, the intent was to reflect the most effective research-supported intervention strategies for eliciting positive behavioural change. The core correctional practices (CCPs) were first introduced in a staff training programme as 'Core Correctional Training' (CCT) in 1998 by Andrews and Carvell. Since 1998 a number of training sessions have focused on shifting officers from 'check-in' supervision to a more skill-focused interaction between the corrections professional and the client, including training curriculums from Trotter (1996) and Taxman et al. (2006) and more recent trainings including the Strategic Training Initiative in Community Supervision (Bonta et al. 2010), Effective Practices in Correctional Settings (EPICS) and Staff Training Aimed at Reducing Rearrest (Robinson et al. 2012). All of these curriculums focus on teaching officers specific skill strategies to be used during client contacts, in the hopes that they will help offenders internalize prosocial thinking and behaviour.

The empirical value of adhering to these CCPs was demonstrated in a meta-analytic review conducted by Dowden and Andrews (2004). The meta-analysis provided strong preliminary evidence supporting CCPs as an important indicator of client outcomes.

Implementation research

The quality of implementation can significantly impact the effectiveness of an intervention. For instance, in a review of cognitive–behavioural programs (CBT) for offenders, Lipsey et al. (2007) found that effective implementation was one of the three main elements that impacted the effectiveness of CBT. In a similar review of juvenile offender interventions, Lipsey (2009) concluded: 'in some analyses, the quality with which the intervention is implemented has been as strongly related to recidivism effects as the type of program, *so much so that a well-implemented intervention of an inherently less efficacious type can outperform a more efficacious one that is poorly implemented*' (p. 127).

Despite the importance of implementation, relatively little attention has been given to researching how to effectively implement interventions. The most recent summary of intervention research (Fixsen et al. 2005) actually tells us more about what doesn't work than what does. Two of the most common practices, providing information and training, without additional supports, do not lead to any significant, sustained changes in programmes or services

(Fixsen et al. 2005). In contrast, the presence of feedback and coaching has led to significant gains in the use of new interventions. For example, Joyce and Showers (2002) reviewed the research on skill acquisition for teachers. When workshops focused on theory and discussion there was little change in skill use in the classroom; even when demonstration and practice within the training were added, there was only a 5 per cent use of the skill in the classroom. It wasn't until on-the-job feedback and coaching were included that substantial gains (95 per cent use in the classroom) were achieved. Similarly, greater proficiency in MI was demonstrated by those individuals who received coaching and feedback (Miller et al. 2004) versus those who only received workshop training. Implementation is also informed by the research on innovation diffusion (Rogers 1962). This research indicates that there are four main elements involved in the diffusion process: aspects of the innovation, communication channels, time and the social system. Although the diffusion of an innovation can be influenced by factors within each of these areas, including characteristics of opinion leaders/change agents, the process of communication about the innovation and the characteristics of those adopting the innovation, for our purpose we focus on characteristics of the innovation itself and their impact on rates of adoption. Rogers (1962) notes that these characteristics include the relative advantage of the innovation over existing practices, the compatibility with existing values and experiences, the complexity of the innovation and the ability to try out and visibly observe the innovation. It is argued that implementation and the rate of adoption may be influenced by these unique aspects, and building an implementation process around these elements will increase the likelihood of successful implementation.

How United States probation went about implementing MI

As a more thorough discussion of our training protocol has been published elsewhere (Alexander et al. 2008), we provide only a brief summary here. The protocol outlined for training officers in MI was built around the existing research on learning MI. There is good evidence that the typical one- to two-day training workshop may not be the ideal format for learning MI (Walters et al. 2005). Although participants often report an increase in *knowledge* or *self-reported skill* following brief workshops, measures of *actual* interactions show much more modest gains (e.g. Miller and Mount 2001). As such, it was important to recognize that a longer training format was necessary. The recommended plan was based on the eight stages of learning MI model outlined by Miller and Moyers (2006). These stages are considered sequential and outline the spirit, skills and strategies necessary to become proficient in MI. The stages include:

Stage 1: The Spirit of Motivational Interviewing. Recognizing the collaborative nature of MI, which focuses on evoking individuals' own reasons, ideas and solutions about behaviour change and respecting their autonomy to choose whether to change their behaviour or not.

Stage 2: OARS – Client-centred Counselling Skills. OARS is the acronym used in MI to refer to skills that are used to demonstrate good listening. It stands for Open-ended questions, Affirmations (positive comments about what clients say/do), Reflections and Summarizations (providing a cohesive picture of what has been discussed).

Stages 3 and 4: Recognizing, Reinforcing and Strengthening Change Talk. MI attempts to increase officers' awareness of client statements that indicate an interest and/or willingness to change, while also teaching strategies that will help draw out additional change statements.

Stage 5. Rolling with Resistance. MI stresses that denial, argumentation and resistance, which in the past were assumed to be a hallmark of an unmotivated client, are instead largely a function of the provider's communication style. Thus, MI focuses on communication skills that decrease resistance.

Stages 6 and 7. Developing and Consolidating Commitment to Change. As clients talk more about change, the officer can move from reinforcing change talk to developing a plan for change. Because people are more likely to act on things they themselves have chosen, advice provision takes a back seat and the provider tries to elicit the offender's *own ideas about change* and emphasize his/her *personal responsibility* in the change process.

Stage 8. Switching Between MI and Other Approaches. MI needs to be integrated into overall session management. No matter what the approach, officers have to make decisions about what topics are important in the moment, and what can be left for later.

If the goal is to have officers who are using MI in a comprehensive, effective way, the most useful training format appears to be a workshop followed by feedback and/or coaching (Miller et al. 2004). Thus, the recommended training plan began with a brief overview of evidence-based practice (EBP) so officers could relate MI to the overall model of EBP and understand its role in effective supervision. Next, officers were to attend a two- or three-day workshop on basic MI skills. Districts chose their own trainer(s) for MI, but the plan recommended choosing a workshop trainer who was both *qualified to train MI* and *familiar with the criminal justice system.* Following the initial training, it was recommended that officers submit audio or video-tapes of their use of MI with clients and receive monthly feedback on their skill development. Additionally, 'booster' sessions at six and 12 months were recommended. Finally, districts were encouraged to utilize a formal coding system, the Motivational Interviewing Treatment Integrity (MITI; Moyers et al. 2003), to document when officers reach proficiency in MI. This formal coding process would allow districts to adequately document officers' skill level and ensure that they are effectively 'doing' MI.

The Model Implementation Plan and accompanying resources (i.e. feedback sheets, coding systems) were distributed to those districts receiving grant funding for MI. Although grantees were required to follow the plan, most did not, in fact, do so.

How United States probation went about implementing STARR

A thorough description of the federal probation STARR rollout strategy has been provided elsewhere (Robinson et al. 2012). Here we provide only a brief description of the training protocol.

Classroom Training: Officers participated in three and a half days of training that included a discussion of the theoretical foundation of STARR, a demonstration of each of the skills, exercises that helped participants relate discussions to everyday tasks, an opportunity to practise and receive feedback, and a discussion that focused on transferring newly learned skills into the work environment. During the classroom training participants were provided with skill cards that detail the steps of each skill. The skill cards were used to introduce each skill and as a resource for officers during practice role play. Officers were also encouraged to use the skill cards during actual client interactions.

Follow-up Activities: Officers who participated in the classroom training were asked to submit recorded interactions at specific intervals following the training. The interactions were coded to determine whether STARR skills were used and the quality of the skill use. Officers were also asked to participate in a number of 'booster session' conference calls. The calls allowed officers to discuss attempts to use the skill and listen to recordings of officers using the skills with offenders and defendants. Additionally, the calls served to provide emotional support, as officers were given the opportunity to discuss anxieties about the skills and receive support from both the coach and other officers who may experience the same thing. Officers were also given access to individual feedback sessions if requested. The individual feedback sessions provided an assessment of the officer's acquisition of the skill and provided feedback on how the officer might improve his use of the skill.

The STARR rollout strategy was similar to the motivational interviewing training plan, in that both interventions used a classroom workshop followed by coaching and feedback.

Method

For both initiatives, officers in the districts completed initial training workshops followed by booster/coaching sessions. In addition, officers were required to submit audio-tape samples of their actual interactions with clients. Specific details for each initiative are outlined below.

Motivational Interviewing

Twenty-two districts participated in the MI training and data collection. Overall, 148 trained officers and 673 untrained officers were included. Districts submitted training information for officers, including the number of days of initial training, the number of booster sessions and the training credentials of the trainers. Officers who had been trained in MI also submitted audio-tape recordings of their MI interactions with clients. The audio-tapes were coded using the Motivational Interviewing Treatment Integrity (MITI) manual, by trained coders. Rearrest rates for offenders were also collected.

STARR

Detailed procedures and data analysis have been published elsewhere (see Robinson et al. 2012) and are only summarized here. Fifty-nine officers (38 trained and 21 untrained) were included in the STARR data analysis. All 38 trained officers completed a three and a half-day initial training, followed by telephone booster sessions. Both trained and untrained officers were asked to submit audio-tape recordings of their client interactions prior to the training, as well as immediately following the initial training and at three months and six months post training. Audio-tapes were coded by trained raters using a structured guide developed for the original research project. In addition to audio-tape recordings, arrest rates for clients on supervision both before and after the training were analysed. Overall, 701 pre-training cases (400 for trained officers and 301 for untrained) and 462 post-training cases (277 for trained officers and 185 for untrained) were included. There were no statistically significant differences between the two offender groups in terms of demographics or risk level.

Results

The initial analyses for MI focused on whether the training protocol was implemented as suggested by the plan. Unfortunately, few officers received the level of training and coaching that was recommended. Although the average for the initial training was two days (range one to five days), which falls within the recommendation, follow-up coaching and feedback were almost non-existent. Most officers only received one follow-up coaching session (range zero to five), and the average for sessions with a highly trained coach (i.e. a coach who was part of the Motivational Interviewing Network of Trainers, MINT) was only 0.66. On average, officers submitted 1.64 audio-tapes (range zero to ten).

Given the lack of follow-up training and audio-tapes, it is not surprising that very few officers were found to have beginning proficiency or competency as measured by the MITI. Of the 125 who were MITI scored, only 10 per cent met criteria for beginning proficiency, and only 2 per cent were judged 'competent' in MI. It is noteworthy that the two 'competent' officers were from the same district, and the average number of coaching sessions for that district was two, rather than the 0.66 average for all districts combined.

Overall, we consider these results to indicate that there was in fact little true Motivational Interviewing happening in interactions with clients. Thus, it is not surprising that there was no significant difference in rearrest rates for offenders supervised by officers trained in MI versus those not trained.

STARR

Since all officers attended the same initial training, there was no variance in the amount of initial training obtained. However, officers were given more flexibility in coaching sessions, and thus there was variability in the amount of follow-up coaching obtained. The number of coaching sessions attended ranged from zero to five, with the mean number being 2.94. The number of tapes submitted ranged from one to 31. Half of the officers submitted five or more audio recordings. The overall mean number of audio-tapes submitted was 7.47, with a standard deviation of 7.19.

The training received seemed to have a significant impact on the use of STARR skills. Effective reinforcement, disapproval or authority was used twice as often by trained officers in the initial and three-month tapings, though the frequency dropped to 1.25 times as likely during the six-month taping. However, this drop may also coincide with a drop in the number of tapes received. The difference in use of core correctional practices was perhaps most profound with regard to teaching and using the cognitive model. Prior to training, fewer than 10 per cent of interactions included use of cognitive–behavioural techniques. After training, use of the cognitive model jumped to 25 per cent and 29 per cent of interactions at three and six months, respectively, while untrained officers' tapes contained no use of the cognitive model. This finding is particularly significant given that cognitive–behavioural techniques have demonstrated some of the most robust reductions in subsequent recidivism (see Lipsey et al. 2007, for a meta-analytic review of findings).

In terms of rearrest rates, offenders supervised by STARR-trained officers demonstrated significantly lower recidivism rates. Overall, the post-training failure rate for offenders supervised by trained officers was approximately 25 per cent lower than for those supervised by untrained officers. However, the results were more interesting when separated by risk. For moderate risk offenders, the relative risk reduction jumped to almost 50 per cent compared with offenders supervised by untrained officers. Although diminished somewhat, this finding has held almost two years after the training, with a 31 per cent relative risk reduction for offenders supervised by trained officers (Lowenkamp et al. 2012). In terms of high-risk offenders, however, when taken alone STARR had less of an impact: there was no difference between the groups, although both groups' recidivism rates dropped 15 per cent relative to pre-training rates. However, analyses that looked at officers trained in both STARR and MI told a very different story. High-risk offenders supervised by officers trained in STARR + MI had significantly lower rearrest rates (37 per cent relative risk reduction) than offenders supervised by officers trained in just STARR. As with the moderate-risk offenders, this finding diminished somewhat at the two-year mark (22 per cent relative risk reduction; see Lowenkamp et al. 2012).

In comparing implementation between the two innovations, it is clear that STARR had more (and maybe better?) implementation. There were significantly more booster sessions attended for STARR versus MI (2.94 vs. .65), in fact, four and a half times as much follow-up training via booster sessions. There were also six times more audio-tapes submitted (10.26 vs. 1.64). Both of these results suggest that officers received significantly more STARR training and practised STARR skills more often than officers trained in MI.

Discussion

The focus of this chapter is on the implementation process for two interventions, versus the intervention itself, as it relates to changes in supervision. The results suggest that STARR was implemented more fully than MI in the United States probation system, as demonstrated by more audio-tapes submitted, more booster sessions attended and better skill attainment. Both of these interventions can be characterized as new innovations in the supervision of offenders; thus, their adoption, or lack thereof, can be informed by the research on the diffusion of innovations (Rogers 1962). For the purposes of this chapter we focus on the characteristics of innovations and how they may influence adoption. These characteristics include the relative advantage of the innovation, the compatibility with existing values/practices, the simplicity of the innovation, the opportunity to try the innovation and the opportunity to observe its effects. Before addressing these, it is important to note that it is the *perception* of these attributes, rather than the actual attributes themselves, which may influence adoption.

In terms of relative advantage, both STARR and MI are likely perceived as relatively equivalent in this arena. Both are presented as 'improvements' over current standard supervision practices, and purport to relate to better outcomes. Rogers (2003) notes that the presence of 'objective' information about the advantage is not as important as factors such as social prestige, convenience and satisfaction. At the time of the implementation in this project, there was very little information for either intervention in terms of these factors; thus, we cannot hypothesize what influence they may have had.

Compatibility relates to how consistent the intervention is with existing values, needs or practices. We postulate that STARR may be an easier transition than MI for most officers. The basic skills are ones that officers may feel they are already doing, and/or may do partially. Thus, the skills are more in line with officers' current perception of their role and duties. In contrast, the basic premise of MI may be more of a philosophical leap for many officers, since the emphasis is on client control and autonomy. Many officers may subscribe to the belief that offenders have 'no choice' since they are on supervision, that they 'must' follow the orders of the court. Thus, the philosophical shift may be a more difficult one. Therefore, MI may be seen as less compatible with their existing practices.

Complexity addresses how difficult an innovation may be to understand and use. STARR may be easier for officers to understand given most of the skills have significant similarities to officers' existing skill sets. Additionally, STARR may be easier to learn given the structure of the STARR curriculum. For each STARR skill specific behavioural steps are included (i.e. 'ask the offender....'). Thus, in some ways officers only have to 'follow the steps' in order to perform the skill. In contrast, there is no similar structure for MI. Rather, the behaviours are more abstract (i.e. demonstrate empathy and a respect for autonomy). Thus, officers must first understand these concepts, then independently figure out how to demonstrate these concepts through concrete behaviours.

In terms of triallability, both MI and STARR are possible to implement on a limited basis. In most districts, for either intervention officers were instructed to try the skills on a limited number of clients, rather than all of their clients. However, STARR could be broken down even further, as officers could focus on one skill at a time. Officers were able to focus their efforts in this way, then receive specific feedback on each skill prior to tackling another skill. This leads to our next point – officers learning STARR attended significantly more booster sessions than those in MI. As such, they received more feedback on their progress. Additionally, they submitted more audio-tapes, which may indicate that they practised the skills more often. Our informal discussions with officers indicate that, in general, the officers audio-taped most, if not all, of their attempts at the skills. Thus, more tapes equated to more practice. As with any new skill, you can expect those who practise more, and receive feedback on their performance, to improve more than those who don't. Finally, while both STARR and MI can be 'seen' in terms of generating different conversations with offenders, STARR again may have the advantage in that it may be more easily observable than MI. As stated previously, the STARR curriculum includes concrete steps that others could easily listen for, whereas MI's more abstract concepts are harder to discern.

The significant differences in the amount of training within each intervention clearly led to greater skill attainment in the STARR intervention, which then translated into an impact on outcomes. Those trained in MI were not rated as actually 'doing' MI and there was no difference in failure rates between those trained and not trained. In contrast, those trained in STARR demonstrated more use of the skills, and that difference translated into significantly better outcomes for offenders.

This study reinforces what we know from both the literature and recent studies on effective interventions: the effectiveness of the intervention is not the only important aspect. Rather, the intervention must be well implemented in order for it to have an impact on outcomes. We hypothesize that differences in the perceived attributes of MI and STARR at least partially explain the different rates of implementation, which in turn impacted the ultimate outcomes of recidivism reduction. The implementation process can be well informed by innovation diffusion research, and future attempts at implementation of either of these interventions should include consideration of this research in order to ensure an optimal implementation process.

References

Alexander, M., Vanbenschoten, S. and Walters, S. (2008) 'Motivational Interviewing Training in Criminal Justice: Development of a Model Plan'. Federal Probation, September 2008.

Andrews, D. A. and Bonta, J. (2010) *The Psychology of Criminal Conduct.* Fifth Edition. New Providence, New Jersey: LexisNexis.

Andrews, D. A. and Kiessling, J. J. (1980) 'Program Structure and Effective Correctional Practices. A Summary of CaVIC Research'. in R. R. Ross and P. Gendreau (Eds) *Effective Correctional Treatment* (pp. 441–463). Toronto: Butterworths.

Anstiss, B., Polaschek, D. L. L. and Wilson, M. (2011) 'A Brief Motivational Interviewing Intervention with Prisoners: When You Lead a Horse to Water, Can It Drink for Itself?' *Psychology, Crime & Law* 17(8), 689–710.

Bonta, J., Rugge, T., Scott, T., Bourgon, G. and Yessine, A.K. (2008) 'Exploring the Black Box of Community Supervision'. *Journal of Offender Rehabilitation* 47(3), 248–270.

Bonta, J., Bourgon, G., Rugge, T., Scott, T., Yessine, A., Gutierrez, L. and Li, J. (2010) *The Strategic Training Initiative in Community Supervision: Risk, Need, Responsivity in the Real World.* Corrections Research: User Report.

Dowden, C. and Andrews, D. A. (2004) 'The Importance of Staff Practice in Delivering Effective Correctional Treatment: A Meta-Analytic Review of Core Correctional Practices'. *International Journal of Offender Therapy and Comparative Criminology* 48(2), 203–214.

Fixsen, D. L., Naoom, S. F., Blase, K. A., Friedman, R. M. and Wallace, F. (2005) *Implementation Research: A Synthesis of the Literature.* Tampa, FL: University of South Florida, Louis de la Parte Florida Mental Health Institute, The National Implementation Research Network (FMHI Publication #231).

Glaze, L. (2010) *Correctional Populations in the United States, 2009.* Washington, DC: US Department of Justice, Office of Justice Programs, Bureau of Justice Statistics.

Joyce, B. and Showers, B. (2002) *Student Achievement Through Staff Development*. Alexandria, Virginia: Association for Supervision and Curriculum Development.

Hettema, J., Steele, J. and Miller, W. R. (2005) 'Motivational Interviewing'. *Annual Review of Clinical Psychology* 1, 91–111.

Lipsey, Mark W. (2009) 'The Primary Factors That Characterize Effective Interventions with Juvenile Offenders: A Meta-Analytic Overview'. *Victims & Offenders* 4(2), 124–147.

Lipsey, M. W., Landenberger, N. A. and Wilson, S. J. (2007) 'Effects of Cognitive-behavioral Programs for Criminal Offenders'. *Campbell Systematic Reviews* 6. DOI: 10.4073/csr.2007.6

Lowenkamp, C., Holsinger, A., Robinson, R. and Alexander, M. (2012) 'Diminishing or Durable Treatment Effects of STARR? A Research Note on 24-month Re-Arrest Rates'. Submitted to the *Journal of Crime and Justice*.

Martinson, R. (1974) 'What Works? – Questions and Answers About Prison Reform'. *The Public Interest* 35 (Spring), 22–54.

McMurran, M. (2009) 'Motivational Interviewing with Offenders: A Systematic Review'. *Legal and Criminological Psychology* 14, 83–100.

Miller, W. R. and Mount, K. A. (2001) 'A Small Study of Training in Motivational Interviewing: Does One Workshop Change Clinician and Client Behavior?' *Behavioural and Cognitive Psychotherapy* 29, 457–471.

Miller, W. R. and Moyers, T. B. (2006) 'Eight Stages in Learning Motivational Interviewing'. *Journal of Teaching in the Addictions* 5, 3–17.

Miller, W. R. and Rollnick, S. (2002) *Motivational Interviewing: Preparing People for Change*. Second Edition. New York: Guilford Press.

Miller, W. R., Yahne, C. E., Moyers, T. B., Martinez, J. and Pirritano, M. (2004) 'A Randomized Trial of Methods to Help Clinicians Learn Motivational Interviewing'. *Journal of Consulting and Clinical Psychology* 72, 1050–1062.

Moyers, T. B., Martin, T., Manuel, J. K. and Miller, W. R. (2003) 'The Motivational Interviewing Treatment Integrity (MITI) Code'. Unpublished manuscript.

National Institute of Corrections (2011) *Motivational Interviewing (with a Criminal Justice Focus) Annotated Bibliography*. Prepared by the NIC Information Center, November 2011. Accession No. 025355

Robinson, C. R., Lowenkamp, C. T., Holsinger, A. M., Vanbenschoten, S., Alexander, M. and Oleson, J. C. (2012) 'A Random Study of Staff Training Aimed at Reducing Re-Arrest (STARR): Using Core Correctional Practices in Probation Interactions'. *Journal of Crime and Justice*, 1–22.

Rogers, E. M. (2003). *Diffusion of Innovations*. New York: Free Press.

Rubak, S., Sandboek, A., Lauritzen, T. and Christensen, B. (2005) 'Motivational Interviewing: A Systematic Review and Meta-Analysis'. *British Journal of General Practice* 55(513), 305–312.

Taxman, F. (2002) 'Supervision – Exploring the Dimensions of Effectiveness'. *Federal Probation* 66(2), 14–27.

Taxman, F. S., Yancey, C. and Bilanin, J. (2006) *Proactive Community Supervision in Maryland: Changing Offender Outcomes*. College Park: University of Maryland, Bureau of Governmental Research.

Trotter, C. (1996) 'The Impact of Different Supervision Practices in Community Supervision: Cause for Optimism'. *The Australian and New Zealand Journal of Criminology* 29(1), 29–46.

Trotter, C. (1999) *Working with Involuntary Clients: A Guide to Practice.* London: Sage.

Walters, S. T., Matson, S. A., Baer, J. S. and Ziedonis, D. M. (2005) 'Effectiveness of Workshop Training for Psychosocial Addiction Treatments: A Systematic Review'. *Journal of Substance Abuse Treatment* 29(4), 283–293.

Walters, S. T., Vader, A. M., Nguyen, N., Harris, T. R. and Eells, J. (2010) 'Motivational Interviewing as a Supervision Strategy in Probation: A Randomized Effectiveness Trial'. *Journal of Offender Rehabilitation* 49(5), 309–323.

15

The Importance of Building Good Relationships in Community Corrections: Evidence, Theory and Practice of the Therapeutic Alliance

Guy Bourgon and Leticia Guiterrez

Across all types of psychotherapy, it has been shown that the therapeutic relationship or working alliance between the therapist and the client is considered one of the most important contributors to change, stronger than what type of intervention is used (Eames and Roth 2000; Horvath and Greenberg 1989, 1994; Mallinckrodt 2000; Martin et al. 2000). As a result, it is a generally accepted view that a positive relationship with the client is both *necessary* and *sufficient* to achieve the desired therapeutic outcomes (e.g. Eames and Roth 2000; Horvath and Greenberg 1989, 1994; Mallinckrodt 2000; Martin et al. 2000). However, it is not known whether or not this view of the critical importance of the relationship is valid within the context of community supervision, where the nature of the relationship and the 'work' being conducted is qualitatively different due to the coercive nature and power differential inherent in community supervision. Within the 'What Works' literature, both the relationship and intervention techniques are components of the Responsivity Principle. This principle is concerned with matching the style and mode of intervention to the abilities, motivation and learning style of the offender. Although the quality of the relationship is considered important, there is considerably more evidence supporting specific core correctional practices which outline the attributes, skills and intervention techniques (i.e. cognitive–behavioural techniques) exhibited by the criminal justice helping professional that are associated with enhanced criminal justice outcomes (Andrews and Bonta 2010). This chapter will examine the relative importance of the quality of the offender–supervisor relationship and the quality of therapeutic interventions and skills exhibited by probation officers to influence criminal justice outcomes, including recidivism. The implications of the results for the policies, practices and staff training efforts of community correctional agencies will be discussed.

Author notes

The views expressed are those of the authors and do not necessarily represent the views of Public Safety Canada. Correspondence concerning this article should be addressed to Guy Bourgon, Corrections Research, Public Safety Canada, 340 Laurier Ave. W., Ottawa, Ontario, Canada, K1A 0P8. email: Guy.Bourgon@ps.gc.ca.

The importance of the relationship between therapist and client in determining outcomes in psychotherapy has a long history in the field of psychology (Horvath and Symonds 1991). Dating as far back as Freud, the therapeutic relationship or therapeutic alliance (TA) can be described as a collaborative bond between therapist and client whereby positive change is achieved for the client via interpersonal processes that exist independently of specific treatment techniques (Green 2006; Martin et al. 2000). Research evaluating the TA has shown that positive relationships and stronger alliances between therapist and client lead to more positive therapeutic outcomes (Baldwin et al. 2007; Elvins and Green 2008; Green 2006; Horvath and Bedi 2002; Martin et al. 2000; Ross et al. 2008).

The relationship between community supervision officers and the clients they supervise has recently received more attention (e.g. Lowenkamp et al. (in press); McNeil et al. 2012). For example, the empirical work of Skeem and her colleagues (2003, 2007) has suggested that the TA in community supervision may have an influence on client outcomes. In addition, newly developed evidence-based supervision officer training programmes now emphasize improving relationship building skills (e.g. Strategic Training Initiative in Community Supervision (Bourgon et al. 2010) and Effective Practices in Correctional Settings II (Lowenkamp et al. 2010). It is evident that an increasing value is being placed on the importance of establishing and maintaining a positive and collaborative relationship to foster and promote prosocial change.

In the following chapter, we will review what the psychotherapeutic literature and the correctional literature have to say about the TA. We will describe what is known about what works in reducing reoffending and, following this, we will propose a more complex reformulation of the TA and where it fits in effective correctional practice. We end the chapter with a discussion of the implications for practice behind the closed doors of community supervision.

Psychotherapy literature and the therapeutic alliance

Ever since Freud developed the 'talking cure', the importance of the relationship between the 'helper' and the client has been recognized. It is believed that the interpersonal processes and the bond that exists between the two account for, in some part, the positive outcomes experienced by the client, which are independent of the specific treatment techniques that are employed (Green 2006; Martin et al. 2000; Ross et al. 2008). It was Bordin (1979) who developed a transtheoretical construct of the therapeutic relationship, which he called the working alliance. This transtheoretical construct of the therapeutic alliance helped foster a renewed interest in assessing and understanding the influence of the TA in helping relationships. Bordin's (1979) working alliance construct was proposed to explain how the therapeutic relationship functions to improve outcomes irrespective of the theoretical orientation of the therapist and the various intervention techniques that are employed. Bordin's (1979) Working Alliance Inventory (WAI) provided a means to assess the TA, and considerable empirical research was carried out to evaluate the effects of the TA on outcomes. The working alliance consists of three main elements: (1) *Tasks*, which assesses the thoughts and behaviours that both the therapist and the client view as productive and relevant elements of the therapeutic process in order to achieve the desired change or outcome; (2) *Goals*, which describes the mutually agreed-upon outcomes that form the targets of therapy; and (3) *Bonds*, which consists of an intricate concept of mutual attachment between the therapist and the client. These three elements were the main determinants of the quality of the working relationship between helper and client. The WAI has been used to assess the quality of relationships in a variety of treatment contexts with a variety of client samples, including offenders on community supervision (Skeem et al. 2007).

To date, the empirical work in this area had led to a strong conviction that positive relationships and stronger alliances between therapist and client lead to more positive therapeutic outcomes (Baldwin et al. 2007; Elvins and Green 2008; Green 2006; Horvath and Bedi 2002; Horvath et al. 2011; Martin et al. 2000; Ross et al. 2008). Numerous outcome studies and a number of meta-analyses from the psychotherapy literature have supported the view that harvesting a positive relationship with a client is, at a minimum, a *necessary* and, to some, a *sufficient* condition for achieving the desired therapeutic outcomes (e.g. Eames and Roth 2000; Horvath and Greenberg 1989, 1994; Mallinckrodt 2000; Martin et al. 2000). Some have gone so far as to say that, in the field of psychotherapy, this alliance construct is 'the quintessential integrative variable of therapy' (Wolf and Goldfried 1988), meaning that the quality of the relationship between the service provider and the client is the *most* important factor in determining the outcomes of therapy, irrespective of treatment type or modality (Safran and Murran 1995).

The therapeutic alliance and correctional literature

Despite the overwhelmingly positive research from the psychotherapy literature, a number of researchers have questioned the applicability of the traditional conception and measurement of alliance to mandated treatment contexts with involuntary clients, particularly within the correctional environment. There is a movement toward the use of formal treatment mandates and legal sanctions that require clients to attend community treatment, such as civil orders (e.g. outpatient psychiatric commitment) and criminal justice sanctions (e.g. probation/parole). The involuntary nature of these arrangements suggests that there are significant differences in the TA between traditional psychotherapy and these involuntary mandated relationships. It has been proposed that the concept of alliance – developed in voluntary treatment settings – does not apply to the unique factors within mandated treatment relationships (Skeem et al. 2007).

In mandated treatment relationships such as the one found in community supervision, there are immediate difficulties associated with trying to establish the collaborative elements of tasks, goals and bonds due to the involuntary nature of the arrangement. Unlike voluntary therapy/treatment, in which the tasks and goals are determined collaboratively or are brought forward by the client, for involuntary clients the tasks and goals are often predetermined (Kozar and Day 2012). For example, in a community supervision setting, clients are required to attend scheduled supervision sessions and are required to comply with a supervision order that has been predetermined by a judge. In this case, the probation/parole officer may face challenges in establishing a collaborative relationship with the client, as s/he must act as the person responsible for monitoring various tasks (e.g. attend prescribed treatment programmes) and goals (e.g. remain crime-free).

In addition to the difficulties associated with establishing a collaborative relationship, there are also difficulties with building trust between clients and service providers in mandated settings. Limits to confidentiality and the reporting requirements regarding compliance with the sentence and information sharing in mandated treatment settings complicate the development of a therapeutic alliance. In other words, if a client is unwilling to disclose information or openly participate in treatment, this may have negative implications for the relationship as well as the outcomes of treatment (Marshall and Serran 2004; Ross et al. 2008).

In relationships in which clients have been mandated to attend a prescribed service, the element of collaboration is more difficult to achieve due to the 'lopsidedness' of the power structure between clients and service providers (Skeem et al. 2007). In other words, rather than functioning on a mutual arrangement of tasks and responsibilities, in mandated treatment the service provider has a level of control over the client and his/her outcomes. The issue of control makes the relationship uneven, thus making collaboration a difficult task.

Balancing the dual role of supervision/rule enforcement and helping is one of the biggest challenges, in contrast to therapists who serve voluntary patients

(Trotter 2006). Striking a balance between the helper role and the surveillance role appears to be the key to promoting a positive therapeutic relationship in mandated treatment settings (Andrews and Bonta 2010; Andrews et al. 1996; Trotter 2006). An examination of therapeutic alliance in a community supervision context with mentally disordered probationers revealed that greater adherence to indicators of 'relational fairness' in balancing this dual role (i.e. caring, fairness, trust and authority) was related to higher-quality therapeutic relationships (Skeem et al. 2003). Relational fairness has also been referred to as an interpersonal form of 'procedural justice' whereby clients perceive mandatory conditions of treatment as less coercive when an element of negotiation on the part of the client and the practitioner is present (Lidz et al. 1995; MacCoun 2005; Skeem et al. 2003). In the community supervision study with mentally disordered offenders, the probationers indicated that probation officers who acknowledged their own punitive role, while conducting themselves with compassion and care, were more 'relatable' compared with those who followed an authoritarian style of supervision (Skeem et al. 2003, 2007).

Although this study did not investigate the relationship between probationers' perceptions of their probation officers and compliance with probation, it provides insight into the types of factors (e.g. relational fairness) that influence how involuntary clients relate to those service providers who occupy a dual role. Although further research is needed, there have been a few recent reviews of the TA within the correctional context (Kozar and Day 2012; Ross et al. 2008). In the most recent review, Kozar and Day (2012) found that the results associating TA with correctional outcome are equivocal. They acknowledged that there are many factors that likely moderate the quality of the TA, such as therapist and client characteristics, as well as external factors such as correctional policies and resource allocation, and more research is needed.

Nonetheless, in a recent article Lowenkamp et al. (in press) stressed the importance of the relationship between officer and client and called for efforts to create and value real relationships between the officer and his/her clients. They provided recommendations to organizations on how they may facilitate that emphasis and, to a lesser extent, some broad suggestions to officers on how to improve their warmth and empathy, and invest in a helping relationship with their clients.

'What Works' framework

The presumptive application of theory and research from the psychotherapeutic literature to corrections has led to the general belief that the TA is an important factor in effective correctional interventions. Although some correctional authors have discussed the TA within corrections (e.g. Ross et al. 2008; Skeem et al. 2007), there has been little elaboration of the TA within the context of the 'What Works' literature. We believe that, by examining the 'What Works' principles of effective correctional interventions and exploring where and how the TA fits into these principles, we may begin to develop a better appreciation of the TA in corrections, understand how to improve the TA, and enhance our efforts at facilitating prosocial change with involuntary criminal justice clients.

The dominant model of effective corrections is the 'What Works' model, with the principles of Risk, Need, and Responsivity (RNR) at its core (Andrews and Bonta 2010). The foundations of this model lie in psychology, social psychology and psychotherapy, focusing on individual behaviour, social learning and the facilitation of individual change that reduces criminal behaviour and reoffending. Over 20 years of research on offender interventions has demon-strated that adherence to these principles results in reductions in reoffending across virtually all offender groups, regardless of age, gender and offence type (Andrews and Bonta 2010; Hanson et al. 2009).

The first component of the RNR model is the risk principle, which states that the risk level of an offender can be predicted and must be matched with the frequency and intensity of the service. In other words, a high-risk offender should receive a higher frequency and dosage of treatment, as they have a higher probability of negative outcomes compared with low-risk offenders. Low-risk offenders, on the other hand, should receive little or no treatment (Andrews and Bonta 2010). Adherence to the risk principle has been shown to increase the effectiveness of programmes for a variety of offender groups (e.g. sex offenders, violent offenders, substance abusers). A meta-analysis of correctional treatment showed that treatment delivered to low-risk offenders had almost no effect (mean effect size $= 0.03$), whereas the appropriate (i.e. treatment that adheres to the RNR principles) treatment delivered to high-risk offenders resulted in a moderate correlation ($r = 0.17$), as expected by the risk principle (Andrews and Dowden 2006).

The second component of the RNR model is the need principle, which addresses the importance of identifying and targeting an offender's criminogenic needs (dynamic risk factors) in order to effectively reduce recidivism (Andrews et al. 1990; Andrews and Bonta 2010). Criminogenic needs are factors that, when improved, are likely to result in a reduction in reoffending. There are eight criminogenic need areas that have been iden-tified in the literature as being the 'Central Eight' correlates of criminal behaviour. These risk/need factors include: antisocial personality, antisocial attitudes/cognitions, antisocial peers, history of antisocial behaviour, fam-ily/marital, employment/education, leisure/recreation, and substance abuse (Andrews and Bonta 2010). One of the main distinctions that must be drawn from the need principle is the difference between criminogenic needs and non-criminogenic needs. As opposed to criminogenic needs, non-criminogenic needs are dynamic factors (e.g. poor self-esteem, anxiety/stress) that are only weakly related to recidivism (Andrews and Bonta 2010). Given that one of the main goals of correctional treatment is to reduce reoffending, prioritizing criminogenic needs rather than non-criminogenic needs increases the likelihood of treatment success (Andrews 2000).

The last principle of the RNR model is the responsivity principle, which refers to delivering treatment in a style and mode that are consistent with the ability and learning style of the offender (Andrews and Bonta 2010; Andrews et al. 1990). The general responsivity principle simply states that cognitive–behavioural interventions work best (Andrews and Bonta 2010), whereas the specific responsivity principle is the matching of the treatment style to that of the client's personality, gender, ethnicity, motivation, age, language and interpersonal style (Bonta 1995). Some have described the responsivity principle as the 'what works for whom' principle (Wormith et al. 2007) and attending to these factors in correctional settings has been shown to result in treatment success and significant reductions in recidivism (Andrews and Bonta 2010).

The TA, which focuses on the interpersonal relationship between the 'helper' and the client, falls under the umbrella of the responsivity principle and has been described by Andrews and Bonta (2010) as the relationship dimension of service provision. They have argued that effectiveness is greatest when the situation (i.e. the relationship between the client and helper) consists of openness, warmth, enthusiasm, non-blaming communication and a collaborative, mutual respect, liking and interest. Much of the evidence for this was founded in the early work of Andrews and Kessling (1980) on staff skills and characteristics that were associated with effective interventions. These skills and characteristics, termed Core Correctional Practice, highlighted a variety of interpersonal skills such as empathy, firm-but-fair attitude and the high-frequency use of reinforcement. They were found to be significantly related ($r = 0.26$) to the size of the treatment effect (Andrews and Bonta 2010). Clearly, these relationship skills are intertwined with any TA between the staff and the client.

Reformulation of the responsivity principle and the therapeutic alliance

Unfortunately, empirical research on the responsivity principle, and TA in particular, has been sparse compared with the amount of research that has focused on risk and need (Polaschek and Ross 2010). It is evident to us that the responsivity principle is concerned with the 'how' of change, not just what works for whom. Rather, the responsivity principle is about the purposeful processes employed through human service that reduce criminal behaviour and enhance prosocial behaviours. Although the general and specific responsivity principles are frequently emphasized, we believe that the creation and maintenance of an attractive 'setting' for change (Andrews and Bonta 2010, p. 381) has often been overlooked as a cornerstone of the responsivity principle. For us, responsivity is 'how' an optimal learning environment is created and maintained for each client. By reformulating the responsivity principle as creating and maintaining the best 'change environment', a more fruitful view of the principle emerges that permits researchers and practitioners with new avenues to explore and examine. Much of the research to date surrounding the responsivity principle has been on the characteristics of the client (e.g. motivation, gender). Although this has led to some client group-specific treatment services, most of these are cosmetic changes to treatment services rather than clearly articulated and empirically demonstrated practices that lead to more effective interventions.

When we look at responsivity in this fashion, we can begin to identify empirically what exactly are the nature and the characteristics of the best learning environments, including fundamental questions of how individuals learn best and, importantly for this chapter, what constitutes an effective and high-quality TA. As all human services involve some form of social interaction with the individual or group in question, the relationship between the 'helper' and client, in other words the way in which the two interact, is critical. This is particularly relevant within the context of community supervision, where the officer and the client typically see each other face to face in a 'supervision session' in which the officer is often expected to not only monitor and ensure compliance, but also help facilitate change and attend to client needs to promote prosocial change.

We begin by examining the fundamental components of the TA. As Hatcher and Barends (2006) stated, 'the alliance describes the degree to which the therapy dyad is engaged in collaborative, purposive work' (p. 293). We prefer this broad definition of the TA, as there are three key components to describe the TA: engagement, collaboration and purpose. Engagement refers to the efforts and energies of both the client and the helper to be involved in interpersonal processes; from the amount of conversation, to demonstrating efforts to understand each other's perspective and efforts to change. Collaboration refers to the cooperativeness of both individuals to have input into what is done during their time together. Finally, purposeful work is a critical aspect in a therapeutic relationship. It is the helper's interpersonal communications, his/her skills and intervention techniques employed that foster client change, and these interactions are purposeful. Taken as a whole, the TA involves a collaborative interaction of client and helper to determine the purpose (i.e. the change for the client) of their interpersonal contact, in which both individuals contribute and the helper purposively behaves in a manner that facilitates and promotes client change toward the mutually shared goal. The client and the helper view their work together as providing a benefit to the client.

Within this framework, we identify a number of major differences between the typical psychotherapy situation and community supervision that merit discussion. The role of the community supervision officer is qualitatively different from the role of a traditional therapist. Community supervision requires officers to have a dual role (Skeem et al. 2007; Trotter 2006). One aspect, often the primary role, is the social control or 'enforcement' element inherent in community supervision. Officers are expected to monitor compliance with the court-ordered sentence, and they are in a position to potentially increase/decrease restrictions on behaviour (e.g. curfew), place additional demands on the client (e.g. attend addictions treatment) and/or initiate formal criminal justice system processes (e.g. failure to comply with conditions can result in breach action and custody). The second aspect, one that is inherent in the traditional therapist role, is that of 'helper'. Many jurisdictions expect community supervision officers to play a 'helper' role to the client. Although helping may be as simple as assisting the client in complying with the sentence or brokering with community resources, it can also be more complex or therapeutic, such as addressing and meeting various client needs.

It appears that one critical aspect of the TA and the learning environment of community supervision is how officers balance these two roles (Skeem et al. 2007). Research by Jennifer Skeem and colleagues with the Dual-Role Relationships Inventory-Revised (DRI-R), an instrument designed to assess the TA within community corrections, suggests that how the officer navigates these two roles has a significant impact on the TA, which in turn is related to outcomes. They found that clients tended to have more positive outcomes when the officer upheld the conditions and compliance aspects of supervision with a firm but fair approach (i.e. an approach that involves both active listening and directive supervision) and demonstrated relational fairness.

A second major difference between psychotherapy and community supervision is the differences in training, skills and abilities of therapists and officers. A therapist is generally schooled and skilled in psychological theories and intervention techniques designed to promote change while working individually or within a family system. The therapist sees him/herself as a change agent; responsible for creating a learning environment for the client, conducting therapeutic interventions, and exhibiting skills and abilities intended to foster learning and change. Many community supervision officers, especially in North America, are not schooled in psychology, nor do they have significant training in therapeutic interventions, and many do not see themselves as change agents. The dominant model in community supervision is case management. Whereas therapists see themselves as change agents, the case management model requires the officer to play less of a change agent role, with the emphasis on motivating, supporting, referring, brokering and managing services (Bourgon et al. 2011). The case manager is not the change agent; rather, s/he is the one who bridges clients with the change agents. Of course, there are other jurisdictions in which social work plays a major role in the training of community supervision officers. Although there is more training in interview techniques and social work skills, there is less focus on psychology, change and psychological intervention techniques.

Another difference between traditional psychotherapy and community supervision is the dynamic by which the client enters the relationship. In psychotherapy, the client seeks out the assistance of the therapist voluntarily and enters the relationship with at least the vague desire of seeking some change in his/her life or circumstance with the assistance of the therapist. The purpose of the work the client and therapist will do is, to a greater or lesser extent, predetermined by the client. The client, at a minimum, determines the goal of the work. In community corrections, this is not the case. Rather, the client is mandated into the relationship with the officer. It is rare that a client sees the officer with a similar desire for personal change; rather, the requirement of change is imposed upon the client. Just as the conditions of the order are set by the court and imposed on the client, so too, to a greater or lesser degree, are the treatment targets imposed on the client by the community correctional officer. As officers are expected to develop a case plan for each client, they typically identify specific and concrete treatment targets. In many of today's correctional organizations, these targets come straight from the standardized risk/needs assessments (adherence to the risk principle) and the treatment targets are the client's criminogenic needs (adherence to the need principle), as the business of corrections is to reduce the risk of reoffending and to enhance public safety (the purpose of the organization's and officer's work). The degree to which the client, in this case the offender, has personal input into what will be the goal or purpose of the work together is minimal. Such a situation will reduce the degree of collaboration, frequently leading to disagreements on the purpose of the work together, and reduce engagement – further eroding the learning environment between the client and the officer.

As we can see, the relationship between a community supervision officer and the client s/he supervises is more complex. From the perspective of the officer, there is a greater challenge to establish and maintain a relationship that promotes engagement, collaboration and purposeful work. As a change agent, the work of the officer must be purposeful. We see community supervision serving two purposes: their responsibility to the court has officers monitoring or administering the sentence handed down by the courts, and their responsibility to the client (and the community at large) is to reduce reoffending via enhanced prosocial functioning. Although this would be a starting point, and sets the parameters of the relationship, the exact client-change purpose of the client–officer interactions, and how this client-change goal is determined, is a direct reflection of the degree of collaboration and the level of engagement. For the most effective learning environments and effective TA, the challenge is for both the client and the officer to have input into their mutually agreed-upon purpose through understanding, compromise and consensus.

Practical implications for community supervision officers

Assuming the organization and the officer place value on the change agent role, one of the first tasks faced by community supervision officers is to develop the TA. This means establishing and creating an environment to maximize learning. The responsivity principle indicates that the community supervision officer's first challenge is to create such an environment. In order to create this learning environment, one must consider client factors first and foremost (e.g. how does this client learn?); and, because community supervision is the dyad of officer and client, the interpersonal relationship between the two must also be considered. After all, the officer is in essence the teacher and the client the student; therefore, the change process is interpersonal.

To enhance the environment for learning, the keys are to enhance collaboration, provide opportunities for engagement, and structure the learning environment so that work is purposeful. For a community supervision officer, the questions are: How can I establish the supervision process as one that is collaborative when there is a dual role component? What can I do to provide ample opportunities and reinforce engagement on the part of the client? How can the client and I find consensus on the purpose of our interactions, yet still adhere to the principles of effective corrections? In addition, we, like many in the field, recognize the challenge of working with criminal justice clients who present with little motivation and poor engagement in the change process (McMurran 2002; Polaschek et al. 2010; Ward et al. 2004). Given this, how can I assist the client in identifying and growing a desire for personal change and leverage this to ensure that any therapeutic work adheres to the need principle? Lastly, what about the strategies and interventions used to facilitate change? How can I play a more active 'change agent role' rather than take the traditional case management and brokerage role? Below, we describe two intervention techniques that are primarily designed to enhance the TA within community supervision by creating a social environment between the officer and client that is most conducive to learning.

Role clarification and collaborative goal setting are two intervention techniques that form the foundation for building effective TA and enhancing the learning environment in community corrections. Both of these techniques are founded on Trotter's work on working with involuntary clients (2006) and are key components of the Strategic Training Initiative in Community

Supervision (STICS). These techniques are designed to create a maximal learning environment for clients on community supervision by facilitating an open and collaborative dialogue regarding the roles and responsibilities of both the officer and the client. The goal is to enhance the collaboration of the dyad and engagement of the client, as well as to collaboratively establish the parameters of the purpose of the sessions (i.e. the change work) during one-on-one sessions.

Role clarification

Chris Trotter (2006) was one of the first individuals who attempted to address the coercive elements that arise with involuntary clients at the onset of contact using a process called role clarification. In STICS, role clarification is an intervention technique that builds the relationship and establishes the roles, responsibilities and expectations of both parties regarding the dual purposes of community supervision, namely, social control and helping. Trotter found that discussions between the client and officer around what is negotiable and what is not (e.g. confidentiality), how case information is accumulated and shared, the general approach and practices of the helper, organizational demands, and client expectations of the officer all help to build a more open, honest, warm, trusting and collaborative relationship. By providing the client with a description of explicit behaviours of the officer that the client can expect, it helps initiate a sense of predictability of the officer's behaviour from the viewpoint of the client, thereby enhancing trust.

At the beginning of a community supervision relationship, most commonly the officer outlines and details what his/her expectations are of the client's behaviour and the potential resultant consequences of non-compliance. Reviewing the client's sentence and community supervision order is, in most jurisdictions, one of the first tasks in the business of community supervision. In our view, 'laying down the law' as the first order of business is counterproductive to creating a collaborative learning environment. Such a process sets an initial tone of us-versus-them, reduces the potential for collaboration, discourages client engagement in the process, and highlights an additional barrier to the interpersonal environment that engages both parties in purposeful work.

In comparison, Trotter described the role clarification process as one in which the officer describes him/herself, professional duties, preferences and responsibilities, and provides reasons or explanations for his/her behaviour and choices. As we see it, Trotter recognized the social control element in services provided to involuntary clients and placed greater emphasis on the helper role and the importance of creating an environment that is more conducive to collaborative and purposeful work. The use of self-disclosure on the part of the officer and providing an opportunity for the client to voice his/her understanding of the role and responsibilities of the officer is an attempt to de-emphasize the social control component of a dual role relationship.

In STICS, which is focused on translating research into practical and concrete real-world skills and techniques, we suggest that role clarification consists of four steps: (1) self-disclosure of the officer about his/her roles, responsibilities and professional personality; (2) soliciting the client's views of the officer's roles, and responsibilities, and likes/dislikes of working with a community supervision officer; (3) client self-disclosure of his/her behaviour/attitude/personality related to community supervisions (e.g., who s/he is, what the officer can expect from him/her); and (4) collaborative agreement on expectations, roles and responsibilities.

The first step is for the officer to spend time talking about him/herself. The key factors are what the officer's role and responsibilities are to the court and to the client (the dual role aspects). This would include many of Trotter's identified components listed above (e.g. what is and what is not negotiable, organizational demands, confidentiality, information sharing). Officers are also encouraged to communicate to the client about how they do their work. In other words, the officer describes his/her interpersonal style and 'professional personality' in order to permit the client to understand who the officer is and begin to build expectations about the officer's behaviour, attitude and interpersonal style when they meet. Lastly, they are also encouraged to describe the general structure of a supervision session and, potentially, how they envision the course of the supervision period. Note that all of these aspects are about the officer and not the client. We recognize that the criminal justice system focuses almost exclusively on the behaviour of the client, both past and present (the criminal behaviour for which s/he was sentenced in court and present/future behaviour in terms of conditions of the sentence). In addition, the enforcer part of community supervision (the social control element) does little to 'humanize' the officer and facilitate an effective TA or enhance the learning environment in the office where they meet. The clients rarely 'get to know' the officer early on in the process before they have a history together.

The second step involves getting input and opinions from the client about what s/he may see as the officer's roles, responsibilities and behaviours: in other words, asking the client what s/he may expect, or would like and not like, from the officer. This provides the client with a voice in the relationship, as well as creating boundaries and parameters for this relationship. This marks the beginning of the negotiations, as it starts with what the officer does/does not do within the context of his/her role and responsibilities.

The third step is engaging the client in a discussion about what the officer can expect from him/her. Similarly to establishing expectations of the officer and his/her behaviour, the roles are reversed and now focus on the client. Rather than assuming what the officer can expect from the client, it provides an opportunity for the client to initiate these expectations. The order is strategic; the initial focus is on the officer and his/her boundaries and professional personality for two reasons. First, it is to recognize the power imbalance and reduce it. Clients are typically the sole focus of interactions between themselves and the criminal justice system; the focus is one-sided, almost exclusively on the client and his/her behaviour. In interpersonal environments (e.g. police interviews, courts and community supervision), the typical demand is for the client to self-disclose about him/herself and what s/he did and will do with minimal, if any, self-disclosure on the part of the criminal justice staff. By having the discussion begin with disclosure about the criminal justice staff, it changes the dynamics and gives the client a little more power through interpersonal information and self-disclosure on the part of the officer. The second reason is that having the officer explain his/her role and expectations first provides an opportunity to model appropriate behaviour and attitudes toward others as well as rules, contracts and agreements. By the manner in which officers speak and describe their roles, responsibilities and expectations of themselves in their work, they can model personal accountability and responsibility; in other words, prosocial attitudes, values and thinking patterns.

The fourth step is collaboratively coming to a mutual agreement on what each person can expect from the other and from themselves. This may involve negotiation and allows a concrete and honest discussion about behavioural expectancies in a reciprocal manner. In other words, this creates a verbal behavioural contract that both the client and the officer contribute to and agree upon. In this fashion, the supervision period begins with a more collaborative and engaged process, building the TA between the client and officer.

Collaborative goal setting

Collaborative goal setting is another technique for building TA with involuntary clients which was first described by Trotter (2006) in what he called problem survey and problem ranking. For Trotter, before initiating work, it was important to have the client generate and identify his/her own problems rather than the officer 'telling' the client what they are, thereby ensuring that any problem is, in fact, considered a problem from the client's perspective. The officer can and should have input here, but, ultimately, Trotter recognized that the client must acknowledge that it is a problem before any work can be done. With criminal justice clients, officers typically identify criminogenic needs through structured risk/need assessments and develop case plans to address these problems. More often than not, clients do not share the same view as the officer regarding these areas of need. Trotter's problem ranking process requires that the client rank orders his/her list of problems in order to prioritize the work. In this fashion, the client is able to have input into what the officer and the client will work on over time. We see this as another important piece of establishing an effective TA, as it is a collaborative process, encourages client engagement, and identifies, at least in general, what the work will entail. The two elements of collaboration and engagement are key factors in effective TA.

In STICS, collaborative goal setting is part of the training for officers and is seen as a process to mutually establish 'what' the officer and client will work on during the period of supervision. In doing this, the officer and client collaboratively set a general 'destination' that they both agree on. It also sets the parameters by which both parties can evaluate the work they do together (i.e., does what we do help in moving us closer to achieving the mutual and collaboratively established goal?). Collaborative goal setting in STICS has three basic steps designed to enhance engagement and collaboration prior to beginning specific change work. These steps are: (1) obtain a general description of the client-generated goal; (2) discuss and elaborate on this goal; and (3) obtain a collaborative agreement on what the goal is and that both parties are invested in working toward it.

Obtaining a general description of a client-generated goal involves asking the client what s/he would like to achieve within the context of the helping aspect of community supervision, which would have been previously established during the role clarification process. Ideally, the goal(s) will be long-term goal(s), and at this stage the officer need not be concerned with whether or not the goal is one that relates directly to the client's criminogenic needs. Rather, the officer should allow the client to identify whatever goals s/he wishes. For the officer, it is important to accept whatever goal(s) the client identifies; however, the officer needs to rephrase whatever goal is identified so that the goal is about the client, his/her thinking, feeling or behaviour, and not about consequences that are under the control of others (e.g. seeking a job is under the control of the client whereas getting a job is dependent on a company offering the job) or desiring changes in other people (e.g. behaving in a fashion that is predictable and trustworthy is under the control of the client, whereas increasing the client's wife's trust in the client is ultimately dependent on the client's wife). The reason for this is simple; goals should be something that is under the control of the client, that is, his/her thinking, feeling and behaviours only, and not those of other people. At a minimum, a client and officer can usually agree to the goal of successful completion of probation.

To aid the officer in understanding the client's goals, there are three fundamental areas that can help guide and reframe the discussions of identifying goals. This includes personality/attitude, relationships and lifestyles, which are reflected in the STICS action plan, a tool designed to translate a risk/need assessment into a prioritized and directive case plan (Bourgon et al. 2011). Keeping the focus on these three broad areas and accepting the initial general goal offered by the client, the officer is now in a position to explore further.

The second step is the goal elaboration process. The officer guides the dis-cussion of the goal to further identify what the goal would look like and what it accomplishes for the client in terms of the client's behaviour, thoughts and feelings. In addition, the officer guides the discussion by seeking to understand the motivation behind the goals and why this goal is important to the client. This process falls in line with the spirit of Motivational Interviewing, in which the helper reflects, paraphrases and summarizes the pros and cons of various choices, as stated by the client. It is very easy for the officer to see how the client's criminogenic needs are typically blatant barriers to the client's success at achieving his/her goal. However, goal elaboration is not the time for the offi-cer to confront the client with these barriers. Rather, just accepting the client's identified goals and reframing them to reflect and identify the client's thoughts, feelings and behaviours sets the stage for having some mutual agreement on the work the officer and client will do during the supervision period.

The last step of collaborative goal setting is obtaining mutual agreement that the goal is one that both the officer and client are willing to work on over the course of the supervision period. One task for the officer is to summarize the goal and offer his/her assistance in achieving it. One frequent problem seen with community supervision officers is their desire to immediately begin the process of problem-solving by generating options and alternatives and placing demands on the client. When an officer moves too quickly into problem-solving, it reduces the amount of collaboration and engagement, thus reducing the TA and adding an unnecessary barrier to the purposeful work that can occur. However, we believe that, before work can begin in earnest, it is better when the client has input into, and agrees to, the goals of the work between the client and officer. This sets a framework for the effective building of a TA, with its core being collaboration and engagement. Once this is established and nurtured, the officer and client can begin their purposeful work.

Conclusion

Outcome studies and meta-analyses from the psychotherapy literature have supported the view that harvesting a positive relationship with a client is both *necessary* and *sufficient* to achieve the desired therapeutic outcomes (e.g. Eames and Roth 2000; Horvath and Greenberg 1989, 1994; Mallinckrodt 2000; Martin et al. 2000). In fact, the therapeutic alliance is viewed as 'the quintessential integrative variable of therapy' (Wolf and Goldfried 1988), meaning that the quality of the relationship between the service provider and the client is the *most* important factor in determining the outcomes of therapy, irrespective of treatment type or modality (Safran and Murran 1995). However, there are oth-ers who note that the TA may be necessary but it is insufficient to bring about behaviour change (Spiegler and Guevremont 2003).

In our opinion, we agree that additional factors are needed to bring about change. To promote change, the officer–client relationship requires what Andrews and Bonta (2010) refer to as 'structuring' – that is, specific and targeted activities intended to teach, enhance, support, reinforce and bring about prosocial thinking and behaviour. Within psychotherapy, it is assumed that there is always some form of 'structuring' involved, but it takes different forms for different therapies (e.g. therapeutic activities in psychodynamic therapy are different from the therapeutic activities involved in cognitive–behavioural therapy, which are also different from humanistic therapeutic activities). However, in many of the helping professions where a case management model is employed, there are questions about what exactly the therapeutic activities are (Bourgon et al. 2011).

Research on the importance of the TA in corrections is equivocal at best (Kozar and Day 2012). We described the principles of risk, need and responsivity and described how the TA fits into a broader view of the responsivity principle, one that includes the relationship and structuring dimensions described by Andrews and Bonta (2010). We encourage community supervision officers to place more value on, and make more strategic and sustained efforts toward, developing and maintaining a quality TA with their clients. We described two specific intervention techniques, role clarification and collaborative goal setting, to aid in this regard. Nonetheless, these intervention techniques are not simple recipes for building better relationships with clients in community supervision. Good communication skills including active listening skills, and the ability to communicate in a non-blaming and non-confrontational manner, as well as motivational interviewing skills, will aid in conducting such interventions and enhance the therapeutic relationships with criminal justice clients in order to achieve change.

We are not alone in recognizing the importance of the relationship in community supervision. In a recent article by Lowenkamp et al. (in press), they stress the importance of the community supervision officers establishing a real and meaningful relationship with their clients, suggesting that, in some ways, we have missed the boat on implementing evidence-based practices when we have forgotten about the individual, the client's own humanness and uniqueness. We believe that community supervision officers need to embrace the role of change agent. By embracing change and recognizing that the relationship with their client can be enhanced, officers may begin to create and maintain a more effective learning environment for their clients through a collaborative, engaged and purposeful process.

References

Andrews, D. A. (2000) Principles of Effective Correctional Programs. *Compendium 2000 on Effective Correctional Programming.* Ottawa, ON: Correctional Service of Canada.

Andrews, D. A. and Bonta, J. (2010) *Psychology of Criminal Conduct*. Fifth Edition. Newark, NJ: LexisNexis.

Andrews, D. A. and Dowden, C. (2006) 'Risk Principle of Case Classification in Correctional Treatment: A Meta-Analytic Investigation'. *International Journal of Offender Therapy and Comparative Criminology* 50, 88–100.

Andrews, D. A. and Kessling, J. J. (1980) 'Program Structure and Effective Correctional Practices: A Summary of the CaVIC Research'. in R. R. Ross and P. Gendreau (Eds) *Effective Correctional Treatment* (pp. 439–463). Toronto: Butterworth.

Andrews, D. A., Bonta, J. and Hoge, R. D. (1990) 'Classification for Effective Rehabilitation: Rediscovering Psychology'. *Criminal Justice and Behaviour* 17, 19–52.

Andrews, D. A., Zinger, I., Hoge, R. D. and Bonta, J. (1996). 'Does Correctional Treatment Work? A Clinically Relevant and Psychologically Informed Meta-Analysis'. in D. F. Greenberg (Ed.), *Criminal Careers* (pp. 437–472). Brookfield, VT: Dartmouth.

Baldwin, S. A., Wampold, B. E. and Imel, Z. E. (2007) 'Untangling the Alliance-Outcome Correlation: Exploring the Relative Importance of Therapist and Patient Variability in the Alliance'. *Journal of Consulting and Clinical Psychology* 75, 842–852.

Bonta, J. (1995) 'The Responsivity Principle and Offender Rehabilitation'. *Forum on Corrections Research*, 7, 34–37.

Bordin, E. S. (1979) 'The Generalizability of the Psychoanalytic Concept of the Working Alliance'. *Psychotherapy: Theory, Research, and Practice* 16, 252–260.

Bourgon, G., Bonta, J., Rugge, T., Scott, T. and Yessine, A. (2010) 'The Role of Program Design, Implementation, and Evaluation in Evidence-Based "Real World" Community Supervision'. *Federal Probation* 74, 2–15.

Bourgon, G., Gutierrez, L. and Ashton, J. (2011) 'The Evolution of Community Supervision Practice: The Transformation from Case Manager to Change Agent'. *Irish Probation Journal* 8, 28–48.

Eames, V. and Roth, A. (2000). 'Patient Attachment Orientation and the Early Working Alliance: A Study of Patient and Therapist Reports of Alliance Quality and Ruptures'. *Psychotherapy Research* 10, 421–434.

Elvins, R. and Green, J. (2008). 'The Conceptualization and Measurement of Therapeutic Alliance: An Empirical Review'. *Clinical Psychology Review* 28, 1167–1187.

Green, J. (2006). 'Annotation: The Therapeutic Alliance – A Significant but Neglected Variable in Child Mental Health Studies'. *Journal of Child Psychology and Psychiatry* 47, 425–435.

Hanson, R. K., Bourgon, G., Helmus, L. and Hodgson, S. (2009) 'The Principles of Effective Correctional Treatment Also Apply to Sexual Offenders'. *Criminal Justice and Behavior* 36, 865–891.

Hatcher, R. L. and Barends, A. W. (2006) 'How a Return to Theory Could Help Alliance Research'. *Psychotherapy: Theory, Research Practice, Training* 43, 292–299.

Horvath, A. O. and Bedi, R. P. (2002) 'The Alliance'. in J. C. Norcross (Ed.) *Psychotherapy Relationships That Work: Therapist Contributions and Responsiveness to Patients* (pp. 37–70). New York: Oxford University Press.

Horvath, A. and Greenberg, L. (1989) 'Development and Validation of the Working Alliance Inventory'. *Journal of Counseling Psychology* 36, 222–233.

Horvath, A. O. and Greenberg. L. (1994) *The Working Alliance: Theory, Research, and Practice*. New York: Wiley.

Horvath, A. O. and Symonds, B. D. (1991) 'Relation Between Working Alliance and Outcome in Psychotherapy: A Meta-Analysis'. *Journal of Counselling Psychology* 38, 139–149.

Horvath, A. O., Del Re, A. C., Fluckiger, C. and Symonds, D. (2011) 'Alliance in Individual Psychotherapy'. *Psychotherapy* 48, 9–16.

Kozar, C. J. and Day, A. (2012) 'The Therapeutic Alliance in Offending Behavior Programs: A Necessary and Sufficient Condition for Change?' *Aggression and Violent Behavior* 17, 482–487.

Lidz, C. W., Hoge, S. K., Gardner, W. and Bennett, N. S. (1995) 'Perceived Coercion in Mental Hospital Admission: Pressures and Process'. *Archives of General Psychiatry* 52, 1034–1039.

Lowenkamp, C. T., Robinson, C. R. and Lowenkamp, M. S. (2010) *EPICS-II: Effective Practices in Correctional Settings.* Unpublished training manual. Contact: mlowenkamp@hotmail.com.

Lowenkamp, C. T., Holsinger, A. M., Robinson, C. and Cullen, F. (in press) 'When a Person Isn't a Data Point: Making Evidence-Based Practice Work'. *Federal Probation*.

MacCoun, R. J. (2005) 'Voice, Control, and Belonging: The Double-Edged Sword of Procedural Fairness'. *Annual Review of Law and Social Science* 1, 171–201.

Mallinckrodt, B. (2000). 'Attachment, Social Competencies, Social Support and Interpersonal Process in Psychotherapy'. *Psychotherapy Research* 10, 239–266.

Marshall, W. M. and Serran, G. A. (2004) 'The Role of the Therapist in Offender Treatment'. *Psychology, Crime, and Law* 1, 309–320.

Martin, D., Garske, J. and Davis, M. (2000) 'Relation of the Therapeutic Alliance with Outcome and Other Variables: A Meta-Analytic Review'. *Journal of Consulting and Clinical Psychology* 68, 438–450.

McMurran, M. (2002) *Motivating Offenders to Change: A Guide to Enhancing Engagement in Therapy.* Chichester: Wiley.

McNeill, F., Farrall, S., Lightower, C. and Maruna, S. (2012) 'Reexamining Evidence-Based Practice in Community Corrections: Beyond "A Confined View" of What Works'. *Justice Research and Policy* 14, 35–60.

Polaschek, D. L. and Ross, E. C. (2010) 'Do Early Therapeutic Alliance, Motivation, and Stages of Change Predict Therapy Change for High-Risk, Psychopathic Violent Prisoners?' *Criminal Behavior and Mental Health* 20, 100–111.

Polaschek, D. L., Anstiss, B. and Wilson, M. (2010) 'The Assessment of Offending-Related Stage of Change in Offenders: Psychometric Validation of the URICA with Male Prisoners'. *Psychology, Crime & Law* 16, 305–325.

Ross, E., Polaschek, D. L. and Ward, T. (2008) 'The Therapeutic *Alliance*: A Theoretical Revision for Offender Rehabilitation'. *Aggression and Violent Behavior* 13, 462–480.

Safran, J. D. and Murran, J. C. (Eds) (1995) 'The Therapeutic Alliance'. *In Session: Psychotherapy in Practice* 1(1).

Skeem, J. L., Encandela, J. and Eno Louden, J. (2003) 'Perspectives on Probation and Mandated Mental Health Treatment in Specialized and Traditional Probation Departments'. *Behavioral Sciences & the Law* 21, 429–458.

Skeem, J. L., Eno Louden, J., Polaschek, D. and Camp, J. (2007) 'Assessing Relationship Quality in Mandated Community Treatment: Blending Care with Control'. *Psychological Assessment* 19, 397–410.

Spiegler, M. D. and Guevremont, D. C. (2003) *Contemporary Behavior Therapy.* Fourth Edition. Pacific Grove, CA: Wadsworth.

Trotter, C. (2006). *Working with Involuntary Clients: A Guide to Practice.* Thousand Oaks, CA: Sage.

Ward, T., Day, A., Howells, K. and Birgden, A. (2004) 'The Multifactor Offender Readiness Model'. *Aggression and Violent Behaviour* 9, 645–673.

Wolfe, B. and Goldfried, M. (1988) 'Research on Psychotherapy Integration: Recommendations and Conclusions from an NIMH Workshop'. *Journal of Consulting and Clinical Psychology* 56, 448–451.

Wormith, J. S., Althouse, R., Simpson, M., Reitzel, L. R., Fagan, T. J. and Morgan, R. D. (2007) 'The Rehabilitation and Reintegration of Offenders: The Current Landscape and Some Future Directions for Correctional Psychology'. *Criminal Justice and Behaviour* 34, 879–892.

Section IV

Offender Diversity: Contextualizing Compliance Theory, Policy and Practice

16

Working with Women in Probation: 'Will You, Won't You, Will You, Won't You, Won't You Join the Dance?'

Loraine Gelsthorpe

Introduction

This chapter addresses a number of issues pertaining to the supervision of female offenders and 'compliance', looking in particular at evidence on gendered aspects of work with women offenders. But what is meant by compliance? As will be clear from other chapters in this book, one of the first tasks in considering 'compliance' is to distinguish between 'compliance', 'completion' and 'desistance.' In common parlance 'compliance' is often assumed to mean a 'cessation of offending behaviour' or 'obedience' to the law on the basis of completion of a programme or other intervention. 'Completion' relates to quantitative measures of whether an individual has met the conditions of the supervision. Set conditions could be a combination of a number of requirements, including attendance at appointments with a probation officer, completion of programmes or work placement, residency orders or working with a drug team (Padfield and Maruna 2006). The measure of 'success' is based on whether the offender has attended the appointment or programme, and not the extent to which the offender has engaged in the process or whether offenders' risk of reoffending has been reduced.

Immediately we are left with a number of questions. Suppose that a programme or intervention is not supported by evidence to show that it works in regard to reducing offending behaviour, yet completion is taken to reflect 'success'. Alternatively, success in regard to 'completion' could mean whether an offender has put their learning into practice. McCulloch (2010) also questions whether the effectiveness of such quantitative measures is a true reflection of success against the intended outcome.

However, in earlier research, Rex and Gelsthorpe (2002) accepted some of the limitations of the measure of 'completion', but also identified the value of the data to the criminal justice system, not least because such measures can give

279

an indication of confidence in the processes. 'Completion' does also offer the potential for offenders to gain something from an intervention or programme simply by virtue of being required to attend.

Chief among researchers who have looked at compliance is Anthony Bottoms (2001), who has identified four types of compliance relevant to community sentence completion: instrumental, constraint-based, routinized and normative compliance. In instrumental compliance, the offender weighs the pros and cons attached to programme completion, concluding that it is in his or her best interests to complete it. For example, s/he may deem it preferable to complete a programme and remain in the community than to refuse and be sent to prison because of being in breach of conditions attached to a community order. Constraint-based compliance is a product of specific restrictions, either physical or social (such as residency requirements, target hardening or curfews – with electronic monitoring to enforce this), which limit an offender's ability to avoid compliance. Routinized compliance, on the other hand, is automated and a function of habit. Here, programme attendance becomes such a regular part of the offender's schedule that s/he no longer needs to actively decide to comply. Finally, normative compliance stems from an offender's belief in the legitimacy of the sentencing authority. For example, an offender recognizes that s/he has a problem (e.g., substance misuse or anger management) that programme compliance might help to solve. It represents an internalization of the values of the supervisory authority and indicates compliance with the spirit (substantive) as well as the letter (formal) dimensions of the sentence or requirements (Carlen 2002; McBarnet 2004). Robinson and McNeill (2010) have taken this work further by giving attention to the idea that 'formal' and 'substantive' dimensions of compliance need to be recognized. Formal compliance here is characterized by an offender who 'technically' complies with the requirements or conditions set, but who does not actively engage beyond that point. Substantive compliance is characterized by the active engagement of an offender who not only meets the requirements or conditions, but also seeks to engage and address issues. It is this '[un] auditable' compliance which Robinson and McNeill (2010: 370) see as problematic, yet essential to 'normative compliance', in which the offender desists from offending behaviour because they have imbibed the good sense in not doing so – for themselves and others.

Thus, compliance can arise from self-interest, social norms, force or simple habit, as well as any combination of these. Ideally, the different dimensions might work together to promote both short (programme completion) and long-term (desistance) compliance. However, the precise mechanisms involved might vary between offenders. Certainly, recognition of gendered 'needs' would need to be considered here alongside the age/crime curve, the seriousness of offences committed, the length of orders and number of requirements or conditions attached.

Official statistics consistently demonstrate that, on the whole, women tend to show more compliance than men (though only marginally so) (see, for example, Section 95 *Statistics on Women and Criminal Justice* (Ministry of Justice 2012a), but it is not at all clear *why* they do. And, as will be shown in this chapter, more nuanced analysis of women's compliance suggests that the content and mode of delivery for programmes may be relevant.

The heart of the dance: women as 'correctional afterthoughts'

One issue which compounds matters here is whether women can be expected to 'comply' with interventions designed for men. The title for the chapter comes from the National Probation Service's document entitled: *The Heart of the Dance: a Diversity Strategy for the National Probation Service for England and Wales, 2002–2006* (National Probation Service 2003) combined with the Mock Turtle's song (the Lobster Quadrille) drawn from Lewis Carroll's *Alice's Adventures in Wonderland* (1865: chapter X). [1] *The Heart of the Dance* was a significant document in terms of highlighting the need to take 'difference' and 'diversity' into account in planning provision for offenders. Women have all too often been 'correctional afterthoughts' (Ross and Fabiano 1986) in the development of interventions and programmes in prisons and in the community, and so there has been increasing recognition that gender differences should be taken into account in devising interventions. Various reviews of the literature support this claim (Blanchette 2002; Hollin and Palmer 2006a; Howden-Windell and Clark 1999; Kaschak 1992). Worrall (2002) criticized the Correction Services Accreditation Panel for failing to provide, in both design and delivery, appropriate opportunities for women offenders or to take into account gender-specific needs and risks. And, arguably, the 'what works' approach, whereby actuarial assessment tools uniformly capture predetermined offender-based risks and needs, and address them as a key design component (Harper and Chitty 2005), neglect the question of whether 'what works' for men also works for women. This is expanded upon by Hollin and Palmer, whose searching review of wide-ranging evidence on what works leads to a conclusion that:

> there are obvious areas of overlap in the criminogenic needs of male and female offenders, but also some areas of difference. This view leads to the suggestion that there may be different pathways to offending among male and female offenders, meaning that it is crucial that these differences are taken into account when designing treatment programmes for women themselves.
>
> (2006b: 260)

Clearly, to accomplish the intended goals, programmes must first be completed. As such, finishing rates and differences in them by gender provide direct insight into programme effectiveness and how it varies by gender. Quantitative analysis of accredited programme completion data can assess this on a grand scale. But there is scant research specifically examining how well women do on community programmes in England and Wales. One study examines recidivism among incarcerated women who participated in single-sex prison-based programmes (Cann 2006), but it provides little insight into community programme compliance. Likewise, the effectiveness of the mixed-gender General Offending Behaviour Programme (GOBP) has remained virtually unexamined (Speed and Burrows 2006). Given recent research which indicates the importance of programme completion to resettlement and preventing recidivism (e.g. Lewis et al. 2007), this lack of attention to women offenders is particularly troubling.

Thus, notwithstanding the general impression created by Section 95 statistics (Ministry of Justice 2012a), which, as noted above, demonstrate that women comply with orders at a higher rate than men, to further comprehend programme compliance, one must also understand the nature of the interventions imposed.

Situational, practical and gender-specific factors that affect how women comply

Situational factors regarding women and compliance: Does the nature of the intervention matter?

Drawing on data generated by the accredited GOBP in 2006–2007 to statistically identify factors involved in why some offenders comply and complete their programme while others are breached, a study by Martin et al. (2009) shows that women's completion rates on General Offending Programmes are significantly lower than men's. The General Offending Behaviour Programmes include *Think first* (TF), *One to One* (OTO), *Enhanced Thinking Skills* (ETS) and *Cognitive Skills Booster* (CSB) programmes.

There were a number of rationales for choosing GOB Programmes as a focus for analysis. First, all of these programmes share a 'cognitive–behavioural' orientation, based on the importance of decision making skills in preventing reoffending (McGuire 2000). Second, they have a common target offender group and are accredited for both sexes. Third, these are the longest-established, most numerous and widespread programmes delivered in the country (Palmer et al. 2007). Fourth, the programme data contain rich descriptive information on both assignment and completion. Finally, nearly half of sentences for women in 2006–2007 were to these programmes, making them one of the most common sentence conditions for women offenders. As indicated, these programme interventions are known as cognitive–behavioural strategies, and the aim is to focus on modifying individuals' behaviour to bring about desistance (McGuire 2006).

While not rejecting societal, situational and proximal causes of crime, cognitive–behavioural approaches recognize that experiences and behaviour arise from circumstances and treatment by others. These, in turn, are dependent upon a wide range of factors, including an individual's gender (Bradley 1996). Theoretically, the development of effective thinking skills will lead offenders to reflect on their previous offending decisions and desist from further criminal activity (regardless of gender) because they have learned better alternatives. Evaluation research suggests that completing a cognitive–behavioural programme is associated with a lower likelihood of reoffending (see Debiden and Lovbakke 2005 for a review of research).

However, women may be sentenced to programmes which do not address their *actual* criminogenic needs,[2] but, rather, their *presumed* needs (Hedderman 2004). GOB Programmes may fail to effectively address women's needs because they remain dependent on male offender-based models of intervention (Shaw and Hannah-Moffat 2004). In addition, while GOB Programmes are designed to address criminogenic needs such as deficits in thinking skills, the criteria that make offenders eligible for such programmes do not necessarily include evidence that there really are *pre-existing deficits* (Hollin and Palmer 2006b; Palmer et al. 2008; see also the critique of cognitive–behaviourism offered by Kendall 2002). Rather, previous convictions or the nature of those previous convictions are often key triggers for inclusion, particularly with female offenders (Worrall 2002). It follows that the constitution of GPB programmes might adversely affect women's completion rates – and, thus, 'compliance'.

Drawing on data from the Interim Accredited Programmes system (IAPS, which contains a record of the performance of all accredited programmes and completions) and OASys data (which comes from a 321-item actuarial risk-assessment tool used to assess individual offenders and inform sentence plans),[3] Martin et al. (2009) focused on predictors of compliance, the influence of static (such as age and previous convictions) and dynamic factors (such as relationships, housing, health and employment), and the predictive utility of cognitive behavioural factors. (It will be recognized that discerning offenders' actual reasons for compliance with GOB Programmes is difficult and that in practice it is easier to focus on attrition or failure to complete or comply.) This study showed that, despite some similarities, the predictors of programme completion not only vary between men and women, but also operate differently between them. In sum, very few OASys items predicted compliance for women, but those that did had larger effects. For example, offence severity and prior record better predict completion of the GOBP for men, while *diversity* of offending better predicts completion for women. Specifically, women who engage in a wide variety of offences have lower compliance rates, which suggests that these women are not invested in social norms; in contrast, that offence severity increases compliance for men suggests that male offenders *instrumentally* recognize when failure to complete will have more detrimental consequences for them as a direct outcome of the greater offence gravity involved. Yet, in regard to unsuitable or unstable accommodation, as another example of the complexity, the higher the score for women, the greater the prediction of completion. This may be the product of women recognizing or believing that the programmes to which they have been assigned can help address the problems which led to their unsuitable or unstable accommodation, indicating acceptance of the legitimacy of the intervention (*normative compliance*).

Importantly, the findings refute the 'what works' supposition that the impact of need is relatively interchangeable for women and men. Rather, they support the 'gender-responsive' position that men and women should be approached differently. In addition, the findings suggest that different forms of compliance are utilized by men and women. More specifically, based on a comparison of positive, negative and irrelevant factors, men seem more likely to engage in *instrumental compliance* (relating to compliance achieved through self-interested calculation) while women appear more likely to achieve *normative compliance* (based on values).[4]

Thus '*will you, won't you, will you, won't you, won't you join the dance?*' highlights questions as to precisely *whose* dance women are being invited to join. Are they being invited, or indeed compelled, to 'comply' with interventions which have been designed for men? In a series of articles about the 'struggle for justice for women' in 2002 Pat Carlen raised some important questions about legitimacy of punishment in relation to women, which obviously have implications for 'compliance' (Carlen 2002). And, as subsequent discussion has shown, what does 'compliance' really mean when the interventions themselves may not make sense? We might make the point here that programmes also need to be culturally sensitive in order to maximize their legitimacy and therefore their impact and potential for achieving compliance (see Gelsthorpe 2001; Durrance et al. 2010; and Calverley 2013 on this issue).

Are there practical factors which influence women's compliance?

Several studies have identified practical factors such as childcare and travel difficulties as factors which might affect how women comply with community orders (see, for example, Roberts 2002). Evidence from a study of a housing project for women leaving prison, however, reveals that compliance with conditions can be difficult alongside childcare. In their study of the early phase of Re-Unite, a project which facilitates the quick return of children from state care to mothers leaving prison, Gelsthorpe and Sharpe (2010) revealed that women might be subject to the vicissitudes of the difficulties of train and bus travel following attendance at school events, or that electronic monitoring might malfunction, suggesting that women were in breach of conditions, in both cases making women vulnerable to discretionary decision making regarding breaches.

In a small-scale study Garnett (2011)[5] interviewed ten women in HMP Drake Hall who had been breached during a period on licence in the community in the previous 12 months and, importantly in the context of this chapter, ten women who had a history of breach of community penalties within the 12 months prior to their being given a custodial penalty. Focusing on the interviews with those who had breached community penalties, the most common reason for breach was for technical violation relating to non-attendance or failing to complete the requirements of the order. The women expressed specific concerns about heavy reporting instructions. Two of the community penalty group stated that they had daily reporting instructions and drug testing requirements. In one case this involved a 30-minute train journey to the probation office. She managed to achieve this for approximately five months, but, despite suggestion of early termination of the order, found it difficult to maintain the required attendance:

> They were on about reducing it as well, 'cos it was a two year community order and they said they would probably reduce it to about a year if I carried on going, and then obviously it went downhill a bit and then I breached ... I know it sounds really bad, but by that point when I breached it was, err, it seemed to be dragging a lot.

The difficulty in maintaining attendance was shared by another woman:

> So it just became really hard work and I think, yeah, okay then, I can't do this anymore.

Such stories find resonance in McCulloch's (2010) study on compliance with community service, which shows that, while compliance is positively influenced by the desire to avoid prison, this factor in itself is not sufficient to limit non-compliance. Offenders also need a 'reason, reward or purpose to comply in the long term' (McCulloch, 2010: 404).

Where the women indicated that they had reoffended during their community order, and had thus been breached, in most cases (nine out of ten) this was to fund a drug habit, or because the influence of substance misuse meant that their lives were chaotic. (In the remaining case there was evidence of a history of alcohol misuse.)

Interestingly, formal compliance among the ten women breached when on community orders was reported simply as 'attendance at a reporting session' without a change to general lifestyle. They viewed the order as a punishment for offending and not as an opportunity to make changes in their lives. The ability of offenders to successfully complete community-based punishments without altering offending behaviours aligns with Morash's (2010) findings in her study of women on probation and parole in the United States, but what is particularly striking in this context is the practical difficulty of maintaining attendance in a context of drug misuse or alcohol dependency, which suggests that further practical support in these directions is necessary.

3. What do we know about gender-specific factors that might be relevant to women's compliance?

The small-scale nature of the studies mentioned supports the idea that a more focused and systematic analysis of women's compliance is required, but we can also draw from other research evidence which suggests that women's engagement in existing interventions is determined by the fact that they learn in different ways from men (Belenky et al. 1986; see also Covington 1998). Women-only environments are also thought to facilitate growth and development (Zaplin 1998), and thus the evidence adds up to a need to work with women in non-authoritarian cooperative settings, where women are empowered to engage in social and personal change. (See Gelsthorpe 2010 for an overview.)

Indeed, in a survey of the research literature and practice-led evidence (looking at models of practice around the country), Gelsthorpe et al. (2007) highlighted nine lessons for the National Offender Management Service (NOMS) commissioners of services charged with the task of deciding upon provision for women offenders in regional and local criminal justice systems. Such provision should: (1) be women-only to foster safety and a sense of community and to enable staff to develop expertise in work with women; (2) integrate offenders with non-offenders so as to normalize women offenders' experiences and facilitate a supportive environment for learning; (3) foster women's empowerment so they gain sufficient self-esteem to directly engage in problem-solving themselves, and feel motivated to seek appropriate employment; (4) utilize what is known about the effective learning styles with women; (5) take a holistic and practical stance to helping women to address social problems which may be linked to their offending; (6) facilitate links with mainstream agencies, especially health, debt advice and counselling; (7) have capacity and flexibility to allow women to return for 'top ups' or continued support and development where required; (8) ensure that women have a supportive milieu or mentor to whom they can turn when they have completed any offender-related programmes, since personal care is likely to be as important as any direct input addressing offending behaviour; and (9) provide women with practical help with transport and childcare so that they can maintain their involvement in the centre or programme.

There is now a national network of women's community services which embody these principles or variants on them (Women's Breakout 2013). But, in describing the government-sponsored prototype for such centres, Hedderman et al. (2011), who evaluated *Together Women*, make a particular plea to learn from women themselves. They comment that women involved with the community projects developed a sense of 'respect and community' which made them feel optimistic about the future (Hedderman et al. 2011: 30). The feeling that *Together Women* workers were genuinely interested in the women's welfare led to positive responses to visits and the telephone calls that they received to remind them of appointments, or missed appointments. As Hedderman et al. (2011, p. 11) indicate, one client returned to the project after not attending some time and found:

> It's nice to know that somebody thinks about you and that, you know, there is somebody there to turn to...I thought it'd be like another authority. I thought it'd be like, erm, police, probation, social services kind of, you know, making these rules, setting down, I must do this, and I must do that, and it's not been anything like that...obviously, they're not gonna put up with my bloomin' nonsense, and all that sort of thing – but they just tell me what I should be doing, really, and then basically they leave it to me whether I take it on board, or phone me and try to encourage me, 'Have you done that?' you know. But it's not like, you know, social services, the authorities, police and things like that.

Another woman explained:

> I went to anger management but then I wasn't so good at coming so I stopped. I got two letters from them writing and saying I haven't been for a few days asking if I'm alright, they said if there's any problems get in touch with them, that they're looking forward to hearing from you. They wrote twice in four days, I live on my own so that was good of them wasn't it? Someone does care. I was thrilled to bits when I opened the letter.
>
> (Cited in Hedderman et al. 2011, p. 11)

Other service users have described matters in similar ways. ISIS is a community service for women offenders in Gloucestershire. In a recent report, one service user explained why she attended in this way: 'It's somewhere I can come and be safe. There's a day centre just down the road, where my doctors is...where I have to go, but all they talk about is drugs, drink, jail, down there, and here they talk about recovery' (ISIS 2012, p. 3).

Such claims are repeated in evaluations of women's community services. In the Turnaround Project in Wales, the clients were unanimously positive about their experiences (Holloway and Brookman 2008). Issues that were highlighted as being particularly positive included: the range of support that was offered, the flexible pace of working, the confidential nature of discussions, the non-judgemental nature of the staff and the ability of staff to uplift them and instil them with confidence and self-esteem. The women were also aware that the project was helping to empower them in various ways; as one woman put it:

> I can do that now. I'll go to this place and that person and it's just giving me all the knowledge or helping me to gain the knowledge because I was making phone calls this morning to the repairs and [she] said 'I'm not making them, you pick up the phone and you do it'. Y'know putting the power back onto me, the responsibility back onto me so I can be responsible for my own life instead of looking to other people to solve everything for me.
>
> (Cited in Holloway and Brookman 2008: 19)

In Scotland, the 218 Service, based in Glasgow, opened in 2003 as a specialist facility (day and residential provision) for women offenders and as a direct response to reviews of experiences (especially the experiences of highly vulnerable women repeatedly sent to prison for short sentences). The 218 service also emerged out of recognition that that there had to be a better way of working with women to offer a safe place and space, help them reintegrate into society and reconnect with their communities (Beglan 2013). As Beglan (2013) describes, regular reviews demonstrate an increase in positive outcomes for the women over time in relation to substance misuse, living situation, social functioning, physical health, psychological well-being and, importantly, criminal activity. As one service user put it:

> ... was just amazing and I'm so glad I had the opportunity and took on board everything that we had done. I didn't think I could have done half of it and I finished and completed it. It's made me look at myself differently as well, and that I can do things and it's given me confidence in myself. I didn't like myself for a long, long time and it's just wee bits, but it's coming together....
>
> (cited in Beglan 2013, p. 164)

Another woman indicated that ' ... if it wasn't for 218 I don't know where I'd be. I'd be in jail or up the road doing something stupid but I'm here and I'm straight and I've never had that in all those years. I don't know where I'd be without this place' (Cited in Beglan 2013, p. 166).

We do not have details in regard to compliance with orders, but there is a strong indication of moves toward compliance in terms of women living less chaotic and more regulated lives.

Similarly, in Belfast, Northern Ireland, the *Inspire Women's Project* was created to develop and deliver in the community a new, enhanced range of women-specific services which directly contribute to reducing women's offending through targeted community-based interventions (DOJ 2010). Here we do have an evaluation which includes compliance; Easton and Matthews (2011) report improvements in compliance with community orders thus: 'The majority (72 per cent) of the 309 women offenders involved with Inspire between 27 October 2008 and 31 July 2010 were compliant with their community sentence. The most common reason for non-compliance was not attending appointments (81 per cent)' (Easton and Matthews 2011: 4).

Non-compliance was subject to standard probation enforcement procedures whereby probation officers contacted each woman offender and made a decision about the reason for non-compliance. If the probation officer deemed it necessary, a woman offender was given a formal warning in the first instance or had formal breach proceedings initiated against her if her non-compliance was deemed serious or frequent enough. Of the 309 women offenders involved in the project during this period, a total of 69 women (22 per cent) breached their community sentence. This compares well with statistics in England and Wales, which show that 58 per cent of women in 2011 completed their community orders (see Table A4 23, Ministry of Justice 2012b). And, again, it appears that it is the holistic approach to women's problems and experiences rather than an exclusive focus on offending behaviour, combined with a supportive non-judgemental approach, which has contributed to the project's success.

As Hedderman et al. (2011) note, the key themes which emerge are that what matters to women as service users is experience of key workers who 'see service users as people, not cases', 'being accepted and respected', 'being in a women only environment' and being in a 'quality' environment (by which is meant a good physical environment where colour schemes were bright and furniture modern and comfortable). As one woman put it:

> Yeah, I've been in trouble with the law again, actually, but that was through me alcohol and through me partner, but I would've possibly been in *more* trouble had I not had this place ... You know, if I didn't have this place to come to, I would've just totally gave up, I think, a couple of time, you know. But instead, I've got myself up and come here instead and it's helped me.
>
> (cited in Hedderman et al. 2011, p. 14)

Concluding reflections

In this chapter I have posed some questions about the meaning of compliance, particularly where programme interventions have not been designed with women in mind. I have also looked at situational, practical and gender-specific factors which may affect the degree to which women comply with orders and requirements. The development of gender-informed community-based services suggests a promising outlook in regard to compliance, given what women themselves say about their experiences.

One recent policy-related initiative revolves around the quality of supervision. In conducting a large-scale literature review of 'quality in supervision', Shapland et al. (2012: 43) conclude that the following points seem to be important to good experiences of supervision and are seen as demonstrating 'quality' by both service users and supervisors:

- Building genuine relationships that demonstrate 'care' about the person being supervised, their desistance[6] and their future, and not just control/monitoring/surveillance.
- Engaging offenders in identifying needs and setting goals for supervision, including supervisory relationships which shows listening by supervisors, who keep on trying to steer supervisees in a desisting direction, through motivating them, encouraging them to solve problems and talk about problems.
- An understanding of how desistance may occur, with thoughtful consideration of how relapses or breaches should be dealt with.
- Attention to relevant practical obstacles to desistance, not just psychological issues.
- Knowledge of and access to the resources of local services/provision, in order to help the supervisee deal with these practical obstacles.
- Advocacy, tailored to individual needs and capabilities, which may involve work by the supervisor, referral to others, or signposting to others, depending on the supervisee's self-confidence and social capital.

There is no reference to any of the evaluations of community services for women in their review, but there might easily be, since the above echoes general findings thus far as to 'what works for women'. While this remains an empirical question in terms of reoffending (as one measurement of compliance),[7] it might be argued that 'what works for women' certainly encourages compliance.

In sum, David Cameron's October 2012 pronouncement that there should be a 'tough but intelligent' response to offending appears to amount to 'punishment' in every sentence (Cameron 2012). What we have learned thus far from the operation of community-based services for women offenders – offering holistic support and a non-judgemental approach – is that 'compliance' might be best achieved through effective relationships with staff. While there is need for further empirical work in this regard, there is at least some promise.[8]

Notes

1. Lewis Carroll (C. L. Dodgson; 1832–1898). The Lobster Quadrille.
   First published in 1865, in *Alice's Adventures In Wonderland*, with revised editions in 1886 and 1897. The first verse is:

   > 'Will you walk a little faster?' said a whiting to a snail.
   > There's a porpoise close behind us, and he's treading on my tail.
   > See how eagerly the lobsters and the turtles all advance!
   > They are waiting on the shingle – will you come and join the dance?
   > Will you, won't you, will you, won't you, will you join the dance?

   Will you, won't you, will you, won't you, won't you join the dance?
2. Criminogenic needs are the factors that are linked to offending; they range from antisocial attitudes and substance misuse to problematic family relationships.
3. OASys is the abbreviated term for the Offender Assessment System, used in England and Wales by Her Majesty's Prison Service and the National Probation Service from 2002 to measure the risks and needs of criminal offenders under their supervision. OASys is designed to enable a properly trained and qualified individual, often a probation officer, to assess how likely an offender is to be reconvicted and identify and classify offending-related needs, including basic personality characteristics and cognitive–behavioural problems, as well as to assess risk of serious harm, risks to the individual and other risks. OASys comprises a series of computer-based forms on which clinical evaluations of offenders are made by staff, and supervision and sentence plans for the forthcoming period of supervision are recorded on a periodic basis – typically every 16 weeks for offenders in the community, and less frequently for imprisoned offenders.
4. A fuller and more technical account of this research can be found in the *British Journal of Criminology*, 49(6), 879–899.
5. Cited with permission of the author, Lisa Garnett, and interviewees who had agreed that their words might be used for research purposes. I am most grateful to Lisa Garnett for allowing me to cite her dissertation.
6. Wider theories of women's pathways into crime may also explain their compliance. Specifically, while men and women have many criminogenic factors in common (antisocial attitudes and depending on drugs, for example), the influence of these factors on men and women may differ (Hedderman 2004; Hollin and Palmer 2006a, 2006b). Similarly, some factors, such as childhood experiences of victimization, may be more salient to women's than men's offending (Gelsthorpe et al. 2007).
7. The Ministry of Justice has commissioned just one study thus far in terms of reconvictions following engagement in community-based services for women. Jolliffe et al.'s (2011) reoffending study following *Together Women* (TW) reveals that the data that were available from TW centres were not sufficiently robust to allow firm conclusions about the impact of TW on later proven reoffending or other desirable social exclusion outcomes (e.g. reduced drug/alcohol use). This does not mean that these projects were not successful at achieving these aims, but it does mean that this cannot be demonstrated with the data that were recorded by the TW centres and with PNC data. These data limitations were the focus of a previous report funded by the Ministry of Justice (Hedderman et al. 2008).
8. I am most grateful to Pamela Ugwudike for helpful comments on an earlier draft of this chapter.

References

Beglan, M. (2013) 'The 218 Experience'. in M. Malloch and G. McIvor (Eds) *Women, Punishment and Social Justice. Human Rights and Penal Practices*. Abingdon, Oxon: Routledge.

Belenky, M., Clinchy, B., Goldberger, N. and Tarule, J. (1986) *Women's Ways of Knowing*. New York: Basic Books.

Blanchette, K. (2002) 'Classifying Female Offenders for Effective Intervention: Application of the Case Based Principles of Risk and Need'. *Forum on Corrections Research* 14, 31–35.

Bottoms, A. (2001) 'Compliance and Community Penalties'. in A. Bottoms, L. Gelsthorpe and S. Rex (Eds) *Community Penalties. Change and Challenges*. Devon: Willan Publishing.

Bradley, H. (1996) *Fractured Identities: Changing Patterns of Inequality*. Cambridge: Polity.

Calverley, A. (2013) *Cultures of Desistance. Rehabilitation, Reintegration and Ethnic Minorities*. Abingdon, Oxon: Routledge.

Cameron, D. (2012) 'We Must Make Prisons Work for Offenders', speech to the Centre for Social Justice, London, 22 October 2012.

Cann, J. (2006) *Cognitive Skills Programmes: Impact on Reducing Reconviction Among a Sample of Female Prisoners*. Research Findings 276. London: Home Office.

Carlen, P. (Ed.) (2002) *Women and Punishment: The Struggle for Justice*. Cullompton: Willan.

Carroll, L. (1865) Mock Turtle's Song (the Lobster Quadrille), drawn from *Alice's Adventures in Wonderland* (Chapter X). London: Macmillan & Co.

Covington, S. (1998) 'The Relational Theory of Women's Psychological Development: Implications for the Criminal Justice System'. in R. Zaplin (Ed.) *Female Crime and Delinquency: Critical Perspectives and Effective Interventions*. Gaithersburg, MD: Aspen Publishers.

Debidin, M. and Lovbakke, J. (2005) 'Offending Behaviour Programmes in Prison and Probation'. in G. Harper and C. Chitty (Eds) *The Impact of Corrections on Re-offending: A Review of 'What Works'*. Third Edition. London: Home Office Research Study 291. London: Home Office.

Department of Justice (DOJ). (2010) *Women's Offending Behaviour in Northern Ireland: A Strategy to Manage Women Offenders and Those Vulnerable to Offending Behaviour 2010–2013*. Belfast: Department of Justice.

Durrance, P., Dixon, L. and Bhui, H. S. (2010) 'Creative Working with Minority Ethnic Offenders'. in J. Brayford, F. Cowe and J. Deering (Eds) *What Else Works? Creative Work with Offenders*. Devon: Willan Publishing.

Easton, H. and Matthews, R. (2011) *Evaluation of the Inspire Women's Project Belfast*. London: South Bank University. http://www.dojni.gov.uk/index/foi/foi_publication_scheme_page/inspire_women_s_project_evaluation_report.pdf (Accessed 2011).

Garnett, L. (2011) *Why Do Women Offenders Breach Licence Conditions and Community Penalties?* M.St dissertation, Institute of Criminology, University of Cambridge.

Gelsthorpe, L. (2001) 'Accountability: Difference and Diversity in the Delivery of Community Penalties' in A. Bottoms, L. Gelsthorpe and S. Rex (Eds) *Community Penalties. Change and Challenges*. Devon: Willan Publishing.

Gelsthorpe, L. (2010) 'What Works with Women Offenders?' in M. Herzog-Evans (Ed.) *Transnational Criminology Manual. Volume 3*. Nijmegen, Netherlands: Wolf Legal Publishers.

Gelsthorpe, L. and Sharpe, G. (2010) *The Way Ahead. The First Two Years* (The Re-Unite Project. Early Development Phase Evaluation Report). London: Commonweal Housing. http://www.re-unite.org.uk/south-london/about-us/evaluation-reports/

Gelsthorpe, L., Sharpe, G. and Roberts, J. (2007) *Provision for Women Offenders in the Community*. London: The Fawcett Society. www.fawcettsociety.org.uk/

Harper, G. and Chitty, C. (2005) *The Impact of Corrections on Re-offending: A Review of 'What Works'*. Third Edition. London: Home Office Research Study 291. London: Home Office.

Hedderman C. (2004) 'The "Criminogenic" Needs of Women Offenders'. in G. McIvor (Ed.) *Women Who Offend*. London: Jessica Kingsley.

Hedderman, C., Palmer, E. and Hollin, C. (2008) *Implementing Services for Women Offenders and Those 'at Risk' of Offending. Action Research with Together Women*. Ministry of Justice Research Series 12/08. London: Ministry of Justice.

Hedderman, C., Gunby, C. and Shelton, N. (2011) 'What Women Want: The Importance of Qualitative Approaches in Evaluating Work with Women Offenders'. *Criminology and Criminal Justice* 11(1), 3–19.

Hollin, C. R. and Palmer, E. J. (2006a) 'Criminogenic Need and Women Offenders: A Critique of the Literature'. *Legal and Criminological Psychology* 11, 179–195.

Hollin, C. R. and Palmer, E. J. (Eds) (2006b) *Offending Behaviour Programmes: Development, Application and Controversies*. Chichester: Wiley.

Holloway, K. and Brookman, F. (2008) An Evaluation of The Women's Turnaround Project. A Report for NOMS CYMRU. Centre for Criminology, University of Glamorgan. http://criminology.research.glam.ac.uk/media/files/documents/2009-01-29/WTP_Final_Version_Report_of_Phase_1_201008.pdf

Howden-Windell, J. and Clark, D. (1999) *Criminogenic Needs of Female Offenders*. London: HM Prison Service.

ISIS (2012) *ISIS Women's Centre and the Nine Lessons of Desistance*. Gloucester: Nelson Trust. http://www.isiswomenscentre.com/

Jolliffe, D., Hedderman, C., Palmer, E. and Hollin, C. (2011) *Re-offending of Women Offenders Referred to Together Women (TW) and the Scope to Divert from Custody*. Ministry of Justice Research Series 11/11. London: Ministry of Justice.

Kaschak, E. (1992) *Engendered Lives: A New Psychology of Women's Experience*. New York: Basic Books.

Kendall, K. (2002) 'Time to Think Again About Cognitive Behavioural Programmes'. in P. Carlen (Ed.) *Women and Punishment. The Struggle for Justice*. Devon: Willan Publishing.

Lewis, S., Maguire, M., Raynor, P., Vanstone, M. and Vennard, J. (2007) 'What Works in Resettlement? Findings from Seven Pathfinders for Short-Term Prisoners in England and Wales'. *Criminology and Criminal Justice* 7(1), 33–53.

Martin, J., Kautt, P. and Gelsthorpe, L. (2009) 'What Works for Women?: A Comparison of Community-Based General Offending Programme Completion'. *British Journal of Criminology* 49(6), 879–899.

McBarnet, D. (2004) *Crime, Compliance and Control*. Farnham: Ashgate.

McCulloch, T. (2010) 'Exploring Community Service. Understanding Compliance'. in F. McNeill, P. Raynor and C. Trotter (Eds) *Offender Supervision: New Directions in Theory, Research and Practice*. Devon: Willan Publishing.

McGuire, J. (2000) 'Cognitive-Behavioural Approaches: An Introduction to Theory and Practice'. in M. Furniss (Ed.) *Evidence-based Practice: A Guide to Effective Practice*. HM Inspectorate of Probation, London: Home Office Publications Unit.

McGuire, J. (2006) 'General Offending Programmes: Concepts, Theory and Practice'. in C. Hollin and E. Palmer (Eds) *Offending Behaviour Programmes: Development, Applications, and Controversies*. Chichester: Wiley.

Ministry of Justice (2012a) *Statistics on Women and the Criminal Justice System: A Ministry of Justice Publication under Section 95 of the Criminal Justice Act 1991*. London: Ministry of Justice.

Ministry of Justice (2012b) Offender Management Caseload Statistics, Annual Probation Statistics. London: Ministry of Justice.

Morash, M. (2010) *Women on Probation and Parole*. Boston: Boston University Press.

National Probation Service (2003) *The Heart of the Dance: A Diversity Strategy for the National Probation Service for England and Wales, 2002–2006*. London: Home Office.

Padfield, N. M. and Maruna, S. (2006) 'The Revolving Door at the Prison Gate: Exploring the Dramatic Increase in Recalls to Prison'. *Criminology and Criminal Justice* 6(3), 329–352.

Palmer, E., McGuire, J., Hounsome, J., Hatcher, R., Bilby, C. and Hollin, C. (2007) 'Offending Behaviour Programmes in the Community: The Effects of Reconviction of Three Programmes with Adult Male Offenders'. *Legal and Criminological Psychology* 12, 251–264.

Palmer, E., McGuire, J., Hounsome, J., Hatcher, R., Bilby, C. and Hollin, C. (2008) 'Importance of Appropriate Allocation to Offending Behavior Programs'. *International Journal of Offender Therapy and Comparative Criminology* 52, 206–221.

Rex, S. and Gelsthorpe, L. (2002) 'The Role of Community Service in Reducing Offending: Evaluating the Pathfinder Projects in the UK'. *The Howard Journal of Criminal Justice* 41(4), 311–325.

Roberts, J. (2002) 'Women-Centred: The West Mercia Community-Based Programme for Women Offenders'. in P. Carlen (Ed.) *Women and Punishment. The Struggle for Justice*. Devon: Willan Publishing.

Robinson, G. and McNeill, F. (2010) 'The Dynamics of Compliance with Offender Supervision'. in F. McNeill, P. Raynor and C. Trotter (Eds) *Offender Supervision: New Direction in Theory, Research and Practice*. Devon: Willan Publishing.

Ross, R. and Fabiano, E. (1986) *Female Offenders: Correctional Afterthoughts*. Jefferson, NC: McFarland.

Shapland, J., Bottoms, A. E., Farrall, S., McNeill, F., Priede, C. and Robinson, G. (2012) *The Quality of Probation Supervision – A Literature Review*. Centre for Criminological Research/University of Sheffield Occasional Paper 3. Sheffield: University of Sheffield and University of Glasgow.

Shaw, M. and Hannah-Moffat, K. (2004) 'How Cognitive Skills Forgot About Gender and Diversity'. in G. Mair (Ed.) *What Matters in Probation*. Cullompton: Willan.

Speed, M. and Burrows, J. (with Burrows, M. H.) (2006) *Sentencing in Cases of Theft from Shops*. Sentencing Advisory Panel Research Report 3. London: Sentencing Advisory Panel.

Women's Breakout (2013) *Women's Breakout – Alternatives to Women's Custody*. www .womensbreakout.org.uk/

Worrall, A. (2002) 'Rendering Women Punishable: The Making of a Penal Crisis'. in P. Carlen (Ed.) *Women and Punishment: the Struggle for Justice*. Cullompton: Devon.

Zaplin, R. T. (1998) *Female Offenders: Critical Perspectives and Effective Interventions*. Second Edition. Sudbury, MA: Jones and Bartlett.

17

Encouraging Compliance, Maintaining Credibility or Fast Tracking to Custody? Perspectives on Enforcement in the Youth Justice System

Tim Bateman

The requirement for 'robust enforcement'

The United Kingdom coalition government's vision for 'effective punishment, rehabilitation and sentencing of offenders' is set out in the criminal justice White Paper, 'Breaking the Cycle', published in December 2010. The document makes clear that community sentences should not be considered – or indeed experienced – as a 'soft option'. To this end, steps to 'improve enforcement' are required to ensure that non-custodial disposals become 'more effective and robust punishments' (Ministry of Justice 2010: paragraph 59). It is apparent that such a rigorous approach is also intended to apply to those below the age of 18 years. The White Paper confirms that community sentences imposed on children must, 'as with adults', be 'robustly enforced' (Ministry of Justice 2010: paragraph 242). The fact that one of the eight questions for consultation in the chapter on youth justice asks for respondents' views as to how to 'increase the effective enforcement of youth sentencing' (Ministry of Justice 2010: question 50) is indicative of the centrality of this issue to government thinking.

Such an emphasis on enforcement is not particular to the present adminis-tration. New Labour's strategy for tackling youth offending, as detailed in the Youth Crime Action Plan, detailed a 'triple track' approach whose first element was 'enforcement and punishment where behaviour is unacceptable' (HM Gov-ernment 2008: 1). While the range of such activity was intended to extend beyond children subject to statutory supervision, it is clear that enforcement of orders imposed by the criminal courts was an important constituent of the broader strategy.

The various editions of National Standards for the supervision of young peo-ple in the community have all linked enforcement directly to breach action. It is therefore unsurprising that the emphasis on enforcement at governmental level finds expression in youth justice practice, with breach accounting for a substantial proportion of court throughput. During 2010/11, for instance, almost one in 12 substantive criminal justice disposals imposed on children below the age of 18 years related to breach of bail or breach of a statutory order (Ministry of Justice 2012a).

Given that prevalence, it is remarkable, as Robinson and McNeill (2010) argue, that the literature on enforcement and breach – both empirically and theoretically – remains relatively slim. Although it may be possible to transfer lessons from the probation context (Canton and Eadie 2005), academic writing that deals with enforcement in the youth justice system in England and Wales is rarer still (though see Bateman 2011; Canton and Eadie 2005; Canton and Patel 2008; Hart 2011; and Nacro 2002). In this context, the current chapter aims to contribute to the limited body of knowledge in this area. It considers different conceptions of enforcement, arguing that, at least until recently, each has been crucially linked to an increasingly punitive environment within which youth justice mechanisms operate. In illustrating the impact of shifts in policy and practice, occasioned by that 'punitive turn', it draws on the results of a survey conducted by the author during 2008 of 22 staff with experience of the youth justice system both before and after the key youth justice reforms of the Crime and Disorder Act 1998, as part of broader research.[1] The chapter concludes with some reflections on the potential for development of a more child-friendly practice.

Why enforcement? The official view

As indicated above, there is a contemporary political consensus as to the necessity of rigorous enforcement within the criminal justice system, but the rationale for that view is frequently not made explicit. Indeed, on occasion, the benefits are presented as self-evident. Home Office research published in 1996, for instance, suggested that responding to the challenge of supervising individuals convicted of serious offences implied that community sentences 'must be complied with and the response to non-compliance must be quick and appropriate' (Ellis et al. 1996: 1). The first edition of National Standards with a specific application to youth justice, issued by the Youth Justice Board (YJB) in April 2000, simply details the actions to be taken when a child fails to attend an appointment (signifying the particular importance of this aspect of practice by underlining the relevant text) without any explanation as to the purpose (Youth Justice Board 2000).[2] More detailed case management guidance, published a decade later (to accompany another set of youth justice standards), devotes four pages to 'enabling and enforcing compliance' (Youth Justice Board 2010a: 8) but similarly neglects to inform practitioners why they should undertake the activities prescribed therein.

This is significant for a number of reasons. In the first place, the focus on enforcement as a key consideration in relation to community-based sanctions is a relatively recent development, dating from the early 1990s and coinciding, in large measure, with the introduction of National Standards (Robinson and Ugwudike 2012). This historical shift suggests that the 'salience of enforcement'-centred policy and practice (Robinson and Ugwudike 2012: 301) has not always been considered an indispensable requirement of the supervisory process, as much contemporary discourse assumes.

Second, while there is widespread agreement that procedures for dealing with children who break the law should differ in important respects from those that apply to adult offenders – reflected in a separate court system, distinct supervisory arrangements and dedicated National Standards – the assumption of equivalent principles and processes for dealing with non-compliance among both groups is rarely questioned.

Third, the failure to interrogate the foundation of what might be termed the 'enforcement paradigm' tends to obscure a range of potential justifications, with varied connotations and practical consequences for children in conflict with the law. In relation to the latter point, it is possible to discern at least three distinct – albeit overlocking – strands of thought in official discourse that purport to explain the desirability of an emphasis on enforcement. These relate to the role of enforcement in:

- encouraging compliance as a prerequisite of effective supervision;
- legitimating community sentences with the courts and the public; and
- providing a manifestation of 'toughness' where court orders are not complied with.[3]

Enforcement as 'effective practice'

One strand of thought posits a relationship between enforcement and the potential for the supervisory process to effect a reduction in offending behaviour. The chapter on supervision orders in the 1995 edition of National Standards, for instance, endorsed just such a position, noting that the 'overall purpose of enforcement is to seek to secure and maintain the child or young person's cooperation and compliance with the order in order to ensure successful completion of the order' to prevent further offending (Home Office 1995: paragraph 4.27). This line of thinking continues to influence present-day policy: 'Breaking the Cycle' asserts that effective case management necessitates that 'all the requirements of a community sentence are delivered and enforced' in the interests of rehabilitation (Ministry of Justice 2010: paragraph 128).

The account also receives some support in the academic literature: Bottoms, in his key contribution to the debate, remarks that effectiveness and compliance are 'inextricably linked' (Bottoms 2001: 89); while Canton and Patel (2008) contend that none of the objectives of a community penalty can be achieved in the absence of sufficient contact between the child and his or her supervisor.

On the face of it, the argument would appear uncontentious – although, as discussed below, there is scope for debate as to what might be regarded as the most appropriate objectives of statutory supervision. There is an increasing recognition that achieving 'engagement' – as manifested by the child being motivated to participate actively in the supervisory process – may be as important as the content of the intervention itself (Mason and Prior 2008; Prior and Mason 2010). Moreover, programme completion is associated with reduced offending (Hedderman and Hearnden 2000) (albeit that 'selection effects' may be responsible, in part, for that relationship; Chitty 2005).

But compliance is not enforcement, and it is a considerable conceptual leap to insist that the latter is also a determinant of lower rates of recidivism (Hedderman and Hough 2004). National Standards make no attempt to explore the relationship between the two, but there is an implied assumption to be found in other government publications of a deterrent effect, whereby rigorous enforcement sends a message that non-compliance 'will not go unpunished' (cited in Robinson and Ugwudike 2012: 303). This account is consistent with New Labour's oft-repeated refrain that children in trouble 'are rarely...confronted with their behaviour and helped to take more personal responsibility for their actions' (Home Office 1997).

Bottoms (2001), however, contends convincingly that, rather than applying coercive pressures to ensure that supervisees stay the distance, developing engagement is better served by practitioners seeking to engender 'normative compliance', whereby cooperation is predicated on a recognition on the part of the person supervised that the supervisor's exercise of authority is legitimate, fair and with regard to the offender's best interest. This is likely to be particularly true in the case of a child, since adolescents are prone to prioritizing short-term advantage over long-term consequences (Farmer 2011) and are accordingly less susceptible to deterrence. Canton and Patel (2008: 157) argue further that many children in conflict with the law may be 'inured to the threat of punishment': the prospect of breach action may be counterproductive since it can impede the development of potentially positive relationships, thereby undermining engagement (Hart 2011).

Nor do empirical studies sustain a conceptual shift from the desirability of fostering compliance to the necessity of robust enforcement practice. Strict adherence to National Standards appears to have little impact on reconviction with adult offenders (Hearnden and Millie 2004). Evaluation of the Intensive

Supervision and Surveillance Programme (ISSP), developed by the YJB as an alternative to youth custody, generated a similar finding.[4] The ten areas which achieved the largest reductions in reoffending were less likely to issue formal warnings, or to return children to court for breach, than the ten schemes with the lowest impact on recidivism, despite having higher levels of recorded non-compliance. Completion rates were also superior in the former: 52.1 per cent of children referred to the most successful schemes finished the programme compared with 39.7 per cent in areas with higher rates of reoffending. The evaluation acknowledges, accordingly, that areas with better outcomes 'were not enforcing the programme in line with national standards' (Gray et al. 2005: 72).

More generally, increased rates of breach over time have not been associated with a reduction in youth reoffending, as would be anticipated if rigorous enforcement was indicative of effective practice. Between 2002/2003 and 2008/2009, breach as a proportion of all offences leading to a substantive youth justice disposal more than doubled, from 3.1 to 6.5 per cent (Bateman 2011). Over the same period, the 12-month recidivism rate for youth community penalties rose slightly from 63.5 to 66 per cent (Ministry of Justice 2012a).

In any event, while encouraging children to comply with court orders has always been a concern of youth justice practitioners, the focus on enforcement as a mechanism for achieving this end is a more recent development. The elision of the two activities is indicative of a philosophical shift. A 1980s youth justice 'orthodoxy' (Haines and Drakeford 1998: 50), grounded in a commitment to diversion and decarceration, was rapidly superseded by a 'punitive turn' whose origins lie, over the longer term, in social and economic changes associated with late modernity (Garland 2001). From a youth justice perspective, the transformation was stimulated more immediately by a developing unease about the extent and nature of youth crime in the early 1990s, cemented by an archetypal moral panic engendered by the murder of two-year-old James Bulger in 1993 at the hands of two boys barely over the age of criminal responsibility (Muncie 2009).[5] The 'discovery' that compliance necessitates rigorous enforcement can accordingly be fruitfully understood as an emanation of a more punitive climate. In that sense, the rationale that sees enforcement as a concomitant of securing compliance merges inextricably with a justification of breach activity as a manifestation of political toughness.

Enforcement as 'legitimation'

'Breaking the Cycle' stresses the centrality of the 'credibility' of community sentences. The government's proposals for children who break the law include ensuring that community orders are 'robustly enforced' as a way of 'securing and maintaining confidence from both sentencers and the public' (Ministry of

Justice 2010: paragraph 242). This line of argument has a pedigree. The YJB, on the introduction of ISSP, set as one of the key objectives for the programme that it should:

> demonstrate that supervision and surveillance is being undertaken consistently and rigorously, and in ways that will reassure the community and sentencers of their credibility and likely success.
>
> (Youth Justice Board 2000a)

The underlying premise is that, in the absence of such reassurance, courts will be less likely to make use of community penalties, with a consequent expansion in the youth custodial population. The intuitive appeal of the argument is such that it is infrequently subject to close scrutiny.

While the two populations – the public and sentencers – generally appear in close juxtaposition, it is not obvious that the issues that pertain to each are the same. The magistracy is supposedly representative of the communities from which it is drawn, but it is obviously true that the former will both be better informed about youth crime and the youth justice process and have greater immediate influence over whether children are deprived of their liberty or benefit from a non-custodial outcome. In these circumstances, it is advisable to consider the confidence of each group separately.

The complexity of measuring, and influencing, public attitudes to law and order in general, and youth crime in particular, is well documented (Allen 2002; Roberts and Hough 2002), and considerations of space preclude an extended treatment here. There is, however, ample evidence to suggest that public opinion is typically supportive of harsher penalties for children who offend, albeit such views are explicable in part by a lack of knowledge of the options available to the youth court or how they are used (Jones 2010). So, the 2010/2011 British Crime Survey suggests that harsher sentencing is the most important factor in improving public confidence in the youth justice system (Ministry of Justice 2012a). This finding might imply that a tougher response to youth crime (including a rigid application of National Standards as regards breach) would go some way to assuaging public opinion. Conversely, the survey also found that more respondents considered that rehabilitation rather than punishment should be the primary aim of the youth justice system (45 per cent against fewer than 14 per cent) (Ministry of Justice 2012a), suggesting scope for a more flexible response to enforcement in the event that such an approach could be shown to generate more positive outcomes in rehabilitative terms.

But either conclusion presumes that the public would be aware of developments in one direction or another, and it is far from clear that that is the case (Jones 2010). The 1980s, for instance, was a decade in which youth justice policy and practice was informed by 'progressive minimalism' (Pitts 2003: 8), premised on an understanding that contact with the criminal justice system could be harmful and a philosophy that aimed to restrict intervention to the minimum necessary to keep children out of court and custody (Smith 2007). Such minimalism led to significant reductions in the prosecution and incarceration of children (Bateman 2012), and, as John Pitts (2004: 141) has noted, this change was effected 'without the public even noticing'. Conversely, there is no evidence that a massive rise in custodial sentencing, in association with an increased focus on robust enforcement, during the 1990s and beyond (Nacro 2003) resulted in any discernible improvements in public approval ratings of the youth justice system. In this context, trusting expert and professional opinion as legitimate sources of authority may be a better guide for youth justice policy than pursuing an elusive public confidence (Tonry 2007).

The views of sentencers, on that analysis, remain of central importance. There is evidence that youth custody is lower in areas where courts are confident in the quality of local service provision for community sentences and that programmes will be properly implemented. For instance, the proportion of sentencers who report being very confident that interventions proposed in pre-sentence reports will be fully delivered is almost twice as high in low-custody areas (Bateman and Stanley 2002). Moreover, research has established a correlation between a lower use of custody and magistrates' confidence that orders will be appropriately enforced (Bateman and Stanley 2002).

Appropriate enforcement does not, however, entail rigid enforcement. Any assumption that courts are wedded to breach action strictly in accord with National Standards may be misplaced – a point made by one Crown Court judge who admonished a senior probation officer for returning a probationer to court, since the problems she presented were precisely those that had led the court to place her on supervision (cited in Canton and Eadie 2005). Moreover, too ready a resort to breach can have the unintended consequence of making it appear that community provision is not an effective mechanism for dealing with young people whose offending may put them at risk of custody (Nacro 2005). Haines and Drakeford (1998: 130) spell out the logic:

> Youth justice practitioners have to reject the entirely fallacious argument that 'credibility' with sentencers depends upon the ability to parade failure before them as quickly and as often as possible.

Even if it can be maintained that strict enforcement reassures the courts, it does not follow that incarceration will be less likely. Indeed, the empirical evidence is consistent with the reverse proposition. The introduction of National Standards and progressively stricter enforcement policy (and practice) coincided with a dramatic expansion in the number of children deprived of their liberty (Bateman 2011).

Particular difficulties are encountered when an order is imposed as an alternative to custody, since sentencers may feel that they have little option but to impose detention in the event of non-compliance. This is problematic, given the tendency for programmes such as ISSP to 'netwiden' (Cohen 1985: 44) by displacing less intensive community penalties rather than diverting children from custodial disposals (Gray et al. 2005). Nearly 60 per cent of those subject to ISSP during the period of the evaluation were breached; one-third were imprisoned in consequence. For some children, then, strict enforcement simply delayed incarceration. Given the netwidening effect, it seems likely that others were subject to 'up-tariffing' (Haines 2008: 351), with breach of ISSP incurring deprivation of liberty for offending that would not have warranted imprisonment in the event that the programme had not existed. While the evaluators were not able to confirm this latter possibility, overall custodial trends were similar in ISSP areas and those which did not have access to the more intrusive forms of provision (Gray et al. 2005).

Conversely, during the 1980s, the fact that practitioners rarely initiated breach action (Bateman 2011) did not prevent the courts from overseeing a fall in the number of custodial sentences imposed on children aged 10–16 years, from 7000 in 1979 to 1400 in 1990.[6] The decrease in 'criminal care orders', from 2700 to 200, was more pronounced still (Home Office 1989, 1993).[7] Although this reduction was partly a function of a falling court population – due to an increased use of formal and informal pre-court measures (Bateman 2012) – custodial penalties also declined as a proportion of total court orders, from 11.9 to 6.1 per cent (Home Office 1989, 1993). Youth justice practitioners during this earlier period were thus able to command sufficient confidence among sentencers to effect what Denis Jones (1989) has called a 'successful revolution' in the arrangements for dealing with children who came to the attention of the system despite returning few to court for non-compliance. In fact, the discourse which fuses enforcement with legitimacy did not emerge in its now familiar form until shortly before the point at which a more punitive climate began to exercise a hold on youth justice policy.

The Criminal Justice Act 1991 was intended to encourage a greater use of community sanctions, through the introduction of a statutory framework predicated on proportionality (Newburn 2003). Reductions in imprisonment were to be effected by proscribing custody unless the seriousness of the offence warranted deprivation of liberty, building on the success of similar statutory measures already in place for young people (Cadman 2005). But the shift implied that probation supervision was to be recast as a punishment rather than an intervention in lieu of a sentence, with a corresponding emphasis on demonstrating the punitive nature of community penalties to inspire the courts' confidence in the new measures (Robinson and Ugwudike 2012).

The statutory provisions were not incompatible with a continued decline in the use of imprisonment for children aged 10 to 16 years (see Nacro 1993), but they were rapidly superseded by further legislative developments that: consciously sought to reverse many of the innovations in the 1991 Act; 'shot great holes' in its underlying principles (Rutherford, cited in Goldson 1997: 131); and presaged the birth of the punitive turn. In this newly unfolding environment, pandering to populism was equated with securing the confidence of the public and the courts (Bateman 2011), and became inextricably linked to demonstrating that community sentences were tough and practices for dealing with non-compliance robust (Robinson and Ugwudike 2012). Enforcement as legitimation – as with enforcement as effective practice – yielded primacy of place to enforcement as 'punishment'.

Enforcement as 'punishment'

The punitive turn emerged under a Conservative administration but survived the change of government in 1997. Punitiveness permeated New Labour's 'new youth justice' (Goldson 2000), exemplified in the transparently titled youth justice White Paper 'No More Excuses' (Home Office 1997). Goldson's (2002: 386) contention that 'punitive imperatives have shaped contemporary policy responses to child "offenders" in England and Wales' is, accordingly, widely accepted (see Matthews 2005 for a dissenting voice). But the relationship of such imperatives to the process of enforcement has rarely been articulated.

As noted above, youth justice practitioners during the 1980s regarded enforcement as peripheral to their role. The orthodoxy described by Haines and Drakeford (1998) was preoccupied with mitigating the worst excesses of the criminal justice system on disadvantaged children. The avoidance of custody was pursued by practitioners with a 'crusading zeal' (Allen 1991: 49), not infrequently with the support of the local authority and the juvenile court (Matthews 1999). Supervision was thus conceived as a mechanism to combat the use of imprisonment and to provide a space for, and a stimulus to, maturational processes of desistance that would allow children to 'grow out of crime' (Rutherford 1992), rather than as an intervention to effect short-term reductions in reoffending. As one practitioner put it at the time, the aim was to:

> Abolish it and enjoy it. Abolish the work, abolish custody, do your best for the kids.
>
> (cited in Haines and Drakeford 1998: 56)

Where such a philosophy prevailed, the role for enforcement was narrow. If the objective was to promote minimum levels of intervention to avoid incarceration, it made little sense to allow the courts a second bite of the cherry where the goal of a non-custodial disposal had been attained (Hedderman and Hough 2004). It should be recalled, too, that, until the passage of the Criminal Justice Act 1988, custody could not be imposed for breach of a supervision order. Thereafter, imprisonment was available only if the court stated, at the point of disposal, that the order was being made 'instead of a custodial sentence' (Great Britain 1988: schedule 10). Given the limited sanctions available, the legislative framework tended to encourage supervisors to pursue normative compliance without the threat of coercion, as evidenced by respondents to the survey of 22 staff with direct experience of the youth justice system, conducted by the author in 2008 (as mentioned at the outset of the chapter). One put it this way:

> Breach cases were rare and normally were pursued when it was clear a case was destined for court proceedings for new offences.
>
> (respondent 9)

In this context, the introduction of the 1992 National Standards, inaugurating as they did a markedly different relationship between the central administration of services and their local delivery (McLaughlin et al. 2001), posed a challenge to practitioners, many of whom would have found it unthinkable, just a few years earlier, that government would attempt to prescribe in detail how they should write court reports, supervise children or enforce court orders. Significantly, too, implementation of the standards, from 1 October (Home Office 1992), occurred just months before the Bulger case transformed the youth justice landscape. In such a climate, the new prescription:

- Carried the germs of a constrained and less reflexive approach to supervision (Eadie and Canton 2002);
- Would mould practitioner responses to the punitive turn when it arrived; and
- Became a conduit through which harsher responses to children in trouble – including in relation to enforcement – were channelled.

Not that national guidance in itself was unwelcome within radical youth justice circles. The Association for Juvenile Justice (AJJ), for instance, a practitioner body advocating 'the immediate and unconditional abolition of prison department custody for young people' (Association for Juvenile Justice 1990: 28), had itself drawn attention to inconsistencies in the administration of statutory supervision, calling for the development of consistent 'standards irrespective of the geographical location of the court' (Association for Juvenile Justice 1990: 21). It was the content of standards that caused concern.

Survey respondents, for instance, described them as being 'too intrusive and far too wide' (respondent 2), and embodying a 'lack of flexibility and discretion' (respondent 11).

In concrete terms, the 1992 standards introduced a presumption that breach action for children should 'normally' occur after no more than three failures to comply with the terms of the court order (Home Office 1992: paragraph 4.34). But this presumption was tempered by a range of concessions to the prevailing ethos:

- Non-compliance might be evidence of the need to change the supervision being undertaken rather than as a failure of the child (paragraph 4.32)
- Supervisors were to seek 'patiently to motivate and assist the child or young person to comply' (paragraph 4.30)
- The process of enforcement was to 'retain the degree of flexibility demanded by the individual's age [and] stage of development' (paragraph 4.30)
- In making a judgement as to the acceptability of any explanation offered by the child, his or her 'personal circumstances and characteristics' were relevant considerations (paragraph 4.32)
- Any enforcement action was to take 'full account of the welfare of the child' (paragraph 4.30).

The role of professional discretion was also fully acknowledged: the stated function of standards was to:

> encourage good practice but avoid unnecessary prescription ... [They] lay down expected norms rather than outright requirements.
>
> (Home Office 1992, p. 1.2(5))

As the angle of the punitive turn tightened, there was a predictable step-change. The role of guidance shifted from offering 'expected norms' to laying down 'required standards of practice' in the second edition of National Standards published in 1995 (Home Office 1995: paragraph 1.2). The dispensations that had permitted an element of practitioner autonomy three years earlier were excised. Whereas the previous standards contained latitude to refrain from breach action if 'strongly in the interests of the objectives of the order' (Home Office 1992: paragraph 4.33), the later edition prescribed, without qualification, that:

> *At most two warnings within any 12 month period may be given before breach proceedings are initiated* ... [Proceedings] should be instituted *within ten working days.* [emphasis in the original]
>
> (Home Office 1995: paragraphs 4.30–31)

Such injunctions did not, of course, guarantee an unquestioning implementation or generate an overnight reversal in practitioner attitudes to enforcement. But the barrage of prescription was bound to impact on day-to-day practice and, in the longer term, on youth justice culture, leading to a dilution of the commitment to the anti-custody ethos over time (Smith 2007). While the ideas of minimum necessary intervention remained 'very influential' (respondent 9), by 1996, the National Association for Youth Justice (the AJJ's successor) had come to accept that responding to instances for non-compliance with supervision 'quickly and consistently' was indicative of good practice (National Association for Youth Justice 1996: 7).

New Labour's declared intent on coming to power in 1997, to 'draw a line under the past' (Straw 1997), was a reference to expunging the last vestiges of welfarist sentiment rather than signalling an end to the increasingly retributive spirit that informed youth justice policy (Goldson 2010). That intent was underlined by provision in section 72 and schedule 5 of the Crime and Disorder Act 1998 which allowed the imposition of custody for breach of any community sentence. The first discrete National Standards for youth justice, published in 2000 (Youth Justice Board 2000b), reinstated the option to stay breach 'in exceptional circumstances' with management approval, but in other respects the provisions in relation to enforcement were more rigorous than those established in 1995. After the first three months of any order, breach action was now required on the second missed appointment, irrespective of performance in the first 12 weeks (Youth Justice Board 2000b: paragraph 7.3.3).[8] The risk of a return to court was in any event heightened by an increase in the minimum level, from one to two, of weekly contacts during the early part of the order (paragraph 7.2.3). Later editions of youth justice standards, issued in 2004 and 2010, reverted to the more familiar formula of breach action on the third missed appointment, but, as if to emphasize pretentions to toughness, required that such action be initiated within five working days rather than ten (Youth Justice Board 2004, 2010b).

The challenges to a progressive youth justice practice were also exacerbated by structural reform. The creation of the YJB and the introduction of multi-agency Youth Offending Teams (YOTs), whatever their other merits, played a key role in dismantling ongoing support for the principle of minimum intervention (Holdaway et al. 2001). The Board was instrumental in promoting change by:

> stifling any 'off message' viewpoints and rubbishing the work of people who had held youth justice together pre-the 1997 Labour government.
>
> (respondent 8)

This process was reinforced by the dilution of the workforce from that earlier era. Existing youth justice staff found themselves outnumbered by colleagues new to the profession whose background did not predispose them to the same ideological identification with principles of diversion and decarceration (Souhami 2007). Pitts (2001: 8) has argued convincingly that these shifts in personnel were conducive to the emergence of an acquiescent practice that discouraged 'diversion from prescribed methods or procedures' – including those pertaining to enforcement.

There are no published data for breach of children during the 1990s. Those for adults subject to various forms of probation supervision show a rise of 176 per cent between 1993 and 2000 (Home Office 2004: table 5.4) and there seems little reason to suppose that a different pattern would prevail for those aged under 18 years. Certainly the views of survey respondents were consistent with such an assumption, reporting that practitioners' previous reluctance to return children to court had given way to a perception, in at least some areas, that breach was 'a success factor!' (respondent 7) or just part of the job: 'workers take the young people back to court at the earliest opportunity for non-compliance. As they are told to do' (respondent 1). The consequence, as one YOT operational manager confirmed, was that: 'We now breach more kids in a week than we used to in a whole year' (respondent 20). This anecdotal evidence is supported by figures from the early part of the last decade which demonstrate a three-fold rise in breach of supervision orders between 2000 and 2004 (Bateman 2006). As noted previously, subsequent data, compiled by the YJB, show an increase in disposals imposed for breach of a statutory order, which rose from 8256 in 2002/2003 to 15,877 in 2008/2009 (Bateman 2011). The 'enforcement paradigm', whether expressed as a mechanism for securing compliance or legitimacy, is thus more accurately represented as a consequence of the increased punitivism that has shaped youth justice policy development for much of the last two decades.

Enforcement as 'fast tracking to custody'

Rising levels of breach have coincided with increases in child imprisonment. There are no distinct youth justice figures for the 1990s, but between 2000 and 2004, as breach of supervision orders rose, so too did the proportion of children returned to court for non-compliance who were incarcerated, from 18 to 25 per cent (Bateman 2006). During 2010/11, 16 per cent of the population of the secure estate for children and young people had been imprisoned for breach of a statutory order (Ministry of Justice 2012a). By the time New Labour left office, non-compliance with orders imposed for offences which were not thought, at the original hearing, to warrant deprivation of liberty had become 'a significant factor' in shaping the size of the child prison population (Jacobson et al. 2010, p. vii).

As noted above, custodial rates for breach of ISSP have been particularly high: the number of children imprisoned for failure to comply with such a programme rose by 12 per cent between 2005/2006 and 2008/2009 (Bateman 2011). Far from robust enforcement increasing confidence in alternatives to custody provision, the capacity to provide such alternatives has been impaired by rigid adherence to breach procedures. Black and mixed heritage children are also more likely to be returned to court for non-compliance, no doubt contributing to continued minority ethnic over-representation within the secure estate (Ministry of Justice 2012a).

The relationship between deprivation of liberty and enforcement is perhaps most strikingly illustrated through the phenomenon of 'justice by geography'. It is well established that there is considerable variation in rates of youth custody from one area to another, which is not fully explained by local patterns of youth crime (Bateman and Stanley 2002). Rates at which children are returned to court for non-compliance with supervision also diverge markedly, and there is a significant positive correlation between enforcement practice and custodial sentencing: YOTs with increased rates of breach tend to exhibit higher levels of child imprisonment, and vice versa (Bateman 2011).

Rigorous enforcement thus appears not to have contributed to effective practice or increased confidence in non-custodial penalties. But, as one of the weapons in the penal arms race, maintained by a consensus politics determined to display its 'tough' credentials, the enforcement paradigm has functioned as a fast track to incarceration.

The prospects for a child-friendly enforcement

There have been welcome developments in the recent period: the number of children entering the youth justice system decreased by more than half between 2007/2008 and 2010/2011 (Ministry of Justice 2012a); and the child population of the secure estate has fallen by almost 40 per cent since April 2008 (Ministry of Justice 2012b). Further reductions in these measures constitute two of the three high-level targets for youth justice (Ministry of Justice 2010). There has been a corresponding decline in numbers of children returned to court for non-compliance – though the incidence of breach as a proportion of offences has remained broadly stable (Ministry of Justice 2012a).

At the same time, the coalition government has sought to distance itself from a target-driven managerialism and committed itself to 'increase discretion and reduce the amount of time frontline workers spend in front of their computers, so as to free up their time to work with young offenders' (Ministry of Justice 2010). In line with that commitment, the YJB has published 'trial National Standards to afford the maximum freedom and flexibility' consistent with maintaining public confidence and effective practice (Youth Justice Board 2012: 3). Provisions on enforcement are considerably altered. Rather than the standards dictating the circumstances when breach is triggered, practitioners are required to seek management approval if they elect not to return a child to court who displays 'a pattern of non-compliance' (Youth Justice Board 2012: 29).[9] This expanded discretion raises the prospect that the enforcement paradigm might give way to encouraging normative compliance through non-coercive, child-friendly, mechanisms built on:

- Ensuring that expectations of supervision are realistic
- Minimizing the potential for non-compliance (paying fares, arranging – or rearranging – appointments at times to suit the young person, home visiting and so on)
- Facilitating participation of children in planning supervision to ensure that they appreciate the relevance of intervention
- Making activities enjoyable (or even fun)
- Developing a relationship that promotes a perception on the part of the child that the supervisor's authority is exercised legitimately
- Acknowledging that the child may be a victim of social injustice as well as an offender
- Displaying empathetic understanding of any difficulties the child may have in complying
- Incorporating flexibility
- Maintaining, and evidencing to the child, a commitment to his or her well-being and to the interests of the order. (Eadie and Canton 2002; Hart 2011; Nacro 2002; Robinson and McNeill 2010:)

There are two considerations that might temper optimism, however. First, while the government is clearly open to the fiscal advantages delivered by a less interventionist youth justice system, and while increased diversion from prosecution and custody are no doubt indicative of a looser punitive grip (Pitts 2012), this relaxation – as the introductory paragraphs of this chapter affirm – continues to run alongside a rhetoric of firm enforcement. Moreover, the response of politicians and the courts to children caught up in the riots of August 2011 confirms that the political appetite for retributive exhortation is not yet exhausted: 32 per cent of children convicted for matters arising out of those episodes were imprisoned compared with 5.3 per cent for equivalent offences during 2010 (Ministry of Justice 2012c). These tensions continue to be played out, and the immediate future direction of policy is in the balance (Bateman 2012).

Second, the turn to punitivism was accompanied by a paradigm shift that saw responses to offending behaviour increasingly predicated on the minimization of risk posed rather than traditional goals of rehabilitation or retribution (Feeley and Simon 1992). While the two trends should not be conflated, Muncie (2006) has cogently argued that risk-led interventions are among the mechanisms by which more punitive outcomes are mediated. One consequence has been the emergence of a risk-averse youth justice culture that prioritizes precaution (Zedner 2008) over reflective practice and endorses toughness over tolerance (Kemshall 2008). Where there is a prospect of an individual allocation of blame in the event of things going awry, prudentialism may militate against a creative use of discretion. Practitioners might in such circumstances adopt a default position of continuing to breach routinely on the third missed appointment even when not required to do so, thereby undermining the potential afforded by less prescriptive guidance.

Such an outcome is not, of course, inevitable, but whether practice in relation to non-compliance is able to maximize the present opportunities to focus on engagement rather than enforcement depends, to a large extent, on the confidence of youth justice staff to operate outside the discourses that have, over the past two decades, dominated discussion of how to respond to children who do not cooperate with orders of the court.

Notes

1. Details are given in Bateman (2011).
2. Youth justice practice was subject to earlier editions of National Standards, but these were generic in nature, applying to children as well as adults. The establishment of the Youth Justice Board, by the Crime and Disorder Act 1998, led to the development of dedicated standards for youth justice.
3. This classification is not intended to be exhaustive. For other potential functions of youth justice enforcement, see Nacro (2002).
4. ISSP was non-statutory, operationalized through a combination of existing court orders. It has more recently been replaced by the ISS requirement of the youth rehabilitation order.
5. For a more extensive overview of the impact of the punitive turn on youth justice, see Bateman (2011).
6. Seventeen-year-olds within the criminal justice system were processed as adults until 1992.
7. The 'criminal care order' was available as a disposal for offending in the juvenile court until its abolition by the Children Act 1989.
8. In fact, this provision might function in contrary ways. Breach action was required on the third failure during the first 12 weeks of supervision, and on the second incident thereafter. Accordingly, a child issued with two warnings within the first three months might miss two further appointments before breach was required (a total of four episodes of non-compliance). Conversely, where a child attended all appointments during the first part of the order, a return to court might be triggered by a total of two missed appointments.
9. Unfortunately, as far as the youth rehabilitation order is concerned, the Criminal Justice and Immigration Act 2008 continues to mandate return to court for the third instance of failure to comply with the order. The revised draft National Standards make no reference to this tension.

References

Allen, R. (1991) 'Out of Jail: The Reduction in the Use of Penal Custody for Male Juveniles 1981–1988'. *Howard Journal for Penal Reform* 30(1), 30–52.

Allen, R. (2002) ' "There Must Be Some Way of Dealing with Kids": Young Offenders, Public Attitude and Policy Change'. *Youth Justice* 2(1), 3–13.

Association for Juvenile Justice (1990) *Guidance for Policy and Practice in Juvenile Justice.* Leicester: Association for Juvenile Justice.

Bateman, T. (2006) 'Large Rise in Breach of Supervision Orders'. *Youth Justice* 6(1), 77–78.

Bateman, T. (2011) ' "We Now Breach More Kids in a Week Than We Used to in a Whole Year": The Punitive Turn, Enforcement and Custody'. *Youth Justice* 11(2), 115–133.

Bateman, T. (2012) 'Who Pulled the Plug? Towards an Explanation of the Fall in Child Imprisonment in England and Wales'. *Youth Justice* 12(1), 36–52.

Bateman, T. and Stanley, C. (2002) *Patterns of Sentencing: Differential Sentencing Across England and Wales.* London: Youth Justice Board.

Bottoms, A. (2001) 'Compliance and Community Penalties'. in A. Bottoms, L. Gelsthorpe and S. Rex (Eds) *Community Penalties: Changes and Challenges* (pp. 87–116). Cullompton: Willan.

Cadman, S. (2005) 'Proportionality in the Youth Justice System'. in T. Bateman and J. Pitts (Eds) *The RHP Companion to Youth Justice.* Lyme Regis: Russell House.

Canton, R. and Eadie, T. (2005) 'Enforcement'. in T. Bateman and J. Pitts (Eds) *The RHP Companion to Youth Justice* (pp. 144–150). Lyme Regis: Russell House Publishing

Canton, R. and Patel, K. (2008) 'Enforcement'. in B. Goldson (Ed.) *Dictionary of Youth Justice* (pp. 157–158). Cullompton: Willan.

Chitty, C. (2005) 'The Impact of Corrections on Reoffending: Conclusions and the Way Forward'. in G. Harper and C. Chitty (Eds) *The Impact of Corrections on Re-Offending: A Review of 'What Works'.* Home Office research study 291. London: Home Office.

Cohen, S. (1985) *Visions of Social Control.* Cambridge: Polity Press.

Eadie, T. and Canton, R. (2002) 'Practicing in a Context of Ambivalence: The Challenge for Youth Justice Workers'. *Youth Justice* 2(1), 14–26.

Ellis, T., Hedderman, C. and Mortimer, E. (1996) *Enforcing Community Sentences: Supervisors' Perspectives on Ensuring Compliance and Dealing with Breach.* Home Office Research Study 158. London: Home Office.

Farmer, E. (2011) 'The Age of Criminal Responsibility: Developmental Science and Human Rights Perspectives'. *Journal of Children's Services* 6(2), 86–95.

Feeley, M. and Simon, J. (1992) 'The New Penology: Notes on the Emerging Strategy and Its Implications'. *Criminology* 30(4): 452–474.

Garland, D. (2001) *The Culture of Control: Crime and Social Order in Contemporary Society.* Oxford: Oxford University Press.

Goldson, B. (1997) 'Children in Trouble: State Responses to Juvenile Crime'. In P. Scraton (Ed.) *Childhood in Crisis.* London: University College Press.

Goldson, B. (Ed.) (2000) *The New Youth Justice.* Lyme Regis: Russell House Publishing.

Goldson, B. (2002) 'New Punitiveness: The Politics of Child Incarceration'. in J. Muncie, G. Hughes and E. McLaughlin (Eds) *Youth Justice: Critical Readings* (pp. 386–399). London: Sage.

Goldson, B. (2010) 'The Sleep of (Criminological) Reason: Knowledge–Policy Rupture and New Labour's Youth Justice Legacy'. *Criminology and Criminal Justice* 10(1), 155–178.

Gray, E., Taylor, E., Roberts, C., Merrington, S., Fernandez, R. and Moore, R. (2005) *Intensive Supervision and Surveillance Programme: The Final Report.* London: Youth Justice Board.

Great Britain (1988) *Criminal Justice Act 1988*. Elizabeth II. Chapter 33. London: The Stationery Office.

Haines, K. (2008) 'Tariff'. in B. Goldson (Ed.) *Dictionary of Youth Justice* (p. 351). Cullompton: Willan.

Haines, K. and Drakeford, M. (1998) *Young People and Youth Justice*. Basingstoke: Macmillan.

Hart, D. (2011) *Into the Breach: The Enforcement of Statutory Orders in the Youth Justice System*. London: Prison Reform Trust.

Hearnden, I. and Millie, A. (2004) 'Does Tougher Enforcement Lead to Lower Conviction'. *Probation Journal* 51(1), 48–58.

Hedderman, C. and Hearnden, I. (2000) *Improving Enforcement: The Second ACOP Audit*. London: ACOP.

Hedderman, C. and Hough, M. (2004) 'Getting Tough or Being Effective: What Matters?' in G. Mair (Ed.) *What Matters in Probation* (pp. 146–169). Cullompton: Willan.

Her Majesty's Government. (2008) *Youth Crime Action Plan 2008*. London: HM Government.

Holdaway, S., Davidson, N., Dignan, J., Hammersley, R., Hine, R. and Marsh, P. (2001) *New Strategies to Address Youth Offending: The National Evaluation of the Pilot Youth Offending Teams*. Occasional paper number 69. London: Home Office.

Home Office (1989) *Home Criminal Statistics: England and Wales 1988*. Cmnd 847. London: HMSO.

Home Office (1992) *National Standards for the Supervision of Offenders in the Community – 1992*. London: HMSO.

Home Office (1993) *Criminal Statistics: England and Wales 1992*. Cmnd. 2410. London: HMSO.

Home Office (1995) *National Standards for the Supervision of Offenders in the Community – 1995*. London: HMSO.

Home Office (1997) *No More Excuses: A New Approach to Tackling Youth Crime in England and Wales*. London: Home Office.

Home Office (2004) *Offender Management Caseload Statistics. Statistical Bulletin 15/04*. London: Home Office.

Jacobson, J., Bhardwa, B., Gyateng, T., Hunter, G. and Hough, M. (2010) *Punishing Disadvantage: A Profile of Children in Custody*. London: Prison Reform Trust.

Jones, D. (1989) 'The Successful Revolution'. *Community Care*, 30 March: i–ii.

Jones, T. (2010) 'Public Opinion, Politics and the Response to Youth Crime'. in D. Smith (Ed.) *A New Response to Youth Crime*. Cullompton: Willan.

Kemshall, H. (2008) 'Risks, Rights and Justice: Understanding and Responding to Youth Risk'. *Youth Justice* 8(1), 21–38.

McLaughlin, E., Muncie, J. and Hughes, G. (2001) 'The Permanent Revolution: New Labour, New Public Management and the Modernisation of Criminal Justice'. *Criminal Justice* 1(3), 301–318.

Mason, P. and Prior, D. (2008) *Engaging Young People Who Offend*. London: Youth Justice Board.

Matthews, R. (1999) *Doing Time: An Introduction to the Sociology of Imprisonment*. Basingstoke: Palgrave.

Matthews, R. (2005) 'The Myth of Punitiveness'. *Theoretical Criminology* 9(2), 175–201.

Ministry of Justice. (2010) *Breaking the Cycle: Effective Punishment, Rehabilitation and Sentencing of Offenders*. Cmnd 7972. London: The Stationery Office.

Ministry of Justice. (2012a) *Youth Justice Statistics 2010/11*. London: Ministry of Justice.

Ministry of Justice. (2012b) *Youth Custody Data April 2012*. London: Ministry of Justice.

Ministry of Justice. (2012c) *Statistical Bulletin on the Public Disorder of 6th to 9th August 2011–June 2012 Update*. London: Ministry of Justice.

Muncie, J. (2006) 'Governing Young People: Coherence and Contradiction in Contemporary Youth Justice'. *Critical Social Policy* 26(4): 770–793.

Muncie, J. (2009) *Youth and Crime*. Third Edition. London: Sage Publications.

Nacro. (1993) *Monitoring the Criminal Justice Act in the New Youth Court: The First Six Months 1 October 1992 to 31 March 1993*. London: Nacro.

Nacro. (2002) *Enforcement in the Youth Justice System*. Youth crime briefing. London: Nacro.

Nacro. (2003) *A Failure of Justice: Reducing Child Imprisonment*. London: Nacro.

Nacro. (2005) *A Better Alternative: Reducing Child Imprisonment*. London: Nacro.

National Association for Youth Justice. (1996) *Policy and Practice Guidelines for Youth Justice*. Glenfield: NAYJ.

Newburn, T. (2003) *Crime and Criminal Justice Policy*. Harlow: Longman.

Pitts, J. (2001) 'Korrectional Karaoke: New Labour and the Zombification of Youth Justice'. *Youth Justice* 1(2), 3–16.

Pitts, J. (2003) 'Changing Youth Justice'. *Youth Justice* 3(1), 3–18.

Pitts, J. (2004) 'What Do We Want? The "SHAPE" Campaign and the Reform of Youth Justice'. *Youth Justice* 3(3), 134–151.

Pitts, J. (2012) 'The Third Time as Farce: Whatever Happened to the Penal State?' in J. Lea and P. Squires (Eds) *Criminalisation and Advanced Marginality: Critically Exploring the Work of Loïc Wacquant*. Bristol: Policy Press.

Prior, D. and Mason, P. (2010) 'A Different Kind of Evidence? Looking for "What Works" in Engaging Young Offenders'. *Youth Justice* 10(3), 211–236.

Roberts, J. and Hough, M. (Eds) (2002) *Changing Attitudes to Punishment: Public Opinion, Crime and Justice*. Cullompton: Willan.

Robinson, G. and McNeill, F. (2010) 'The Dynamics of Compliance with Offender Supervision'. in F. McNeill, P. Raynor and C. Trotter (Eds) *Offender Supervision: New Directions in Theory, Research and Practice* (pp. 367–383). Cullompton: Willan.

Robinson, G. and Ugwudike, P. (2012) 'Investing in "Toughness": Probation Enforcement and Legitimacy'. *Howard Journal of Criminal Justice* 51(3), 300–316.

Rutherford, A. (1992) *Growing Out of Crime*. Second Edition. Winchester: Waterside Press.

Smith, R. (2007) *Youth Justice: Ideas, Policy and Practice*. Second Edition. Cullompton: Willan.

Souhami, A. (2007) *Transforming Youth Justice: Occupational Change and Identity*. Cullompton: Willan.

Straw, J. (1997) 'Preface by the Home Secretary'. in Home Office *No More Excuses: A New Approach to Tackling Youth Crime in England and Wales*. London: Home Office.

Tonry, M. (2007) 'Determinants of Penal Policies'. in M. Tonry (Ed.) *Crime, Punishment and Politics in Comparative Perspective. Crime and Justice: A Review of Research* 36, 1–48.

Youth Justice Board. (2000a) *Intensive Supervision and Surveillance Programmes*. London: YJB.

Youth Justice Board. (2000b) *National Standards for Youth Justice – April 2000*. London: YJB.

Youth Justice Board. (2004) *National Standards for Youth Justice Services – 2004*. London: YJB.

Youth Justice Board. (2010a) *Case Management Guidance: Planning and Delivering Interventions in the Community*. London: YJB.

Youth Justice Board. (2010b) *National Standards For Youth Justice Services – 2010.* London: YJB.

Youth Justice Board. (2012) *National Standards Trial: April 2012–April 2013.* London: YJB.

Zedner, L. (2008) 'Fixing the Future? The Pre-Emptive Turn in Criminal Justice'. In B. McSherry, A. Norrie and S. Bronitt (Eds) *Regulating Deviance: The Redirection of Criminalisation and the Futures of Criminal Law.* Oxford: Hart.

18

Achieving Compliance with Drug-Misusing Offenders: Challenges for the Probation Service

Paul Sparrow

Introduction

Drug misusers, especially those at the heavier end of the addiction spectrum, have always posed a number of challenges for the probation service. An increase in the level of criminality, often a feature of habitual drug use, combined with a propensity toward a chaotic lifestyle and an inclination toward relapse make drug users particularly difficult to hold in treatment and vulnerable to breaching the terms and conditions of court-mandated supervision (Turnbull et al. 2000). While in the past both courts and probation officers have had the opportunity to respond to drug users in breach of community orders in a variety of ways, recent legislation, designed to firm up probation, has resulted in an erosion of practitioner autonomy, a significant curtailment of the courts' powers and the imposition of limited number of options available to sentencers when dealing with instances of offender non-compliance.

Getting to grips with drugs: The arrival of HIV and the new modes of practice

Although the problem of drug misuse among offenders is not entirely new to the probation service (see Dawtry 1968), prior to the early 1980s the absence of a critical mass of criminally active users meant that the service was able to regard its existence as a minority activity, catered for in the main by the medical profession and bolstered by the support of a small number of voluntary agencies and an even smaller number of interested probation officers (Bean 1974; Page 1992; Turner 2005). From the early 1980s, however, the United Kingdom was witness to an unprecedented and dramatic influx of heroin and, as a consequence, a noticeable and significant increase in the number of notified addicts (Pearson 1991). The Advisory Council on the Misuse of Drugs (AMCD)

315

commented at the time that its best estimate suggested that by the mid-1980s Britain would have had somewhere between 75,000 and 150,000 misusers of notifiable drugs.

Given estimations such as these, it is perhaps not entirely surprising that existing drug service providers found both the scale of the problem and the rapidity of the escalation almost entirely overwhelming. Numbers alone, however, were not the defining feature of this new wave of illicit drug users; in terms of geographical distribution, mode of administration, economic position and connection with crime, these new users differed radically from their predecessors. Preferring to source their supplies on the street and to support their habit through crime, this new wave of young, white heroin users proved significantly more difficult to entice into the drug clinic than their predecessors. Within this context it was no longer possible for the probation service to regard the drug abuser as outside its official focus of attention.

The policy and practice agenda in illicit drug use has always struggled to maintain pace with variations in the user population (MacGregor 1989a). To this end, there was broad agreement that the medical profession alone was ill equipped to bring the rapidly increasing drugs problem under control (Stimson and Oppenheimer 1982). In recognizing the fact that drug clinics, established some 20 years earlier to deal with a very different user population, were unlikely to be in a position to deal with the range of social, personal and legal problems presented by the 'new addict', the ACMD saw considerable merit in widening the practice community's understanding of the drug user. '[W]e consider that the traditional orientation towards the treatment of specific forms of addiction, often substance based, is too narrow; a broader approach oriented towards responding to a whole range of problems encountered by drug misusers will facilitate the development of more effective services' (ACMD 1982: 2). The Council's suggestion, therefore, was that the addict, traditionally understood by reference to compulsion and craving (MacGregor 1989a, 1989b), ought to be reconceptualized as 'the problem drug taker'. The approach, they suggested, needed to be 'problem oriented rather than specifically client or substance labelled' (ACMD 1982, para. 5.13). This definition sought to encompass 'any person who experiences social, psychological or legal problems related to intoxication and/or regular excessive consumption and/or dependence as a consequence of his own use of drugs or other chemical substances (excluding alcohol and tobacco)' (ACMD 1982, para. 11.4).

Not only did this new definition seek to encompass the broad range of needs likely to be found in the new drug-using population, but, more importantly, the Advisory Council saw the need to open the field of addictions to a whole range of new service providers that could support the pre-existing system of medical intervention. The Council called for 'a more co-ordinated approach, at both national and local levels, which can ensure an effectively structured organisation of existing specialized services working with non-specialists' (ACMD 1982, p. 2). Within this context probation was defined as a non-specialist, but nevertheless crucial, service. 'In areas where there are few specialist services it is clear that the probation and after-care service is likely to be a major source of advice and support' (ACMD 1982, para. 6.41).

The 1991 Criminal Justice Act and drug misusers: An opportunity not quite realized

The bulk of research into the 'new' drug users during the 1980s had provided compelling evidence of a group of disenfranchised, multiply disadvantaged individuals whose relentless criminal inclinations (mostly acquisitive in nature) propelled them invariably toward custody. It was this category of offender, the persistent petty criminal whose prison sentence often owed far more to the number of court appearances than it did to the seriousness of the crime, that the 1991 Act hoped to subsume under its punishment in the community rubric. In terms specifically of drug users, therefore, the 1991 Act offered, at least in theory (Goodsir 1992; Lee 1994), a legislative framework capable of diverting the chaotic, petty, recidivist offender away from the routine cycle of short-term imprisonment (Kothari et al. 2002).

The emergence of HIV during the late 1980s had forced the issue of drug use to a prominent position on the government's agenda. Indeed, three years prior to the 1991 Act the Advisory Council had announced that 'HIV is a greater threat to public and individual health than drug misuse. The first goal of work with drug misusers therefore must be to prevent them from acquiring or transmitting the virus' (ACMD 1988: 1). In its follow-up report, the ACMD (1989) noted with great concern that drug users formed the fastest-growing population with AIDS in the country at that time, and, premised on the belief that the probation service was likely to come into contact with more drug users than most generic statutory agencies (ACMD 1988), the service was tasked with both the identification of drug users and developing a model of practice that incorporated a public health dimension into the community supervision of offenders.

The Advisory Council stated categorically what many involved with the Service had suspected for some time: 'that drug misusers form a significant part of their caseload' (ACMD 1991: para 2.6). The AMCD maintained that the probation service ought to be regarded as 'a crucial agent for change in the way that drug misusers are dealt with by the criminal justice system' (ACMD 1991: para 2.11). Above all, the report had high hopes for the 1991 Criminal Justice Act. It noted that the ACMD had 'long argued that community sentences are likely to be a more effective way than prison of dealing with less serious drug-misusing offenders, in terms of the protection of the public, the prevention of

reoffending and the successful re-integration of the offender in the community'
(ACMD 1991: para 2.8). In clear support of the legislation, it stated that the Act
'will lead to fewer drug misusing offenders receiving custodial sentences and
that greater use will be made of alternative disposals' (ACMD 1991: para 4.7).

Coming into effect in October 1992, the 1991 Criminal Justice Act introduced, for the first time, a statutory framework for attaching to probation orders
a condition of treatment for drug or alcohol dependency where the court was
satisfied, first, that such dependency had contributed to the commission of
the offence, and, second, that the dependency was likely to be responsive to
treatment (see Wasik and Taylor 1994). According to the ACMD, the probation
service was 'in an ideal position to promote the early disclosure of drug misuse.
We recommend that Probation Officers should ask all offenders about the possibility of drug misuse. We believe this is good practice even in cases where there
is no obvious indication that drug misuse is an issue' (ACMD 1991: para 3.14).

Drug users' experience of the criminal justice system, however, had not
always been positive (Hough 1996; Rumgay 2000). Fear of harsher sentences in
court (Collison 1993, 1994) and an unrealistic focus on abstinence had created a
climate within which probation clients could claim good reason to engage with
supervision at no more than a superficial level (Briton 1995; Nee and Sibbitt
1993). However, driven by the belief that HIV was a greater threat to both public and individual health than drug misuse (ACMD 1988), the Advisory Council
made it clear that it was 'imperative for services to make contact with many
more of the large hidden population of injecting drug misusers and to offer
them services on terms they are willing to accept: where courses of treatment
which demand total abstinence prove unacceptable to misusers, they must be
supplemented by interventions such as needle exchanges and substitute prescribing which recognize the existence of a hierarchy of goals and mitigate
the worst consequences of misuse. This harm reduction philosophy has been
widely accepted by workers in the field of drug misuse, and we believe that
the circumstances of drug misusing offenders require an analogous approach'
(ACMD 1991: para 3.9).

While being supported in the continuation of drug use was an approach with
which most addicts felt able to engage, permitting drug users to continue with
an illicit lifestyle was not something that reconciled easily with the service's
duty to the court. The solution, as far as the AMCD was concerned, lay in the
development of partnerships between probation and drug service providers.
'In our view the very real difficulties which arise from the tension between
health and law and order objectives can be solved if all parties – criminal
justice agencies, treatment providers and misusers themselves – have a clear
understanding of each other's expectations' (para. 3.11). Such a view, however, was always overly optimistic and failed to acknowledge the chasm which
existed between the criminal justice sector and the range of agencies that had

begun to emerge in response to the problem of drug misuse. As Smith et al. (1993) noted at the time, 'much counselling in the voluntary sector (and in the health service) depends for its success on confidentiality and on a low-key, non threatening approach, often stressing harm minimisation (e.g. smoking heroin instead of injecting it, or injecting it sensibly rather than stupidly) rather than abstinence... But abstinence, in the case of heroin and other widely used drugs, is a legal requirement, and one which an agency charged, as the probation service now is, with delivering "punishment in the community" cannot readily ignore' (pp. 34–35).

There is no doubt that the opportunities which the AMCD saw in the 1991 Act fell some way short of what the probation service was able to deliver. Perhaps not surprisingly, therefore, just two years after the Advisory Council's recommendations Nee and Sibbitt reported that 'very few probation services had a formal policy on drug misuse' (p. iv), and in the same year the Probation Inspectorate described the service's work with drug users as 'piecemeal and... as a response to individual events or pressures rather than as part of any strategic planning' (HMIP 1993: para 5.1). In terms specifically of harm reduction, Nee and Sibbitt (1993) observed that, while individual probation officers often attempted to mirror the harm reduction approach of local drug service providers, the probation services in their survey '... were often unaware of the full implications of this or had failed to resolve the resultant dilemmas created for probation practice' (p. 42).

For all the optimism around the 1991 Act, the legislation had deliberately distanced probation from its 'welfare' origins (Sparrow and Webb 2004), and in introducing nationally agreed standards of supervision it had removed much of the discretion which probation officers might previously have used in trying to engage those at the chaotic end of their caseload. A good deal of the 1991 Criminal Justice Act's potency had rested on its intention to match seriousness of the offence with an appropriate sentence. In so far as drug misusers were concerned, then, the expectation was that the Act would shield such individuals from prison sentences based simply on their accumulation of petty offences and as a consequence reserve the treatment condition for those who were at serious risk of custody. During the first six months of the Act, however, only 61 conditions were made; over half of these were in the magistrates' court and most of them had been imposed on low-level acquisitive offenders. While the profile of these offenders was broadly in line with the new heroin users identified in the late 1980s, the fact that such individuals found themselves in receipt of sanctions that exceeded the proportionality criteria was a serious cause for concern, and certainly contrary to the intentions of the 1991 legislation.

In truth, the optimism offered by the new sentencing structure of the 1991 Act had been relatively short-lived. Amendments contained in the 1993 Criminal Justice Act and the 1994 Criminal Justice and Public Order Act reconnected sentencing practice with the 'culture of severity' that had been identified some years earlier (Allen 1990), and this, combined with the tendency of probation officers to overestimate the level of seriousness for fear of appearing unrealistic with sentencers, resulted in the doling out of disproportionately harsh sentences (Drakeford 1993). As far as the drug users were concerned, while this meant a return to punishment at the expense of treatment (Henham 1994, 1996), it also reaffirmed the legitimacy of their long-standing strategy of minimizing their drug use in dealings with probation officers. For many drug users, then, engagement with the service amounted to little more than perfunctory adherence to the routine of appointments where that was possible, and where it was not offenders often abandoned supervision altogether, based on the belief that there was little, if anything, of relevance on offer (HMIP 1993; Nee and Sibbitt 1993).

Despite the early expectations of the 1991 Act, the standardization of supervision and the reduction in probation officer discretion that accompanied the legislation worked against a number of the more chaotic offender groups, drug users included. As a number of authors have shown (Collison 1993; Lee 1994), once drawn into the criminal justice system drug users often lose their victim status and are dealt with 'via the logic(s) of punishment and deterrence...' (Collison 1993: 384) Although, arguably, one of the key tasks of the probation officer is to militate against the worst excesses of the judiciary, there is some evidence to suggest that probation officers themselves regarded drug users as an unpalatable group, and as a consequence a number within the profession struggled to contradict the court's view of the 'typical addict' (Collison 1993; Lee 1994).

The limited success of the 1991 Criminal Justice Act for drug users cannot be understood simply as a result of the punitive drift which emerged in the early 1990s (Raynor and Vanstone 2007), and neither is it just a function of individual probation officers having a dislike of chaotic offenders. The hopes for the treatment condition originally contained within the Act, and its subsequent failure to deliver drug users into the hands of specialist services, need to be understood within the much broader context of the fight against drugs and drug users which emerged in the mid-1990s and which, as a consequence, shifted the agenda for drug treatment from health to crime reduction.

Drug treatment and testing orders: Achieving abstinence by instruction

Just over a decade ago Garland (2001) observed that 'the once-dominant welfarist criminology that depicted the offender as poorly socialized or disadvantaged...has become increasingly irrelevant to policy-makers...' (p. 137). As a consequence, the once imprecise ground between deviant and patient occupied by the drug user, a position typified in the harm reduction model, has become ever more intolerable to politicians and policy makers alike. Perhaps not surprisingly, therefore, one of the key objectives of government over the past 15 years or so has been to focus much more overtly on reducing levels of repeat offending among drug users (HM Government 1998). Underpinned by evidence which suggested that a small number of addicts were responsible for a disproportionately large amount of crime (Gossop 1996), successive governments have felt ever more justified in demanding treatment programmes that clearly demonstrate a reduction in criminal behaviour. Thus, while not entirely negating the value of harm reduction, certainly from the mid-1990s onward there has been a conspicuous step change in the agenda for working with drug users; one that has seen crime reduction elevated above health.

Introduced as part of the 1998 Crime and Disorder Act, the Drug Treatment and Testing Order (DTTO) was rooted in the presumption that dependency was the key driver to drug users' criminality. Intended for those whose persistent offending placed them at serious risk of custody (Kothari et al. 2002) and designed broadly with the American Drug Court system in mind (Bean 2002), the purpose of the order was the achievement of total abstinence and, as a consequence, a cessation of all criminal behaviour (see Home Office 1998). Most crucially, the DTTO differed from the treatment condition contained in the 1991 CJA in two important respects. First, the order explicitly required the offender to submit themselves to routine testing for the use of illegal substances, and, second, the Act allowed for the court to receive regular review hearings, and with these the right to amend or even revoke the order depending on the progress made by the offender.

The initial pilot of the DTTO in Gloucestershire, Croydon and Liverpool gave considerable cause for concern. Many of the implementation difficulties were reminiscent of those that had beset the 1991 Act, most particularly the difficulties of creating working partnerships between drug treatment providers and the probation service. If these had been important for the effective working of the 1991 Act's treatment condition, they were critical to an order which had at its heart a contractual arrangement between the probation service, in terms of providing judicial oversight of the order, and treatment providers, in terms of providing specialist input to reduce dependency on drugs. There is no doubt that the imbalance in power in the DTTO, which favoured the criminal justice agencies (probation service and courts) over treatment providers, was deliberate, and thus not only reaffirmed the DTTO as a sanction of the court but also reasserted the order's primary objective as a reduction in offending (Kothari et al. 2002).

The DTTO was officially rolled out in England and Wales in October 2000, before the pilot evaluation had been completed. Bean (2002) concluded that this hasty implementation of the order amounted to a political decision, and certainly not one based on the weight of empirical evidence. Indeed, following the final evaluation, Bean further concluded that the results pointed to a failure in training, preparation and planning which, collectively, did not lead to a measure of confidence in the new order. While a full national evaluation of the DTTO was never commissioned, in the years thereafter there was every reason to believe that services around the country continued to experience many of the same problems identified in the initial pilot regions (Turner 2004; Falk 2004).

The suppression of harm minimization to the requirement to become drug free, combined with the implementation of National Standards which required supervising officers to initiate breach proceedings after two unacceptable absences, tested, during the pilot and beyond, the very best efforts of a significant number of DTTO clients (Quinn and Barton 2000). By the end of the DTTO pilot, and despite significant variations in enforcement regimes between the piloting areas, over half of the offenders (57 per cent) had breached the terms and conditions of their order, 46 per cent had had their sentence revoked (Turnbull et al. 2000), and, in the two years following national rollout, Cuppleditch and Evans (2005) reported that the 24-month reconviction rate for DTTOs stood at 89 per cent.

While the idea of using the probation service as a conduit to treatment for drug users has considerable merit, and certainly this was not a new idea (Dawtry 1968), the drugs to crime equation upon which the DTTO was based was unrealistically simplistic (Stevens et al. 2005; see also Burr 1987). Drug users present with a multiplicity of problems, and a successful response is one that manages to mirror that complexity. Notwithstanding the myriad of implementation problems, however, and in no small part due to the relentless efforts of interested officers, for some the DTTO was a workable and constructive sanction that paid significant dividends (Hales 2002; HM Inspectorate of Probation 2003). Between 2002 and 2004 completion rates for the DTTO rose from 25 per cent to 34 per cent (Home Office 2005), and, where services (probation and drugs) were able to successfully engage offenders and, crucially, where drug users were 'held' in treatment even following a breach, the DTTO was able to demonstrate success in terms of reducing both drug use and associated criminality (Hough et al. 2003; Turnbull et al. 2000).

2003 Criminal Justice Act: Not exactly the therapeutic court!

Despite its best efforts to implement the DTTO, 'the probation service's spirited attempts to make a success out of an order whose legacy owed at least as much to political posturing as it did to strategic foresight was never likely to guarantee protection from future policy upheaval' (Sparrow and McIvor 2013).

As the probation service continued to work through the complexities presented by health and criminal justice partnerships (see Rumgay 2000), the government embarked on its next round of legislative upheaval (Fowles 2006) in the form of the 2003 Criminal Justice Act.

While a full discussion of the 2003 Act is beyond the scope of this chapter, certainly as it applies to the sentencing of drug misusers the legislation presents a number of challenges. Chief among these is the removal of the principle not to sentence offenders based on their previous record (Ashworth and Player 2005). Proportionality had been the linchpin of the 1991 CJA, and, although provisions in the 1993 CJA had meant that the primacy of the current offence had been relatively short-lived, section 143 (2) of the 2003 Act states clearly that 'courts must treat each previous conviction as an aggravating factor if the conviction is recent and relevant to the current offence' (Ashworth and Player 2005: 827).

In terms specifically of sentences available to the courts, the 2003 Act finally brings to an end the range of community sentences that had previously been available and replaces them with a single generic community sentence, to which sentencers attach one or more of 12 possible requirements. Where previously the court would have imposed a DTTO, the judiciary now imposes a Drug Rehabilitation Order (DRR).

There is no doubt that the old DTTO and the DRR share a common heritage. Like its predecessor, the DRR can range from six months to three years, and it is broadly designed to 'catch' those who are dependent on, or have a propensity to misuse, drugs, and where the drug user is likely to benefit from treatment (Sparrow and McIvor 2013). Above all, the DRR contains the two defining features of its predecessor, namely, the court's right to monitor progress through regular review and the requirement that offenders submit to repeated drug testing.

Beyond these similarities, however, the DRR differs from the DTTO in two very important ways. First, the DRR is intended for a wider drug-using population than the DTTO, which had, generally, been reserved for class A drug users. The intention here is to increase access to court-ordered treatment for those whose drug use might, hitherto, have been considered below the threshold necessary for the DTTO (Hollingworth 2008). Second, and perhaps most significantly, courts will no longer have the option to take no action on a breach (McSweeney et al. 2007). Instead, courts now choose one of the three options available to them: they can revoke the order and resentence, having regard to any progress made during the order; impose a period of imprisonment on the offender, even when the original offence was not imprisonable, but only up to a maximum of 51 weeks; or add additional requirements to the existing DRR in order to make the remaining period of supervision more onerous (Gibson 2004).

As has been argued elsewhere, any one of these responses to non-compliance poses potentially serious problems for offenders (Sparrow and McIvor 2013). Given that for many appearing before the breach court a period of imprisonment now tends to look like a distinct possibility, the prospect of additional requirements added to an existing DRR appears, at first sight, to be a successful outcome.

As Ashworth and Player (2005) have observed, however, 'fundamental to sentencing guidelines, and particularly to any kind of comprehensive system, is agreement on the purposes of sentencing' (p. 825). Under previous sentencing regimes, and certainly under the 1991 Act, sentencers were encouraged to strike a balance between punishment and rehabilitation. For this process to be meaningful, however, it must involve 'thinking about what offenders are capable of managing, and whilst not "overloading" offenders might appear to hark back to the days when probation was indistinguishable from social work, this does not stop such an approach having considerable merit' (Sparrow and McIvor 2013 p. 304). Within this context, then, the possibility of demanding more from offenders who have already demonstrated an inability to abide by the terms and conditions of an order might run counter to what passes for encouraging compliance.

The ultimate justification of court-mandated drug treatment is that coercion is effective, but in truth this represents a somewhat imprecise and loose interpretation of the evidence. Certainly research does suggest that coerced intervention is no less effective than voluntary involvement (Stevens et al. 2005), but, as the National Treatment Outcome Reconviction Study (Gossop et al. 2001) has shown, there is still much to be gained from ensuring that the mode of treatment is a match to the needs of the particular client. It is not simply that any treatment works, but, rather, that some treatment works with some people in certain circumstances (Raynor and Vanstone 2007). As McSweeney et al. (2007) recognized, 'desistence from drug use and offending behaviours will not necessarily be triggered by corralling an ever increasing number of drug-using offenders into treatment' (p. 486).

Drug addiction, or more accurately recovery from drug addiction, rarely emerges as a 'one go success story' (see Klingermann 1994; Prins 1994; Washton 1989). As McIntosh and McKeganey (2002) have observed, while addicts will regularly embark on 'numerous attempts to escape from their addiction . . . the great majority of these end in failure' (p. 90). Given that substance misuse stands as one of the strongest predictors of breach for community sentences (Gyateng et al. 2010; Kirby et al. 2011), it is not surprising that failure in the addict community emerges as a regular and expected feature of probation-based supervision. Within the context of a court-enforced order, however, viewing 'relapse as a near certainty in the cycle of recovery . . . poses, potentially, a number of very serious problems' (Sparrow and McIvor 2013 p. 308).

While McIntosh and McKeganey (2002) would not necessarily dismiss the benefit of relapse, arguing that even brief spells of abstinence provide a crucial opportunity for an addict to draw a contrast between their old self and the aspiration for a different future, it might be difficult to argue the same for breach of a community sentence. If the idea that returning offenders to court is either beneficial, or at least not damaging to them, has always been difficult to defend (Sparrow and Webb 2004), then under the restrictive provisions of the 2003 CJA these positions seem even more insecure.

As has been noted elsewhere, probationers comply with the conditions of their order for a whole variety of reasons (Farrall 2002). For some, compliance will amount to no more than formal obedience with the rules of the order, whereas for others, and this must surely be the aspiration for the probation service, offenders will demonstrate substantive, long-term compliance whereby they actively engage with the content of the order and seek to bring about lasting change in their beliefs and behaviour. As Robinson and McNeill (2008: 438) have pointed out, however, such compliance behaviour 'will not necessarily remain static over time'. Indeed, the 'elasticity of compliance', to which they refer, is particularly true for drug-addicted offenders, for whom the motivation to become drug free has a well-evidenced tendency to ebb and flow (McIntosh and McKeganey 2002).

For a number of authors (Kirby et al. 2011; McIntosh and McKeganey 2002; Stimson and Oppenheimer 1982), a successful route out of addiction rests on timing. 'The decision to stop taking drugs is, of course, fundamental to any attempt to recovery. Although it carries no guarantee of success, it is nevertheless a decisive moment in the addict's career since, without it, it is unlikely that recovery will take place at all' (McIntosh and McKeganey 2002: 42). Whether entered into voluntarily or under a legal obligation, engendering a motivation to end drug use and then sustaining that desire is crucial to success. As we have noted earlier, however, both the initial enthusiasm and then the continuing drive to achieve abstinence are rarely constant features on the road from dependency. Accepting failure as an integral feature of recovery, the crucial issue, and the one which distinguishes a voluntary undertaking from court-mandated treatment, is how the various services respond to this failure.

Certainly during the early stages of treatment, staying drug free can be a major challenge for a large proportion of dependent users (Sparrow and McIvor 2013). In addition to the physical craving for drugs (Gossop et al. 1991), ex-users regularly experience a sense of loss as they shift away from a familiar lifestyle and feelings of isolation and vulnerability as old coping mechanisms become prohibited (Bradley et al. 1989). Under these circumstances, breach of a DRR and a return to the court has the potential to be a pivotal moment in the cycle of recovery.

Under the provisions of the 2003 CJA, the only sanction now available to the breach court, short of prison, is the addition of extra requirements. While this does have the obvious attraction of avoiding incarceration, 'the likelihood of breach and reconviction has been shown to increase significantly in line with the number of requirements imposed on an offender' (Kirby et al. 2011: 3). Thus, a system which is high on short-term compliance (Robinson and McNeill 2008) and which, as a consequence, prioritizes frequency of contact over quality of intervention is unlikely to serve well those clients who might be committed to long-term change, but whose lifestyles, in the case of drug misusers, work against a regimented regime.

Despite the dangers for those offenders returning to court for non-compliance, there is an increasing body of research which suggests that, under the right circumstances, courts can exercise a very positive influence over the outcome of treatment. To date, the so-called 'therapeutic court' has performed well across a variety of areas, and certainly in the field of drug abuse the American Drug Court has shown considerable success (Belenko 1998). Notwithstanding the variations in the American Drug Court model that have emerged since its inception in the late 1980s, they nevertheless continue to unite around notions of positive reinforcement, individualized sentences and an operational procedure that has moved away from the tradition of an adversarial approach to justice.

While there is little doubt that Drug Courts in the United States have proved both popular and successful, the level of flexibility which has come to define them is certainly not mirrored in the legislative framework currently at play in England and Wales. Indeed, as Kirby et al. (2011) have pointed out, despite calls from within both the criminal justice and substance misuse arenas, 'probation and court services have tended to be punishment-orientated in approach and involved the imposition of negative sanctions in response to non-compliance' (p. 6). By way of some contrast, however, it is worth noting that recent legislation in Scotland in the form of the 2010 Criminal Justice and Licensing (Scotland) Act has attempted to build in more judicial flexibility than is the case in the 2003 CJA, and as a consequence Scottish courts have had some degree of success with their more traditional version of the Drug Court. There may be much to be learned from following developments in the Scottish jurisdiction in the years to come (see McIvor 2009; McIvor et al. 2006).

Conclusion

Engaging drug misusers in treatment, particularly within the restrictive framework of the 2003 CJA, poses a number of significant challenges. By its very nature, drug addiction is a chronic and relapsing condition (Kirby et al. 2011), and as a consequence drug users have a tendency to be chaotic, unreliable and prone to drifting in and out of treatment (McIntosh and McKeganey 2002). As I have argued elsewhere, we should not deny the fact that in funding their habit through crime drug users do pose a very real threat to communities. At the same time, however, and certainly at the heavier end of the abuse spectrum, those engaged in habitual drug abuse also do considerable harm to themselves (Sparrow and McIvor 2013). The challenge for criminal justice policy, then, is the reconciliation of these two seemingly incompatible goals, the protection of the public on the one hand and the effective rehabilitation of the offender on the other.

'[T]he assumption that swifter and surer enforcement will ultimately drive up rates of compliance (e.g. HMIP 2007, p. S3.1) is arguably misconceived, and it is not supported by the research to date. Indeed, the opposite appears to be true' (Robinson and McNeill 2008: 443). Currently, around two-fifths of all community orders end in breach, and, comparing them with the range of orders that pre-date the 2003 CJA, Mair and Mills (2009) have noted that both the Community Order and the Suspended Sentence Order have higher breach rates than their predecessors; a fact which they describe as 'not surprising...' but most definitely 'disturbing...' (p.14).

Establishing the punitive credentials of the probation service has been a near obsession for policy makers over the past two decades, and this has certainly been noticeable where drug users are concerned. The quest to intensify the constraining qualities of community sentences has collided with a war on both drugs and drug abusers (Buchanan and Young 2000) to produce sentences which now, arguably, misunderstand the very nature of the problem they seek to address. As a possible antidote to this deep-rooted, punishment-orientated approach to non-compliance, McSweeney (2010) has suggested that there may be more to gain by considering criminal justice-based interventions 'within a 'career' perspective as described by the broader recovery and criminological desistance literature. These perspectives have charted the trajectories of drug use and offending careers – with a beginning (initiation/onset), middle (increased frequency of use/offending and associated problems) and end (recovery/desistance) – over the course of many years, with intermittent contact with drug treatment services and the criminal justice system during this time' (p. 179).

The reasons why offenders do or do not engage with probation supervision are numerous and complex. At the same time, the decision to stop using drugs can be equally convoluted and tortuous. Within the intricate process of interaction between officer and client, a number of key mechanisms do emerge as potentially salient factors in facilitating compliance. First, evidence suggests that when goals of supervision are agreed between officer and client they are more likely to promote engagement than when objectives are imposed by the officer on the offender (Compton and Galaway 1994). Second, offenders are more likely to shift from requirement compliance to active engagement if supervision offers them something that is both useful and meaningful to them (see Farrall 2002). Finally, addiction is a relapsing condition; there is much to be gained from working with this reality and seeing relapse as an inevitable occurrence during the process of achieving abstinence.

It seems unlikely that the current legislative framework, in the form of the 2003 CJA, allows probation practitioners to deliver a flexible and responsive service to drug-misusing offenders. The desire to establish what works in terms of reducing offending appears to have taken place with relatively scant attention given to what works in compliance. While there is little evidence to suggest elevating threat over persuasion, the current approach to enforcement appears strangely fixated with the quantity rather than the quality of contact. As I have argued elsewhere, any approach to enforcement which focuses on the number of absences at the expense of other salient features of a case is unlikely to encourage compliance (Sparrow and McIvor 2013). Indeed, working on the 'assumption that the driver to effective intervention with offenders is a robust assessment of risk and need, then surely any response to non-compliance needs to be just as firmly rooted in these judgements. It is the assessment of risk and an appraisal of progress therefore, rather than simply the calculation of absences, which might form the basis of a more flexible approach to enforcement with, logically, a more graduated range of penalties from which to respond' (Sparrow and McIvor 2013).

References

Advisory Council on the Misuse of Drugs. (1982) *Treatment and Rehabilitation*. London: HMSO.

Advisory Council on the Misuse of Drugs. (1988) *AIDS and Drug Misuse Part 1*. London: HMSO.

Advisory Council on the Misuse of Drugs. (1989) *AIDS and Drug Misuse Part 2*. London: HMSO.

Advisory Council on the Misuse of Drugs. (1991) *Drug Misusers and the Criminal Justice System, Part 1: Community Resources and the Probation Service*. London: HMSO.

Allen, R. (1990) 'Punishment in the Community'. in P. Carter, T. Jeffs and D. Smith (Eds) *Social Work and Social Welfare Yearbook 2* (pp. 29–41). Buckingham: Open University Press.

Ashworth, A. and Player, E. (2005) 'Criminal Justice Act 2003: The Sentencing Provisions'. *The Modern Law Report* 68(5), 822–838.

Bean, P. (1974) *The Social Control of Drugs*. Martin Robertson and Company.

Bean, P. (2002) *Drugs and Crime*. Cullompton: Willan.

Belenko, S. (1998) *Research on Drug Courts: A Critical Review*. New York: National Centre on Addiction and Substance Abuse at Columbia University.

Bradley, B. P., Phillips, G., Green, L. and Gossop, M. (1989) 'Circumstances Surrounding the Initial Lapse to Opiate Use Following Detoxification'. *British Journal of Psychiatry* 154, 354–359.

Briton, C. (1995) 'Mind Your Own Business'. Druglink, Jan./Feb, 16–17.

Buchanan, J. and Young, L. (2000) 'The War on Drugs – A War on Drug Users'. *Drugs: Education, Prevention and Policy* 7(4), 409–422.

Burr, A. (1987) 'Chasing the Dragon: Heroin Misuse, Delinquency and Crime in the Context of South London Culture'. *British Journal of Criminology* 27(4), 333–357.

Collison, M. (1993) 'Punishing Drugs: Criminal Justice and Drug Use'. *British Journal of Criminology*, 33(3), 382–399.

Collison, M. (1994) 'Drug Crime, Drug Problems and Criminal Justice'. *Howard Journal of Criminal Justice* 33(1), 25–40.

Compton, B. and Galaway, B. (1994) *Social Work Processes.* Fifth Edition. Homewood: Dorsey.

Cuppleditch, L. and Evans, W. (2005) 'Re-Offending of Adults: Results from the 2002 Cohort'. *Home Office Statistical Bulletin 25/05.* London: Home Office.

Dawtry, F. (Ed.) (1968) *Social Problems of Drug Abuse: A Guide for Social Workers.* London: Butterworths.

Drakeford, M. (1993) 'The Probation Service, Breach and the Criminal Justice Act 1991'. *Howard Journal of Criminal Justice* 32(4), 291–303.

Falk, C. (2004) 'Are DTTO's Working: Issues of Policy, Implementation and Practice'. *Probation Journal* 51(4), 398–406.

Farrall, S. (2002) 'Long-Term Absences from Probation: Officers' and Probationers' Accounts'. *The Howard Journal of Criminal Justice* 41(3), 263–278.

Fowles, T. (2006) 'Counterblast: The Criminal Justice Act 2003 – The End of an Era?' *Howard Journal of Criminal Justice* 45(1), 71–73.

Garland, D. (2001) *The Culture of Control: Crime and Social Order in Contemporary Society.* Oxford University Press.

Gibson, B. (2004) *Criminal Justice Act 2003: A Guide to the New Procedures and Sentencing.* Winchester: Waterside Press.

Goodsir, J. (1992) 'A Strategic Approach to the Criminal Justice Act'. *Druglink*, Sept./Oct., pp. 12–14. London: ISDD.

Gossop, M. (1996) *National Treatment Outcome Research Study. Summary of the Project, the Clients and Preliminary Findings.* London: Department of Health.

Gossop, M., Battersby, M. and Strang, J. (1991) 'Self-detoxification by Opiate Addicts: A Preliminary Investigation'. *British Journal of Psychiatry* 159, 208–212.

Gossop, M., Marsden, J. and Stewart, D. (2001) *NTORS After Five Years: The National Treatment Outcome Research Study.* London: Department of Health.

Gyateng, T., McSweeney, T. and Hough, M. (2010) *Key Predictors of Compliance with Community Supervision in London. A Report Prepared for the London Criminal Justice Partnership.* London: ICPR.

Hales L (2002) Do Drug Treatment and Testing Orders really work? Criminal Justice Matters, 42(Spring): 18–19.

Henham, R. (1994) 'Criminal Justice and Sentencing Policy for Drug Offenders'. *International Journal of the Sociology of Law* 22(3), 223–238.

Henham, R. (1996) 'Drug Offenders and Sentencing Policy'. *Web Journal of Current Legal Issues*, No. 2.

HM Government. (1998) *Tackling Drugs to Build a Better Britain: The Government's 10 Year Strategy for Tackling Drug Misuse.* London: HMSO.

HM Inspectorate of Probation. (1993) *Offenders Who Use Drugs: The Probation Service Response.* Report of a Thematic Inspection. London: Home Office.

HM Inspectorate of Probation. (2003) A Long Way in a Short Time: Inspection of the Implementation of Drug Treatment and Testing Orders by the National Probation Service. London: Home Office.

Hollingworth, M. (2008) 'An Examination of the Potential Impact of the Drug Rehabilitation Requirement on Homeless Illicit Drug-Using Offenders'. *Probation Journal* 55, 127.

Home Office. (1998) *Drug Treatment and Testing Order, Background and Issues for Consultation*. London: Home Office.

Home Office. (2005) 'Offender Management Caseload Statistics 2004: RDS NOMS'. Home Office Statistical Bulletin 17/05. London: Home Office.

Hough, M. (1996) *Drug Misuse and the Criminal Justice System: A Review of the Literature*. Drugs Prevention Initiative Paper 15. London: Home Office.

Hough, M., Clancy, A., McSweeney, T. and Turnbull, P. J. (2003) *The Impact of Drug Treatment and Testing Orders on Offending: Two Year Reconviction Results*. Home Office Research Findings, No. 184. London: Home Office.

Kirby, A., McSweeney, T., Turnbull, P. and Bhardwa, B. (2011) *Engaging Substance Misusing Offenders: A Rapid Review of the Substance Misuse Treatment Literature*. London: Institute for Criminal Policy Research.

Klingermann, H. (1994) 'Environmental Influences Which Promote or Impede Change in Substance Behaviour'. in G. Edwards and M. Lander (Eds) *Addiction: Processes of Change*. Oxford: Oxford University Press.

Kothari, G., Marsden, J. and Strang, J. (2002) 'Opportunities and Obstacles for Effective Treatment of Drug Misusers in the Criminal Justice System in England and Wales'. *British Journal of Criminology* 42(2), 412–432.

Lee, M. (1994) 'The Probation Order: A Suitable Case for Treatment?' *Drugs: Education, Prevention and Policy* 1(2), 121–133.

MacGregor, S. (1989a) 'Choices for Policy and Practice'. in S. MacGregor (Ed.) *Drugs and British Society: Responses to a Social Problem in the 1980s*. London: Routledge.

MacGregor, S. (1989b) 'The Public Debate in the 1980s'. in S. MacGregor (Ed.) *Drugs and British Society: Responses to a Social Problem in the 1980s*. London: Routledge.

McIntosh, J. and McKeganey, N. (2002) *Beating the Dragon: The Recovery from Dependent Drug Use*. Harlow: Pearson.

McIvor, G. (2009) 'Therapeutic Jurisprudence and Procedural Justice in Scottish Drug Courts'. *Criminology and Criminal Justice* 9(1), 5–25.

McIvor, G., Barnsdale, L., Malloch, M., Eley, S. and Yates, R. (2006) *The Operation and Effectiveness of the Scottish Drug Court Pilots*. Edinburgh: Scottish Executive Social Research.

McSweeney, T. (2010) 'Recovery, Desistance and "Coerced" Treatment', in R. Yates and M. Malloch (eds.), *Tackling Addiction: Pathways to Recovery*. London: Jessica Kingsley.

McSweeney, T., Stevens, A., Hunt, N. and Turnbull, P. J. (2007) 'Twisting Arms or a Helping Hand?: Assessing the Impact of "Coerced" and Comparable "Voluntary" Drug Treatment Options'. *British Journal of Criminology* 47(3), 470–490.

Mair, G. and Mills, H. (2009) *The Community Order and the Suspended Sentence Order: Three Years on. London*: Centre for Crime and Justice Studies.

Nee, C. and Sibbitt, R. (1993) *The Probation Response to Drug Misuse. Research and Planning Unit Paper 78*. London: Home Office.

Page, M. (1992) *Crime Fighters of London*. London: Inner London Probation Service Development Trust.

Pearson, G. (1991) 'Drug-Control Policies in Britain'. in M. Tonry (Ed.) *From Crime and Justice: A Review of Research*. Chicago: University of Chicago Press.

Prins, E. H. (1994) 'Maturing Out: An Empirical Study of Personal Histories and Processes in Hard Drug Addiction'. University of Amsterdam Press.

Robinson, G. and McNeill, F. (2008) 'Exploring the Dynamics of Compliance with Community Penalties'. *Theoretical Criminology* 12(4), 431–449.

Quinn, C. and Barton, A. (2000) 'The Implications of Drug Treatment and Testing Orders'. *Nursing Standard*, 14/27, 38–41.

Raynor, P. and Vanstone, M. (2007) 'Towards a Correctional Service'. in L. Gelsthorpe and R. Morgan (Eds) *Handbook of Probation*. Cullompton: Willan.

Rumgay, J. (2000) *The Addicted Offender: Developments in British Policy and Practice*. Basingstoke: Palgrave.

Smith, D., Paylor, I. and Mitchell, P. (1993) 'Partnerships Between the Independent Sector and the Probation Service'. *Howard Journal of Criminal Justice* 32(1), 25–39.

Sparrow, P. and McIvor, G. (2013) 'Sentencing Drug Offenders Under the 2003 Criminal Justice Act: Challenges for the Probation Service'. *Criminology and Criminal Justice* 13(3), 298–316.

Sparrow, P. and Webb, D. (2004) 'Discipline and Flourish: Probation and the New Correctionalism'. in R. Hopkins Burke (Ed.) *Hard Cop, Soft Cop: Dilemmas and Debates in Contemporary Policing*. Cullompton: Willan.

Stevens, A., McSweeney, T, van Ooyen, M. and Uchtenhagen, A. (2005) 'On Coercion'. *International Journal of Drug Policy* 16(4), 203–206.

Stimson, G. and Oppenheimer, E. (1982) *Heroin Addiction: Treatment and Control in Britain*. London: Tavistock.

Turnbull, P. J., McSweeney, T., Webster, R., Edmunds, M. and Hough, M. (2000) *Drug Treatment and Testing Orders; Final Evaluation Report. Research Study 212*. London: Home Office.

Turner, D. (2005) 'The Voluntary Sector'. in J. Strang and M. Gossop (Eds) *Heroin Addiction and The British System: Origins and Evolution*. London: Routledge.

Turner, R. (2004) 'The Impact of Drug Treatment and Testing Orders in West Yorkshire: Six Month Outcomes'. *Probation Journal* 5(2), 116–132.

Wasik, M. and Taylor, R. D. (1994) *Blackstone's Guide to the Criminal Justice Act 1991*. Second Edition. London: Balckstone Press Ltd.

Washton, A. M. (1989) *Cocaine Addiction: Treatment, Recovery and Relapse Prevention*. New York: Norton.

19
Conclusion: What Works in Offender Compliance

Pamela Ugwudike and Peter Raynor

Introduction

The contributions to this volume offer wide-ranging empirical and theoretical analysis of offender compliance from diverse theoretical orientations and various academic disciplines which include criminology, law and psychology. This is quite intentional. Our primary aim has been to draw together international empirical and theoretical insights that can enhance knowledge and inform policy and practice in the field of offender compliance. Therefore, we invited leading international experts (who have researched and published widely in the field of offender compliance policy and practice) to contribute chapters. Experts based in diverse academic disciplines and in jurisdictions across Europe, Australia, the United States and Canada have contributed chapters that provide rich insights into: theories of compliance; the views of the key actors involved in compliance transactions-namely, criminal justice practitioners and the people they supervise; and emerging empirical work in the field of offender compliance.

Despite the theoretical eclecticism of the book, it has been possible to uncover three main themes that can help us answer the question: what works in offender compliance? The first section of this book draws attention to the nature of compliance as a constructed concept that can emerge from policy prescriptions and practice imperatives. Indeed, Section 1 and several other chapters in the book do provide detailed accounts of the policy dynamics that can shape compliance. Similarly, several chapters in our second section also explore how the views and experiences of the key actors shape compliance. The section reminds us that the key actors involved in securing compliance (frontline practitioners and the people they supervise) do provide useful insights into effective compliance strategies. In exploring the views and experiences of the key actors, Section II focuses on how the actors define and 'do' compliance. Section III of the book draws on several theoretical and empirical frameworks to present detailed insights into the practices that can enhance offender compliance. It brings together emerging international perspectives on evidence-based supervision practices. Importantly, the section provides empirical insights that demonstrate the relevance of 'responsivity' to substantive compliance. Along with the 'risk' principle and the 'need' principle, responsivity represents a principle of effective practice.[1] Unlike the 'responsivity' principle, the 'risk' and need' principles of effective practice have been extensively theorized in the academic literature. In addition, several Western governments have funded the development of increasingly sophisticated risk/need assessment tools (Bonta and Andrews 2007). Meanwhile, 'responsivity' remains the least developed of the three principles of effective practices (Bonta et al. 2011). The principle has two dimensions – general responsivity and specific responsivity. General responsivity involves using cognitive social learning strategies that can influence behaviour. The specific responsivity principle emphasizes the need to tailor practices so that they can suit the learning styles of the individual offender and also build on the offender's motivations and strengths. Section III presents studies which demonstrate the relevance and application of both dimensions of the responsivity principle. What follows below is a more detailed account of the three key themes the book covers.

Compliance and its policy dynamics

As Maurice Vanstone's, Gwen Robinson's and Trish McCulloch's chapters demonstrate, to understand compliance during probation supervision and how best to promote it, we have to recognize the impact of the policy contexts in which practitioners operate. Policy provisions from central government and at organizational level may inform practice priorities even where the policies do not entirely obliterate historical professional ideals. In Chapter 2 Maurice Vanstone takes us through the trajectory of probation policy developments in England and Wales. The chapter demonstrates how shifts in policy have altered practice contexts but not necessarily the welfarist practice ideology that operated through much of the service's early history. It appears that this welfarist ideology underlines the compliance strategies some practitioners adopt. The welfarist approach is an individualized approach that is very much geared toward enabling motivated offenders to successfully complete their orders. The approach is tailored to suit the circumstances of each case of non-compliance. It takes into account the specific causes of non-compliance and it also attempts to help the offender address obstacles to compliance (see also Robinson and Ugwudike 2012; Ugwudike, this volume). It follows that the welfarist approach is very much consistent with the 'care' aspect of the 'care/control' dualism that characterizes probation practice. Enforcement (warnings, court action and sanctions for non-compliance) would fall within the 'control' dimension of this dualism. Although many practitioners adopt a more welfarist approach, enforcement has always been a feature of probation policy. The Probation of

Offenders' Act 1907, which formally introduced probation in England and Wales, placed enforcement practice on a statutory footing. The Act granted statutory powers of coercion to probation officers by transforming probation supervisors into officers of the court and also by transforming probation conditions into enforceable court orders (Brownlee 1998). The Act also provided that an offender could be returned to court for bad behaviour. The court could then impose a fine, although the order was not automatically subject to revocation (Hedderman and Hough 2004: 147).

Notwithstanding these provisions, in the period after the implementation of the 1907 Act, it was apparent that enforcement was a marginal aspect of practice. The officers had considerable scope to apply their professional discretion during enforcement decision making. There appeared to be a lack of concern with streamlining enforcement practice, and it was officially acknowledged that the primary role of probation supervision is to provide a welfare-based response to offending. Indeed, the 1907 Act provided that the role of probation officers was 'to advise, assist and befriend' the probationer.

In Chapter 3, Gwen Robinson extends these themes about probation policy and practice and their impact on compliance. The chapter examines how probation policy in England and Wales has evolved since the formal introduction of probation, and also the policy developments that may shape the nature of offender compliance during supervision. The chapter discusses the seismic changes to probation policy particularly from the 1990s onwards. It was in the 1990s that centralized probation policies including tough and standardized enforcement strategies became key policy priorities for probation. Official constructions of compliance were tailored to suit the new image of community orders as punishments which imposed limitations on the supervisees' liberty. Therefore, for the first time, compliance had an official definition which was less oriented toward promoting desistance and more focused on improving attendance and reporting arrangements (see, generally, Home Office 1995, 2002; National Probation Service 2005; National Offender Management Service 2007). Enforcement also became central to practice and enforcement rates became a measure of the service's effectiveness. Several interwoven ideals, including political expediency and pragmatism, may explain this 'toughening up' of community orders from the 1990s onwards. From a political perspective, since the late 1970s, several politicians have come to believe that talking tough about crime and punishment is a potential vote-winner. From a pragmatic perspective, espousing punitive rhetoric, such as the intention to promote 'tough' enforcement, now represents a key element of the effort to enhance the credibility of community orders with the public and with sentencers in order to encourage their use instead of custodial sentences (see also Nellis 1999, 2002). Successive governments have sought to stem the rise in the prison population by encouraging the courts to impose community penalties instead. This fits in with the managerialist agenda of contemporary penal policy, which some argue has heralded a shift away from transformative penal ideals toward systemic ideals of improving efficiency and reducing costs (Scheerer 2000). Whatever the reasons for the shift toward tough enforcement, as Robinson points out in Chapter 3, it has posed several implications for practice and the nature of compliance. To cite one example, the demand on practitioners to comply with tough enforcement standards and to improve enforcement rates may have led to a rise in breach rates in recent years. But, if community penalties are to be seen as credible alternatives to custody by the courts and the public, then high breach rates are likely to undermine their credibility. It is therefore perhaps not surprising that in recent years successive governments have sought to reduce breach rates by granting front-line practitioners greater discretion to apply individualized compliance strategies during enforcement decision making (Ministry of Justice 2007, 2011a; Ministry of Justice 2011b). For example, departing from the prescriptive enforcement approach promoted by the previous standards, the 2007 enforcement standards which were introduced by the previous Labour government encouraged individualized enforcement based on professional discretion (National Offender Management Service 2007). The current National Standards also grant practitioners greater discretion during enforcement (Ministry of Justice 2011a). But, although it appears that there is now greater discretion available to practitioners to adapt their practices to the needs of the supervisees during enforcement (individualized enforcement), Robinson (this volume) found that, for some of the respondents in her study, the discretion available was limited by the implicit expectation that the practitioners would limit costly enforcement action and meet compliance targets. Once again it appears that practitioners are having to contend with new demands to pursue practices that are consistent with managerialist cost saving ideals. This time, the objective seems to be to reduce the fiscal costs that excessive enforcement rates pose because they are accompanied by costly court breaches and they can inflate the prison population.[2] As Gwen Robinson observes in Chapter 3, just as enforcement was intended to serve as a means of improving the credibility of the service, but failed to do so given that it heralded high rates of breach (an indication of the service's inability to engage offenders), the current focus on compliance rates may produce adverse consequences. It may encourage practitioners to focus on forms of compliance that are quantifiable, while the more qualitative forms, such as active engagement and commitment (substantive compliance), which practitioners should actively encourage may be overlooked. Reinforcing the themes covered by Gwen Robinson, Trish McCulloch in Chapter 4 draws on a study that demonstrates how practitioners are being encouraged to promote compliance not by working with offenders to develop their motivation, engagement and commitment but by employing strategies that can reduce breach rates and enhance quantifiable or measurable forms of compliance such as attending statutory appointments. Similarly, several probation practitioners who participated in Gwen Robinson's study revealed the perceived pressure to 'avoid enforcement action at almost any cost'. In addition, as Gwen Robinson rightly points out, where practitioners are enjoined to overlook acts of non-compliance in order to improve compliance rates, incidents of non-compliance which pose risks of harm and victimization to the public may also be overlooked, with adverse consequences for the credibility of the service. In sum, Chapters 2–4 demonstrate how policy changes since the introduction of the service have altered the nature and mechanisms of compliance during community-based supervision in England and Wales.

Compliance from the perspective of the key actors

Building on the themes discussed in the first section of the book, Section II directs attention to how the key actors involved in penal supervision experience and/or define compliance. Recently some desistance theorists have rightly decried the apparent marginalization of the views of those wishing to desist from offending (McNeill et al. 2012). The 'what works' or effective practice literature for example, mainly employs meta-analytic methods although recent studies have used innovative techniques such as observation methods and self-assessment among other methods (Raynor et al. 2010; Alexander et al., this volume; Bourgon and Gutierrez, this volume). Nevertheless, there is also a need to explore how the key actors themselves define their experiences of compliance during supervision and their desistance journeys (McNeill et al. 2012; McCulloch, this volume).

In Chapter 5 Anthony Bottoms presents a theoretical and empirical account of a specific compliance mechanism – the offender's internal motivations. He presents the findings of a study that revealed how offenders draw on their internal resources to avoid criminogenic situations and outcomes. As Anthony Bottoms rightly notes, the chapter is unique in its focus on compliance strategies that are primarily self-motivated, given that they involve self-applied Situational Crime Prevention (SCP) strategies. Although various possible techniques may be applied during supervision to help enhance self-applied SCP strategies, the Core Correctional Practices (CCPs) referred to by several chapters in this book may also be useful strategies.

In an interesting departure from what they describe as a 'paternalistic' approach, in which the practitioner is considered to be the active change agent, Ralph Serin and his colleagues (in Chapter 6) also address the importance of harnessing offender skills and self-motivation. In their view, it is useful to move beyond the view of the offender as the 'passive observer' of the change process. From this perspective, which echoes the arguments presented by Anthony Bottoms in Chapter 5, there is much to be gained from building on the offender's inner predisposition to change. Ralph Serin argues for a greater alignment of the 'what works'/effective practice model with desistance research which emphasizes the active role of the offender in the change process. They argue that to encourage offender 'cooperation' it is necessary to pay greater attention to the skills, dispositions and motivations offenders develop to refrain from offending and ensure desistance. Offender cooperation that stems from willing submission should be a primary goal rather than offender compliance which in their view implies a degree of compulsion and may as such require the use of incentives and disincentives (see also Bottoms 2001).

It is worth noting that Anthony Bottoms in Chapter 5, and Ralph Serin and colleagues in Chapter 6 make interesting points about the importance of recognizing and building on offender strengths to encourage long-term change. Indeed, a major criticism of a key model of offender supervision (which has been mentioned by several chapters in this volume) and which is known as the 'what works'/effective practice approach or the Risk, Need, Responsivity Model (RNR), is that it emphasizes offenders' flaws (their risks and needs) rather than their strengths (see, for example, Ward and Maruna 2007). Several desistance theorists offer this criticism. Some critics of the approach advocate a shift away from what they describe as an undue focus on 'offender deficits', toward a focus on promoting positives such as the offender's motivation and strengths (Maruna and LeBel 2010: 66). There is also a call for a greater recognition of individual and wider social factors that can affect desistance (Ward 2012). Proponents of the Good Lives Model of offender supervision argue that the effective practice approach overlooks human motivation and agency, and with its focus on criminogenic needs, overlooks what they describe as the needs that help offenders fulfil personal goals such as developing good relationships and securing the jobs they enjoy (Ward 2010; Ward and Maruna 2007). In response to this, it is important to point out that the effective practice literature is replete with theories, studies and other work that point to the importance of building on the offender's strengths and motivation during supervision. Indeed, individualizing supervision approaches by building on offenders' strengths and adapting programmes to suit their abilities and particular circumstances forms the core of the responsivity principle we described earlier. Andrews and Bonta point out that:

> Specific responsivity individualises treatment according to strengths, ability, motivation, personality and bio-social characteristics such as gender, ethnicity and age.
>
> (2010: 20–21)

It is however, important to acknowledge that further work is required to promote better understanding of the Risk-Need-Responsivity (RNR) approach and how it should be implemented in practice to help encourage compliance. The responsivity principle in particular and the concept of 'programme integrity' (using the relevant skills to implement the effective practice approach), require further theorization. As Andrews et al. (2011) rightly acknowledge, more work is required to: promote better understanding of RNR; emphasize programme integrity factors, including staff skills and supervision relationships; and refocus on offender motivation. Unfortunately, as we pointed out in Chapter 1, there is a dearth of empirical and theoretical knowledge about programme integrity which, according to Andrews and Bonta (2010: 23), 'is of extraordinary significance' (see also Dowden and Andrews 2004; Lowenkamp et al. 2006). This means that it is difficult to ascertain the extent to which practitioners use the relevant skills to implement the effective practice approach and encourage substantive compliance. Bonta and colleagues acknowledge this in the statement below:

> Do probation officers use offender risk assessments in assigning intensity of intervention and identifying criminogenic needs that should be addressed? Do probation and parole officers use cognitive-behavioural techniques during their supervision sessions? Answers to these questions are lacking and yet answers are sorely needed to improve supervision practices.
>
> (Bonta et al. 2008: 252–253)

Section III of this book provides much-needed insights into the 'responsivity' principle and the supervision skills that enhance programme integrity and encourage compliance during and after supervision.

Returning to our earlier discussion about the issues covered in Section II of the book, Chapters 7– 9 also draw on recent empirical studies to highlight yet another key concept that can help us understand compliance as perceived by those who are required to comply with the directives of people in authority in penal contexts.[3] In Chapter 7, Peter Raynor explores probation managers' and clients' views about the nature and purposes of compliance, and shows how a problem-solving approach can involve practitioners in actively improving their own compliance. A key concept these chapters and indeed several other chapters in this book highlight is the perceived legitimacy of authority. Below we explore this concept in more detail.

Perceived legitimacy and substantive compliance

In Chapter 8, Ben Crewe emphasizes the views of those subject to supervision in prison. Like several other contributors to this volume, including Gwen Robinson, Trish McCulloch and Ralph Serin, Ben Crewe also problematizes the concept of compliance by observing the differences between the way policy makers construct compliance (mainly by labelling quantifiable behaviour as compliance) and the way the key actors experience and define compliance. Ben Crewe's chapter is a very interesting departure from the traditional focus of compliance studies on compliance in probation settings because it explores the dynamics of compliance in prisons. In arguments similar to Mike Nellis's (this volume) description of the nature of control involved in Electronic Monitoring (EM) supervision, Ben Crewe notes that the degree of control in prison contexts is markedly different from what obtains in probation settings. Imprisonment subjects people to more restrictive control in ways that may trigger perceptions of unfair treatment. Several studies have identified links between perceived unfair treatment during penal supervision (in the community or in prison) and the perceived legitimacy of authority. These studies persuasively show that perceptions of unfair treatment can undermine the perceived legitimacy of authority and trigger non-compliance (Bottoms 2001; Ugwudike 2008, this volume; McNeill and Robinson 2013). In Chapter 8, Ben Crewe also draws attention to the association between legitimacy and compliance. The concept of legitimacy has been theorized across diverse disciplines. For example, arguing from a socio-psychological perspective, Tyler (1990, 2013) points out that compliance is normative when internalized perceptions that an authority is legitimate trigger a perceived obligation to obey irrespective of self-interest (see also Jackson et al. 2012). Normative compliance may perhaps require the use of less costly strategies unlike instrumental compliance, which may rely on the use of potentially costly incentives (rewards) or disincentives (e.g. costly court hearings and custodial sentences). Moreover, Ben Crewe outlines several possible impediments to the effective use of incentives in prison contexts. These range from anti-authoritarian values that may trigger prisoner resistance to official rewards, to suspicion of the motives of people in authority (the prison officers offering the rewards).

As Ben Crewe observes in Chapter 8, the quality of the interactions between individuals who are subject to authority and the representatives of legal authorities such as the prison service can reinforce or undermine perceived legitimacy. Bottoms (1999) also considers these issues in the context of maintaining order within prisons (see also Sparks et al. 1996). He argues that transactions between prison officers and prisoners produce implications that transcend the situational context within which such transactions occur. Ultimately, interactions between both parties shape the prisoners' perceptions of the legitimacy of the prison officers' authority and also of the prison service as a whole:

> ordinary everyday encounters between staff and prisoners can have crucial implications for the nature of the power relations in the prison, and to the validity of the staff's claims to justified authority – that is, to legitimacy.
>
> (Bottoms 1999: 256)

Ben Crewe (this volume) observes that the perception that one has received 'humane and respectful treatment' and the view that a prison regime is 'legal, decent and consistent' can trigger an obligation to obey even when the regulations are inconsistent with the prisoner's personal inclination. Several studies point to the crucial role of perceived legitimacy in encouraging normative compliance in other penal contexts, including: during police encounters (Tyler 1990; Paternoster et al. 1997; Jackson et al. 2013) and during probation supervision (McNeill and Robinson 2013; Ugwudike 2008, this volume).

The concept of perceived legitimacy of authority and its association with normative compliance have also been explored from a socio-legal perspective. Murphy's (2005) longitudinal study of tax evasion explored the role of legitimacy in producing tax compliance compared with the influence of deterrent strategies. Like other legitimacy studies, the study found that perceptions of legitimacy ultimately affect the decision to defer to authority, and such perceptions are typically based on the nature of the encounter with legal authorities and, in particular, the nature of treatment received – 'procedural justice judgements' (Murphy 2005: 585). Coercive or punitive compliance strategies tended to generate perceptions of unfair treatment and non-compliance.

A key implication of the findings of the legitimacy literature is that the manner of exercising authority may have a direct influence on the perceived legitimacy of that authority. It is important not to ignore this finding because studies also reveal that links exist between the perceived legitimacy of authority and normative compliance. When applied to the specific context of penal supervision it is possible that subjective assessments of the fairness of decision making processes may affect perceptions of legitimacy and ultimately the willingness to comply with the directives of supervising officers.

Trish McCulloch's chapter (mentioned earlier) also draws on the key actors' views in its discussion about normative compliance. Moving away from the managerialist definition of compliance in quantifiable terms such as attendance, Trish McCulloch's chapter refers to recent studies that have drawn on supervisees' accounts to show how specific strategies and contexts can support normative compliance. The chapter emphasizes the role of the offender as an active contributor to the compliance process. This according to Trish McCulloch, departs from contemporary trends which vest all the control and responsibility for compliance in criminal justice officials and overlook the offenders' capacity to engage with the compliance process during penal supervision. The question of how to encourage the active commitment of the offender deserves even more consideration when we recognize that long-term compliance ultimately relies on the continuing commitment of the offender after the order expires. During supervision, practitioners seeking to promote long-term compliance can help the offenders develop the tools they need to continue on the desistance journey after the order expires. According to Trish McCulloch, one way of achieving this is to promote normative compliance during penal supervision. Patricia McCulloch argues that normative compliance, relying, as it does, to a significant degree on factors that are within the offender's control (e.g. their perceptions of the legitimacy of authority and their moral values), is a form of compliance that emerges from the offender's active role in evaluating the quality of treatment they have received and the perceived legitimacy of authority. Some commentators persuasively argue that human actors do not always exercise the degree of rationalization implicit in the normative view of compliance (see, for example, Decoene and Beyens, this volume). One may add that habit compliance mechanisms (as described in Chapter 1) are particularly relevant because they can help ensure that offenders are able to play active roles in the change process by, for example, taking active steps to develop non-criminogenic routines that can, over time, evolve into habit compliance. Importantly, unlike normative compliance, habit compliance does not rely on detailed evaluations of the actions of people in authority.

In Chapter 9, Mike Nellis draws on international research to provide a rich review of the purposes of EM, how EM operates and the compliance issues associated with the sanction. The chapter also highlights the importance of perceived legitimacy of authority and compliance. Perceived legitimacy also has some significance in EM settings, not least because as Mike Nellis observes, EM involves direct and more intense surveillance than other community penalties. Offenders are required (though not necessarily as physically constrained as prisoners are) to routinely perform specific behaviour, such as observing set schedules. Therefore, the effective implementation of EM requires the cooperation of the offender. As Mike Nellis puts it, compliance remains 'an active, willed process'. Again, as noted above, just as the quality of treatment received during community-based supervision can affect perceived legitimacy and compliance, Mike Nellis writes that, with EM, 'the rigour and perceived legitimacy' of the EM regime which the offender should comply with can affect decisions to comply. Drawing on several studies, Mike Nellis demonstrates that perceptions of EM as onerous and constraining can trigger formal compliance or even worse, wilful acts of non-compliance. Offenders lacking adequate motivation may also engage in acts of wilful non-compliance. Mike Nellis describes attempts to improve compliance with EM sanctions by adding rehabilitative programmes to the sanctions. Unlike 'stand-alone' EM, these programmes to varying degrees provide 'assisted compliance' through mechanisms that aim to address criminogenic routines and dispositions in order to encourage rehabilitation or change. A notable limitation of this approach is that it could encourage a focus on compliance during supervision without a corresponding commitment to promoting longer-term desistance.

Chapter 10 presents the findings of a study that explored *inter alia*: the views of front-line probation practitioners regarding the compliance strategies they employ. The study found a general commitment to welfarist compliance strategies that seek to help the offender address the socioeconomic, practical and other obstacles to compliance. Most of the participating officers also reported that they employ individualized enforcement strategies that are responsive to the needs of the offenders and to the specific circumstances of each incident of non-compliance. The chapter echoes the findings of several existing studies that highlight the continuing commitment to the Social Work principles that informed early probation practice in England and Wales. The chapter also attempts to place the study's findings in the context of recent theories of compliance and the emerging evidence base on effective compliance strategies. It acknowledges that although responsive and welfarist compliance strategies are useful, not least because they may promote perceived fair treatment and perceived legitimacy of authority, there is also a need to pursue practices that can promote habit compliance as defined by Bottoms (2001). The chapter argues that this is necessary given that, compared with other mechanisms of compliance outlined in the literature, habit compliance occurs automatically and is, as such, more likely to transcend the specific contexts of penal supervision and to persist even after supervision ends.

Compliance as the product of correctional skills and practices

Unlike Section II, Section III of the book focuses more closely on the sites in which supervisors and supervisees interact to produce substantive compliance across diverse Western jurisdictions. The section describes how supervision practices, skills and approaches can affect compliance. In Chapter 11, Martine Herzog-Evans addresses the impact of supervision practices on compliance. Martine Herzog-Evans offers a very interesting perspective on the impact of criminal justice practices on offender compliance. Martine's chapter focuses on practices in France and unlike the other chapters, addresses the actions of sentencers. Nevertheless, like several other chapters in the book, Chapter 11 demonstrates that compliance is a likely outcome where there is procedural fairness through for example, individualized responses to non-compliance in which the client is also given the opportunity to state their case and a respectful attitude to clients. This is directly comparable to Tyler's (1990) findings in his study of how people draw their beliefs about police legitimacy from their interactions with individual police officers. The chapter also holds the converse to be true – rigid enforcement which overlooks the specific circumstances of each case can trigger defiance and non-compliance. The chapter draws on a study which demonstrates these issues. It also illuminates how constraints such as the demand to complete bureaucratic tasks can impinge on practices. Importantly, it describes how sentencers can contribute to the compliance process. This topic has attracted limited attention. However, it is worth noting that a recent study by McIvor (2009) also demonstrated how the actions of sentencers presiding over Drug Courts in Scotland can promote procedural justice and substantive compliance among drug-using offenders serving community orders.

Stef Decoene and Kristel Beyens offer a multidisciplinary account of compliance in Chapter 12. Basing their work on Belgian contexts, they draw on insights from medicine and psychology. From the medical literature, they identify three forms of compliance. Concordance emphasizes the collaborative nature of communication and decision making between the two parties involved (the doctor and the patient, or, in correctional supervision contexts, the practitioner and the client). It recognizes the rights of the person who is expected to comply with directives. Adherence suggests that the client has a more active role in implementing the objectives of treatment. Crucially, intertwined with these forms of compliance is the relational element of compliance. Decoene and Beyens cite several studies that identify positive relationships with people in authority such as healthcare providers and criminal justice practitioners, as vital for encouraging compliance: 'A trusting, supportive relationship' is required for compliance. Interestingly, the medical literature outlines a range of strategies for encouraging compliance which mirror the Core Correctional Practices (CCPs) mentioned earlier and also further below.

From the psychological literature, the authors draw on studies that explore how people who are perceived to be in authority can influence others. These studies reveal that effective compliance mechanisms target not only behavioural change (such as attending appointments) but also attitudinal change (such a commitment to the objectives of the order). Although they posit otherwise, it appears that Beyens and Decoene's descriptions of the psychological literature echoes Robinson and McNeill's (2008) conceptual analysis of 'compliance', which comprises formal compliance (primarily behavioural) and substantive compliance (attitudinal change, possibly identity change and also behavioural change).

Their chapter also presents insights into enforcement practices in Belgium. In doing so, it adds to the growing body of knowledge about practices in diverse jurisdictions. An emerging theme is that judiciously applied practitioner discretion which facilitates individualized enforcement can in turn, promote perceived legitimacy of authority and enhance substantive compliance. Again, like some of the previous chapters, Chapter 12 identifies several contextual factors that can affect compliance. A key example is the conflicting ideologies and practice cultures of the sentencers (those responsible for imposing sanctions for non-compliance) and the probation officer equivalent in Belgium – the justice assistant. The justice assistants operate at the caring dimension of the care/control dynamic, while the sentencers operate at the control spectrum of the dynamic.

Carrying forward the theme of Section III of the book, which addresses the skills and practices that can enhance substantive compliance, in Chapters 13 to 15 the respective authors draw on the findings of recent studies that have explored links between evidence-based supervision skills (Core Correctional Practices – CCPs) and long-term compliance (reduced reoffending). As such, the chapters uncover the nature and impact of CCPs, and the importance of training practitioners in these skills.[4]

As mentioned earlier, the CCPs can be summarized as follows:

- Effective use of authority
- Appropriate modelling and reinforcement
- Problem-solving
- Use of community resources – Brokerage/Advocacy
- Quality of interpersonal relationships

Emerging international insights, including those presented in this volume, suggest that there is significant potential for developing these skills in ways that make them easy to implement and more likely to enhance compliance. Studies also suggest that adequate training in the use of the evidence-based skills is required if staff members are to implement the skills effectively.

What follows below is a more detailed examination of the chapters in Section III of the book. In Chapter 13, Christopher Trotter focuses on the impact of the skills practitioners use in youth justice contexts in Australia. He reviews the relevant literature on the impact of supervision skills and highlights the emphasis of much of the research on the relational dimension of supervision, that is, the relationships or interactions between the key actors. To add further insights to this field of research, Christopher Trotter draws on a recent study that examined whether specific skills such as role clarification and prosocial modelling may encourage offender engagement (in cases where the offender is not engaged in the supervision process) even in the absence of effective relationship or interpersonal skills. Christopher's study is quite unique because unlike most of the existing studies, the study focused on practices involving young people. It examined the impact of skills across several domains including: the set-up of the interview; structure of the interview; role clarification; needs analysis; problem -solving; developing strategies; relapse prevention/cognitive–behavioural techniques; prosocial modelling and reinforcement; nature of the relationship; empathy; confrontation; termination; use of referral/community resources; non-verbal cues; and incidental conversations. Like other emerging studies in this field, the study found that practitioners who used most of the skills had probationers who later had lower rates of reoffending after 2 years compared with practitioners who used fewer skills. Interestingly, the study suggests that of all the skills studied, the two skills that have the strongest correlation with reduced reoffending are 'the use of rewards by the worker and a non-blaming approach'. Both strategies represent essential components of the CCPs. The study also suggests that practitioner skills have an impact on outcomes, particularly in supervision contexts involving offenders who appear to be less engaged during supervision. Christopher Trotter acknowledges that there is compelling evidence to support the efficacy of the supervision skills as effective mechanisms of short-term and long-term substantive compliance.

Alexander and colleagues address the issue of programme integrity in Chapter 14 by exploring how supervision skills may affect programme integrity and outcomes. Their chapter illuminates the implications of training practitioners to implement evidence-based supervision skills. They draw on a research study that examined how practitioners respond to training on Motivational Interviewing (MI) techniques and other approaches that are based on the CCPs. The study persuasively suggests *inter alia*, that practitioners are more likely to employ approaches that are less complex (easier to learn, understand and apply) and are perceived to be more compatible with existing practices. Providing booster sessions where practitioners receive feedback on their progress, and practising the skills more often can help improve the positive impact of the skills on outcomes (reduced reoffending).

In Chapter 15, Bourgon and his colleagues draw on the 'what works' literature and the psychotherapeutic literature to develop an understanding of how the relationship between practitioners and clients (in the form of a 'therapeutic alliance' – TA) can improve longer-term compliance. The chapter reviews the literature on TA within correctional settings. These studies draw attention to the importance of the relational element of supervision. The studies also highlight the skills practitioners can use to improve this element of supervision and encourage long-term change. Bourgon and colleagues examine the intersections between the 'what works' approach and TA, and they argue that TA is an essential component of the responsivity principle which directly relates to how best to improve offender engagement with the change process. Principally, this concerns how to develop and sustain 'an optimal learning environment' for each client. As mentioned earlier, Bonta and Andrews (2009) describe this as the key dimension of specific responsivity, which is one of several principles of effective practice. The specific responsivity principle states that effective programmes take offenders' learning styles and other learning needs (cultural, gender-related, practical, etc.) into account and allocate offenders to appropriate staff (see Andrews and Bonta 2010). Central to the responsivity principle of practice is the ability of practitioners to prioritize client-centred factors such as the potential correlates of learning. A key factor here pertains to orientating the quality of the interpersonal relationship with the client in directions that can help elicit collaboration, enhance engagement and construct purposeful work. Bourgon and colleagues draw on Trotter's (2006) work to identify two strategies for achieving these objectives and for creating an effective TA: role clarification, in which practitioners use specific skills to clarify the roles, responsibilities and expectations of both parties, and collaborative goal setting, which affords the client an active role in the identification of problems, goals and solutions.

In sum, these studies demonstrate that, as Alexander and colleagues (this volume) put it: 'the effectiveness of the intervention is not the only important aspect. Rather, the intervention must be well implemented in order for it to have an impact on outcomes.' To implement interventions effectively, practitioners should receive adequate training on evidence-based skills and techniques. Another key requirement for effective outcomes (substantive compliance) is tailoring these skills and practices to the needs of individual offenders. Bonta and Andrews (2009) describe this requirement as the essence of the responsivity principle which as noted earlier, is one of the three principles of effective practice identified in the international literature (see, specifically, Andrews and Bonta 2010; McGuire 1995, 2002, 2007). Below we summarize what the final chapters of this book tell us about the importance of tailoring policies and practices according to the needs of diverse offender groups.

The importance of 'specific responsivity'

Because it emphasizes the importance of tailoring practices to suit the learning needs and other needs of the offender, an individualized approach lies at the heart of the specific responsivity principle. If the objective of supervision is to promote long-term desistance, then it is important to help each individual offender address the factors that can impede their ability to attain this objective. There are two important ways of achieving this and fulfilling the specific responsivity principle. First, practitioners should formally assess the strengths and motivations of the offenders and build on these during supervision (Bonta and Andrews 2009). Second, practitioners should help identify and remove the obstacles or impediments to learning. These obstacles differ across diverse offender demographics. Bonta and Andrews (2007) provide useful examples of the specific approaches that may suit specific offenders. For example: 'providing childcare so that the mother can attend treatment' (where the mother is the primary carer of the child) is one way of implementing the specific responsivity principle.

Each chapter in the final section of the book attempts to identify the specific compliance issues that practitioners may consider during supervision interactions involving diverse offender groups, namely, women, young people and drug-using offenders. In doing so, the chapters provide rich theoretical and empirical insights that can enhance knowledge and enrich specific responsivity practices. In Chapter 16, Loraine Gelsthorpe presents an account of compliance that draws on studies that have explored gendered dimensions of work with female offenders. Gelsthorpe outlines Bottoms's (2001), and Robinson and McNeill's (2008) conceptualizations of compliance and explores how practitioners can apply these in contexts involving female offenders. She argues that general offender behaviour programmes are designed for men. As such, they do not adequately address the treatment needs of female offenders. This poses implications for how female offenders comply. She presents the findings of a study that revealed that, while men are more likely to demonstrate instrumental compliance, women are likely to comply for normative reasons. The factors that affect compliance are also different for both genders. Specific factors like childcare and travel difficulties have been found to have a greater impact on how women comply. Other factors include drug and alcohol misuse which may in turn, fuel chaotic lifestyles that make compliance with routine attendance requirements quite difficult. The setting and the quality of the intervention may also affect compliance. 'Women only' environments appear to be more productive in this context, as does a more cooperative and less authoritarian setting in which the women feel empowered.

In Chapter 17 which focuses on compliance in youth justice contexts, Tim Bateman demonstrates the relevance of normative compliance mechanisms that are 'non-coercive, child-friendly' and built on realistic supervision expectations. The chapter identifies additional strategies that can encourage normative compliance. These strategies include: removing obstacles to compliance such as travel problems; using compliance-oriented techniques and home visits; encouraging collaborative identification of areas to focus on; improving the quality of relationships to improve perceived legitimacy of authority; and developing individualized approaches to responding to non-compliance. Tim Bateman persuasively argues that, just as in adult supervision contexts, there are policy provisions that affect how effectively supervisors can deploy these mechanisms. Two examples are: the rhetoric of 'tough' enforcement; and the focus on risk management rather than transformative goals such as rehabilitation. Echoing Mike Nellis's (this volume) arguments, Tim Bateman points out that the risk management agenda could encourage the greater surveillance and control of young people who offend.

Chapter 18 addresses the compliance issues that pertain to drug-misusing offenders. In the chapter, Paul Sparrow argues that reconciling public protection goals and rehabilitative objectives represent two challenges that confront those seeking to encourage compliance among this group of offenders. There is little empirical evidence to suggest that tough enforcement in the form of expedited and certain enforcement produces desired outcomes (substantive compliance). In Chapter 18, Paul Sparrow demonstrates how the quest for punitive community orders has been counterproductive. Again, an emerging theme is the importance of the quality of supervision relationships, collaborative identification of supervision goals, offering purposeful interventions and possibly providing relapse prevention sessions.

The book adds to the growing academic and official interest in offender compliance by drawing on new and emerging research to demonstrate the most effective strategies for encouraging compliance. Given its premise and the broad range of issues covered, it is envisaged that the book will also be relevant to practitioners and other observers interested in the dynamics of compliance within diverse criminal justice settings, including probation supervision, prisons and youth justice settings. These insights will prove useful in current policy and practice contexts of shrinking budgets/reduced spending on criminal justice provision alongside a 'payment by results' policy agenda. Criminal justice practitioners will increasingly have to secure compliance in contexts of ever-increasing competition with external providers amidst the threats of, or what now appears to be the growing reality of privatization. The need for evidence-based effective practices cannot be overestimated. By collating the existing and emerging international perspectives on the skills and strategies that can inform effective work with offenders to encourage compliance during supervision, this volume addresses a surprising gap in knowledge.

Notes

1. International researchers have identified several evidence-based principles of effective practice. These comprise three core principles: the risk principle; the need principle and the responsivity principle (please see Andrews and Bonta 2010, and Bourgon and Guiterrez (this volume) for further elucidation of these principles).
2. As mentioned in Chapter 1, official statistics show that 'tough' enforcement is one factor that has contributed to the growth in the prison population (Ministry of Justice 2010).
3. People in authority in these contexts include probation practitioners and prison officers.
4. Several chapters in this book also explore the CCPs in some detail. See generally, Chapters 6, 10, 14 and 15. Motivational Interviewing techniques are also considered to be effective practice skills (see generally, Alexander et al. this volume; Raynor et al. 2010).

References

Andrews, D. A. and Bonta, J. (2010) *The Psychology of Criminal Conduct*, Fifth Edition. Cincinnati, OH: Anderson.

Andrews, D. A., Bonta, J. and Wormith, S. (2011) 'The Risk-Need-Responsivity Model: Does Adding the Good Lives Model Contribute to Effective Crime Prevention?' *Criminal Justice and Behaviour* 38(7), 735–755.

Andrews, D. A. and Kiessling, J. J. (1980) 'Program Structure and Effective Correctional Practices: A Summary of the CaVic Research'. in R. R. Ross and P. Gendreau (Eds) *Effective Correctional Treatment*. Toronto: Butterworth.

Bonta, J. and Andrews, D. A. (2007) *Risk-Need-Responsivity Model for Offender Assessment and Rehabilitation*. http://securitepubliquecanada.gc.ca/res/cor/rep/_fl/Risk_Need_2007-06_e.pdf (accessed 10 March 2009)

Bonta, J., Rugge, T., Scott, T., Bourgon, G. and Yessine, A. (2008) Exploring the Black Box of Community Supervision. *Journal of Offender Rehabilitation* 47(3), 248–270.

Bonta, J., Bourgon, G., Rugge, T., Scott, T.-L., Yessine, A. K., Gutierrez, L. and Li, J. (2011) 'An experimental demonstration of training probation officers in evidence-based community supervision'. *Criminal Justice and Behaviour* 38, 1127–1148.

Bottoms, A. E. (2001) 'Compliance and Community Penalties'. in A. E. Bottoms, L. Gelsthorpe and S. Rex (Eds) *Community Penalties: Change and Challenges.* Devon: Willan.

Brownlee, I. (1998) *Community Punishment: A Critical Introduction.* Harlow: Longman.

Dowden, C. and Andrews, D. A. (2004) 'The Importance of Staff Practice in Delivering Effective Correctional Treatment: A Meta-Analytic Review of Core Correctional Practice'. *International Journal of Offender Therapy and Comparative Criminology* 48(2), 203–214.

Hedderman, C. and Hough, M. (2004) 'Getting Tough or Being Effective: What Matters?' in G. Mair (Ed.) *What Matters in Probation.* Devon: Willan.

Home Office. (1995) *National Standards for the Supervision of Offenders in the Community.* London: Home Office.

Home Office. (2002) *National Standards for the Supervision of Offenders in the Community, 2000* (Amended, 2002). London: Home Office.

Jackson et al. (2013) 'Compliance with the Law and Policing by Consent: Notes on Police and Legal Legitimacy'. in A. Crawford and A. Hucklesby (Eds) *Legitimacy and Compliance in Criminal Justice* (pp. 116–137). NY, London: Routledge.

Lowenkamp, C. T., Latessa, E. J. and Holsinger, A. M. (2006) 'The Risk Principle in Action: What Have We Learned from 13,676 Offenders and 97 Correctional Programmes?' *Crime Delinquency* 52, 77–93.

Maruna, S. and LeBel, T. (2010) 'The Desistance Paradigm in Correctional Practice: From Programmes to Lives'. in F. McNeil, P. Raynor and C. Trotter (Eds) *Offender Supervision: New Directions in Theory, Research and Practice* (pp. 41–64). New York, NY: Willan.

McGuire, J. (1995) *What Works: Reducing Re-offending.* Chichester: Wiley Press.

McGuire, J. (2002). 'Integrating Findings from Research Reviews'. in J. McGuire (Ed.) *Offender Rehabilitation and Treatment: Effective Programmes and Policies to Reduce Re-offending* (pp. 3–38). Chichester, UK: John Wiley & Sons.

McGuire, J. (2007) 'Programmes for Probationers'. in G. McIvor and P. Raynor (Eds) *Developments in Social Work with Offenders.* London, Jessica Kingsley.

McIvor, G. (2009) 'Therapeutic Jurisprudence and Procedural Justice in Scottish Drug Courts'. *Criminology and Criminal Justice*, 9(1), 5–25.

McNeill, F., Farrall, S., Lightowler, C. and Maruna, S. (2012) 'Re-Examining Evidence-based Practice in Community Corrections: Beyond a "Confined View" of What Works'. *Justice Research and Policy*, 14(1), 35–60.

McNeill, F. and Robinson, G. (2013) 'Liquid Legitimacy and Community Sanctions'. in A. Crawford and A. Hucklesby (Eds) *Legitimacy and Compliance in Criminal Justice* (pp. 116–137). NY, London: Routledge.

Ministry of Justice. (2007) *National Standards for the Management of Offenders: Standards and Implementation Guidance.* London: NOMS, Ministry of Justice.

Ministry of Justice. (2011a) *National Standards for the Management of Offenders*. Ministry of Justice press release 5 April 2011. http://www.justice.gov.uk/downloads/publications/corporate-reports/MoJ/national-standards-management-offenders-2011.pdf (accessed on 13 May 2011).

Ministry of Justice. (2011b) The Offender Engagement Programme: An overview from programme director, Martin Copsey. http://www.essexprobationtrust.org.uk/doc/The_Offender_Engagement_Programme_Overview_July_11.pdf (accessed on 13 December 2011).

Murphy, K. (2005) 'Regulating more Effectively: the Relationship Between Procedural Justice, Legitimacy, and Tax Non-Compliance'. *Journal of Law and Society* 32(4), 562–589.

National Probation Service. (2005) *National Standards.* London: National Probation Directorate.

Nellis, M. (1999) 'Towards the Field of Corrections: Modernising the Probation Service in the Late 1990'. *Social Policy and Administration.* 33 (3) 303:323.

Nellis, M. (2002) Community Justice, Time and the New National Probation Service'. *Howard Journal of Criminal Justice,* 41 (1).

Paternoster, R., Bachman, R., Brame, R. and Sherman, L. R. (1997) 'Do Fair Procedures Matter? The Effect of Procedural Justice on Spouse Assault'. *Law and Society Review* 31(1), 163–204.

Raynor, P., Ugwudike, P. and Vanstone, M. (2010) 'Skills and Strategies in Probation Supervision: The Jersey Study'. in McNeill, P. Raynor and C. Trotter (Eds) *Offender Supervision: New Directions in Theory, Research and Practice.* Cullompton: Willan.

Raynor, P., Ugwudike, P. and Vanstone, M. (forthcoming) 'The impact of skills in probation work: A reconviction study.' *Criminology and Criminal Justice.*

Robinson, G. and McNeill, F. (2008) Exploring the dynamics of compliance with community penalties, Theoretical Criminology 2008; 12; 431.

Robinson, G. and Ugwudike, P. (2012) 'Investing in "Toughness": Probation, Enforcement and Legitimacy'. *Howard Journal of Criminal Justice,* 51(3), 300–316.

Scheerer, S. (2000) 'Three Trends into the New Millennium: The Populist and the Road Towards Global Justice'. in A. Rutherford and P. Green (eds) *Criminal Policy in Transition.* Oxford: Hart Publishing.

Sparks, R., Bottoms, A. E. and Hay, W. (1996) Prisons and the Problem of Order. Oxford: Clarendon Press.

Trotter, C. (2006) *Working with Involuntary Clients.* Sydney: Allen & Unwin.

Tyler, T. R. (1990) *Why People Obey the Law.* New Haven, CT: Yale University Press.

Tyler, T. (2013) 'Legitimacy and Compliance: The Virtues of Self-Regulation', in A. Crawford & A. Hucklesby (Eds.), *Legitimacy and Compliance in Criminal Justice.* NY, London: Routledge.

Ugwudike, P. (2008) *Developing an Effective Mechanism for Encouraging Compliance with Community Penalties.* PhD thesis, Swansea University.

Ugwudike, P., Raynor, P. and Vanstone, M. (forthcoming) 'Supervision Skills and Practices: The Jersey Study'. in I. Durnescu and F. McNeill (eds) *Understanding Penal Practice.* Routledge.

Ward, T. (2010). 'The Good Lives Model of Offender Rehabilitation: Basic Assumptions, Aetiological Commitments, and Practice Implications'. in F. McNeil, P. Raynor and C. Trotter (Eds) *Offender Supervision: New Directions in Theory, Research and Practice* (pp. 41–64). New York, NY: Willan.

Ward, T. (2012) 'Moral Strangers or Fellow Travellers? Contemporary Perspectives on Offender Rehabilitation'. *Legal and Criminological Psychology* 17, 37–40.

Ward, T. and Maruna, S. (2007) *Rehabilitation: Beyond the Risk Paradigm.* London: Routledge.

Index

Printed and bound by CPI Group (UK) Ltd, Croydon, CR0 4YY